Metropolitan
HILARION ALFEYEV

JESUS CHRIST

His Life and Teaching

In Six Volumes

VOLUME TWO

THE SERMON ON THE MOUNT

S T VLADIMIR'S SEMINARY PRESS

YONKERS, NEW YORK

2019

Library of Congress Cataloging-in-Publication Data

Names: Ilarion, Metropolitan of Volokolamsk, 1966– author.
Title: The Sermon on the Mount / Metropolitan Hilarion Alfeyev.
Other titles: Nagornai︠a︡ propoved: English
Description: Yonkers : St Vladimir's Seminary Press, 2019. | Series: Jesus Christ: his life
    and teaching; volume 2 | Includes bibliographical references. | In English; translated
    from Russian. | Summary: "Met. Hilarion Alfeyev devotes the entire second volume
    of the series Jesus Christ: His Life and Teaching to an exposition of the Sermon on
    the Mount, drawing upon the tradition of the Orthodox Church, patristic exegesis,
    and modern biblical scholarship"—Provided by publisher.
Identifiers: LCCN 2019031248 (print) | LCCN 2019031249 (ebook) | ISBN 9780881416534
    (paperback) | ISBN 9780881416541 (kindle edition)
Subjects: LCSH: Sermon on the Mount—Commentaries. | Jesus Christ—Person and
    offices.
Classification: LCC BT380.3 .I53 2019 (print) | LCC BT380.3 (ebook) | DDC
    226.9/06—dc23
LC record available at https://lccn.loc.gov/2019031248
LC ebook record available at https://lccn.loc.gov/2019031249

COPYRIGHT © 2019

ST VLADIMIR'S SEMINARY PRESS
575 Scarsdale Road, Yonkers, NY 10707
1-800-204-2665
www.svspress.com

ISBN 978–088141–653–4 (paper)
ISBN 978–088141–654–1 (electronic)

Unless noted otherwise, scriptural quotations are taken from the King James Version,
with some modifications for accuracy or ease of comprehension. Quotations from
the Psalms are taken from *The Psalter According to the Seventy* (Brookline, MA: Holy
Transfiguration Monastery), and are cited according to the Septuagint (LXX) numbering,
which differs from the Hebrew numbering (used by most English translations) in
Pss 9–147: LXX Ps 9 = Heb. Pss 9–10; LXX Pss 10–112 = Heb. 11–113;
LXX 113 = Heb. 114–115; LXX 114 = Heb. 116.1–9; LXX 115 = Heb. 116.10–19;
LXX 116–145 = Heb. 117–146; LXX 146 = Heb. 147.1–11; LXX 147 = Heb. 147.12–20.

TABLE OF CONTENTS

FOREWORD

The present volume continues our series of studies dedicated to the life and teaching of Jesus Christ.

In the first volume,[1] we laid out the general principles on which the whole series would be built, as well as information concerning the four Gospels, which are the primary source of information about Jesus' life and teaching. We also talked about the main directions in which modern New Testament studies is developing, paying attention to the need to take a critical approach to its findings and achievements. Then, we examined the opening chapters of the four Gospels, including the narratives of Jesus' birth, his baptism by John, his temptation in the wilderness, his going out to preach, and the calling of his disciples. Individual chapters of the book were dedicated to Jesus' prophetic ministry, the beginning of the conflict between him and the Pharisees, and also a description of some of the most characteristic features of his personality and character.

The present volume is dedicated to the Sermon on the Mount, which contains the quintessence of Jesus Christ's moral teaching. Regardless of the fact that different theories exist regarding the sermon's origins (there is the opinion that the Sermon is a collection of sayings uttered at various times),[2] we shall examine it as a single coherent text—in the form in which it has reached us.

The Sermon on the Mount occupies a special place in the Gospel of Matthew. It follows the story of Jesus embarking upon his ministry, and precedes the narratives of his miracles and parables. Its very position in this Gospel, and in the entire corpus of the four Gospels, compels one to

[1]Metropolitan Hilarion Alfeyev, *Jesus Christ: His Life and Teaching*, vol. 1, *The Beginning of the Gospel* (Yonkers, NY: St Vladimir's Seminary Press, 2018).

[2]See, in particular, Hans Dieter Betz, *Essays on the Sermon on the Mount*, trans. L. L. Welborn (Philadelphia, PA: Fortress, 1985), 42.

see in it a sort of spiritual and moral program that is further uncovered on the pages of the New Testament.

The Sermon on the Mount is the longest of all of Jesus' speeches contained in the Synoptic Gospels. This also compels one to distinguish it from other didactic material as a discourse that possesses independent significance. At the same time, the Sermon on the Mount cannot be examined in isolation from the Gospel of Matthew as a whole, from the other books of the New Testament, or even from Old Testament moral law, to which it is directly connected. Moreover, it should not be examined separately from the subsequent church tradition, in which it has a rich history of interpretation and practical application.

All these considerations lie at the basis of the exegetical[3] method that will be consistently applied to each section of the Sermon of the Mount in the present book. First of all, we will examine the text of the Sermon itself, noting, where necessary, the extant textual variants in the manuscript tradition, as well as parallels to the verses of the Sermon of the Mount in the other Gospels. In cases where a topic laid out in the Sermon is developed in more detail in other teachings of Jesus, the reader's attention will be called to these teachings and their interpretation.

Special attention will be paid to Old Testament parallels to the Sermon on the Mount, particularly to texts that the Sermon directly refers to, comments upon, expands on, or enriches. The Sermon's genetic dependence on Old Testament texts makes it necessary in some cases to refer to Jewish concepts that were the likely prototypes of the Greek terms and expressions used in the Sermon.

As for the subsequent Jewish tradition as reflected in rabbinical literature,[4] contrary to the opinion of various researchers, studying it can hardly enrich our understanding of the Sermon on the Mount in any substan-

[3]*Exegesis* (Greek *exēgēsis*): interpretation, explanation; *exegetics*: the science of interpretation; *exegetical*: connected with interpretation.—*Ed.*

[4]As a rule, classical rabbinical literature is understood to refer to the corpus of texts originating from the rabbinical academies of Palestine and Babylonia in the first millennium after Christ. This corpus includes standard texts (the Mishnah and Talmud, as well as the Tosefta), commentaries (midrashim), Aramaic translations (targumim) of biblical books, the responsa of the Geonim (written responses by the Jewish spiritual leaders of the late sixth century to the mid-eleventh century to questions sent to them from diaspora communities), and collections of prayers.

The Sermon on the Mount, Carl Heinrich Bloch, 1877

tial way. The problem here does not consist only in the chronological gap between the New Testament and rabbinical literature, the main corpus of which took shape significantly later than the appearance of the books of the New Testament.[5] The main problem seems to us to be that rabbinical literature belongs to a tradition that consciously opposes itself to Christianity. This tradition is the direct heir and successor to the teaching of the Pharisees and scribes, which Jesus harshly criticized, including in the Sermon on the Mount.

In contrast, the subsequent Christian tradition became the fertile ground in which the seeds sown by Jesus put forth abundant shoots. Already the first generations of Christians, including the apostle Paul and the authors of the Catholic Epistles of the New Testament in the second half of the first century, as well as the apostolic fathers in the second

[5]Menahem Kister, "Words and Formulae in the Gospels in the Light of Hebrew and Aramaic Sources," in *The Sermon on the Mount and Its Jewish Setting,* ed. Hans-Jürgen Becker and Serge Ruzer, Cahiers de la Revue biblique 60 (Paris: Gabalda, 2005), 119–120.

century, were engaged in the systematic interpretation of Jesus' spiritual and moral teaching. This work was continued by the church fathers of the third, fourth, and subsequent centuries. Even today, their interpretations are of great help to anyone who wishes to understand how the Sermon on the Mount can be lived out in the community of those who follow Jesus, who perceive his teaching not as abstract moralizing or an unattainable ideal, but as a guide to action.

The works of contemporary scholars dedicated to the text of the Sermon on the Mount and its theological interpretation will be referred to insofar as doing so would be necessary for attaining a better understanding of certain passages.

We have not set ourselves the task of giving an exhaustive analysis of the views of ancient and modern commentators on the Sermon on the Mount. It is much more important for us to understand how the Sermon on the Mount can be applied in contemporary conditions.

Very often, modern commentaries on Jesus' sayings are reduced to attempts to understand what he could have "had in mind" when he uttered certain things in his own historical context. For all the importance of finding the original meaning that Jesus' teachings could have had for his original audience, their significance is not at all limited to this meaning. In limiting the meaning of Jesus' words solely to the historical circumstances in which these words were pronounced, the scholar inevitably creates a distance between their supposed meaning in those circumstances and their practical application in other circumstances. Yet, in expounding his teachings, Jesus did not simply "have something in mind": he was inviting a response.[6] And this response must be expressed in very concrete actions on the practical level—in actions that are conditioned by neither historical era nor circumstance.

The present volume, which is a continuation of the volume *The Beginning of the Gospel*, is in turn a prologue to the study of Jesus' miracles and parables. The next two books in the series *Jesus Christ: His Life and Teaching* will be dedicated to these two topics.

[6]Jonathan T. Pennington, *Reading the Gospels Wisely: A Narrative and Theological Introduction* (Grand Rapids, MI: Baker Academic, 2012), 132.

Chapter 1

THE OVERALL CONTEXT OF THE SERMON ON THE MOUNT

The Gospel of Matthew includes five lengthy speeches by Jesus Christ. The first of them is the Sermon on the Mount, which constitutes about a ninth of the entire book. No other Gospel contains such an extended and systematic exposition of Jesus' spiritual and moral teaching, although we do find multiple parallels with the Sermon on the Mount in the other Gospels, especially in Luke.[1] It is possible that, at some very early stage of the development of Christian literary texts, the Sermon on the Mount existed as an independent literary work and was incorporated as a whole into Matthew's narrative. It is also possible that the Sermon on the Mount was woven together from various shorter thematic blocks that were found in the oral or written tradition. However, the scholarship does not lay out any textual data confirming such a possibility.

In contemporary scholarly literature, the Sermon on the Mount is most often viewed not as a speech by Jesus that was recorded by one of his disciples, but as the work of the Evangelist Matthew, based, at best, on

---

[1] Of the total text of the Sermon on the Mount, approximately twenty-seven percent of it has parallels in the Sermon on the Plain in Luke; about another thirty-three percent has parallels in other passages of the Gospel of Luke; and about five percent has parallels in the Gospel of Mark. The remaining thirty-five percent of the text has no parallel in the other Synoptic Gospels. See R. T. France, *The Gospel of Matthew*, The New International Commentary on the New Testament (Grand Rapids, MI: Eerdmans, 2007), 154–55.

The Evangelist Matthew,
miniature, 13th century

separate sayings uttered by Jesus, and sewn together into a single literary fabric by the evangelist. Georg Strecker, the author of one of the modern commentaries on the Sermon on the Mount, writes:

> No proper exegesis of the Sermon on the Mount can ignore the results of more than two hundred years of historical-critical research into the New Testament. One of these results is the determination that the Sermon on the Mount in the First Gospel is not a speech made by Jesus but the literary work of the Evangelist Matthew, for between the historical Jesus

and the composition of the New Testament Gospels there is a broad domain of oral and written tradition within the early Christian communities. Here, under the changing conditions of community thought and life, the gospel of Jesus was interpreted.[2]

The picture sketched by many researchers boils down to approximately the following: around the year AD 70, the shortest of the four Gospels appeared—the Gospel of Mark. It lay at the basis of the two other Synoptic Gospels, the Gospels of Matthew and Luke. The material that was in the Gospels of Matthew and Luke but absent from Mark must have been taken from another primary source; scholars called this source "Q."[3] Despite the fact that Q has never been found, many scholars have believed in its existence to such an extent that they even refer to it as a concretely existing text. In 2000, a "critical edition" of this imaginary primary source was published, based on individual verses from the Synoptic Gospels and

---

[2]Georg Strecker, *The Sermon on the Mount: An Exegetical Commentary*, trans. O. C. Dean Jr. (Edinburgh: T&T Clark, 1988), 11.

[3]From the German *Quelle*, "source." In the first volume of our series we spoke in more detail on the Q source and the hypothesis that all the canonical Gospels were created within Christian communities at the end of the first century and were intended for the members of these communities. See Metropolitan Hilarion Alfeyev, *Jesus Christ: His Life and Teaching*, vol. 1, *The Beginning of the Gospel* (Yonkers, NY: St Vladimir's Seminary Press, 2018), 61–63, 73–81.

the apocryphal Gospel of Thomas, torn out of context and presented in the form of parallel columns.[4]

The assertion became commonplace that the Gospel of Matthew appeared "at least fifty years after the death of Jesus,"[5] that is, in the 80s of the first century.[6] Researchers who proceed from the assumption that Matthew composed his Gospel after the fall of Jerusalem, at the height of the perse-cution of the Church, see confirmation of this posi-tion first and foremost in the part of the Sermon on the Mount that begins with the words, "Blessed are

The Evangelist Luke,
miniature, 13th century

they which are persecuted for righteousness' sake" (Mt 5.10). They suppose that the "entire verse [i.e., the eighth Beatitude] was composed by Mat-thew.... In this verse the situation of the Matthean community becomes visible. The congregation lives in persecution.... Matthew is writing in Gentile territory; his congregation is predominantly composed of Gen-tile Christians. The persecutions come, accordingly, not primarily from the Jews, but from Gentile compatriots."[7] The community to which the Sermon on the Mount is addressed is, "without doubt, a Jewish-Christian minority in distress.... Thus the [Sermon on the Mount] bears witness to a community that finds itself in the midst of a profound internal crisis."[8] The Matthean community "looks back on what may be a fifty-year history of Christian preaching of grace.... By ethicizing the Beatitudes,[9] Matthew

---

[4]James M. Robinson, Paul Hoffmann, and John S. Kloppenborg, eds., *The Critical Edition of Q: Synopsis Including the Gospels of Matthew and Luke, Mark and Thomas with English, German, and French Translations of Q and Thomas,* Hermeneia (Minneapolis, MN: Fortress, 2000).

[5]Richard B. Hays, *The Moral Vision of the New Testament: Community, Cross, New Creation; A Contemporary Introduction to New Testament Ethics* (San Francisco, CA: HarperSanFran-cisco, 1996), 323.

[6]John P. Meier, *Law and History in Matthew's Gospel: A Redactional Study of Mt. 5:17–48,* Analecta Biblica 71 (Rome: Biblical Institute Press, 1976), 7.

[7]Strecker, *Sermon on the Mount,* 42–44.

[8]Hans Dieter Betz, *Essays on the Sermon on the Mount,* trans. L. L. Welborn (Philadelphia, PA: Fortress, 1985), 21.

[9]That is, attributing to these Beatitudes an ethical character that they supposedly did not originally have.

The Evangelist Mark,
miniature, 13th century

and/or the community before him have accommo-
dated themselves to their changed situation. . . .
Obviously a basic problem for the Matthean community was how it would remain faithful to the faith
given it. And with his ethical interpretation Matthew wanted to help it do just that."[10]

The statements above testify to a tradition,
firmly established in contemporary scholarly circles, of ascribing that which the author of the first
Gospel himself ascribes to Jesus to a certain person, conventionally designated by the name "Matthew." Rather than preferring the direct witness of
the Gospel text, scholars prefer their own fantasies
concerning what was supposedly taking place in some "Matthean community." It is entirely likely that this community is the same sort of scholarly
phantasm as the Q source. Nevertheless, throughout the entire twentieth century, the notion migrated from one scholarly work to another that
the Sermon on the Mount was not delivered by Jesus to his immediate
audience, but was composed by Matthew on the basis of some of Jesus'
aphorisms by expanding them, "enriching" them, and "ethicizing" them
(that is, by giving them content that they did not originally have) for some
hypothetical community, with the goal of comforting this community during its persecution and to lead it out of crisis.[11]

[10]Ulrich Luz, *Matthew 1–7: A Commentary*, trans. James E. Crouch, ed. Helmut Koester, Hermeneia (Minneapolis, MN: Fortress, 2007), 201.

[11]Hans Windisch, *The Meaning of the Sermon on the Mount*, trans. S. MacLean Gilmour (Philadelphia, PA: Westminster, 1951), 26–27, 87–88; Martin Dibelius, "Die Bergpredigt," in *Botschaft und Geschichte*, Bd. 1 (Tübingen: Mohr, 1953), 120; Jacques Dupont, *Les Béatitudes*, new ed., vol. 1, *Le problème littéraire: les deux versions du Sermon sur la montagne et des Béatitudes* (Bruges: Abbaye de Saint-André, 1958), 254–58; Robert A. Guelich, *The Sermon on the Mount: A Foundation for Understanding* (Waco, TX: Word Books, 1982), 33–36; Ulrich Luz, *The Theology of the Gospel of Matthew*, trans. J. Bradford Robinson, New Testament Theology (Cambridge: Cambridge University Press, 1995), 11–21; Graham N. Stanton, "Matthew's Sermon on the Mount," in *Tradition and Interpretation in the New Testament: Essays in Honor of E. Earle Ellis for His 60th Birthday*, ed. Gerald F. Hawthorne and Otto Betz (Grand Rapids, MI: Eerdmans, 1987), 188–189; V. George Shillington, *The New Testament in Context: A Literary and Theological Textbook* (New York, NY: T&T Clark, 2008), 87–88; Martin Hengel, *The Four Gospels and the*

This view persists even today. One recent example is found in a book by the American scholars Charles E. Carlston and Craig A. Evans, *From Synagogue to Ecclesia: Matthew's Community at the Crossroads*, which was published in 2014. In this work, these two distinguished New Testament experts rehearse the hypotheses concerning the Matthean community that have become established in twentieth-century New Testament scholarship. The Sermon on the Mount, to which a considerable part of the book is devoted,[12] is presented as the product of Matthew's theological work, built on substantially expanded material from the Q source, to which was added material belonging to the evangelist's hand.[13] In the opinion of these scholars,

The Inspiration of Saint Matthew, Caravaggio, 1602

although the Beatitudes (Mt 5.3–12), the antitheses (Mt 5.21–47), and the Lord's Prayer (Mt 6.9–13) do not exhaust the content or meaning of the Sermon on the Mount, they "reflect in a significant way Matthew's pastoral concerns."[14] The entire discussion revolves around the theological vision of "Matthew": the presentation of the material is constructed in such a way that the figure of Jesus is not even discernible as a possible source of his own theological views. Obviously, the scholars are proceeding from the same methodological assumption: that between the "historical Jesus" and "Matthew" so much time has passed that almost nothing of the original "Gospel of Jesus" is left in Matthew.

In *The Beginning of the Gospel*, we spoke of the necessity of demythologizing New Testament scholarship—cleansing it of the myths and conjectures with which it had become overgrown over the course of the

---

One Gospel of Jesus Christ: An Investigation of the Collection and Origin of the Canonical Gospels, 1st North American ed. (Harrisburg, PA: Trinity Press International, 2000), 180–181.

[12] Charles E. Carlston and Craig A. Evans, *From Synagogue to Ecclesia: Matthew's Community at the Crossroads*, Wissenschaftliche Untersuchungen zum Neuen Testament 334 (Tübingen: Mohr Siebeck, 2014), 186–244.

[13] Carlston and Evans, *From Synagogue to Ecclesia*, 104–106 and elsewhere.

[14] Carlston and Evans, *From Synagogue to Ecclesia*, 192.

nineteenth and twentieth centuries.[15] This task remains urgent today, since, as one modern critic of "critical biblical studies" noted, "By the late twentieth century, the *Neutestamentler's* cappucino had too frequently become all froth and no coffee."[16] Thanks to various kinds of fanciful scholarly conceptions, the most important thing has disappeared from the researchers' field of vision: the Gospel text as a single, coherent narrative. The image of Christ as the Author of the sayings, sermons, and parables that the evangelists ascribe to him has disappeared. Drowning in conjectures concerning the reason for the appearance of a particular story, phrase, or word, many scholars refuse on principle to believe in the simple and artless testimony of the Gospels, a holistic view of which has been carefully preserved in church tradition.

At present the scholarly community has embarked on a radical revision of the views on the Gospel text that prevailed in the literature on the New Testament in the twentieth century. The "new perspective on Jesus," advocated in particular by James D. G. Dunn, rejects the opposition between the "historical Jesus" and the "Christ of faith" that dominated scholarly literature in the twentieth century,[17] as well as many hypotheses concerning the supposed primary sources of the Gospels. Also subject to revision is the "two-source hypothesis," which until recently seemed to be unshakeable; according to this hypothesis, Mark and Q formed the basis for all the Synoptic Gospels. Finally, scholars have begun to move the dating of the Synoptic Gospels earlier—to the 50s or even the 40s of the first century.[18]

This turn in New Testament studies toward the traditional approach to the text of the Gospels offers hope that, sooner or later, the scholarly community will agree with what ancient commentators did not doubt: that the Sermon on the Mount in the Gospel of Matthew is a record of a speech

[15]Metropolitan Hilarion Alfeyev, *The Beginning of the Gospel*, 71–82.

[16]Markus Bockmuehl, *Seeing the Word: Refocusing New Testament Study* (Grand Rapids, MI: Baker Academic, 2006), 37.

[17]James D. G. Dunn, *A New Perspective on Jesus: What the Quest for the Historical Jesus Missed* (Grand Rapids, MI: Baker Academic, 2005), 15–22.

[18]See, for example, Andreas J. Köstenberger, L. Scott Kellum, and Charles L. Quarles, *The Cradle, the Cross, and the Crown: An Introduction to the New Testament* (Nashville, TN: B&H Academic, 2009), 187, 234, 264.

that was given at some point by Jesus Christ. The question of whether this record is a word-for-word reproduction or a paraphrase of what Jesus said will evidently continue to be discussed. From our point of view, however, given the absence of any other alternate sources, such a discussion cannot lead to any convincing conclusions. In our opinion, an analysis of the text that has come down to us in its totality is a much more promising and fruitful pursuit.

1. The Sermon on the Mount and the Sermon on the Plain

One of the premises of the historical-critical method of studying the New Testament was the belief that only the shortest and most succinct sayings ascribed to Jesus actually belonged to him. Where two versions of a single saying appeared in the Synoptic Gospels—a shorter version and a more expanded version—preference was given to the former: it was this version that would be recognized as authentic. It was believed that, as the sayings of Jesus—always distinguished by their simplicity and laconism—underwent editorial revision, they acquired additions tacked on to them by the evangelists in order to allow the text to be better assimilated by their church communities.

In light of this, scholars often compare the Sermon on the Mount with the so-called Sermon on the Plain in the Gospel of Luke (Lk 6.20−49). At first glance, the Sermon on the Plain is a much reduced version of the Sermon on the Mount,[19] on the basis of which many scholars infer the former's primacy in relation to the latter. The hypothetical Q source

---

[19]For a table of parallels, see Charles H. Talbert, *Matthew*, Paideia (Grand Rapids, MI: Baker Academic, 2010), 71 (the author counts nine parallel passages between the Sermon on the Mount and the Sermon on the Plain, and eight between the Sermon on the Mount and other passages in the Gospel of Luke).

The Sermon on the Mount, Károly Ferenczy, 1896

supposedly contained precisely such a brief version, which is given by Luke and which Matthew substantially expanded and added to.[20]

This position seems to us to be objectionable, unsound, and tenuous for a whole range of reasons. First, it is not absolutely necessary that the brief version be the source of the fuller version: it may very well be the other way round. Second, the integrity and compositional completeness of the Sermon on the Mount does not permit us to interpret it as being a work constructed through the mechanical expansion of some shorter original source. Third, the Sermon on the Plain contains material absent from the Sermon on the Mount. Finally, between the two speeches, alongside the thematic similarities, there are also substantial differences, including differences of meaning.

It seems much more likely that the Gospel of Matthew presents a speech that Jesus delivered under one set of circumstances, while the Gospel of Luke presents another speech delivered at another place and time.[21] In Luke, the Sermon on the Plain precedes the story of the choosing of the

[20]See, for example, Luz, *Matthew 1–7*, 174–176. See also Strecker, *Sermon on the Mount*, 12; Graham N. Stanton, *A Gospel for a New People: Studies in Matthew* (Edinburgh: T&T Clark, 1992), 286–289, 299; John Reumann, *Jesus in the Church's Gospels: Modern Scholarship and the Earliest Sources* (Philadelphia, PA: Fortress, 1968), 230–232.

[21]Cf. W. F. Albright and C. S. Mann, *Matthew: Introduction, Translation and Notes by W. F. Albright and C. S. Mann,* Anchor Yale Bible 26 (New Haven, CT: Yale University Press, 2011; first published 1971 by Doubleday), 48.

Twelve (Lk 6.12–16). In Matthew, the choosing of the Twelve (Mt 10.1–4) takes place significantly later than the Sermon on the Mount. In Matthew, Jesus, seeing the people, "went up into a mountain," sat down with his disciples around him, and began to speak (Mt 5.1). In Luke, Jesus descended from a mountain after choosing the Twelve, stood in a plain, and began to speak, looking at his disciples, but addressing the people around them (Lk 6.17–20). Jesus delivers the Sermon on the Mount while seated, and the Sermon on the Plain while standing; the audience listens to the former seated, and the latter presumably standing. Just this fact alone could have led Jesus to speak for a much shorter time in the second instance than in the first.

To be convinced that the Sermon on the Mount is by no means an editorial expansion upon the Sermon on the Plain, it is sufficient to look at the opening segment of both speeches. In Matthew, Jesus' sermon opens with nine Beatitudes, each beginning with the word "Blessed," and the blessed are spoken of in the third person ("for *theirs* is the kingdom of heaven," "for *they* shall be comforted"). In the parallel passage in the Gospel of Luke (Lk 6.20–23), there are only four Beatitudes beginning with the same word, and the blessed are spoken of in the second person ("for *yours* is the kingdom of God," "for *ye* shall be filled"). This indicates that in the Sermon on the Plain, Jesus is directly addressing his actual listeners in the crowd: blessed are *ye*—the poor, the hungry, the weeping. In Matthew, on the other hand, he gives general exhortations that concern all who are ready to follow him.

In many editions of the New Testament, in both Matthew and Luke, the Beatitudes begin with the words "Blessed are the poor in spirit" (Mt 5.3; Lk 6.20). However, in the most ancient manuscript copies, the Gospel of Luke reads: "Blessed be ye poor" (this reading is given as the most authoritative in the critical edition of the New Testament).[22] It is also distinctive that in Matthew, Jesus speaks of the blessedness of those who "hunger and thirst after righteousness," while in Luke he speaks simply of those who "hunger." The appearance of the expression "poor in spirit" in later manuscript

---

[22]This is the reading accepted by the most recent critical edition of the New Testament, the twenty-eighth edition of the Nestle-Aland text: *Novum Testamentum Graece*, 28th rev. ed. (Stuttgart: Deutsche Bibelgisellschaft, 2012), commonly abbreviated as NA28.

The Twelve Apostles, miniature, 13th century

copies of Luke is usually attributed to harmonistic alteration of the text: copyists, comparing the text of Luke with the text of Matthew, added the words "in spirit," supposing that they had been left out in Luke. However, we cannot exclude the possibility that Jesus used different expressions in different situations.

Ultimately, Matthew and Luke do not simply have different points of emphasis: the logic of Jesus' speech in the two cases is different. The text in Luke can be summarized thus: blessed are those who suffer now, for in the future they will receive their recompense. It is no coincidence that in Luke's version the word "now" is added in reference to both those who hunger and those who weep, which points to the temporary nature of suffering and implies that the recompense for suffering does not come at the present time, but most likely beyond the threshold of death. It is there, in the kingdom of God, that the poor will gain the kingdom of heaven, those who hunger will be filled, and those who weep will laugh.

In the Sermon on the Mount in Matthew, what emerges at the forefront is not the suffering for which a person will receive recompense in the

future, but the acquisition of specific spiritual and
moral qualities in order to achieve blessedness. The
word "now" is absent in Matthew's version, and the
reward for suffering is not necessarily thought of as
relating exclusively to a person's posthumous fate:
the very existence in a person of the moral qualities mentioned makes him blessed already here and
now. Only the last two lines are practically identical
in both evangelists (Mt 5.11–12; Lk 6.22–23), while
the entire sequence of Beatitudes in Matthew is different from that in Luke.

The Evangelist Luke,
El Greco, c. 1608

As with the Sermon on the Mount as a whole,
many scholars give preference to Luke's version of the Beatitudes as being
more authentic: the Beatitudes in the Sermon on the Mount supposedly
"represent a filling-out of their original form."[23] How was this version created? In the original list of the Beatitudes there were only the poor, those
who hunger, and those who weep, but when Matthew edited it, he added
the meek, the merciful, the pure in heart, the peacemakers, and those
persecuted for righteousness' sake, at the same time turning the poor into
the poor in spirit, and those who hunger into those who hunger and thirst
after righteousness: "While the beatitudes were originally prophetic cries
of comfort and promise directed to the afflicted, [Matthew] has infused
into them his own moral parenesis on Christian attitudes and conduct."[24]

This implies that Luke's version is close to the original version of these
"prophetic cries," of which there were presumably three, which sounded
approximately like this:

> Blessed are the poor, for theirs is the kingdom of God.
> Blessed are those who hunger, for they shall be filled.
> Blessed are those who weep/grieve, for they shall laugh.

---

[23]Ernst Käsemann, *New Testament Questions of Today*, trans. W. J. Montague (Philadelphia,
PA: Fortress, 1969), 100.
[24]Meier, *Law and History*, 42.

*Joy of All who
Sorrow*, icon,
18th century

The above reconstruction[25] is essentially a sort of "common denominator" between the Beatitudes presented in Matthew and Luke, arrived at by pruning away everything not shared by the two evangelists. Following the footsteps of many other researchers, Ulrich Luz suggests that only three reconstructed Beatitudes "go back to Jesus in approximately their Lukan form." To these three Beatitudes, in his opinion, a fourth was added in Q ("Blessed are ye, when men shall revile you . . ."); then the Beatitudes were reformulated in light of the book of Isaiah and certain psalms, and entered the Gospel of Matthew in this redacted form.[26]

[25]Quoted from Anna Wierzbicka, *What Did Jesus Mean?: Explaining the Sermon on the Mount and the Parables in Simple and Universal Human Concepts* (Oxford: Oxford University Press, 2001), 31.
   [26]Luz, *Matthew 1–7*, 186–187.

However, in approaching the matter thus, we cannot avoid the conclusion that in the process of "redaction" the author who calls himself Matthew changed Jesus' original preaching practically to the point of complete unrecognizability. Moreover, the Gospel text itself does not give any basis for such suppositions with regard to either the Beatitudes or the Sermon on the Mount as a whole.

It appears fairly obvious to us that Matthew and Luke present two different sermons that echo each other thematically but are far from identical. Jesus could well have—and must have—repeated the same truths multiple times in various contexts, giving them different nuances depending on the circumstances, the audience, and other factors. Even within a single Gospel we can observe how Jesus, in his conversations with the disciples and when addressing the people, returns to the same ideas and uses similar verbal formulas—sometimes in a strictly fixed form, and sometimes with minor divergences. This is what any teacher would do in order to help students grasp a lesson well. Perhaps this is precisely why Jesus' words were seared into the memory of the disciples with such word-for-word fidelity that they could reproduce them from memory even many years after his resurrection.

Augustine of Hippo touches on the topic of the relationship between the Sermon on the Mount and the Sermon on the Plain in his treatise *The Harmony of the Gospels*. At first he seems to allow the possibility that Luke "introduced the self-same discourse of the Lord, but that at the same time he has omitted certain sentences which Matthew has inserted." Moreover, he points out that Luke "has also brought in other sayings which Matthew has not mentioned; and that, in a similar manner, he has expressed certain of these utterances in somewhat different terms, but without detriment to the integrity of the truth." At the same time, turning his attention to the fact that Jesus delivers the speech on a mountain in Matthew, but on a plain in Luke, Augustine poses the following question: "And what should there be, indeed, to hinder [us from supposing] Christ to have repeated elsewhere some words which He had already spoken, or from doing a second time certain things which He had already done on some previous occasion?" Augustine comes to the conclusion that on the mountain Jesus "delivered

The Church of the Icon of the Mother of God "Joy of All Who Sorrow" in Moscow on the street Bol'shaya Ordynka

that discourse which Matthew has introduced, and which Luke has left unnoticed . . . and that thereafter, when He had now come down, He spoke in the plain a second discourse similar to the first, on which Matthew is silent, but which is detailed by Luke."[27]

In the Sermon on the Plain, the four Beatitudes are followed by three antitheses beginning with the words "Woe unto you":

> But woe unto you that are rich, for ye have received your consolation! Woe unto you that are full, for ye shall hunger! Woe unto you that laugh now, for ye shall mourn and weep! Woe unto you, when all men shall speak well of you! For so did their fathers to the false prophets. (Lk 6.24–26)

All this material is absent from the Sermon on the Mount in Matthew. This material thematically echoes the teaching of Jesus presented in other places: for example, the assertion that "it is hard for a rich man to enter into the kingdom of heaven" (Mt 19.23). But we do not find any textually similar material. This must mean either that Luke used material unknown to Matthew, or that which we are attempting to demonstrate: the Sermon on the Mount and the Sermon on the Plain are two different sermons that were delivered at different times before different audiences. In the case of

[27]Augustine of Hippo, *Harmony of the Gospels* 2.19.44–45 (NPNF¹ 6:124–125).

the Sermon on the Plain, we have a clear contrast between the poor and the rich, those who hunger and those who are full, those who weep and those who laugh. In the Sermon on the Mount, this contrast is completely absent.

---

2. The Composition and Structure of the Sermon on the Mount

The Sermon on the Mount in the Gospel of Matthew is a whole, coherent text that has its own clearly thought-out structure and composition. At its middle stands the Lord's Prayer ("Our Father"), from which thematic clusters radiate in various directions, to the beginning and to the end of the text, like concentric circles: each of these can be considered the symmetrical reflection of another cluster located on the other side of the composition's center. All this creates an internal symmetry and leads scholars to speak of the ring-shaped composition of the Sermon (in particular, a certain symmetry can be observed between Mt 6.1–6 and Mt 6.16–18, between 5.21–48 and 6.19–7.11, between 5.17–20 and 7.12, between 5.3–16 and 7.13–27, and between 5.1–2 and 7.28–8.1).[28] The Beatitudes that begin the Sermon on the Mount (Mt 5.3–12) form a thematic arch with the words about the house on the rock that conclude the Sermon (Mt 7.24–27). Though this kind of structural analysis is not without question, it helps us to understand why the Sermon on the Mount is understood as a whole, complete, and clearly structured composition. Despite the presence of many apparently unconnected thematic passages within it, the Sermon has its own internal logic and its own arc of development from beginning to end.

The compositional completeness of the Sermon on the Mount could be ascribed to the author of the First Gospel, but there is much more ground for seeing in it the distinctive speaking style of its author—Jesus Christ.

---

[28]Luz, *Matthew 1–7*, 172–173.

Anyone who has had to preach a sermon or read a lecture knows that in order for material to be optimally mastered, it must not only be articulately presented, but also clearly structured. The key points of the speech must be underlined and emphasized, and the main ideas repeated many times. All of this is taught in rhetoric lessons, which Jesus, we assume, did not take. The beauty, elegance, internal proportionality, and clearly structured quality of his speech was not a result of lessons learned from someone else, but a reflection of his particular way of thinking and a means of expressing his thought. In contrast to many preachers, who do not know what they want to say, improvise along the way, and are unable to structure their speech clearly, Jesus knew what he wanted to say and how he wanted to say it. The compositional completeness of his speech is the direct result of the inner integrity his thinking and his conviction about the truth of his words.

Like many of Jesus' other speeches, the Sermon on the Mount is "stitched" through with certain constantly repeated words or formulas that make it possible to better remember and assimilate the material. Thus, for example, in the beginning of the text, the word "blessed" is repeated nine times; further on, the refrain "Ye have heard that it was said. . . . But I say unto you" is heard six times; and an entire series of six commandments is given in the negative ("Take heed that ye give not your alms before men"; "Thou shalt not be as the hypocrites are"; "Be not, as the hypocrites, of a sad countenance"; "Lay not up for yourselves treasures upon earth"; "Judge not"; "Give not that which is holy unto the dogs"). The word "kingdom" is encountered nine times in the Sermon on the Mount, and the formula "the law and the prophets" is heard thrice.

As a rule, scholars imagine the evangelist as a person sewing the fabric of his narrative together from scraps of material at hand many decades after the events that lie at the foundation of the narrative; hence the many hypotheses about original sources and their subsequent editorial revisions. But why could we not suppose that either Matthew himself, or one of the thousands of people who were listening to Jesus when he was delivering his sermon, was capable of taking it down in shorthand? If this person was not able to do so directly on the spot, he could have done it a little later,

*The Sermon
on the Mount,*
Cosimo Rosselli
and Piero di
Cosimo, fresco,
1481

from memory. Even if he had reproduced the sermon significantly later, why could he not have committed it to memory word for word—all the more so if he had heard the same sermon more than once?[29]

In each person's life there are conversations that one remembers with literal precision, which a person can reproduce word for word even many decades later. These are conversations that have exerted a special influence on someone's fate or worldview, or conversations with especially significant people whose every word sears itself into one's memory. Why could Jesus' disciples, who spent so much time with him and heard his teachings, not have remembered them word for word and passed them on to succeeding generations—all the more since all of them heard what he said, and consequently, when one disciple orally recalled Jesus' words, the others could double-check them? The text of the Gospels—if not in their final form, then in the form of fragments—had already taken shape in the apostles' lifetimes, and we have no reason to distrust it and everywhere suspect the work of later redactors, who supposedly put into Jesus' mouth sayings that he did not in fact say.

In the Sermon on the Mount, Jesus comes across to the reader as a moral teacher first and foremost. However, he is different from typical

[29]Memorization was a much more common and necessary skill in the context of first century Palestine than many moderns understand. For a helpful summary of recent New Testament scholarship on different models of oral tradition, see Richard Bauckham, *Jesus and the Eyewitnesses: The Gospels as Eyewitness Testimony*, 2nd ed. (Grand Rapids, MI: Eerdmans, 2017), 240–63.—*Ed.*

The Greek
Orthodox
Church of the
Holy Trinity on
the peak of Sinai
(the mount of
Moses)

teachers, whose mission is finished after their disciples have learned the lesson. Jesus remains necessary as a person even after his teaching has been presented:

> Christ is a teacher in a unique way, for what he teaches depends on his own person for its truth, validity, and permanence. Teacher and teaching become inextricably bound together. You do not fully understand what the teaching is unless you understand who the teacher is. You cannot fully accept the teaching as true unless you accept the teacher as your Lord, as the Son of God and Son of Man. In short, accepting his teaching involves following him in the path of discipleship, permanently.[30]

Already in the early Christian period interpreters were drawing attention to the parallelism between the Sermon on the Mount and the narrative in Exodus of how on Mount Sinai Moses received the tablets on which God had inscribed the Ten Commandments: in both instances the action takes place on a mountain; Jesus emerges as a new Moses, who renews the law of Sinai.[31] The Sermon on the Mount possesses a programmatic

[30]John P. Meier, *The Vision of Matthew: Christ, Church, and Morality in the First Gospel* (Crossroad, 1991; repr. Eugene, OR: Wipf & Stock, 2004), 43.

[31]Gregory of Nyssa, *The Beatitudes* 7. English translation in Gregory of Nyssa, *The Lord's Prayer; The Beatitudes*, trans. Hilda C. Graef, Ancient Christian Writers 18 (Mahwah, NJ: Paulist Press, 1954), 154.

character: it is the quintessence of the spiritual program that Jesus offers his followers. At the same time, it is conceived as a fulfillment of the law of Moses, as the new interpretation of the law and its correction.

Thus, on the one hand, Jesus emphasizes the importance of the law ("one jot or one tittle shall in no wise pass from the law, till all be fulfilled") and speaks of himself as not the destroyer, but the fulfiller of the law ("Think not that I am come to destroy the law, or the prophets: I am not come to destroy, but to fulfill"). But, on the other hand, starting out from what "was said by them of old," he consciously and consistently reinterprets the law of Moses.

What are the main differences here? If the commandments given by God through Moses were addressed to the people of Israel as a whole, then the commandments of Jesus are addressed to the individual listener. If the law of Moses sets up a defined moral standard, then Jesus raises this standard significantly higher. If, in the law of Moses, God speaks almost exclusively of the external aspects of a person's behavior, then Jesus devotes more attention to a person's internal condition. The Beatitudes do not abolish the Ten Commandments, and the remaining material of the Sermon on the Mount does not abolish the other statutes of the law of Moses. However, in the Sermon on the Mount, the relationship between God and man is brought to a new spiritual and moral level, thanks to which the entire system of relationships between people is also rebuilt afresh.

3. "He Went up into a Mountain"

The Sermon on the Mount is preceded by the words of the evangelist: "And seeing the multitudes, he went up into a mountain: and when he sat down his disciples came unto him. And he opened his mouth, and taught them, saying . . ." (Mt 5.1–2).

Mountains have always held a special significance for mankind. Even in our day, in the minds of many people, being in the mountains

is associated not only with fresh air and beautiful landscapes, but also freedom from cares and the opportunity to be alone with oneself, with nature, and with God. In the understanding of ancient Israel, mountains were unambiguously associated with the presence of God. The psalmist says, "I have lifted up mine eyes to the mountains, from whence cometh my help. My help cometh from the LORD, who hath made heaven and the earth" (Ps 120.1–2).

If it is enough to raise one's eyes to the hills in order to receive help from God, then it is necessary to go up into the mountain in order to meet with God. God often arranges to meet a person not just anywhere, but specifically on a mountain.

One example that was undoubtedly well known to Jesus' listeners and Matthew's readers is the biblical story of how Abraham offered his son Isaac as a sacrifice. The story begins with God saying to Abraham, "Take now thy son, thine only son Isaac, whom thou lovest, and get thee into the land of Moriah; and offer him there for a burnt offering upon *one of the mountains*[32] which I will tell thee of." Abraham sets out without hesitation and, after three days' journey, arrives at the mountain indicated by God. There he sets up an altar, binds his

A depiction of Abraham in the Kiev Psalter, 1397

son, and raises a knife over him, but the voice of an angel from heaven stops him with the words: "Lay not thine hand upon the lad, neither do thou any thing unto him, for now I know that thou fearest God, seeing thou hast not withheld thy son, thine only son from me." Abraham brings a ram for the sacrifice in place of his son and names the place *Jehovahjireh* ("the Lord will see [to it]"). The account concludes with

[32]Emphasis added.

the words: ". . . as it is said to this day, '*In the mount*[33] of the LORD it shall be seen'" (Gen 22.2–14).

Another example is God's appearance to Moses in the wilderness of Sinai. According to the account in Exodus, Moses ascends the mountain, and God calls to him from the mountain. Moses goes down to the people, relates God's words to them, and then goes up again to hear God's command to return to the people and sanctify them over the course of three days:

The Prophet Moses,
icon, 1571

> And it came to pass on the third day in the morning, that there were thunders and lightnings, and a thick cloud *upon the mount* [Sinai], and the voice of the trumpet exceeding loud, so that all the people that was in the camp trembled. And Moses brought forth the people out of the camp to meet with God; and they stood *at the lower part of the mount*. And *mount Sinai* was altogether smoking, because the LORD descended upon it in fire: and the smoke thereof ascended as the smoke of a furnace, and *the whole mount* quaked greatly. And when the voice of the trumpet sounded long, and waxed louder and louder, Moses spake, and God answered him by a voice. And the LORD came down *upon mount Sinai, on the top of the mount*; and the LORD called Moses up to the *top of the mount*; and Moses went up. (Ex 19.16–20)[34]

But this time, too, God commands Moses to return to the people and warn them not to approach the mountain, lest they die. Only after Moses ascends Mount Sinai the fourth time does God give the commandments that form the basis of the so-called law of Moses. Moses relates them to the people and records them. But the theophany at Sinai does not end with this. God calls Moses once more, and again the meeting takes place on a mountain:

[33]Emphasis added.
[34]Emphases added.

And the LORD said unto Moses, "Come up to me *into the mount*, and be there: and I will give thee tables of stone, and a law, and commandments which I have written, that thou mayest teach them." And Moses rose up, and his minister Joshua, and Moses went up *into the mount* of God. And he said unto the elders, "Tarry ye here for us, until we come again unto you: and, behold, Aaron and Hur are with you. If any man have any matters to do, let him come unto them." And Moses went up *into the mount*, and a cloud covered *the mount*. And the glory of the LORD abode *upon mount Sinai*, and the cloud covered it six days; and the seventh day he called unto Moses out of the midst of the cloud. And the sight of the glory of the LORD was like devouring fire *on the top of the mount* in the eyes of the children of Israel. And Moses went into the midst of the cloud, and went up *into the mount*: and Moses was *in the mount* forty days and forty nights. (Ex 24.12–18)[35]

When Moses comes down from the mountain, he notices that the people have turned away from God during his forty-day absence and begun to worship a golden calf. In his anger, he breaks the tablets that have the commandments of God written upon them. But God calls him again: "Cut two tables of stone like unto the first [and come up to me on the mount]: and I will write upon these tables the words that were in the first tables, which thou didst break. And be ready in the morning, and come up in the morning unto mount Sinai, and present thyself there to me in the top of the mount" (Ex 34.1–2). Again the meeting between God and Moses takes place on a mountain, and again Moses receives instructions from God that he must relate to the people after coming down from the mountain.

Mount Sinai, which is also known as Mount Horeb, is also associated with God's appearance to the prophet Elijah. Elijah journeyed toward this mountain forty days and forty nights. As he approached it, God said to him:

"Go forth, and stand upon the mount before the LORD." And, behold, the LORD passed by, and a great and strong wind rent the mountains, and broke in pieces the rocks before the LORD, but the LORD was not

[35]Emphases added.

in the wind; and after the wind an earthquake, but the LORD was not in the earthquake; and after the earthquake a fire, but the LORD was not in the fire; and after the fire a still small voice [and the LORD was there]. (1 Kg 19.11–12)

Besides Sinai, there was another mountain that was of special significance to the people of Israel: Mount Zion. It was on this mountain that David built his city (2 Sam 5.7–10). He extolled it many times in the Psalms:

The Ascent of the Prophet Elijah, Veliky Novgorod, 13th century

> They that trust in the Lord shall be as Mount Sion; he that dwelleth at Jerusalem, nevermore shall he be shaken. Mountains are round about her, and the Lord is round about his people from henceforth and forevermore. (Ps 124.1–2)
> The Lord bless thee out of Sion: and mayest thou see the good things of Jerusalem all the days of thy life. (Ps 127.5)
> Let them be put to shame and turned back, all they that hate Sion. (Ps 128.5)
> For the Lord hath elected Sion, he hath chosen her to be a habitation for himself. (Ps 131.13)
> The Lord bless thee out of Sion, he that made heaven and the earth. (Ps 133.3)
> Blessed be the LORD out of Sion, who dwelleth in Jerusalem. (Ps 134.21)

According to Jewish tradition, Mount Zion is the same mountain in the land of Moriah that Abraham ascended in order to offer Isaac as a sacrifice. According to Christian tradition, the first man, Adam, was buried on this mountain; on this same mountain Jesus Christ was crucified.

Over the course of his earthly life, Jesus went up on mountains many times. In the Gospel of Matthew alone we find eight such episodes.[36] In the

---

[36]On the symbolism of mountains in Matthew, see Dorothy A. Lee, *Transfiguration*, New Century Theology (New York, NY: Continuum, 2004), 43–46.

Jesus Ascending the Cross,
Dečani, Serbian Orthodox
monastery, Balkans,
14th century

beginning of this Gospel we read of how the devil took Jesus "up into an exceeding high mountain, and showed him all the kingdoms of the world, and the glory of them" (Mt 4.8). Then Jesus went up into a mountain to deliver his first sermon (Mt 5.1). After Jesus fed the five thousand with five loaves and two fishes in the wilderness, he went up a mountain in order to pray by himself (Mt 14.23; Mk 6.46). Further on we see how, having gone up into a mountain, he healed the "lame, blind, dumb, maimed, and many others" (Mt 15.30). One of Jesus' main miracles, the Transfiguration, also took place on a mountain (Mt 17.1–3; Mk 9.2–4; Lk 9.28–30). On the Mount of Olives, Jesus answered the disciples' questions regarding the signs of his second coming (Mt 24.3; Mk 13.3). At the conclusion of the Last Supper, Jesus and the disciples, "when they had sung an hymn . . . went out into the mount of Olives" (Mt 26.30; Mk 14.26; Lk 22.39). At the same place, in the garden of Gethsemane, Jesus prayed to the Father that, if it were possible, this cup should pass from him (Mt 26.36–46; Mk 14.32–42; Lk 22.41–46). Finally, after Jesus' resurrection, the eleven disciples "went away into Galilee, into a mountain where Jesus had appointed them. And when they saw him, they worshipped him, but some doubted" (Mt 28.16–17).[37]

We can add to these episodes the account in Mark and Luke of how Jesus "[went] up into a mountain, and [called] unto him whom he would, and they came unto him. And he ordained twelve" (Mk 3.13–14; Lk 6.12–13). We should also note that, according to John, the feeding of the five thousand with five loaves took place on a mountain (Jn 6.3). John mentions that Jesus, after visiting the temple, went to the Mount of Olives, and went

---

[37]Some scholars propose that Jesus met his disciples after the resurrection on the same mountain in Galilee where he delivered the Sermon on the Mount, the Sermon being the kernel of what the disciples were to "teach all nations." See Udo Schnelle, *Theology of the New Testament,* trans. M. Eugene Boring (Grand Rapids, MI: Baker Academic, 2009), 438.

to the temple again in the morning (Jn 8.1–2). From Luke we learn that going up into the mountain was Jesus' habitual practice: "In the day time he was teaching in the temple; and at night he went out, and abode in the mount that is called the mount of Olives" (Lk 21.37). Luke is the only evangelist who specifies that after the Last Supper Jesus went to the Mount of Olives "as he was wont" (Lk 22.39).

The Evangelist Mark, miniature, Codex Aureus, 778–820

For an itinerant preacher such as Jesus, it would seem that it was not necessary for him to go up into the mountains. All the main roads lay on the plains, and one could easily avoid the mountains if one wished, and interact with the people in the towns and villages. Yet we see Jesus going up into various mountains again and again. Sometimes he goes up alone, in order to be alone with the Father. Sometimes he takes the disciples with him. But at times entire crowds of people go up after him, in order to hear a word from him or to receive healing.

The image of Jesus going up a mountain in order to give instruction to the disciples, and through them to the people, is reminiscent of Moses, who went up a mountain in order to receive instruction from God and relate it to the people. However, there is a substantial difference between the two images. Moses goes up alone, and the people are strictly forbidden to approach the mountain; Jesus takes with himself to the mountain those to whom he intends to impart a new teaching—one that fulfills the law of Moses and is henceforth to serve as a moral standard for his followers. Moses goes up into the mountain to meet with God; Jesus is himself God, who invites people to the mountain to meet with him. Moses goes up into the mountain several times, and each time comes down and relates to the people what he has heard from God; Jesus goes up into the mountain together with the people and tells them what they must hear.

According to a tradition that appeared in the fourth century, the mountain on which the Sermon on the Mount was delivered is located not far from the Sea of Galilee: it is called the Mount of Beatitudes, and from it

The Mount
of the Beatitudes

one has a picturesque view of the Sea of Galilee and the surroundings.[38] In contrast to the rocky Mount Sinai, whose peak stands at 7,497 feet, the Mount of Beatitudes stands only 509 feet high,[39] and climbing it does not pose any particular difficulty. The external appearance of this mountain, which is surrounded by fertile land, is reminiscent of the humility of the Teacher, who came not to proclaim to the people of Israel harsh laws in thunder and lightning, but to proclaim new God-revealed truths to mankind in a "still small voice."

Jesus' words in the Sermon on the Mount are not the fruit of book-learned wisdom. They are the words of God himself addressed to mankind. They differ from ordinary human words in both form and content. And it is precisely the awareness that the words of the Sermon on the Mount belong to God and not simply to a man—even though he may be a prophet and teacher—that is the key to understanding the Sermon's meaning and significance. It was God who called Moses to Mount Sinai to give him the tablets of stone with commandments for the people of Israel. And it is God who initiates the new covenant with the new Israel through his Son, who

---

[38]Donald L. Brake and Todd Bolen, *Jesus, a Visual History: The Dramatic Story of the Messiah in the Holy Land* (Grand Rapids, MI: Zondervan, 2014), 89.

[39]The summit of the Mount of the Beatitudes is 509 feet above the Sea of Galilee, but its base is 190 feet below sea level.—*Ed.*

*At the Sea of
Galilee*, V. D.
Polenov, 1888

solemnly proclaims in the Sermon on the Mount what God himself wishes to say to the people through him.

4. To Whom Was the Sermon on the Mount Addressed?

To whom was the Sermon on the Mount addressed—the disciples, or the people? The answer is not clear from the evangelist's introductory words: "And seeing the multitudes, he went up into a mountain; and when he sat down, his disciples came unto him. And he opened his mouth, and taught them, saying . . ." (Mt 5.1–2). On the one hand, the multitudes are mentioned; on the other hand, the disciples are also mentioned, to whom the words "taught them" apply. However, at the conclusion of the Sermon of the Mount, the evangelist writes, "And it came to pass, when Jesus had ended these sayings, the people were astonished at his doctrine: for he taught them as one having authority" (Mt 7.28–29). At this point "taught them" applies to the people and not only to the disciples. From this it follows that when Jesus was delivering his sermon, both the disciples and the people were with him: he addressed his words either to both the disciples and the people, or to the disciples only, but in such a way that the people could hear them also. Consequently, his teaching had universal meaning.

Which of Jesus' disciples could have been present at the Sermon on the Mount? In the first four chapters of the Gospel of Matthew preceding the Sermon, only four disciples are mentioned: Peter, Andrew, James, and John. The accounts of the calling of Matthew (Mt 9.9) and the choosing of the Twelve (Mt 10.1–4) follow later. However, inasmuch as according to the other evangelists (Mk 3.13–19; Lk 6.13) the Twelve were chosen from the general, larger number of Jesus' followers, it is possible to suppose that besides the four disciples mentioned above, there were others who were also on the mountain with Jesus, some of whom were later numbered among the Twelve.

Was Matthew, the author of the First Gospel, among them? This possibility cannot be excluded. In such a case, if he had been present at the Sermon on the Mount, it would mean that when Jesus later called Matthew they were already known to each other before that point (recall that the other disciples whose calling is described in the Synoptics were known to Jesus before he called them).[40]

The expression "opened his mouth" draws our attention: it introduces an element of solemnity in the description of the event and emphasizes the significance of what Jesus is about to say. Up to this point in the Gospel of Matthew, Jesus has said practically nothing, besides his answer to John the Baptist (Mt 3.15), three brief retorts in answer to the devil's temptation (Mt 4.4, 7, 10), the words adopted from the Forerunner, "Repent: for the kingdom of heaven is at hand" (Mt 4.17), and the words addressed to Peter and Andrew, "Follow me, and I will make you fishers of men" (Mt 4.19). The preaching of the Forerunner is presented fairly completely (Mt 3.7–12), but Jesus has not yet been presented as a preacher. And here he opens his mouth to expound the essence of the "gospel of the kingdom" that he was preaching throughout Galilee (Mt 4.23).

Jesus begins his speech without any preamble. In contrast to ordinary orators, lecturers, and teachers, who specify the topic of their speech at its beginning and alert their listeners beforehand to what will be said, Jesus begins immediately with the very pith of what he wants to say. We cannot exclude the possibility that in reality some opening words were spoken

[40]See Metropolitan Hilarion Alfeyev, *The Beginning of the Gospel*, 379–382, 384–385.

and were later left out by the evangelist. But it is in this form, the form in which the Sermon on the Mount has reached us—without any opening words—that the Sermon produces the distinctive impression that is reflected in the words of the evangelist concerning the audience's reaction to it: "For he taught them as one having authority, and not as the scribes" (Mt 7.29).

5. Interpreting the Sermon on the Mount

The moral radicalism of the Sermon on the Mount has often puzzled commentators. How realistic were Jesus' calls to spiritual perfection? For example, could a man absolutely never look at a woman with lust? How is it possible to offer one's left cheek in response to being struck on the right cheek? Is a person able to love his or her enemies? How is it possible to live without storing up any sort of treasure on earth? The impression might arise that the sermon is addressed to some abstract superhuman who lacks normal earthly desires, passions, and attachments, or that Jesus is over-idealizing human beings, demanding from them the obviously unachievable. Scholars speak of the "irrational, utopian, and rigoristic injunctions" of the Sermon on the Mount "that often seem out of place in the real world."[41]

Early Christianity perceived the Sermon on the Mount as a call to action. Certain instructions in the Sermon on the Mount are mentioned in the *Didache* (also known as *The Teaching of the Twelve Apostles*), which is the earliest Christian literary work after the New Testament (dating to the end of the first century), and also in the works of second-century authors such as Justin Martyr, Irenaeus of Lyons, and Tertullian (the latter lived at the turn of the third century).

[41]Wolfgang Schrage, *The Ethics of the New Testament*, trans. David E. Green (Philadelphia, PA: Fortress, 1988), 9.

The *Didache*

The first full commentary on the Sermon on the Mount was written by Origen (third century). This was part of his *Commentary on the Gospel of Matthew*, which is divided into twenty-five books. However, of the first ten books, including the second book, which contains the commentary on the Sermon on the Mount, only minute fragments have survived. As an adherent of the allegorical method of interpretation, Origen consistently applied this method to all of Holy Scripture, including the Gospels.

In the first three Christian centuries, the Sermon on the Mount was used in Christian literature as a classic exposition of Christian ethics and also to refute the teachings of heretics. In particular, Irenaeus of Lyons and Tertullian appealed to the part of the Sermon on the Mount that speaks of "the law and the prophets" to refute Marcion's belief that Christ came not to fulfill the law, but to destroy it. The Sermon on the Mount was first and foremost seen as a manual, addressed to the Christian community, that was to be fulfilled literally.[42] The idea that certain instructions in the Sermon were impossible or difficult to fulfill is absent in early Christian literature.[43]

In the fourth century, the Sermon on the Mount attracted the attention of the church fathers who were working on creating a Christian spiritual and moral code in this period, particularly the three great Cappadocian fathers: Basil the Great, Gregory the Theologian, and Gregory of Nyssa. Yet only one of them, Gregory of Nyssa, wrote a complete commentary on the initial segment of the Sermon on the Mount—the Beatitudes. In his commentary, Gregory turns to a wide range of sources, including the

[42]Scholars view the Sermon on the Mount as the original Christian catechesis. See C. H. Dodd, "The Primitive Catechism and the Sayings of Jesus," in *New Testament Essays: Studies in Memory of Thomas Walter Manson, 1893–1958*, ed. A. J. B. Higgins (Manchester: Manchester University Press, 1959), 111; Joachim Jeremias, *Jesus and the Message of the New Testament*, ed. K. C. Hanson, Fortress Classics in Biblical Studies (Minneapolis, MN: Fortress, 2002), 27–30.

[43]Warren S. Kissinger, *The Sermon on the Mount: A History of Interpretation and Bibliography*, ATLA Bibliography Series 3 (Metuchen, NJ: Scarecrow, 1975), 9.

Old Testament and the Epistles of the apostle Paul. Being an expert on ancient philosophy, Gregory interpreted certain elements of the Sermon on the Mount in light of the teaching of Greek philosophers concerning moral perfection. In the subsequent Eastern Christian tradition, his commentary on the Beatitudes acquired the status of a classic.

The earliest complete commentary on the Gospel of Matthew preserved in full was written by John Chrysostom. It was composed at the end of the fourth century and consists of a series of homilies delivered in Antioch in approximately AD 390. The part of the work dedicated to the Sermon on the Mount contains the most ancient and complete commentary on the Sermon among all patristic works of the East. Chrysostom does not consider any of the commandments in the Sermon on the Mount to be impossible to fulfill. He cites monastics as an example of literal adherence to these commandments:

Sts Basil the Great, John Chrysostom, and Gregory the Theologian, Greece, 18th century

> Let us not therefore suppose His injunctions are impossible: for there are many who duly perform them. . . . even now there are many who show forth the apostolical life. . . . And if we believe not, it is not because there are none who do well, but because we are far from so doing. . . . he who connects himself with numberless women [does not easily believe] that it is easy to live in virginity; nor he that extorts other men's goods, that one shall readily give up even his own: so neither will those, who daily melt themselves down with innumerable anxieties, easily receive this thing. Now as to the fact, that there are many who have attained unto this, we might show it even from those, who have practised this self-denial even in our generation.[44]

Further on, however, Chrysostom says that not all are capable of immediately fulfilling all that Christ commands. If a person cannot give away

[44]John Chrysostom, *Homilies on Matthew* 21.5 (NPNF[1] 10:149).

all his possessions completely, he can at the very least "learn not to covet, and that almsgiving is a good thing," and "impart of what [he has]." As an example, Chrysostom cites John the Baptist, who "when he was discoursing with those that were employed upon the tribute, and with the soldiery, enjoined them 'to be content with their wages.' Anxious though he was to lead them on to another, and a higher self-command, yet since they were still unfit for this, he speaks of lesser things. Because, if he had mentioned what are higher than these, they would have failed to apply themselves to them, and would have fallen from the others."[45]

Thus, in Chrysostom's understanding, Jesus' commandments are divided into two categories: the higher and the lower (or "lesser"). The fulfillment of the former falls to those who are striving toward spiritual perfection (particularly monastics); the fulfillment of the latter is compulsory for all Christians. Correspondingly, Christians are also divided into two categories: those who are capable of literally fulfilling that which Christ commanded, and those who are called to fulfill the commandments only to a certain extent. In this way, Chrysostom significantly softens the radicalism of the moral imperatives in the Sermon on the Mount, leaving space in the Christian community for those who are not capable of literally fulfilling them.

The first complete commentary on the Sermon on the Mount that appeared in the West was a cycle of exegetical discourses by Augustine of Hippo, composed between 392 and 396. He called his work *Our Lord's Sermon on the Mount, according to Matthew* (*De sermone Domini in monte secundum Matthaeum*). From then on, in the Western tradition, the teaching of Jesus contained in Matthew 5–7 began to be called the "Sermon on the Mount" (this title came into the Eastern tradition much later). According to Augustine, each person who reads the Sermon on the Mount will find in it "a perfect standard of the Christian life" (*perfectum vitae christianae modum*), inasmuch as it is "perfect in all the precepts by which the Christian life is moulded" (*omnibus praeceptis quibus christiana vita informatur esse perfectum*).[46]

---

[45] John Chrysostom, *Homilies on Matthew* 21.5–6 (NPNF[1] 10:149).
[46] Augustine of Hippo, *Our Lord's Sermon on the Mount* 1.1 (NPNF[1] 6:3).

In his commentary on the Sermon on the Mount, Augustine outlines the understanding of salvation that he elaborates on in his polemic with Pelagius. The latter believed that one could acquire salvation by one's own efforts, since one has sufficient personal resources to overcome sin and achieve perfection. Augustine, in contrast, insisted that without divine grace, which is given to a person by supernatural means, salvation is impossible. According to him, grace "is not given according to our merits, but is given according to [God's] own most secret and at the same time most righteous, wise, and beneficent will; since those whom He predestinated, them He also called [Rom 8.30], with that calling of which it is said, 'The gifts and calling of God are without repentance' [Rom 11.29]."[47]

St Augustine, mosaic,
12th century

Augustine believed that the decisive role in salvation is played by divine election: from the beginning, God predestined some people for salvation, and others for judgment, while a person's free will plays no role in salvation. The ones predestined for salvation are all those to whom God gives the gift of faith, and if God gives faith, then the will of a person cannot resist it. God teaches faith to some and not to others; the former are taught according to his mercy, and the latter are not taught according to his righteous judgment.[48] Insofar as all people after Adam have received righteous condemnation, God would not deserve any reproach even if no one were delivered from condemnation.[49]

From these views of Augustine follows the idea that those who have not heard the preaching of the gospel, those who have not responded to this preaching, and unbaptized infants are not saved and cannot be saved; they are not predestined for salvation. Only those who have been predestined beforehand, and who by virtue of predestination merit the gift of

---

[47] Augustine of Hippo, *The Gift of Perseverance* 13.33 (NPNF[1] 5:538).
[48] Augustine of Hippo, *The Predestination of the Saints* 8.14 (NPNF[1] 5:505).
[49] Augustine of Hippo, *The Predestination of the Saints* 8.16 (NPNF[1] 5:506).

faith and saving grace, are saved. They—not by virtue of their own works, but exclusively thanks to the "grace of the Mediator," being justified by the blood of the second Adam—are withdrawn from the "mass of perdition" (*perditionis massa*), separated "from that original condemnation" (*ab illa originali damnatione*), and elected in order to be saved, "because they were called according to the purpose—the purpose, however, not their own, but God's."[50]

The Eastern Christian tradition, in the person of John Chrysostom, expressed a different view on predestination and calling: "Now if all have sinned, how come some to be saved, and some to perish? It is because all were not minded to come to Him, since for His part all were saved, for all were called."[51] In other words, all are predestined and called to salvation without exception, but only those who voluntarily respond to God's call are saved; those who reject God's call are not saved.

From the point of view of the Eastern church fathers, all people created by God are predestined for salvation; there is no one who is destined beforehand for perdition, condemnation, or damnation. In his polemics with those who say, "What good is it to me if I throw myself into many labors, if I give proof of repentance and conversion, when I am neither foreknown nor predestined by God to be saved?," Symeon the New Theologian writes:

> Do you not hear the Savior crying out every day: "As I live . . . I have no pleasure in the death of the wicked, but that the wicked turn from his way and live" [Ezek 33.1]? Do you not hear Him Who says: "Repent, for the Kingdom of Heaven is at hand" [Mt 3.2]; and again: "Just so, I tell you, there is joy in heaven over one sinner who repents" [Lk 15.7, adapted]? Did He ever say to some: "Do not repent for I will not accept you," while to others who were predestined: "But you, repent! because I knew you beforehand"? Instead, throughout all the world and in every church He shouts: "Come to me, all who labor and are heavy laden, and

---

[50]Augustine of Hippo, *On Rebuke and Grace* 7.12–14 (NPNF[1] 5:476–477).
[51]John Chrysostom, *Homilies on Romans* 16 (NPNF[1] 11:464).

I will give you rest" [Mt 11.28]. Come, He says, all you who are burdened with many sins, to the One Who takes away the sin of the world.[52]

Every human being is called to salvation; consequently, anyone who desires it can be justified and glorified. God wants all people, without exception, to become gods by grace:

> The grace of the all-holy and adorable Spirit seeks to enkindle our souls. . . . Thus they too may draw near to the fire and one by one, or, if possible, all of them together, may be enkindled and shine like gods. . . . This, in my opinion, is the truth of the matter, and such is God's counsel toward us.[53]

In the West, Augustine's teaching—that all people are rightly to be condemned, and that only by God's mercy some would be chosen for salvation—was embraced and developed by many theologians.

Thomas Aquinas (thirteenth century), who dedicated part of his magnum opus, the *Summa Theologiae*, to a commentary on the Sermon on the Mount, constantly refers to Augustine. Examining the relationship between the law of Moses and the commandments given in the New Testament, Aquinas draws a distinction between "counsels" and "commandments": a commandment must necessarily be obeyed, while whether a counsel is followed depends on the person to whom it is given. The new law is the law of love; therefore, in the new law, counsels were added to the commandments of the old law, which was the law of bondage. Fulfilling these commandments is necessary for obtaining eternal happiness, while following these counsels is necessary for obtaining it as quickly as possible. The commandments are required of all people, while a person may follow the counsels selectively, depending on his disposition toward them.[54]

---

[52]Symeon the New Theologian, *Ethical Discourses* 2.12–25. English translation from *On the Mystical Life: The Ethical Discourses*, vol. 1, *The Church and the Last Things*, by Symeon the New Theologian, trans. Alexander Golitzin, Popular Patristics Series 14 (Crestwood, NY: St. Vladimir's Seminary Press, 1995), 83–84.

[53]Symeon the New Theologian, *Catechetical Discourses* 34. English translation from *The Discourses*, by Symeon the New Theologian, trans. C. J. deCatanzaro, Classics of Western Spirituality (Mahwah, NJ: Paulist Press, 1980), 354.

[54]Thomas Aquinas, *Summa Theologiae* 2.1.108.

The Triumph of St Thomas Aquinas, Benozzo Gozzoli, 1471

At the same time, following Augustine, Aquinas emphasizes that a person cannot fulfill the commandments and achieve salvation by his own strength alone, through his own natural abilities. In order to love God with one's whole heart, soul, and mind (Mt 22.37), as well as to fulfill the other commandments, one needs the grace of God in addition to one's free will.[55] Aquinas shared Augustine's opinion regarding the predestination of some for salvation and others for perdition, drawing a distinction between the antecedent will of God that "all men . . . be saved" (1 Tim 2.4) and the consequent will of God, according to which only some will be saved.[56]

The theologians of the Reformation further developed the Augustinian understanding of predestination. The idea of "double predestination" became the cornerstone of the theological doctrine of Martin Luther (1483–1546) and John Calvin (1509–64). Calvin asserted that Adam "fell because the Lord had judged it to be expedient," although he fell "by his own fault."[57] Both Calvin and Luther denied the existence of free will in

[55] Thomas Aquinas, *Summa Theologiae* 2.1.109.3–4.

[56] Thomas Aquinas, *Summa Theologiae* 1.23.4.

[57] John Calvin, *Institutes of the Christian Religion* 3.23.8. English translation from *Institutes of the Christian Religion*, vol. 2, by John Calvin, trans. Ford Lewis Battles, ed. John T. McNeill (The Westminster Press, 1960; reissued, Louisville, KY: Westminster John Knox, 2006), 957.

fallen mankind and the possibility of its influencing a person's salvation. Speaking of the feats of the martyrs, Luther asserts that the reason for their steadfastness was exclusively the grace of God, and not their own free will: "So not even here is there any free choice, or freedom to turn oneself in another direction or will something different, so long as the Spirit and grace of God remain in a man."[58] The battle for each person's soul takes place not within that person, but outside him or her—between God and the devil. Like a beast of burden, the person's will finds itself between the will of God and the will of Satan: if God gains possession of the person, he or she follows God, while if Satan takes over, he or she follows Satan.[59] The person himself thus remains merely a passive observer of his or her own salvation or condemnation.

The problems of the relationship between human will and divine grace directly influenced the understanding of the Sermon on the Mount in the Protestant tradition, beginning with Luther, Calvin, and Ulrich Zwingli (1484–1531).[60] Luther, in particular, dedicated a series of sermons to the Sermon on the Mount, directed against an understanding of the Sermon that, in his opinion, was characteristic of "papistic and factious jurists," who distorted Christ's teaching under the influence of the devil.[61] Luther viewed drawing a clear distinction between what belongs to the kingdom of Christ and what belongs to the reality of earthly life as the key to a correct understanding of the Sermon on the Mount.[62] The founder of the German Reformation believed that God ruled earthly kingdoms through secular authorities, and the spiritual kingdom through his word.[63]

---

[58]Martin Luther, *On the Bondage of the Will*, in *Luther and Erasmus: Free Will and Salvation*, ed. and trans. E. Gordon Rupp, A. N. Marlow, Philip S. Watson, and B. Drewery, The Library of Christian Classics (The Westminster Press, 1969; reissued, Louisville, KY: Westminster Fort Knox Press, 2006), 140.

[59]Luther, *On the Bondage of the Will*, in *Luther and Erasmus*, 140.

[60]Concerning the views of these writers on the Sermon on the Mount, see Kissinger, *Sermon on the Mount*, 20–29.

[61]Martin Luther, *Commentary on the Sermon on the Mount*, trans. Charles A. Hay (Philadelphia, PA: Lutheran Publication Society, 1892), ix.

[62]Luther, *Sermon on the Mount*, 187 (commentary on Mt 5.38–42).

[63]Kissinger, *Sermon on the Mount*, 21.

Martin Luther, Lucas
Cranach the Elder, 1526

In Luther's opinion, some of the commandments in the Sermon on the Mount, such as to "resist not evil," belong to the sphere of personal and not societal morality. Luther made a clear distinction between the person and his social role, service, and profession; that which concerns a person as an individual may not concern his professional activity. For example, if a Christian goes to war, or if he sits as a judge and metes out punishment to his neighbor, or if he takes up a formal complaint, "this he does not as a Christian, but as a warrior, judge, jurist." At the same time, he must retain a "Christian heart": he must not wish harm on anyone, and it grieves him when sorrows befall his neighbor. Thus, he lives simultaneously as a Christian toward everyone and as a person of the world, fulfilling his duties as prescribed by local laws.[64]

In the twentieth century, this understanding found a serious critic within the Lutheran tradition. This critic was the brilliant theologian Dietrich Bonhoeffer (1906–1945), who died a month before the end of the Second World War in the Nazi concentration camp of Flossenbürg. He emphasized that Jesus' teachings did not distinguish between a private person and his role in society.[65] In his commentary on the words "resist not evil," he wrote:

> At this point, the Reformation interpretation introduced a decisively new concept, namely, that we should differentiate between harm done to me personally, and harm done to me as bearer of my office. . . . In the former case I am to act as Jesus commands, but in the latter case I am released from doing so. Indeed, for the sake of true love, I am even obligated to behave in the opposite way, to answer violence with violence in order to resist the inroads of evil. . . . But this distinction between private person and bearer of an office as normative for

[64]Luther, *Sermon on the Mount*, 200.
[65]Stanley Hauerwas, *Matthew*, Brazos Theological Commentary on the Bible (Grand Rapids, MI: Brazos, 2006), 73.

my behavior is foreign to Jesus. He does not say a word about it. He addresses his disciples as people who have left everything behind to follow him. "Private" and "official" spheres are all completely subject to Jesus' command. The word of Jesus claimed them undividedly. He demands undivided obedience. In fact, the distinction between private and official is vulnerable to an insoluble dilemma. Where in real life am I really only a private person and where only the bearer of my office? Wherever I am attacked, am I not simultaneously the father of my children, the pastor of my congregation, the statesman of my people?[66]

By the time Bonhoeffer wrote his commentary on the Sermon on the Mount, the history of the latter's interpretation had been enriched by a multitude of works in which the Sermon was examined from various perspectives. In particular, the leading German expert on the New Testament, Albert Schweitzer (1875–1965), viewed the Sermon on the Mount as "interim ethics" based on a "thoroughgoing eschatology." The essence of Schweitzer's idea was that Jesus preached renewal and repentance in light of the imminent coming of the kingdom of God; the radical and uncompromising nature of his positions on moral questions, as presented in the Sermon on the Mount, was directly connected with the perception of the urgency with which it was necessary to prepare for the coming of this kingdom.

Schweitzer's teachings influenced the author of one of the key twentieth-century works dedicated to the Sermon on the Mount, the German theologian Hans Windisch (his work, *The Meaning of the Sermon on the Mount*, was first published in 1929). In Windisch's opinion, the Sermon on the Mount was correctly understood by those who interpreted it literally, such as Leo Tolstoy, with his teaching on not resisting evil with force. Such people could not be considered fanatics or sectarians: "If this is what they are, then Jesus himself was a fanatic and the founder of a sect. . . . Polemic against 'fanatics' is to a large extent polemic against the Sermon on the Mount and criticism of Jesus himself."[67]

[66]Dietrich Bonhoeffer, *Discipleship*, trans. Barbara Green and Reinhard Krauss (Minneapolis, MN: Fortress Press, 2015), 104–105.

[67]Windisch, *Sermon on the Mount*, 172.

Windisch saw in the commandments of the Sermon on the Mount
two types of moral teaching: eschatological ethics, which were contingent
on the expectation of the imminent coming of the kingdom of God, and
wisdom ethics, which were unconnected with any eschatological expectations. In summary, Windisch's theory looks like this:

> Jesus' predominant ethics is eschatological and essentially diverse
> from wisdom ethics. It is new legislation, i.e., rules of admittance to
> the eschatological Kingdom; therefore it is to be understood literally
> and fulfilled completely. Its radical character is not conditioned by the
> imminence of the Kingdom but by the absolute will of God. . . . The
> religion of the Sermon on the Mount is predominantly a religion of
> works. However, this eschatological ethic is an extreme, heroic, abnor-
> mal ethic that Jesus himself was unable to fulfill.[68]

Examining the various interpretations of the Sermon on the Mount,
ancient as well as new, the prominent twentieth-century German scholar
of the New Testament Joachim Jeremias distinguishes among three of
the most widespread views in the exegesis of the Sermon's meaning. The
"perfectionistic" conception proceeds from the view that in the Sermon
on the Mount, Jesus described the ideal of Christian perfection: human
beings cannot achieve it, but can strive toward it. The scholar calls another
conception the "theory of the impossible ideal": according to this theory,
Jesus, knowing that his demands were impossible to fulfill, presented them
in order that people might understand that they could not attain salvation
by their own efforts, for a person is saved only by faith in Jesus Christ (Gal
2.16) and not by any kind of works. Finally, the third conception proceeds
from the view that the Sermon on the Mount offers people an "interim-
ethic": Jesus' demands are not for the long term, but are motivated by the
idea that the end of the world would come soon.[69] The first of these positions is close to the view of John Chrysostom, the second is close to that of
Martin Luther, and the third is close to that of Albert Schweitzer.

[68]George Eldon Ladd, *A Theology of the New Testament*, rev. ed., ed. Donald A. Hagner
(Grand Rapids, MI: Eerdmans, 1993), 120.

[69]Joachim Jeremias, *The Sermon on the Mount*, trans. Norman Perrin (London: Athlone,
1961), 11–15.

Georg Strecker, for his part, puts in first place the "theory of the impossible ideal," following Jeremias in tracing it back to the apostle Paul and Luther with his teaching on justification by faith. In second place he puts the interpretation that he calls the "fanatical type of exegesis": according to this type, the demands of the Sermon on the Mount are realistic and must be carried out literally (Leo Tolstoy's teachings about not resisting evil with force are given as an example). The third understanding, called the "liberal type of exegesis," is based on the view that Jesus offers in the Sermon on the Mount not an "ethic of action," but an "ethic of attitude": his commandments are to be interpreted not literally, but merely as a general call to renew one's consciousness.[70]

Albert Schweitzer,
photograph

Some scholars emphasize the paradoxical, challenging nature of Jesus' sayings in the Sermon on the Mount: "He keeps making strong, paradoxical statements without the qualifications that we must supply in some situations." To interpret such statements literally is to "repeat the method of the scribes whom he denounces so strongly."[71] Jesus' sayings in the Sermon on the Mount are compared with parables and proverbs, which have "an unexpected, paradoxical, and absolute manner of speaking that sharply accentuates a particular side of the truth without considering the possible exceptions to the rule."[72]

All these perspectives on the Sermon on the Mount unavoidably narrow down the possibilities for its interpretation, insofar as they attempt to put it on a Procrustean bed of an already formulated concept or theory. This is pointed out by the well-known mid-twentieth-century Welsh Protestant preacher D. Martyn Lloyd-Jones in the introduction to his own commentary on the Sermon on the Mount: the mistake of many consists in that they "approach the Bible with a theory"; with this approach,

[70]Strecker, *Sermon on the Mount*, 15–18.

[71]Leon Morris, *The Gospel According to Matthew*, The Pillar New Testament Commentary (Grand Rapids, MI: Eerdmans, 1992), 91.

[72]Herman N. Ridderbos, *Matthew*, trans. Ray Togtman, Bible Student's Commentary (Grand Rapids, MI: Zondervan, 1987), 112.

The Sermon on the Mount, Aurél Náray, 1940s

everything that they read out of the Bible is controlled by the theory, and they cannot find anything in the biblical text besides that which supports their own theory.[73]

But the Sermon on the Mount does not fit into any theory. The various sections of the Sermon on the Mount require a differentiated approach. The ancient commentators, such as John Chrysostom and Augustine of Hippo, did not give themselves the task of finding a single hermeneutic[74] key that would be equally applicable to all sections of the Sermon. Nevertheless, they proceeded from the view that the Sermon was a guide to action, and not simply a description of some obviously unattainable ideal.

The question of to what degree the demands of the Sermon on the Mount are realistic would be justified if the one who formulated these demands were not a human being himself. In that case, both the Beatitudes and the other exhortations in the Sermon on the Mount could be understood as directives given from above, directly from God, but unrealizable from the point of view of an ordinary, real, earthly human being. The Ten Commandments of the Old Testament, according to such an approach, would look much more realistic than the Beatitudes, and the law of Moses as a whole would seem much more possible to fulfill than the Sermon on the Mount. Thus was the Sermon on the Mount understood by one of the

[73]D. Martyn Lloyd-Jones, *Studies in the Sermon on the Mount*, 2nd ed. (Grand Rapids, MI: Eerdmans, 1976), 15.

[74]Hermeneutics (from *hermēneuō*—to explain, to interpret) is interpretation and explanation. The term "hermeneutics" is often used as a synonym for the term "exegesis."—Ed.

Christ's Sermon on the Mount, Germany, 12th century

Jewish scholars sympathetic to Christianity in the middle of the nineteenth century: "the defect in the ethical teaching of Jesus is that it is strung so high that it has failed to produce solid and practical results just where its admirers vaunt that it differs from, and is superior to, the ethical codes of the Pentateuch, the Prophets, and the Rabbis."[75]

However, when reading the Sermon on the Mount, one must remember that its author sets goals that he proves to be attainable by his own experience: he leads an unmercenary way of life, not gathering up treasures on earth; he is surrounded by women, but does not look at them with lust; he does not resist evil with force; he loves his enemies and prays on the cross for those who crucify him.

From this perspective, the Sermon on the Mount becomes the projection of Jesus' own life experience onto the situation of an ordinary person, and all the subsequent text of the Gospel of Matthew becomes proof that Jesus' commandments in the Sermon on the Mount are by no means impossible to fulfill: he himself is the first to fulfill them. In his footsteps thousands and millions of his followers—each to his or her own degree—would attempt to fulfill these commandments: for some these commandments remain an unattainable ideal, but for many they become

[75]C. G. Montefiore, *The Synoptic Gospels*, vol. 2 (London: Macmillan, 1909), 523.

John the Theologian, El
Greco, 1595–1605

an opportunity here on earth to attain to the kingdom of heaven, to acquire in their earthly life the higher dimension that is not accessible on the basis of fulfilling the law of Moses alone.

The Sermon on the Mount is by no means an exhaustive exposition of Christian morality. In it Jesus addresses only certain ethical topics. Jesus' moral teaching would be supplemented in other chapters of the Gospel of Matthew, as well as in the three other Gospels. It would be substantially expanded and enriched in the Catholic Epistles and in the Epistles of the apostle Paul. But even the entire New Testament as a whole does not give us a full exposition of all aspects of Christian morality. Many topics were to be developed, supplemented, and interpreted by the church fathers, while certain moral topics have arisen in our time and require new answers.

It seems to us that Jesus did not conceive of the Sermon on the Mount as an exhaustive exposition of his moral teaching. In it he first and foremost gives his listeners fundamental moral guidelines and sets forth his understanding of morality as exemplified in certain concrete topics. Some other topics are developed in his other exhortations and parables. It is assumed that, on the basis of these guidelines, Christians would build their lives on the foundation of the approach to the realities of life that is revealed in the Sermon on the Mount.

The prologue to the Gospel of John concludes with these words: "For the law was given by Moses, but grace and truth came by Jesus Christ" (Jn 1.17). These words pertain directly to Jesus' entire ministry and teaching, including that which is expressed in the Sermon on the Mount. The Old Testament commandments were the law that the people of Israel were supposed to follow. What Jesus brought was not just a new form of the law: he brought grace and truth. Grace is the divine gift that is necessary in order for people to fulfill Jesus' commandments and to live in truth. With the help of grace, and not by their own efforts alone, his followers are called to seek and attain the kingdom of heaven.

Chapter 2

THE BEATITUDES

The Beatitudes, which begin the Sermon on the Mount, occupy a special place in the New Testament. Even within the context of the Sermon on the Mount, the Beatitudes constitute a complete spiritual program: in them Jesus enumerates the qualities that his followers are called to possess.

The Greek term *makarios* in the Septuagint, including in the translation of the Psalms, is used to translate the ancient Hebrew word *'ešer* ("happiness," "blessedness").[1] It is most likely that it was this term that Jesus used in the Beatitudes in the Sermon on the Mount. As in the Psalms, this term refers not only to ordinary, earthly, human happiness, but also to a state with a clearly expressed religious dimension.[2] Practically everywhere in the Psalms this term is connected with a person's faith in God, hope and trust in him, fear before him, obeying his law, dwelling in his house, and also the remission of sins.

We find such a use of this term in the book of Proverbs, where the Wisdom of God takes on the role of mediator between God and man: here blessedness is connected with the acquisition of wisdom and understanding (Prov 3.13, 18), keeping the ways of Wisdom and listening to her (Prov 8.32, 34), having mercy on the poor (Prov 14.21), hoping in the Lord (Prov 16.20), abiding in fear (Prov 28.14), and observing the law (Prov 29.18). If we recall that in the Christian tradition the Wisdom of God was understood

---

[1] This word is attested in the Old Testament only in the plural and only with a noun or pronoun dependent on it; for example: *'ašrê hā-'îš* ("blessed is the man"; literally, "blessings of the man," or "blessings [belong to] the man"). See Ludwig Koehler and Walter Baumgartner, *Hebräisches und aramäisches Lexikon zum Alten Testament*, 3rd ed., Lfg. 1, ed. Walter Baumgartner (Leiden: Brill, 1967), 96.

[2] Note that in Greek the term *makarios* was originally used with reference to the gods and was only later applied to people. In the Christian tradition, it again acquired its own religious dimension, signifying a special spiritual state and a special type of holiness.

---

to be one of the Old Testament foreshadowings of Christ, the connection between the book of Proverbs and the Beatitudes becomes clear.

The word "blessed" begins a whole variety of verses in various parts of the Old Testament. In the Psalter we find quite a long list of beatitudes scattered throughout the whole book. Here are some of the more representative verses:

> Blessed is the man that hath not walked in the counsel of the ungodly, nor stood in the way of sinners, nor sat in the seat of the pestilent. (Ps 1.1)
> Blessed are all that have put their trust in him. (Ps 2.12)
> Blessed are they whose iniquities are forgiven, and whose sins are covered. Blessed is the man unto whom the Lord imputeth not sin, and in whose mouth there is no guile. (Ps 31.1–2)
> Blessed is the nation whose God is the Lord, the people whom he hath chosen for his inheritance. (Ps 32.12)
> Blessed is the man that hopeth in him. (Ps 33.9)
> Blessed is the man, whose hope is in the Name of the Lord, and who hath not looked upon vanities and false frenzies. (Ps 39.5)
> Blessed is the man that hath understanding for the poor man and the pauper; in an evil day the Lord will deliver him. (Ps 40.2)
> Blessed is he whom thou hast chosen and hast taken to thyself; he shall dwell in thy courts. (Ps 64.5)
> Blessed are they that dwell in thy house; unto ages of ages shall they praise thee. Blessed is the man whose help is from thee; he hath made ascents in his heart. (Ps 83.5–6)
> Blessed is the man that hopeth in thee. (Ps 83.13)
> Blessed is the people that knoweth jubilation. O Lord, in the light of thy face shall they walk. (Ps 88.16)
> Blessed is the man whom thou shalt chasten, O Lord; and out of thy law shalt thou instruct him. (Ps 93.12)
> Blessed are they that keep judgment and do righteousness at all times. (Ps 105.3)

The Roman Catholic Church of the Beatitudes on the northwest bank of the Sea of Galilee, near Tabgha

Blessed is the man that feareth the Lord; in his commandments shall he greatly delight. (Ps 111.1)

Blessed are the blameless in the way, who walk in the law of the Lord. Blessed are they that search out his testimonies; with their whole heart shall they seek after him. (Ps 118.1–2)

Blessed are all they that fear the Lord, that walk in his ways. (Ps 127.1)

Blessed is the people whose God is the Lord. (Ps 143.15)

Blessed is he that hath the God of Jacob for his help, whose hope is in the LORD his God. (Ps 145.5, KJV Ps 146.5)

The Psalms were the basis of temple worship, and their text was well known not only to Jesus, but also to his audience. Some Psalms that people knew by heart, including the opening psalm, Psalm 1, and the well-known Psalm 118, begin with the word "blessed." The choice of such a method of exposition for the beginning of the Sermon on the Mount was not a coincidence: Jesus was using verbal formulas familiar to his listeners. Besides this, the Psalms were works of Hebrew poetry, and Jesus begins his Sermon on the Mount with words that possess all the characteristic features of a poetic text. In particular, each verse of a psalm is divided into two parts, and each verse in the Beatitudes is also divided into two parts: the first begins with the word "blessed" (*makarioi*), and the second with the word "for" (*hoti*).

Let us also not forget that it is in the Gospel of Matthew that Jesus is presented foremost as the "Son of David," and David, according to tradition, was the author of most of the Psalms. In this sense, in the Sermon on the Mount, Jesus comes across not only as a new Moses, but also as a new David—a prophet and a poet in a single person.

One more parallel to the evangelical Beatitudes is found in the beatitudes in the books of the Wisdom of Solomon and Proverbs, as well as in the book of the Wisdom of Sirach:

> Wherefore blessed is the barren that is undefiled, which hath not known the sinful bed: she shall have fruit in the visitation of souls. (Wis 3.13)

> Happy is the man that findeth wisdom, and the man that getteth understanding. (Prov 3.13)

> Blessed is the man that heareth me, watching daily at my gates, waiting at the posts of my doors. (Prov 8.34)

> Happy is the man that feareth always, but he that hardeneth his heart shall fall into mischief. (Prov 28.14)

> Blessed is the man that hath not slipped with his mouth, and is not pricked with the multitude of sins. Blessed is he whose conscience hath not condemned him, and who is not fallen from his hope in the Lord. (Sir 14.1–2)

> Blessed is the man that doth meditate good things in wisdom, and that reasoneth of holy things by his understanding. (Sir 14.20)

> Blessed is the soul of him that feareth the Lord: to whom doth he look? And who is his strength? (Sir 34.15)

> Blessed are they that saw thee, and slept in love; for we shall surely live. (Sir 48.11)

> Blessed is he that shall be exercised in these things; and he that layeth them up in his heart shall become wise. (Sir 50.28)

A list of beatitudes contained in one of the recently discovered Qumran manuscripts is close in content to the beatitudes from the wisdom literature. The manuscript dates to the period between 50 BC and AD 50; its text was first published in 1991. The beginning has been lost. A more

Fragments of the Qumran scrolls on display in the Jordan Archaeological Museum in Amman

or less coherent text begins with the following verses, which refer to the Wisdom of God:

> [Blessed is he who speaks truth] with a pure heart and who does not slander with his tongue.
> Blessed are those who cling to his statutes and who do not cling to her ways of perversity.
> Blessed are those who rejoice because of her and who do not spread themselves in the ways of folly.
> Blessed is he who seeks her with pure hands and who does not go after her with a deceitful heart.
> Blessed the man who has attained Wisdom and walks in the law of the Most High and applies his heart to her ways, who cherishes her lessons and ev[e]r rejoices in her corrections, but who does not repel her in the pain of [his] misfortune[s?] (or in the distress of tri[al?]) and in bad times does not abandon her who does not forget her [in days of] terror and in his humility of soul does not reproach [her].[3]

[3] English translation as printed in F. Manns and E. Alliata, eds., *Early Christianity in Context: Monuments and Documents*, Collectio Maior 38 (Jerusalem: Franciscan Printing Press, 1993), 355. For the original text, see Émile Puech, ed., *Qumrân Grotte 4.XVIII: Textes Hébreux (4Q521–4Q528, 4Q576–4Q579)*, Discoveries in the Judaean Desert 25 (Oxford: Clarendon Press, 1998), 115–178.

The Beatitudes,
icon, 16th
century

Researchers are turning their attention to the possible terminological and thematic convergences between the Qumran beatitudes and the list of Beatitudes that begins the Sermon on the Mount.[4] For example, the expression "pure hands" (*bôr kappayim*) in the Qumran beatitudes recalls the expression "pure in heart" (*katharoi tē kardia*) in the evangelical Beatitudes. The theme of joy and sorrows (trials) is present in both lists of beatitudes. However, that is the extent of the similarity. The overall subject and orientation of the beatitudes are different between those in the Qumran and those in the Gospel. The former beatitudes praise the wisdom

[4]Pino Di Luccio, *The Quelle and the Targums: Righteousness in the Sermon on the Mount/ Plain*, Analecta Biblica 175 (Rome: Pontificio Istituto Biblico, 2009), 55; George J. Brooke, *The Dead Sea Scrolls and the New Testament* (Minneapolis, MN: Fortress, 2005), 228–234.

that comes from following the law of Moses, while the latter have as their central theme the kingdom of heaven. In the evangelical Beatitudes Jesus speaks of a reward for righteousness and sufferings on earth, while in the Qumran beatitudes this theme is absent:

> The Qumran beatitudes lack the apocalyptic reversal of fortune. For example, in them no poor become rich or well fed. They offer their readers no paradox to ponder. . . . It is the theme of God's kingdom that more than any other distinguishes the Beatitudes of Jesus from those found at Qumran or in Sirach.[5]

> The Qumran beatitudes are different from those of Jesus in that they are centered on one topic, wisdom or the *tôrāh*, and its influence in human conduct. There is little of the eschatological nuance that characterizes the Matthean or Lucan beatitudes, just as there is little of the sapiential content or formulation in the Matthean or Lucan collection of Jesus' beatitudes.[6]

A direct link between the Qumran beatitudes and the evangelical Beatitudes must be excluded. Nevertheless, in individual instances an indirect link is possible through a common original source in the Old Testament, first and foremost in the wisdom literature. As we examine each of the Beatitudes, we will point out the possible Old Testament roots of the concepts used in them. We will also address the overall context of the life and preaching of Jesus to uncover the meaning of each Beatitude. The commentaries of the church fathers on the Beatitudes will be used as supporting material.

---

[5]Benedict T. Viviano, *Matthew and His World: The Gospel of the Open Jewish Christians; Studies in Biblical Theology*, Novum Testamentum et orbis antiquus 61 (Fribourg: Academic Press; Göttingen: Vandenhoeck & Ruprecht, 2007), 66–68.

[6]Joseph A. Fitzmyer, *The Dead Sea Scrolls and Christian Origins*, Studies in the Dead Sea Scrolls and Related Literature (Grand Rapids, MI: Eerdmans, 2000), 116.

1. "Blessed Are the Poor in Spirit"

The first Beatitude is the opening sentence of the whole Sermon on the Mount: "Blessed are the poor in spirit: for theirs is the kingdom of heaven" (Mt 5.3). We recall that the parallel text in the Gospel of Luke reads thus in many ancient manuscripts: "Blessed be ye poor: for yours is the kingdom of God" (Lk 6.20). Scholars see this as a reflection of Luke's interest in the theme of wealth and poverty, which occupies much more space in his Gospel than in the other Gospels.[7] However, there is no need to see in the two different versions of the first Beatitude a reflection of a difference of interests between Matthew and Luke. If anything, one could say that each of them emphasized certain aspects of Jesus' teaching to greater or lesser degrees.

The poor, the destitute, the lowly, the oppressed—these are the ones of whom the Old Testament speaks with sympathy and compassion. The Bible never faults a person for destitution and poverty, for the Lord himself "maketh poor, and maketh rich: he bringeth low, and lifteth up" (1 Sam 2.7). The sufferings of the poor on earth are temporary: "For the poor man shall not be forgotten to the end; the patience of the paupers shall not perish forever" (Ps 9.19). Beggars and the poor, according to the Old Testament, are under God's special protection: he "saveth the poor from the sword" (Job 5.15), sees "the distress of the beggars and the groaning of the poor" (Ps 11.6), hears the poor man and saves him from tribulations (Ps 33.7), delivers the weak from the strong and the poor and beggars from their despoilers (Ps 34.10), and hearkens unto the poor and does not disregard the prisoners (Ps 68.34). The sons of Israel are called to be merciful to the poor and destitute (Deut 15.4, 7–11). Insulting the poor is a grievous sin: "Whoso mocketh the poor reproacheth his Maker; and he that is glad at calamities shall not be unpunished" (Prov 17.5).

---

[7]Jonathan T. Pennington, *Reading the Gospels Wisely: A Narrative and Theological Introduction* (Grand Rapids, MI: Baker Academic, 2012), 72.

The Greek word *ptōchos* ("poor") can correspond to several Hebrew terms: *rāš* ("poor"), *dal* ("helpless"), *'ebyôn* ("beggar"), *'ānî* ("destitute," "poor," "needy"), *'ānāw* ("lowly," "bent down"). In view of the multiple meanings of the possible Hebrew equivalents to the Greek *ptōchoi* ("poor ones"), attempts to reconstruct the original Hebrew expression for "poor in spirit" are hypothetical.[8] The attempts of some commentators to see in the expression "poor in spirit" a reference to the action of the Holy Spirit in the poor are unfounded.[9] In this case, the word "spirit" has nothing to do with the Holy Spirit, but rather it refers to one of the components of the human being.

Determining the precise meaning of the expression "poor in spirit" (*ptōchoi tō pneumati*) becomes a practically insoluble exegetical task if we attempt to divorce its interpretation from the ecclesiastical tradition: in this case, the meaning of Jesus' words depends on the sense in which the term "poor" is used (literally or metaphorically), and also on the understanding of the term "spirit," which is in the dative case in the Greek text of the Gospel.

In the church tradition this expression had a twofold interpretation. On the one hand, in the words of Basil the Great, the "poor in spirit" are "those who are poor for no other cause but for that teaching of the Lord who said: *Go and sell all that you have and give to the poor* [Mt 19.21; Lk 18.22]."[10] It follows that material poverty is in view here.[11]

On the other hand, very many commentators have understood the expression "poor in spirit" as a reference to spiritual qualities. In the words of Macarius the Great, to be poor in spirit means to be "never thinking [oneself] to be anything, but holding [oneself] in a lowly and humble

---

[8]In speaking of the "poor," Jesus supposedly used the term *'ănāwîm* ("oppressed," "humble," "meek"). In the Greek Psalter the term *'ānāw* is translated variously as *ptōchos* ("poor" or "beggar"), *penēs* ("poor"), and as *praus* ("meek"); it is semantically close to "poor" in the first Beatitude and "meek" in the third Beatitude.

[9]See, for example, Margaret Ann Hannan, *The Nature and Demands of the Sovereign Rule of God in the Gospel of Matthew*, Library of New Testament Studies 308 (New York, NY: T&T Clark, 2006), 47–48.

[10]Basil the Great, *Shorter Responses* 205. English translation from *The Rule of St. Basil in Latin and English: A Revised Critical Edition*, trans. Anna M. Silvas (Collegeville, MN: Liturgical Press, 2013), 215.

[11]Compare Morris, *The Gospel according to Matthew*, 96.

attitude as one knowing or having nothing, even though [one] does know and does have much."[12] In this way, spiritual poverty is synonymous with humility. John Chrysostom says:

> What is meant by "the poor in spirit?" The humble and contrite in mind. . . . He blesses them first, who by choice humble and contract themselves. But why said he not, "the humble," but rather "the poor?" Because this is more than that. For He means here them who are awe-struck, and tremble at the commandments of God.[13]

Some light can be shed on the meaning of the phrase "poor in spirit" by similar expressions encountered in the Old Testament, such as "of a contrite heart . . . the humble of spirit" (Ps 33.19), "to be of an humble spirit" (Prov 16.19), "the humble in spirit" (Prov 29.23), "poor and of a contrite spirit" (Is 66.2). All these expressions only serve to support the correctness of the second of the two traditional readings of the first Beatitude: it speaks of humility.

Neither in the Old Testament nor in ancient literature was humility viewed as a quality that could be placed first in the list of virtues. Humility is mentioned in the book of Psalms (Ps 9.38–39; 33.19; 50.19; 137.6; 146.6; 149.4) and the book of Proverbs (Prov 3.34; 11.2; 15.33; 18.13; 22.4; 29.23): in most instances humility is contrasted with pride. But in Jesus' teaching, humility occupies such an exceptional place that it is this quality that opens the entire spiritual program outlined in the Sermon on the Mount.

What exactly is meant by humility and poverty in spirit? The expression "poor in spirit" is partly explained by the subsequent content of the Sermon on the Mount: the poor in spirit are those who do not resist evil with force, but offer their left cheek when they are struck on their right cheek; they are those who love their enemies; they are those who pray not for show, but in secret. Jesus' teaching on humility is also excellently illustrated in the parable of the publican and the Pharisee: the Pharisee lists

---

[12]Pseudo-Macarius, *Homilies* 12.3. English translation from *The Fifty Spiritual Homilies and the Great Letter*, by Pseudo-Macarius, trans. George A. Maloney, Classics of Western Spirituality (New York, NY: Paulist Press, 1992), 98.

[13]John Chrysostom, *Homilies on Matthew* 15.2 (NPNF[1] 10:92).

his accomplishments in his prayer to God, while the publican, "standing afar off, would not lift up so much as his eyes unto heaven, but smote upon his breast, saying, 'God be merciful to me a sinner'" (Lk 18.10–14). In the latter instance, humility is presented as a quality that characterizes a person's attitude toward God.

Christ Pantocrator,
Bulgaria, 13th century

However, the strongest and most vivid example of humility is Jesus himself. The entire course of his life is the path of humility and impoverishment. The Evangelist Matthew applies to Jesus the words from the book of the prophet Isaiah about the Servant of God, who "shall not strive, nor cry; neither shall any man hear his voice in the streets. A bruised reed shall he not break, and smoking flax shall he not quench" (Mt 12.19–20; Is 42.2–3). The apostle Paul speaks of Christ using the concepts of humility, obedience, humiliation, and poverty. In his words, Christ is the one who "made himself of no reputation, and took upon him the form of a servant, and was made in the likeness of men, and being found in fashion as a man, he humbled himself, and became obedient unto death, even the death of the cross" (Phil 2.7–8). He himself, "though he was rich, yet for [our] sakes he became poor, that [we] through his poverty might be rich" (2 Cor 8.9).

Gregory of Nyssa (fourth century) cites these words of Paul in his commentary on the first Beatitude, when he says that God alone is truly blessed (1 Tim 6.15), and the acquisition of blessedness is possible for human beings through the imitation of God. And what in the Divine is desirable for imitation? The poverty in spirit by which Gregory understands "voluntary humility" [*dokei moi ptōcheian pneumatos, tēn hekousion tapeinophrosynēn onomazein ho Logos*]."[14] Jesus' entire life is the greatest example of humility and impoverishment:

> What greater poverty is there for God than the form of a servant? What more humble for the King of creation than to share in our poor nature?

[14]Gregory of Nyssa, *The Beatitudes* 1 (trans. Graef, 90).

The Ruler of rulers, the Lord of lords puts on voluntarily the garb of servitude. The Judge of all things becomes a subject of governors; the Lord of creation dwells in a cave; He who holds the universe in His hands finds no place in the inn, but is cast aside into the manger of irrational beasts. The perfectly Pure accepts the filth of human nature, and after going through all our poverty passes on to the experience of death. Look at the standard by which to measure voluntary poverty! Life tastes death; the Judge is brought to judgement; the Lord of the life of all creatures is sentenced by the judge; the King of all heavenly powers does not push aside the hands of the executioners. Take this, He says, as an example by which to measure your humility.[15]

According to Isaac the Syrian, humility is a quality that God possesses to the highest degree. The humility of God was revealed to the world in the incarnation of the Son of God. In the Old Testament, God remained invisible and inaccessible to anyone who approached him, but when God clothed himself in humility and concealed his greatness under human flesh, he became visible and accessible:

For humility is the raiment of the Godhead. The Word Who became man clothed Himself in it, and therewith He spoke to us in our body. Every man who has been clothed in it has truly been made like unto Him Who came down from His own exaltedness, and hid the splendor of His majesty, and concealed His glory with humility, lest creation should be utterly consumed by the contemplation of Him.[16]

Every Christian, in the words of Isaac the Syrian, is called to imitate Christ in his humility. By acquiring humility, a person becomes like God and is clothed in him: "Wherefore every man has put on Christ when he is clothed with the raiment[17] wherein the Creator was seen through the body that He put on. For the likeness in which He was seen by His own creation and in which He kept company with it, He willed to put on in His inner

[15]Gregory of Nyssa, *The Beatitudes* 1 (trans. Graef, 91).

[16]Isaac the Syrian, *Ascetical Homilies* 77. English translation from *The Ascetical Homilies of Saint Isaac the Syrian*, by Isaac the Syrian, trans. Holy Transfiguration Monastery, rev. 2nd ed. (Boston, MA: Holy Transfiguration Monastery, 2011), 534.

[17]That is, in the raiment of humility.

man, and to be seen therein by His fellow servants."[18] Humility combined with Christian asceticism makes a person "a god upon earth."[19]

The Christian teaching about humility was often attacked by philosophers of an anti-Christian bent, such as Friedrich Nietzsche. They saw humility as a quality characteristic of slaves (of which the early Christian Church supposedly was primarily composed), as abjection, subjugation, an inability to stand up for oneself or to defend one's interests.[20] The Russian philosopher Nicolas Berdyaev wrote about the unfairness of such a view of humility. He contrasts this "false and decadent" understanding of Christian humility with the understanding by which it is viewed as a "manifestation of spiritual power in the conquest of selfhood," that is, of egoism and egocentrism:

> Man is shut up within himself and sees everything from his own point of view and in relation to himself. He is obsessed by the idea of his own self. We are all guilty of self-centredness. Looked at objectively, nothing could be more comical. Self-centredness distorts all the perspectives of life; everything is seen in a false light, nothing has its proper place assigned to it. In order to see the world in a true light and everything in its proper shape, in order to contemplate the wide horizon, we must climb out of the pit of self-centredness and rise to a height. We must see the centre of being not in ourselves but in God, where it truly is, and then everything will fall into its right place. Humility in its ontological meaning is the heroic conquest of selfhood and ascent to the heights of theocentrism. Humility means escape from one's hardened selfhood and the asphyxiating atmosphere of one's own limited self into the pure air of cosmic life.[21] Humility is not only not a denial of one's identity,

---

[18]Isaac the Syrian, *Ascetical Homilies* 77 (trans. Holy Transfiguration Monastery, 535).

[19]Isaac the Syrian, *Ascetical Homilies* 6 (trans. Holy Transfiguration Monastery, 178).

[20]See Friedrich W. Nietzsche, *The Antichrist*, trans. H. L. Mencken (New York, NY: Alfred A. Knopf, 1920), 62–67.

[21]Nicolas Berdyaev, *The Destiny of Man*, trans. Natalie Duddington (London: G. Bles, The Centenary Press, 1937), 116. [The rest of the passage has been translated by the present translator as Duddington's translation skips over it, although it is found in the Russian original. See Nicolas Berdyaev, *O naznachenii cheloveka: Opyt paradoksal'noy etiki* (Paris: Sovremennye zapisi, 1931), 124.—Trans.]

but it is the finding of one's own identity, for identity can be found only in God, and not in hardened and inveterate egoism.

According to Berdyaev, "So far from being opposed to freedom, humility is an act of freedom." Nothing can compel a man to humility, which is "part of our inner, hidden life." Humility frees a person from the torment caused by wounded vanity:

> Humility is directed in the first place against self-love and is the power which heals wounded pride.
>
> Christianity alone teaches how to be completely free from the external world which thwarts and injures us. Even the words "obey your master" may be interpreted as the acquisition of inner spiritual freedom and independence. Be free in spirit, do not be a slave in spirit. . . . The acceptance of circumstances which have fallen to one's lot must be interpreted as mastery over the external world, as the victory of the spirit. . . . Holiness is the highest spiritual force and a victory over the world. Love is a force, a radiation of beneficent, life-giving energy. Victory over passions is power. It is to that power that Christianity calls us. . . . Christianity bids us to overcome the world and not to submit to it. Humility is not submission, on the contrary, it is a refusal to submit, and movement along the line of the greatest resistance.[22]

In this way, humility is spiritual valor, the ability of a person to overcome and eliminate in himself vain self-enclosedness, to sacrifice his "I" for the sake of higher ideals. Humility is impossible if a person does not place himself before the face of God, if in light of the presence of God in his life he does not re-examine his moral values, if he does not turn to God for help to fulfill his commandments. In the final reckoning, all of Christian morality acquires its meaning only if it is apprehended as a morality that is "divinely human," based on the "interaction between man and God."[23] This can be seen from the example of the other Beatitudes.

---

[22]Berdyaev, *Destiny of Man*, 116–117.
[23]Berdyaev, *Destiny of Man*, 117.

The Beatitudes are framed by the words "for theirs is the kingdom of heaven" at the beginning and at the end; these words are heard again in the eighth Beatitude. According to John Chrysostom, the promise of the kingdom of heaven includes all the other promises associated with the other Beatitudes:

> But thou, though thou hearest not of a kingdom given in each one of the blessings, be not discouraged. For although He give different names to the rewards, yet He brings all into His kingdom. Thus, both when He saith, "they that mourn shall be comforted;" and, "they that show mercy shall obtain mercy;" and, "the pure in heart shall see God;" and, the peacemakers "shall be called the children of God;" nothing else but the Kingdom doth He shadow out by all these sayings. For such as enjoy these, shall surely attain unto that [i.e., the kingdom of heaven].[24]

The use of the expression "the kingdom of heaven" in the first Beatitude, which opens the entire Sermon on the Mount, is not incidental. The kingdom of heaven is the overarching idea that holds together all of Jesus' teaching.[25] The entire Sermon on the Mount as a whole, and the Beatitudes in particular, are a guide to the way to the kingdom of heaven, which should not at all be thought of merely as the end point of the journey. The kingdom of heaven is present in a person's spiritual journey to God, as the dimension that allows a person to fulfill commandments that are seemingly impossible to fulfill.

We spoke earlier of the meaning of the concept of the "kingdom of heaven" in our first volume, *The Beginning of the Gospel*. There we noted

---

[24]John Chrysostom, *Homilies on Matthew* 15.7 (NPNF[1] 10:95).

[25]The literature dedicated to the concepts of the "kingdom of heaven" and the "kingdom of God" is immense. See, in particular, Jack Dean Kingsbury, *Matthew: Structure, Christology, Kingdom* (Philadelphia, PA: Fortress, 1975), 128–160; Jonathan T. Pennington, *Heaven and Earth in the Gospel of Matthew*, Supplements to Novum Testamentum 126 (Leiden: Brill, 2007; repr., Grand Rapids, MI: Baker Academic, 2009), 279–330; Ladd, *Theology of the New Testament*, 42–132; Robert D. Rowe, *God's Kingdom and God's Son: The Background in Mark's Christology from Concepts of Kingship in the Psalms*, Arbeiten zur Geschichte des antiken Judentums und des Urchristentums 50 (Leiden: Brill, 2002), 115–161; John P. Meier, *A Marginal Jew: Rethinking the Historical Jesus*, vol. 2, *Mentor, Message and Miracles*, Anchor Bible Reference Library (New York, NY: Doubleday, 1994), 237–506 (the most detailed investigation into the topic).

that the kingdom of heaven is, in Jesus' language, an all-encompassing concept: it cannot be reduced to the present, nor to the future, nor to an earthly reality, nor to eternity; it does not have concrete earthly features, nor a concrete verbal expression; it cannot be localized in time or space; it is oriented not to the here, the now, the external, but to the heavenly, the future, the internal. The kingdom of heaven is eternity superimposed on time, but not merged with it.[26]

2. "Blessed Are They That Mourn"

The second Beatitude is connected with the first and follows from it: "Blessed are they that mourn [*penthountes*]: for they shall be comforted [*paraklēthēsontai*]" (Mt 5.4). In the parallel text from the Sermon on the Plain, different terms are used: "Blessed are ye that weep now [*klaiontes nyn*]: for ye shall laugh [*gelasete*]" (Lk 6.21). The semantic difference between the verbs *pentheō* and *klaiō* is not easy to grasp: both of them refer to weeping occasioned by sorrow, grief, and mourning, including mourning for the deceased. The difference between the second pair of verbs is more substantial. They refer respectively to two different states: being comforted, and laughter. One may say that according to Luke's version, as a reward for weeping due to various lamentable circumstances (including poverty and hunger), a person will receive joy (laughter), while in Matthew's version mourning as an inner spiritual state is transformed into being comforted, which again is of a spiritual nature.

Those who mourn can be understood in a broad sense to refer to all who suffer,[27] who find themselves in desperate circumstances,[28] in sor-

---

[26]Metropolitan Hilarion Alfeyev, *Beginning of the Gospel*, 342–343.

[27]M. D. Muretov, *Evangelie po Matfeyu* [The Gospel of Matthew], in *Izbrannye trudy* [Selected works] (Moscow: Izd. Svyato-Vladimirskogo Bratstva, 2002), 217.

[28]France, *Gospel of Matthew*, 165.

rows, and under persecution,[29] who sense their own helplessness and vulnerability.[30]

The second Beatitude has a possible parallel in the book of the prophet Isaiah—in the very same passage that Jesus read in the synagogue in Nazareth (Lk 4.16–20). Here it is in the version of the Septuagint: "The Spirit of the Lord is upon me, because he has anointed me; he has sent me to preach glad tidings to the poor, to heal the broken in heart. . . . to comfort all that mourn [*parakalesai pantas tous penthountas*]; that there should be given to them that mourn [*penthousin*] in Sion glory instead of ashes, the oil of joy to the mourners, the garment of glory for the spirit of heaviness" (Is 61.1–3 LXX, trans. Brenton).

The verbal correspondence between the two Greek translations—of the book of the prophet Isaiah and the words of Jesus—is obvious; the Hebrew originals probably must have had a similar correspondence. Jesus' words contain a direct allusion to the text of Isaiah.[31] The fact that Jesus applies the words of the prophet to himself in the synagogue in Nazareth demonstrates that it is he himself whom he sees as the source of joy: he is the one called to "comfort all that mourn." This comfort is focused in his person, just as the kingdom of heaven, which is promised to the poor in spirit, also has him as its source. The Christocentrism of both Beatitudes is obvious. Jesus does not merely announce the blessedness of people who possess certain qualities: he himself is the giver of this blessedness.

Here it is appropriate to recall Jesus' words about sorrow and joy that he addressed to his disciples at the Last Supper: "Ye shall weep and lament, but the world shall rejoice; and ye shall be sorrowful, but your sorrow shall be turned into joy" (Jn 16.20). Jesus compares the disciples' sorrow at parting with him to the suffering of a woman in labor, and the joy of his resurrection to the joy at the birth of a child. Again, he himself is the source of joy: "And ye now therefore have sorrow, but I will see you again, and your

[29]David L. Turner, *Matthew*, Baker Exegetical Commentary on the New Testament (Grand Rapids, MI: Baker Academic, 2008), 150–151.

[30]Guelich, *Sermon on the Mount*, 100–101.

[31]Some scholars believe that the Beatitudes are entirely based on Isaiah 61.1–11. See, for example, Darrell L. Bock, *Jesus according to Scripture: Restoring the Portrait from the Gospels* (Grand Rapids, MI: Baker Academic, 2002), 128.

The Last Supper,
Fra Angelico,
1450

heart shall rejoice, and your joy no man taketh from you" (Jn 16.22). The comfort of which Jesus speaks in the Beatitudes and the joy of which he would speak to his disciples at the Last Supper are eternal and timeless and spring from encountering him—the one who is God incarnate.

It is not incidental that the sixth Beatitude—which is about the pure in heart—concludes with the words "for they shall see God" (Mt 5.8). Thus the connection extends between the second and sixth Beatitudes: the source of comfort for those who mourn is God himself, whom the pure in heart shall see.

The second Beatitude, like the first, has a rich history of interpretation. In the Eastern Christian tradition, the interpretation that became established connected this Beatitude with the theme of repentant mourning, which must be the Christian's lifelong labor.[32] John Chrysostom speaks of repentance as a "second baptism," citing the example of Peter, who mourned over his sin of denying the Lord.[33] Chrysostom understands the second Beatitude as referring to the mourning of repentance:

---

[32]Origen, *Commentary on the Psalms* 37.7 (J. B. Pitra, ed., *Analecta sacra spicilegio solismensi parata* [Venice, 1882–1883], 3:21). The attribution of this work to Origen is doubtful. The fragments on the Psalms that are ascribed to Origen are traced back to the *Scholia on the Psalms* of Evagrius Ponticus.

[33]John Chrysostom, *Homilies on Repentance* 3.4. English translation from *On Repentance and Almsgiving,* by John Chrysostom, trans. Gus George Christo, Fathers of the Church 96 (Washington, DC: Catholic University of America Press, 1998), 40.

Pain is good for those who repent sincerely; the sorrow, matching the sin, suits those who sin. *"Blessed are those who mourn, for they shall be comforted"* [Mt 5.4]. Mourn for the sin so you may not lament for the punishment. Apologize to the judge before you come to the court. Or do you not know that all who want to win the judge flatter him, not when the case is being tried, but before they enter the court, or through friends, or through guardians, or through another way they coax the judge? The same with God: you cannot persuade the Judge during the time of the tribunal. It is possible for you to plead with the Judge before the time of judgment.[34]

Another kind of mourning is found in tears of compunction. John Climacus (seventh century) emphasizes that these tears are a consolation in themselves: "When I consider the actual nature of compunction, I am amazed at how that which is called mourning and grief should contain joy and gladness interwoven within it, like honey in the comb. . . . [S]uch compunction is, in a special sense, a gift of the Lord."[35]

According to the teaching of Isaac the Syrian, tears of repentance first arise out of a person's consciousness of his own sinfulness; these tears are accompanied by bitterness of heart and contrition. However, a person's spiritual growth requires a gradual movement from this type of weeping to another—the sweet tears of compunction.[36] These tears of compunction, which are accompanied by a sense of spiritual joy, are given to a person when he or she attains purity of heart and passionlessness. Speaking of this, Isaac links the second and fifth Beatitudes:

> Blessed, therefore, are the pure in heart, for there is no time when they do not enjoy the sweetness of tears, and in this sweetness they see the Lord at all times [Mt 5.8]. While tears are still wet in their eyes,

---

[34]John Chrysostom, *Homilies on Repentance* 7.6 (trans. Christo, 102–103).

[35]John Climacus, *The Ladder of Divine Ascent* 7.49. English translation from *The Ladder of Divine Ascent*, by John Climacus, trans. Holy Transfiguration Monastery, rev. ed. (Boston, MA: Holy Transfiguration Monastery, 2001), 76.

[36]Isaac the Syrian, *Ascetical Homilies* 37 (trans. Holy Transfiguration Monastery, 306–307).

they are deemed worthy of beholding His revelations at the height of their prayer; and they make no prayer without tears. This is the meaning of the Lord's saying, "Blessed are they that mourn, for they shall be comforted" [Mt 5.4]. For a man comes from mourning into purity of soul. But when the Lord said that they will be comforted, He did not explain what sort of comfort. When by means of tears a monk is deemed worthy of traversing the land of the passions and of reaching the plains of purity of the soul, then he encounters there consolation. . . . For it is not possible that a man who continually mourns and weeps should be disquieted by the passions. . . . All the saints strive to reach this entrance-way, because by means of tears the door is opened before them to enter the land of consolation.[37]

The above interpretations are quite distant from the literal meaning of Jesus' words about the blessedness of those who mourn. However, they reveal the inner richness of the content of these words and the possibility of interpreting them on many levels. Almost every Beatitude can be interpreted on different levels of understanding. We find a similar phenomenon when we study the parables of Jesus.

3. "Blessed Are the Meek"

The third Beatitude—"Blessed are the meek: for they shall inherit the earth" (Mt 5.5)—is a paraphrase of the words of Psalm 36. In this psalm evildoers and those who work iniquity are contrasted with those who hope in the Lord and do good, delight in the Lord, and submit to the Lord and hope in him (Ps 36.1–7). Meekness is contrasted with wrath and anger:

Cease from wrath and forsake anger; fret not thyself so as to do evil. For evil-doers shall utterly perish, but they that wait on the Lord, they

---

[37]Isaac the Syrian, *Ascetical Homilies* 37 (trans. Holy Transfiguration Monastery, 307).

shall inherit the earth. And yet a little while, and the sinner shall not be, and thou shalt seek for his place, and shalt not find it. But the meek shall inherit the earth and shall delight themselves in an abundance of peace. (Ps 36.8–11)

Thus, in his phrasing of the third Beatitude, Jesus again appeals to a verbal formula familiar to his listeners.

The Greek term *praüs* ("meek") is used in the Septuagint to translate a whole range of ancient Hebrew words. In particular, it is used to convey the words *tām* ("meek," lit. "whole," "perfect" in both a physical and religious sense), *'ānāw* ("humble," "stooping"), and *'ānî* ("destitute," "poor," "needy," "uncomplaining," "submissive").[38] The word *marpē'* ("calmness, softness") in the expressions *lēḇ marpē'* ("meek heart," lit. "a heart of calm") and *marpē' lāšôn* ("meek tongue," lit. "calmness of tongue"), as well as the word *raḵ* ("soft," "meek") are close in meaning to the term *tām* ("meek").[39]

In the book of Genesis, Jacob, who dwelled in tents, was called "plain" (or "meek," *tām*), unlike Esau, who was skilled at hunting (Gen 25.27). In the Psalter, people whom God guides toward truth and to whom he teaches his ways are called meek (Ps 24.9), as are those who are glad in the Lord (Ps 33.3); the meek are contrasted with the evildoers (Ps 36.11). In the book of Proverbs, meekness is contrasted with envy, wrath, anger, lack of restraint, and pride:

> A sound heart [*lēḇ marpē'*] is the life of the flesh; but envy the rottenness of the bones. (Prov 14.30)
> A soft [*raḵ*] answer turneth away wrath; but grievous words stir up anger. (Prov 15.1)
> A wholesome tongue [*marpē' lāšôn*] is a tree of life; but perverseness therein is a breach in the spirit. (Prov 15.4)

---

[38]Koehler and Baumgartner, *Hebräisches und aramäisches Lexikon*, 3:809, 810; 4:1604. Certain scholars believe that the original text of the Beatitudes as they were uttered in Aramaic contained a play on words based on the phonetic similarity between the terms *'ānî* ("poor") and *'ānāw* ("meek"). See, in particular, Robert H. Gundry, *Matthew: A Commentary on His Literary and Theological Art* (Grand Rapids, MI: Eerdmans, 1982), 69.

[39]See Koehler and Baumgartner, *Hebräisches und aramäisches Lexikon*, 2:602, 4:1147.

> Better it is to be of an humble spirit with the lowly ['ănāwîm], than
> to divide the spoil with the proud. (Prov 16.19)

Some Old Testament passages about meekness are interpreted in the New Testament as foreshadowings of Jesus Christ. The most well-known of these is from the prophet Zechariah: "Rejoice greatly, O daughter of Zion; shout, O daughter of Jerusalem: behold, thy King cometh unto thee: he is just, and having salvation; lowly ['ānî], and riding upon an ass, and upon a colt the foal of an ass" (Zech 9.9). The Evangelist Matthew refers to this prophecy when he describes how Jesus entered Jerusalem on a young ass (Mt 21.5).

In the New Testament, Jesus is called a Lamb multiple times (Jn 1.29, 36; 1 Pet 1.19; Rev 5.6, etc.). The prophecy of Isaiah is applied to him: "He was led as a sheep to the slaughter; and like a lamb dumb before his shearer, so opened he not his mouth" (Acts 8.32; Is 53.7). In the Old Testament, the lamb is a symbol of meekness: "But I, like an innocent lamb led to be slaughtered, did not know. They devised an evil scheme against me" (Jer 11.19, NETS). It was not incidental that this symbol was chosen for Jesus: it points to his redemptive work, the culmination of which would be Jesus' death on the cross. But, at the same time, it points to Jesus as an image of meekness and humility:

> Take my yoke upon you, and learn of me; for I am meek and lowly in
> heart: and ye shall find rest unto your souls. For my yoke is easy, and
> my burden is light. (Mt 11.29–30)

The word "yoke" translates the Greek *zygos*, which refers to a wooden collar for harnessing oxen together. Metaphorically, this term refers to the duties and responsibility associated with following Jesus' commandments.[40] The term *phortion*, translated as "burden," can also mean "weight" or "load." The same term in the plural is used in relation to the Pharisees, who "bind heavy burdens [*phortia*] and grievous to be borne, and lay them on men's shoulders" (Mt 23.4). The word "heavy-laden" (*pephortismenoi*)

---

[40]Celia Deutsch, *Hidden Wisdom and the Easy Yoke: Wisdom, Torah and Discipleship in Matthew 11.25–30*, Journal for the Study of the New Testament Supplement Series 18 (Sheffield: JSOT Press, 1987), 42–43.

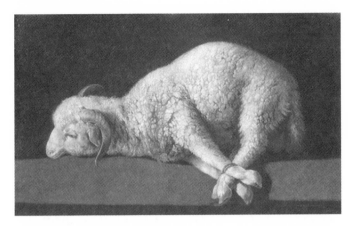

Agnus Dei,
Francisco de
Zurbarán,
1635–1640

comes from the same root, but in the given instance refers to a burden of a different sort—the burden and weight of earthly cares.

Jesus' commandments can seem difficult to fulfill, but fulfilling them brings peace to the soul, because doing so frees the soul from the burden of earthly cares. The means of acquiring this inner peace is meekness and humility. Chrysostom paraphrases Jesus' call thus:

> Not this or that person, but all that are in anxiety, in sorrows, in sins. Come, not that I may call you to account, but that I may do away with your sins; come, not that I want your honor, but that I want your salvation. "For I," saith He, "will give you rest." He said not, "I will save you," only; but what was much more, "I will place you in all security". . . . Thus, "be not afraid," saith He, "hearing of a yoke, for it is easy: fear not, because I said, 'a burden', for it is light". . . . Whilst thou art careless, whilst thou art supine; whereas, if thou duly perform His words, the burden will be light; wherefore also He hath now called it so. But how are they duly performed? If thou art become lowly, and meek, and gentle. For this virtue is the mother of all strictness of life. Wherefore also, when beginning those divine laws, with this He began.[41] And here again He doeth the very same, and exceeding great is the reward He appoints. . . . For, "Of what art thou afraid?" saith He, "lest thou shouldest be a loser by thy low estate? Look to me, and to all that is

---

[41] Here Chrysostom is speaking of the first Beatitude.

mine; learn of me, and then shalt thou know distinctly how great [is] thy blessing."[42]

Inasmuch as the third Beatitude is a direct allusion to an Old Testament passage, we should look for the meaning of the expression "inherit the earth" in the context of the Old Testament understanding of the promised land. The key image here is that of Abraham, of whom it is said in the Epistle to the Hebrews,

> By faith Abraham, when he was called to go out into a place which he should after receive for an inheritance, obeyed; and he went out, not knowing whither he went. By faith he sojourned in the land of promise, as in a strange country, dwelling in tabernacles with Isaac and Jacob, the heirs with him of the same promise: for he looked for a city which hath foundations, whose builder and maker is God. (Heb 11.8–10)

The story of Abraham, whom God commanded to go to an unknown land, and the entire history of his descendants, who fought for this same land, are reinterpreted in Christianity as a type of the spiritual journey that has as its goal the new promised land—the kingdom of heaven. In this sense we may say that the words "for they shall inherit the earth" are close in meaning to the words "for theirs is the kingdom of heaven." What is being spoken of here is one and the same promise, one and the same goal.

Meekness, alongside humility, is one of the qualities that distinguish the Christian idea of spiritual perfection from analogous ideas in other religious and philosophical traditions. In none of them does humility or meekness occupy a prime position on the list of virtues. In the apostolic Epistles, meekness is one of the oft-mentioned qualities that a Christian ought to possess:

> Wherefore lay apart all filthiness and superfluity of wickedness, and receive with meekness the engrafted word, which is able to save your souls. (Jas 1.21)

---

[42]John Chrysostom, *Homilies on Matthew* 38.3 (NPNF[1] 10:252–253).

Who is a wise man and endowed with knowledge among you? Let him show his works by good conduct with meekness of wisdom. (Jas 3.13)[43]

... whose adorning let it not be that outward adorning of plaiting the hair, and of wearing of gold, or of putting on of apparel; but let it be the hidden man of the heart, in that which is not corruptible, even the ornament of a meek and quiet spirit, which is in the sight of God of great price. (1 Pet 3.3–4)

But sanctify the Lord God in your hearts; and be ready always to give an answer to every man that asketh you a reason of the hope that is in you with meekness and fear. (1 Pet 3.15)

Now I Paul myself beseech you by the meekness and gentleness of Christ, who in presence am base among you, but being absent am bold toward you. (2 Cor 10.1)

But the fruit of the Spirit is love, joy, peace, longsuffering, gentleness, goodness, faith, meekness, temperance: against such there is no law. (Gal 5.22–23)

I therefore, the prisoner of the Lord, beseech you that ye walk worthy of the vocation wherewith ye are called, with all lowliness and meekness, with longsuffering, forbearing one another in love, endeavoring to keep the unity of the Spirit in the bond of peace. (Eph 4.1–3)

Let your moderation be known unto all men. The Lord is at hand. (Phil 4.5)

Put on therefore, as the elect of God, holy and beloved, bowels of mercies, kindness, humbleness of mind, meekness, longsuffering. (Col 3.12)

---

[43]On the theme of meekness in the Epistle of James and the connection between Jas 1.21 and Mt 5.5, see, in particular, Gerhard Maier, *Poslanie Iakova* (Wuppertal: Brockhaus, 2004) .

And the servant of the Lord must not strive, but be gentle unto all men, apt to teach, patient, in meekness instructing those that oppose themselves, if God perhaps will give them repentance to the acknowledging of the truth. (Tim 2.24–25)

Put them in mind to be subject to principalities and powers, to obey magistrates, to be ready to every good work, to speak evil of no man, to be no brawlers, but gentle, showing all meekness unto all men. (Tit 3.1–2)

Judging by the large number of times meekness is mentioned, the apostles considered this quality to be an important part of Christian witness, both within the Christian community and toward outsiders. Along with humility and patience, meekness is one of the characteristic features of the new spiritual and moral image being created in the church community under the direct influence of the person of Jesus Christ.

In the subsequent Eastern Christian tradition, a significant amount of attention is devoted to meekness. In the classic guide to monastic life, *The Ladder of Divine Ascent*, an entire chapter is dedicated to meekness. In it meekness is treated first of all as being synonymous with freedom from anger and the opposite of the mad and shameful passion of anger: in contrasting meekness with anger, John Climacus follows Psalm 36. In his words, "Meekness is an immovable state of soul which remains unaffected, whether in evil report or in good report, in dishonour or in praise. . . . it is a mark of extreme meekness, even in the presence of one's offender, to be peacefully and lovingly disposed towards him in one's heart."[44]

---

[44]John Climacus, *The Ladder of Divine Ascent* 8.3, 13 (trans. Holy Transfiguration Monastery, 81–82).

4. "Blessed Are They Which Do Hunger and Thirst after Righteousness"

The fourth Beatitude differs quite substantially in Matthew's version from the parallel text in Luke. In the Sermon on the Plain, Jesus speaks of physical hunger (Lk 6.21), while in the Sermon on the Mount, he is speaking of spiritual hunger and spiritual thirst: "Blessed are they which do hunger and thirst after righteousness: for they shall be filled" (Mt 5.6).

In the Old Testament, particularly in the book of Psalms, the image of thirst is used to describe a person's strong and burning desire for God, to fulfill his law and commandments:

> As the hart panteth after the fountains of water, so panteth my soul after thee, O God. My soul thirsted for God, the mighty, the living. (Ps 41.2–3)
>
> O God, my God, unto thee I rise early at dawn. My soul hath thirsted for thee; how often hath my flesh longed after thee in a land barren and untrodden and unwatered. (Ps 62.2)
>
> I opened my mouth and drew in my breath, for I longed for thy commandments. (Ps 118.131)
>
> I have longed for thy salvation, O Lord, and thy judgments will help me. (Ps 118.174)
>
> I stretched forth my hands unto thee; my soul thirsteth after thee like a waterless land. (Ps 142.6)

Our understanding of the fourth Beatitude depends on the meaning of the word "righteousness." As a rule, in the Septuagint, the word *dikaiosynē* corresponds to the Hebrew *sedeq*, or *sədāqā* ("righteousness"). The term *dikaiosynē* is usually translated as "righteousness," "justice." In the overall context of the Beatitudes, this term has an emphatically religious meaning. It is no coincidence that it is encountered there twice: first in the fourth

*The Joy of the
Righteous in
the Lord, V.
M. Vasnetsov,
1885–1896*

Beatitude, then in the eighth. It is encountered seven times in total in the Gospel of Matthew (Mt 3.15; 5.6, 10, 20; 6.1, 33; 21.32), five instances of which are in the Sermon on the Mount.

Righteousness is the quality that, according to the Sermon on the Mount, is to be the distinguishing mark of Jesus' disciples, who constitute the Church.[45] What is being spoken of foremost here is righteousness that derives from the law of God or will of God.[46] It was precisely of this that Jesus spoke to John the Baptist: "Permit it to be so now: for thus it becometh us to fulfill all righteousness [*dikaiosynēn*]" (Mt 3.15). In Jesus' words, John the Baptist came "in the way of righteousness [*dikaiosynēs*]," but the scribes and Pharisees did not believe him (Mt 21.32). At the Last Supper, as he promised to send the Holy Spirit to his disciples, Jesus spoke again about righteousness:

> Nevertheless I tell you the truth; it is expedient for you that I go away: for if I go not away, the Comforter will not come unto you; but if I depart, I will send him unto you. And when he is come, he will reprove the world of sin, and of righteousness [*dikaiosynēs*], and of judgment: of sin, because they believe not on me; of righteousness, because I go to my Father, and ye see me no more; of judgment, because the prince of this world is judged. (Jn 16.7–11)

Righteousness is a key biblical concept. In the language of the Old Testament, it referred primarily to following the commandments of God; the

---

[45] Augustine Stock, *The Method and Message of Matthew* (Collegeville, MN: Liturgical Press, 1994), 69.

[46] Martin Goldsmith, *Matthew and Mission: The Gospel through Jewish Eyes* (Carlisle: Paternoster, 2001), 66.

calling of the people chosen by God was to "keep the way of the LORD, to do justice and judgment" (Gen 18.19). The pursuit of justice is a necessary condition for taking possession of the promised land: "That which is altogether just shalt thou follow, that thou mayest live, and inherit the land which the LORD thy God giveth thee" (Deut 16.20). In the Psalms, the concept of righteousness is used both in the sense of human righteousness as well as in relation to God, and both understandings of righteousness are tightly intertwined:

St John the Baptist, icon, 14th–15th century

> When I called upon thee, O God of my
> righteousness, thou didst hearken unto me.
> (Ps 4.2)
> O Lord, guide me in the way of thy righteousness. (Ps 5.9)
> Judge me, O Lord, according to my righteousness, and according to
> mine innocence within me. (Ps 7.9)
> I will give praise unto the Lord according to his righteousness, and I
> will chant unto the Name of the Lord Most High. (Ps 7.18)
> For the Lord is righteous and hath loved righteousness; upon
> uprightness hath his countenance looked. (Ps 10.7)
> Good and upright is the Lord; therefore will he set a law for them
> that sin in the way. He will guide the meek in judgment, he will
> teach the meek his ways. (Ps 24.8–9)
> O continue thy mercy unto them that know thee, and thy
> righteousness unto the upright of heart. (Ps 35.11)
> My mouth shall declare thy righteousness, all the day long thy
> salvation; for I know not the reckoning thereof. I will commence
> in the might of the Lord; O Lord, I will make mention of the
> righteousness which is thine alone. (Ps 70.15–16)
> Mercy and truth are met together, righteousness and peace have
> kissed each other. Truth is sprung up out of the earth, and
> righteousness hath looked down from heaven. Yea, for the

Christ's Sermon on the Mount, fresco, 1870–1890

Lord will give goodness, and our land shall yield her fruit. Righteousness shall go before him and shall set his footsteps in the way. (Ps 84.11–14)

Clouds and darkness are round about him; righteousness and judgment are the establishment of his throne. (Ps 96.2)

Behold, I have longed after thy commandments; in thy righteousness quicken me. (Ps 118.40)

Mine eyes have failed with waiting for thy salvation, and for the word of thy righteousness. (Ps 118.123)

Thy righteousness is an everlasting righteousness, and thy law is truth. . . . Thy testimonies are righteousness forever; give me understanding and I shall live. (Ps 118.142, 144)

In this way, righteousness in the Old Testament stands out as one of the qualities of God himself. Human righteousness, on the other hand, is a direct reflection of this divine righteousness. The righteousness of God has a timeless, eternal character, but it is reflected in the commandments that God has given to human beings, who live in time. In this context, those who "hunger and thirst after righteousness" are those who fervently seek to fulfill the commandments of God. One may also say that those who hunger and thirst after righteousness are the ones who seek God with all their heart, since God is the source of all righteousness.

Being simultaneously God and man, Jesus manifests in his life both the righteousness of God and the righteousness of man. In the experience of his life, these two concepts become inseparable. As with the other Beatitudes, the true meaning of the fourth Beatitude is revealed through Jesus. Gregory of Nyssa emphasizes the theocentrism and Christocentrism of this Beatitude: "The true virtue, the good that is unmixed with evil. . . . is God the Word Himself. . . . and rightly have those who hunger for this justice of God been called blessed. For if, as the Psalmist says, a man has truly tasted the Lord [Ps 33.9]; that is, if he has received God into himself, he is filled with Him for whom he has thirsted and hungered."[47]

5. "Blessed Are the Merciful"

The fifth Beatitude speaks of yet another very important human quality that directly reflects one of the characteristics of God: "Blessed are the merciful: for they shall obtain mercy" (Mt 5.7).

Already in the Old Testament God is called merciful and gracious: God appears to Moses on Sinai with the name "The LORD, the LORD God, merciful and gracious, longsuffering, and abundant in goodness and truth" (Ex 34.6). These words are repeated almost word for word in Psalm 85: "But thou, O Lord my God, art compassionate and merciful, long-suffering and plenteous in mercy, and true" (Ps 85.15). Psalm 102 says, "Compassionate and merciful is the Lord, long-suffering and plenteous in mercy" (Ps 102.8).

[47]Greogy of Nyssa, *The Beatitudes* 4 (trans. Graef, 128–129).

We find similar expressions in the books of the prophets: "He is gracious and merciful, slow to anger, and of great kindness, and repenteth him of the evil" (Joel 2.13).

To refer to divine mercy in the Old Testament, the terms *hesed* ("loving-kindness") and *rahāmîm* ("mercy," "benevolence," "compassion") are used. These terms often appear in a pair, as though complementing each other (for example, in Ps 24.5; 39.12; 50.3; 68.17; 102.4; 105.45–46; 118.76–77, 156, 159; 144.9–10; Lam 3.22; Neh 9.17, 19, 27, 28, 31; Is 54.7–8; 63.7; Jer 16.5). The term *rahāmîm* is related to the word *rehem*, which means "maternal womb": the Greek *eusplanchnia* conveys its meaning more precisely than the word "compassion."

One may say that the Old Testament idea of God's compassion is akin to the idea of maternal love. The compassion of God, his *eusplanchnia*, is akin to the feeling that is described in the story of Solomon's trial of the two women who tried to get custody of the same child: when Solomon suggested dividing the child in two in order to give him to both women equally, the real mother objected, "for her bowels [*rahāmêhā*[48]] yearned for her son" (1 Kg 3.16–28). God the Father also has such pity and compassion toward human beings as his children.

At the same time, the God of the Old Testament remains primarily a just Judge who gives to each according to his deeds. In the Old Testament God's mercy toward someone is directly connected with that person's conduct: "With the holy man wilt thou be holy, and with the innocent man wilt thou be innocent. And with the elect man wilt thou be elect, and with the perverse wilt thou be perverse" (Ps 17.26–27).

In the New Testament, on the other hand, the emphasis is placed on mercy as a characteristic of God, independent of human conduct: God "maketh his sun to rise on the evil and on the good, and sendeth rain on the just and on the unjust" (Mt 5.45). In the New Testament the idea of divine justice is almost completely superseded by the idea of divine mercy. Many of Jesus' parables are dedicated to this theme, including the parable of the laborers in the vineyard: each laborer receives an equal reward from God independent of the hour that he began working (Mt 20.1–16).

---

[48]This is the plural form of the word *rehem* with a pronominal suffix.

At this point, it is appropriate to once again recall the words of Isaac the Syrian, who insisted that "mercy is opposed to justice,"[49] and that therefore one should not speak of the justice of God, but only of the mercy that surpasses all justice: "As a grain of sand cannot counterbalance a great quantity of gold, so in comparison God's use of justice cannot counterbalance His mercy. As a handful of sand thrown into the great sea, so are the sins of all flesh in comparison with the mind of God."[50]

According to Isaac the Syrian, the Old Testament idea of God as the punisher of sinners, "visiting the iniquity of the fathers upon the children unto the third and fourth generation of them that hate me" (Ex 20.5; Num 14.18), does not correspond to the revelation that we receive through Christ in the New Testament. Although in the Psalms David calls God righteous and just (Ps 118.137), the Son of God showed rather that he is good and gracious. Christ affirmed the "injustice" of God and his goodness in the parables of the laborers in the vineyard and of the prodigal son, but even more so by his redeeming work, accomplished for the salvation of sinners. Isaac asks, "Where, then, is God's justice?—for while we are sinners Christ died for us!"[51] In another passage, he says emphatically, "Justice does not belong to the Christian way of life, and there is no mention of it in Christ's teaching."[52]

Divine mercy is reflected in the human quality that is called, in biblical language, mercy or compassion. Isaac the Syrian's well-known passage on the "merciful heart," through which a person becomes like God, is notable:

> "And what is a merciful heart?" "It is the heart's burning for the sake of the entire creation, for men, for birds, for animals, for demons, and for every created thing; and at the recollection and sight of them, the eyes of a merciful man pour forth abundant tears. From the strong and vehement mercy that grips his heart and from his great compassion, his heart is humbled and he cannot bear to hear or to see any injury

[49]Isaac the Syrian, *Ascetical Homilies* 51 (trans. Holy Transfiguration Monastery, 379).
[50]Isaac the Syrian, *Ascetical Homilies* 51 (trans. Holy Transfiguration Monastery, 379).
[51]Isaac the Syrian, *Ascetical Homilies* 51 (trans. Holy Transfiguration Monastery, 387).
[52]Isaac the Syrian, *Ascetical Homilies* 51 (trans. Holy Transfiguration Monastery, 382).

or slight sorrow in creation. For this reason he offers up prayers with tears continually even for irrational beasts, for the enemies of the truth, and for those who harm him, that they be protected and receive mercy. And in like manner he even prays for the family of reptiles, because of the great compassion that burns without measure in his heart in the likeness of God."[53]

Note that Isaac the Syrian was writing in the same language that Jesus was speaking six centuries before. In the Syrian tradition, the gospel teaching was interpreted in its own special way: here we encounter some motifs absent in the Greek writers. In particular, Isaac's idea of prayer for demons, animals, birds, and reptiles is alien to Greek patristic writings. It is likewise absent in the Gospels themselves. However, through the words cited above, Isaac, unlike any other author in the patristic era, succeeded in conveying the emotional content that characterizes the concept of "love" in the Christian tradition. Love exerts a transformative effect on a person's entire view of the world. The one who has acquired love begins to look at people and the surrounding world in a different way: this person sees the latter not through the prism of his or her own egoistic perception, but as if through the eyes of God himself. This person also sees people as God sees them, seeing beneath their outer shell the image of God that all people possess, regardless of whether they are friend or foe.

The merciful (*eleēmones*) who are spoken of in the fifth Beatitude are those who possess the compassion and love that reflect divine love, who do not divide people into friends or enemies, evil or good, righteous or unrighteous. Like the sun, God illumines both the one and the other with his light: like rain, he showers them with his love and mercy. The "merciful heart" in a person is the image of the divine mercy that extends over all creation. Thus, from the Christian perspective, to be merciful means not simply to behave mercifully toward one's neighbors, but also to have in one's heart the mercy that reflects the divine mercy. What is being spoken of here is not only a pattern of behavior, but an inner quality as well.

---

[53]Isaac the Syrian, *Ascetical Homilies* 71 (trans. Holy Transfiguration Monastery, 491).

The Beatitudes say of the people who possess this quality that they "shall obtain mercy [*eleēthēsontai*]." As in the Old Testament, a direct connection can be traced here between a person's attitude toward his neighbor and God's attitude toward that person. This connection will be emphasized later on in the Sermon on the Mount in the words of the Lord's Prayer, "And forgive us our debts, as we forgive our debtors," as well as in the commentary that Jesus provides on these words: "For if ye forgive men their trespasses, your heavenly Father will also forgive you; but if ye forgive not men their trespasses, neither will your Father forgive your trespasses" (Mt 6.12, 14–15).

The Blind, A. A. Plastov, first half of the 20th century

The act of having mercy is a fundamental biblical concept. The Psalmist addresses God with the appeal "have mercy" (*eleēson*) many times; the Christian Church adopted it from the Psalms, and it has firmly entered into the divine services as the main petition that believers address to God. With this same phrase those who wished to receive healing from Jesus also addressed him (Mt 9.27; 15.22; 17.15). For his part, Jesus heals, having "had compassion [*splanchnistheis*]" on the infirm (Mt 20.34; Mk 1.41). His human mercy is inseparably linked with the mercy that he possesses as God.

Jesus calls all his followers to this mercy through the fifth Beatitude, as well as through the words in the Sermon on the Plain: "Be ye therefore merciful [*oiktirmones*], as your Father also is merciful" (Lk 6.36). Here the word used is close in meaning to the term *eleēmones* and also means "merciful," "compassionate."

6. "Blessed Are the Pure in Heart"

The sixth Beatitude also does not speak of a pattern of behavior but of an inner quality in a person: "Blessed are the pure in heart: for they shall see God" (Mt 5.8).

The expression "pure in heart" (*katharoi tē kardia*) is from the Psalter: "Who shall ascend into the mountain of the Lord? Or who shall stand in his holy place? He that is innocent in hands and pure in heart . . ." (Ps 23.3–4). Again we see how Jesus uses an expression that many knew by heart. In order to understand its meaning, we must examine the two key concepts that it contains: "purity" and "heart."

In the language of the Old Testament, the concept of purity is connected primarily with sacred objects, divine service, the offering of sacrifices, the altar, the tabernacle, and the temple: nothing impure is to touch what is sacred. At the same time, impurity can be physical, connected with diseases, injuries, or bodily imperfections (Lev 21.17–23), as well as spiritual impurity (Is 1.10–17). The source of purity and cleansing is God, to whom David turns in prayer in his penitential psalm: "Wash me thoroughly from mine iniquity, and cleanse me from my sin. . . . Thou shalt sprinkle me with hyssop, and I shall be made clean; thou shalt wash me, and I shall be made whiter than snow" (Ps 50.4, 9).

In the Old Testament tradition, the heart is understood to be not merely a physical organ or the center of a person's emotional activity. It is also a spiritual center that determines a person's actions, life choices, and attitude toward God and other people. It is in the heart that thoughts and decisions take shape; it is in the heart that a person conducts a dialogue with himself and with God. The heart is the spiritual depth into which God looks in a person (1 Sam 16.7; Jer 17.10). It is not just human beings who have a heart; God has a heart as well (Gen 6.6; 8.21; Ps 32.11).

Purity of heart is impossible to attain through a person's own efforts alone; God's help is necessary: "Create in me a clean heart, O God, and renew a right spirit within me" (Ps 50.12). What is expected of a person is repentance: "A sacrifice unto God is a broken spirit; a heart that is broken and humbled God will not despise" (Ps 50.19). As one modern scholar notes, the renewal of the heart is the main theme of the Sermon on the Mount. However, Jesus does not just require a new heart of his followers: he himself gives it to them.[54]

Purity of heart is a precondition for communion with God: "Who shall ascend into the mountain of the Lord? Or who shall stand in his holy place? He that is innocent in hands and pure in heart. . . . This is the generation of them that seek the Lord, of them that seek the face of the God of Jacob" (Ps 23.3–4, 6). Without purity of heart it is impossible to touch the sacred, to meet God, to see the face of God.

The promise "for they shall see God" brings to mind a whole series of biblical passages that talk about seeing God.[55]

On the one hand, in both the Old and the New Testaments we find emphatic assertions that it is impossible for a human being to see God. When Moses ascends Mount Sinai, God promises to cause his glory to pass before him, but at the same time he declares, "Thou canst not see my face: for there shall no man see me, and live" (Ex 33.19–20). In the words of the apostle Paul, "no man hath seen, nor can see" God (1 Tim 6.16). The assertion that no one has ever seen God is found twice in the corpus of John's writings (Jn 1.18; 1 Jn 4.12).

On the other hand, some passages speak of the possibility of seeing God. Jacob, who wrestled with God, exclaims, "I have seen God face to face, and my life is preserved" (Gen 32.30). Job expresses his hope that he would see God with his own eyes: "For I know that my redeemer liveth, and that he shall stand at the latter day upon the earth; and though after my skin is destroyed, yet in my flesh shall I see God, whom I shall see for myself, and mine eyes shall behold, and not another" (Job 19.25–27). The apostles John and Paul speak of seeing God in the life to come (1 Jn 3.2; 1 Cor 13.12).

[54]Frederick Neumann, *The New Heart: An Introduction to the Sermon on the Mount* (Princeton, NJ: Princeton University Press, 1991), 9.

[55]Here and below on pages 83–85 we repeat the conclusions made earlier in Hilarion Alfeyev, *St Symeon the New Theologian and Orthodox Tradition* (Oxford: Oxford University Press, 2000), 215–218, 224.

Job on the Ash Heap, miniature, 11th century

The inherent paradox of the theme of seeing God is vividly expressed by Gregory of Nyssa in his commentary on the sixth Beatitude:

> *Blessed are the clean of heart, for they shall see God* [Mt 5.8]. God is promised to the vision of those whose heart has been purified. But "No man hath seen God at any time," as says the great John [Jn 1.18]. And the sublime mind of Paul confirms this verdict when he says, "Whom no man hath seen, nor can see" [1 Tim 6.16]. . . . all possibility of apprehension is taken away by this explicit denial, "No man can see the Lord and live" [Ex 33.20]. Yet to see the Lord is eternal life. . . . Do you realize the vertigo of the soul that is drawn to the depths contemplated in these words? If God is life, then the man who does not see Him does not see life. On the other hand, the Divinely inspired prophets and apostles testify that God cannot be seen. Is not the hope of man annihilated?[56]

In the patristic literature we find various approaches to the paradox of "visible/invisible."

The first explanation is that God, by his nature, cannot be seen, but he can be seen in his energies (actions), his glory, his goodness, his revelations, his condescension. In the words of Gregory of Nyssa, "He is invisible by nature, but becomes visible in his energies."[57] John Chrysostom, recalling God's appearance to Moses, Isaiah, and other prophets, speaks of the "condescension" (*oikonomia*) of God shown to them:

---

[56]Gregory of Nyssa, *The Beatitudes* 6 (trans. Graef, 143–144).
[57]Gregory of Nyssa, *The Beatitudes* 6 (trans. Graef, 147).

All these were instances of (His) condescension, not the vision of the Essence itself unveiled. For had they seen the very Nature, they would not have beheld It under different forms. . . . [W]hat God really is, not only have not the prophets seen, but not even angels nor archangels. . . . [M]any have seen Him in the mode of vision permitted to them, but no one has beheld His Essence.[58]

St Ignatius of Antioch,
fresco, 16th century

The second way to resolve the problem of "visible/invisible" assumes a Christological dimension: God is invisible in his essence, but has revealed himself in the human flesh of the Son of God. Ignatius of Antioch says that God is "who is invisible . . . [became] visible for us" in the person of his Son.[59] Irenaeus of Lyons asserts that "the Father is the invisible of the Son, but the Son the visible of the Father."[60] In the words of John Chrysostom, the Son of God, being by his divine nature as invisible as the Father, became visible when he put on human flesh.[61] Theodore the Studite writes,

Previously, when Christ was not in flesh, He was invisible
For "no man," as it is said, "hath seen God at any time" [Jn 1.18].
But when he put on coarse human flesh . . .
He deliberately becomes palpable . . .[62]

The third possible approach to the problem is to attempt to resolve it from an eschatological perspective: God cannot be seen in the present life, but the righteous will see him after death. However much a person may perfect himself before God, says Isaac the Syrian, in this life he sees God from behind, as in a mirror, seeing only his image; in the age to come,

---

[58]John Chrysostom, *Homilies on John* 15.1 (NPNF[1] 14:51–52).

[59]Ignatius of Antioch, *Epistle to Polycarp* 3.2 (*Ignatius of Antioch: The Letters*, trans. Alistair Stewart, Popular Patristics Series 49 [Yonkers, NY: St Vladimir's Seminary Press, 2013], 103).

[60]Irenaeus of Lyons, *Against Heresies* 4.6.6 (ANF 1:469).

[61]John Chrysostom, *Homilies on John* 15.1 (NPNF[1] 14:52).

[62]Theodore the Studite, *Iambs* 33; see *Theodoros Studites: Jamben auf verschiedene Gegenstände*, ed. Paul Speck, Supplementa Byzantina 1 (Berlin: de Gruyter, 1968), 181. English translation by the author in Hilarion Alfeyev, *St Symeon the New Theologian and Orthodox Tradition*, 217.

however, God will show him his face.[63] Theodore the Studite considers seeing God a reward given in the life to come: it is necessary to struggle and suffer here in order to see in the age to come "the immeasurable beauty and ineffable glory of the face of Christ."[64]

Finally, the fourth possible way of explaining the contradiction of "visible/invisible" is to place it in the context of the idea of purifying the soul: God is invisible to a person in a fallen state, but becomes visible to those who have achieved purity of heart. We find this idea in Theophilus of Antioch, who believed that it is necessary to be purified of sin in order to see God.[65] When a person's heart is cleansed, Gregory of Nyssa says, "he will see the Image of the Divine Nature in his own beauty."[66]

Which of these four approaches is the closest to the original meaning of Jesus' saying concerning the blessedness of the pure in heart? It seems that it would be the fourth, in which seeing God is directly connected with purity of heart, but nevertheless nothing is said of *when* a person might see God: in this earthly life or beyond the grave. Unlike the Sermon on the Plain in the Gospel of Luke, where all the promises are relegated to the future, which is contrasted with that which takes place "now," such a contrast is lacking in the Sermon on the Mount in the Gospel of Matthew. Between purity of heart and seeing God there is no temporal gap, just as there is no such gap between the other Beatitudes and the promises that derive from them. This gives Symeon the New Theologian the right to dispute an eschatological interpretation of the sixth Beatitude, and to say that seeing God comes simultaneously with attaining purity of heart:

> [They] will reply: "Yes, certainly the pure in heart will see God, but this will happen only in the future, not in the present age." My dear friend, just why or how will this happen? If He said that God will be seen by purity of heart, then clearly when this purity comes to pass the vision

---

[63]Isaac the Syrian, *Ascetical Homilies* 48 (trans. Holy Transfiguration Monastery, 365).

[64]Theodore the Studite, *Great Catechism* 1.12; see *Patris nostri Theodori Studitae parvae et magnae catecheseos sermones*, ed. Josephus Cozza-Luzi, t. 9, pt. 1–2 of *Novae patrum bibliothecae* (Rome, 1888). English translation by present translator.

[65]Theophilus of Antioch, *To Autolycus* 1.2 (ANF 2:89).

[66]Gregory of Nyssa, *The Beatitudes* 6 (trans. Graef, 148).

will follow in consequence. . . . For if the purification takes place in this life, then so does the vision. On the other hand, if you should say that the seeing is for after death, then you certainly posit the purification as also after death, and thus it will turn out that you will never see God since after death there will be no work for you by which you might find purification.[67]

At the same time we must point out that the second of the aforementioned patristic interpretations also has a direct parallel in the Gospels, in particular, in the dialogue between Philip and Jesus at the Last Supper. In reply to Jesus' words, addressed to the disciples, that they know and have seen the Father, Philip says, "Lord, show us the Father, and it will be enough for us." Jesus replies, "Have I been so long with you, and yet hast thou not known me, Philip? He that hath seen me hath seen the Father; and how sayest thou then, 'Show us the Father'?" (Jn 14.7–9). Jesus equates seeing God the Father with the appearance of the Son of God: through the human face of Jesus, the way to seeing the divine face of the invisible Father is opened to human beings. Thus, as with the other Beatitudes, the sixth Beatitude has a vividly expressed Christological dimension.

7. "Blessed Are the Peacemakers"

The seventh Beatitude, unlike the ones preceding it, speaks not so much of an inner quality of a person as it does of his conduct: "Blessed are the peacemakers: for they shall be called the children [or 'sons', Gr. *huioi*] of God" (Mt 5.9).

An expression close to the word "peacemakers" is encountered in the Old Testament once, in the book of Proverbs: "Deceit is in the heart of

[67]Symeon the New Theologian, *Ethical Discourses* 5.112–125. English translation from *On the Mystical Life: The Ethical Discourses*, by Symeon the New Theologian, vol. 2, *On Virtue and Christian Life*, trans. Alexander Golitzin, Popular Patristics Series 15 (Crestwood, NY: St Vladimir's Seminary Press, 1996), 47–48.

them that imagine evil, but to the counselors of peace is joy" (Prov 12.20). This expression comes from the biblical idea of peace (Hebrew *šālôm*) as an antonym of war, enmity, and hate. The entire history of the people of Israel was full of wars, conflicts, and clashes with neighboring tribes; times of peace and stability came rarely and did not endure for long. In the Old Testament peace is understood as a divine gift that is given to people as a reward for fulfilling the commandments of God (Ex 26.3–7). We find exhortations to peace in the Psalter: "Turn away from evil, and do good; seek peace, and pursue it" (Ps 33.15).

Peacemakers are not simply peaceable people: they are the ones who "make peace," that is, they actively work to bring peace to people.[68] As in the above citation from the book of Proverbs, this Beatitude is about making peace—first and foremost in the relationships between a concrete person and the people around him or her. Herein lies one of the differences between Jesus' moral program and the moral law laid out in the law of Moses. The law of Moses is addressed to the entire society of Israel and directed at the preservation of its spiritual integrity as the chosen people of God. Jesus' commandments are addressed to the individual who lives in the world but is called to live according to laws different from the ones on which ordinary human communal life is built.

We find further elucidation of the meaning of this same Beatitude later on in the Sermon on the Mount. The following words are a direct continuation of the seventh Beatitude: "But I say unto you, love your enemies, bless them that curse you, do good to them that hate you, and pray for them which despitefully use you, and persecute you" (Mt 5.44–45). Making peace is conceived of not as the passive expectation of the development of events, but as a person's intervention in events that are not developing in the way they ought to from a religious point of view. We will return to this topic when we discuss how the Old Testament principle of "an eye for an eye, a tooth for a tooth" is replaced in Jesus' teaching by a new moral paradigm based on the principle of non-resistance to evil.

---

[68]Richard B. Gardner, *Matthew*, Believers Church Bible Commentary (Scottsdale, PA: Herald, 1991), 97.

The expression "sons of God" (or "children of God") is encountered in multiple places in the Old Testament. The book of Genesis mentions the "sons of God" who "came in unto the daughters of men" (Gen 6.1–4). The angels, one of whom being the fallen angel, Satan, are called sons of God (Job 1.6; 2.1). The people of Israel are called the children of the Lord God (Deut 14.1).

The expression "sons/children of God" in Jesus' usage refers to the adoption by God that takes place through the fulfillment of his commandments. Active peacemaking entails, among other things, loving one's enemies: this love causes people to be adopted by God, to become children of their

The Apostle Paul, Andrei Rublev, 15th century

heavenly Father (Mt 5.44–45). Active peacemaking entails, among other things, loving one's enemies: this love causes a person to be adopted by God.

The theme of adoption by God plays a significant role in the writing of the apostle Paul. In his words, "as many as are led by the Spirit of God, they are the sons of God," thanks to the Spirit of adoption, which those who have believed in Jesus have received (Rom 8.14–15). In the Epistle to the Galatians, Paul writes. "For ye are all the children of God by faith in Christ Jesus" (Gal 3.26). In the same Epistle, the apostle says, "And because ye are sons, God hath sent forth the Spirit of his Son into your hearts, crying, 'Abba, Father.' Wherefore thou art no more a servant, but a son, and if a son, then an heir of God through Christ" (Gal 4.6–7).

In the above quotations from the apostle Paul, he is speaking of the adoption of human beings by God because of their faith in Jesus Christ and of the acceptance of the gift of the Holy Spirit that comes about from this faith. In the seventh Beatitude, adoption by God is thought of as the result of moral labor. This labor, as in the other Beatitudes, consists first of all in imitating Jesus, who was a peacemaker. In the words of John Chrysostom, peacemakers carry out Christ's work, since "the work

Only Begotten Son,
Russia, 17th century

of the Only Begotten [was] to unite the divided, and to reconcile the alienated."[69]

Taking into account the overall context of the Beatitudes and the Sermon on the Mount as a whole, the original meaning of Jesus' Beatitude about making peace concerns the personal sphere, and not societal morality. Nevertheless, in the broad sense, the seventh Beatitude can also be applied to political activity as well as to the role of the Church as a mediator between opposing sides in military, political, and civil conflicts. In fulfilling this Beatitude, the Church is called to "carry out her peace service both on national and international scale, trying to help resolve various contradictions and bring nations, ethnic groups, governments and political forces to harmony." In particular, the Church "opposes the propaganda of war and violence, as well as various manifestations of hatred capable of provoking fratricidal clashes."[70]

8. On the Persecution of Christians

The eighth, ninth, and tenth Beatitudes are closely connected with each other and therefore must be examined as a whole:

> Blessed are they which are persecuted for righteousness' sake, for theirs is the kingdom of heaven.

---

[69]John Chrysostom, *Homilies on Matthew* 15.7 (NPNF[1] 10:95).

[70]Moscow Patriarchate, *The Basis of the Social Concept of the Russian Orthodox Church* VIII.5. The document was presented at the Bishops' Council, Moscow, August 13–16, 2000; online version at https://mospat.ru/en/documents/social-concepts/viii/.

> Blessed are ye, when men shall revile you, and persecute you, and
> shall say all manner of evil against you falsely, for my sake.
> Rejoice, and be exceeding glad, for great is your reward in heaven.
> For so persecuted they the prophets which were before you.
> (Mt 5.10–12)

All three Beatitudes are linked by the recurring theme of persecution. The verb *diōkō*, which is encountered thrice in these verses in different forms, means "to pursue," "to follow after." With these three concluding Beatitudes, Jesus uncovers a theme that will be a leitmotif throughout all the Gospels. In his first instruction to the Twelve after their selection, Jesus would speak to them of the persecution and harassment that awaited them (Mt 10.17–22). Not long before his death, while conversing with his disciples in the Jerusalem temple, he would again return to this theme (Mt 24.9–13; Lk 21.12–18). Finally, at the Last Supper, Jesus would again warn his disciples that they would be persecuted (Jn 15.18–20).

The juxtaposition of the eighth and ninth Beatitudes is of special interest: while the former speaks of those who are persecuted for righteousness' sake, in the latter Jesus speaks of those who would be persecuted, reviled, and unjustly maligned for his sake. Here, truth and Jesus become synonymous.

We have said that all the Beatitudes are, as a whole, deeply Christocentric, since they contain a moral portrait of Jesus. But while in the first eight Beatitudes this portrait is, as it were, hidden beneath a list of human qualities, in the ninth Beatitude Jesus finally reveals himself not only as the source of these Beatitudes, but also as the main reason that his followers will be persecuted. They will be persecuted not because they are poor in spirit, weep, are meek, hunger and thirst after righteousness, are merciful, are pure in heart, or are peacemakers, but because they believe in him, and are his followers, and fulfill his commandments. In other words, they will be persecuted not for a particular quality or for following a particular moral precept, but because they do all this in his name: it is as Christians that they will be persecuted.

The eighth Beatitude, like the first, concludes with the following words: "for theirs is the kingdom of heaven." We have already noted that these words about the kingdom of heaven bookend eight of the Beatitudes at their beginning and end. One may say that all eight of these Beatitudes are oriented toward the kingdom of heaven and evince its presence in the community of Jesus' disciples, who will be comforted, filled, shown mercy, be called the sons of God, inherit the earth, and see God.[71]

The eighth Beatitude concludes the sequence of Beatitudes in which Jesus speaks of people in the third person. Beginning with the ninth Beatitude, he addresses his words directly to his listeners: "Blessed are ye." While the Sermon on the Plain begins with a direct appeal to his listeners, in the Sermon on the Mount Jesus' speech has a more universal character at first, and only at this point is the third person replaced by the second.

Some scholars believe that the ninth Beatitude "not only does not belong to the same stratum as the previous ones which are all in the third person but also looks back to persecutions already suffered by the community and explicitly promises apocalyptic reward in return."[72] We have already mentioned that the verses in the Sermon on the Mount dedicated to persecution are often treated in the scholarly literature as the fruit of the literary activity of the Evangelist Matthew, and not as Jesus' direct speech.

Yet warning about coming persecutions is a leitmotif of the preaching of Jesus himself. He speaks of the persecution of his followers not only in the Sermon on the Mount and not only in the Gospel of Matthew. The prophetic meaning of Jesus' words was revealed not only in the era of persecutions under Nero: the persecution of Christians has continued over the course of the entire history of the Church, right up to the present time.

Jesus' prophecies have a timeless quality: they concern the very essence of the Christian faith. Being an expression of the righteousness of God, this faith always encounters resistance from the forces of evil. In the global war between good and evil, Christians are called to stand on the side of

---

[71]Cf. Günther Bornkamm, *Jesus of Nazareth*, trans. Irene McLuskey, Fraser McLuskey, and James M. Robinson (New York, NY: Harper & Row, 1960), 77.

[72]Käsemann, *New Testament Questions of Today*, 100–101.

*Candlesticks
of Christianity
(Nero's Torches),*
Henryk
Siemiradski, 1876

good, even if doing so costs them their lives. In exchange for the feat of confession and martyrdom, they are promised a reward in heaven. The thought of this reward should be for them a source of joy. But the reward in heaven is none other than Christ himself. It is he who contains in himself the entirety of the good things that are described in the promises that accompany each of the Beatitudes.

It is not incidental that the list of Beatitudes concludes with the words concerning the persecution of Jesus' followers. These words are by no means a mere addendum to the preceding Beatitudes, nor are they an editorial addition meant to comfort the persecuted Christians of the first century in their suffering. They follow naturally from the preceding Beatitudes. To see blessedness in spiritual poverty, weeping, meekness, the search for righteousness, mercy, purity of heart, and peacemaking, means to radically break with the generally accepted idea of happiness, to live by laws different from those by which the world lives, to place before oneself different ideals and goals. Such a view of the world unavoidably leads to conflict with the world. Those who possess such a worldview will inevitably be outcasts in the world, where happiness is measured in the categories of material wealth, success, and wellbeing.

Speaking to his disciples at the Last Supper, Jesus would say:

If the world hate you, ye know that it hated me before it hated you. If ye were of the world, the world would love his own; but because ye are not of the world, but I have chosen you out of the world, therefore the world hateth you. Remember the word that I said unto you, the servant is not greater than his lord. If they have persecuted me, they will also persecute you; if they have kept my saying, they will keep yours also. (Jn 15.18–20)

Through the Beatitudes the community of Jesus' disciples is called to imitate its Teacher, to dwell where he is found. The Beatitudes are sometimes interpreted as being like a ladder, requiring a gradual ascent from the lower steps to the higher ones.[73] But this ladder ultimately leads a person to Golgotha, and ascending this ladder makes conflict with the world unavoidable:

> In judgment and action those who follow Jesus will be different from the world in renouncing property, happiness, rights, righteousness, honor, and violence. They will be offensive to the world. That is why the disciples will be persecuted for righteousness' sake. Not recognition, but rejection, will be their reward from the world for their word and deed. . . . Here at the end of the Beatitudes the question arises as to where in this world such a faith-community actually finds a place. It has become clear that there is only one place for them, namely, the place where the poorest, the most tempted, the meekest of all may be found, at the cross on Golgotha. The faith-community of the blessed is the community of the Crucified. With him they lost everything, and with him they found everything. Now the word comes down from the cross: blessed, blessed.[74]

Thus the cross of Jesus Christ stands not only at the center of the Christian faith, but also of Christian ethics.[75] And the followers of Jesus in different eras have joyfully and readily gone to their personal Golgothas. In becoming the victims of persecution and harassment, they did not simply surrender to fate: they saw in this the opportunity to put into practice the

---

[73]Gregory of Nyssa, *The Beatitudes* 2.1 (trans. Graef, 97).

[74]Bonhoeffer, *Discipleship*, 77–78.

[75]F. Scott Spencer, *What Did Jesus Do?: Gospel Profiles of Jesus' Personal Conduct* (Harrisburg, PA: Trinity Press International, 2003), 253.

moral exhortations of the Sermon on the Mount and, through suffering and death, come to Jesus himself.

At the beginning of the second century, Ignatius, the bishop of Antioch, was sentenced to death for refusing to sacrifice to the pagan gods. After the sentence was handed down, Ignatius was put in chains and sent to Rome in the company of soldiers, where he was to be torn apart by lions in front of the public. The bishop's journey took him through various cities, and he sent his epistles to the Christians of these cities. Addressing the Christians of Rome, Ignatius asks the Romans not to intercede on his behalf for his punishment to be revoked or lightened:

Christ Carrying the Cross,
El Greco, 1580

> I am writing to all the churches and I am instructing everyone that I am willingly dying for God, unless you prevent me. I beseech you, do not become an unseasonable kindness for me. Leave me to be bread for the beasts, through which I may be able to attain to God. I am God's wheat and through the beasts' teeth I shall be found to be pure bread for Christ. Rather encourage the beasts, so that they may be my tomb and nothing be left over of my body, so that I become no burden to anyone when I am dead. . . . Beseech the Lord on my behalf, so that I may be found a sacrifice for God through these instruments. . . . I am fighting wild beasts from Syria to Rome, through earth and sea, day and night. I am guarded by ten leopards, which is a military unit, who become worse by being well-treated. In their injustices I am becoming more of a disciple, "but I am not made just on this account." May I delight in the beasts prepared for me, and I pray they may be found ready for me. . . . May nothing, visible or invisible, show jealousy towards me, only let me attain to Jesus Christ. Fire and cross, packs of wild beasts, cuttings, rendings, the scattering of bones, the chopping up of limbs, the grinding of the whole body, the evil torments of the devil can come upon me, only let me attain to Jesus Christ. Neither the ends of the world nor

The hieromartyr Benjamin
of Petrograd, photograph

the kingdoms of this age profit me anything. It is better for me to die in Jesus Christ than to reign over the ends of the earth.... Him I seek, the one who died on our behalf. Him I desire, him who rose up for us.... Allow me to receive the pure light.... Allow me to be an imitator of the passion of my God.[76]

Eighteen centuries later, another Christian martyr, Metropolitan Benjamin of Petrograd (1873–1922), who was sentenced to death by firing squad on a false charge, would write from prison a few days before his death:

In my childhood and youth I voraciously read the lives of the saints and marveled at their heroism, their holy enthusiasm, and I regretted with all my soul that times were different, and it would not fall to my lot to experience what they experienced. Times have changed: the opportunity has come to endure, for Christ's sake, suffering from friend and foe. It is difficult, it is hard to suffer, but, to the measure of our suffering, consolation from God also abounds.... Now, it appears, I have to endure almost everything: prison, court, public ridicule; the doom and requirement of this death; the applause of, supposedly, the common folk; human ingratitude, venality; inconstancy and the like; anxiety and responsibility for the fate of others and even for the Church herself. The sufferings have reached their apogee, but the consolation has also increased. I am joyful and at peace, as always. Christ is our life, light, and peace. With him, it is always, and everywhere, good.[77]

In the two passages quoted, one of which belongs to the very beginning of the history of Christian martyrdom, and the other to an altogether recent era, what we see is not simply human steadfastness and courage.

[76]Ignatius of Antioch, *Epistle to the Romans* 4–6.3 (PPS 49:69, 71).
[77]As cited in S. A. Zegzhda, *Aleksandro-Nevskoe bratstvo* [The Alexander Nevsky Brotherhood] (Saint Petersburg, 2008), 20–21. Translated by present translator.

As in a multitude of other documentary records left by Christian martyrs of different eras, we see in them a completely peculiar phenomenon: at the center of the entire feat of martyrdom stands Jesus Christ. His person has a power that allows one to staunchly endure torments, rejoice in persecution and affliction, and readily accept death. His invisible presence is felt by those sentenced to death, and this presence fills their hearts with the joy and gladness of which Jesus spoke in the concluding words of the Beatitudes.

Saint Eustace,
Albrecht Dürer, c. 1501

The theme of persecution, which unites the New Testament with all the subsequent history of the Christian Church, became one of the links between the New and Old Testaments in Jesus' preaching. It is not incidental that the Beatitudes conclude with the words "for so persecuted they the prophets which were before you." Not only in the Sermon on the Mount, but also in other exhortations, including in his polemics with the Jews, Jesus would turn many times to the question of the attitude of the people of Israel toward the prophets. Not long before his death, he would harshly denounce the scribes and Pharisees for building tombs for the prophets while being the sons of those who killed the prophets; Jesus foretells that, continuing the work of their fathers, they would go on to kill "prophets, and wise men, and scribes" whom God would send to them (Mt 23.29–34).

In adding the words about the prophets to the Beatitudes, Jesus thereby introduces a new topic that would occupy an important place in the Sermon on the Mount: the topic of the relationship between "the law and the prophets," that is, the Old Testament on the one hand and New Testament morality on the other. The continuity between the New and Old Testaments is expressed not only in that the commandments of Jesus are an extension and fulfillment of the Old Testament moral precepts, but also in that a prophetic mission is entrusted to his followers: to witness to God and to God's righteousness by all of one's way of life. This witness is realized contrary to the will and standards of this world, which "lieth

The Sermon on the Mount, N. P. Lomtev, 1841

in wickedness" (1 Jn 5.19), often becomes the way to martyrdom. But in their suffering and their own deaths, Christians of all eras imitate Jesus, who witnessed to the truth "unto death, even the death of the cross" (Phil 2.8). His suffering and death marked the beginning of the long history of Christian martyrdom—a history that continues to this day.

What does Jesus promise his followers in exchange for their faithfulness and martyrdom? A reward in heaven. We will encounter the term "reward" (*misthos*) more than once later in the Sermon on the Mount. On Jesus' lips this term referred primarily to the recompense that a person would receive in the life to come. He speaks in particular of the "reward of your Father which is in heaven," which is lost by those who receive a reward from other people (Mt 6.1–2). This heavenly reward can be identified with the kingdom of God in its eschatological sense—as the posthumous blessedness of the righteous.

* * *

It is not incidental that we have analyzed each of the Beatitudes in such detail. Unlike the contemporary scholars who believe that these Beatitudes are the fruit of the moralizing efforts of the Evangelist Matthew, we are deeply convinced that they belong to Jesus himself and contain the quintessence of his spiritual and moral teaching. It is in this capacity that they were conceived of and uttered by Jesus—this is why he imparted to them a special solemnity, which is expressed not only in the fact that he began the Sermon on the Mount with them, but even in their external poetic form. Like the subsequent sections of the Sermon on the Mount, the whole story of Jesus' life, passion, and death would become a revelation of the meaning of the Beatitudes. This story is reflected in them, as in a mirror, and together with it the entire centuries-long history of Christian witness, inscribed in the blood of martyrs and confessors, is reflected as well.

The Beatitudes vividly testify to the paradoxical character of Christian morality. In them Jesus speaks of how genuine happiness (blessedness) is possessed by the one who, by human standards, is deeply unhappy; he cites as positive qualities those that are not so highly valued in human society (for example, humility and meekness):

> We have already seen how great was the change made by the Gospel in moral valuations. It meant the most radical revaluation of values in the whole of the world's history. Everything becomes strange and different from that which the world values and by which it lives. . . . The blessed are not those whom the world considers blessed—blessed are those who weep, the meek, the merciful, the pure in heart, those who hunger and thirst after righteousness. . . . But for the world the blessed are the rich, the well born, the powerful, the strong, the famous, the gay. . . . The Gospel and the world are utterly opposed and incompatible.[78]

From the very first words of the Sermon on the Mount, the foundation is laid for the teaching that the apostle Paul would call "foolishness" (1 Cor 1.21–23), in view of its radical opposition to the measures and standards by which happiness is ordinarily measured. Jesus offers people a scale of values, which in many of its positions is contrary to what is usual for them and what appears to be generally accepted: "The Beatitudes limn an upside-down reality, or—more precisely—they define reality in such a way that the usual order of things is seen to be upside down in the eyes

---

[78]Berdyaev, *Destiny of Man*, 124–125.

The Last Supper,
icon, 1497

of God."[79] To a certain extent, this statement applies to the entire spiritual
and moral program that Jesus presents in the Sermon on the Mount and
in his other teachings preserved in the Gospels.

The evangelical Beatitudes have firmly entered into the liturgical practice of the Christian churches.[80] In the Orthodox Church the Beatitudes
are sung, according to the typikon, at every Sunday liturgy (in practice,
they are included also in liturgies served on weekdays). Their singing is
preceded by the following words based on the prayer of the wise thief (Lk
23.42): "In thy kingdom remember us, O Lord, when thou comest in thy
kingdom." In this liturgical context, the Beatitudes are read as Jesus' moral
and spiritual testament, which the Church considers its duty to remind
believers of when they gather to celebrate the Eucharist.

[79]Hays, *Moral Vision of the New Testament,* 321.
    [80]See Metropolitan Hilarion Alfeyev, *Orthodox Christianity, volume 4: The Worship and
Liturgical Life of the Orthodox Church* (Yonkers, NY: St Vladimir's Seminary Press, 2016), 117.

Chapter 3

"THE SALT OF THE EARTH" AND "THE LIGHT OF THE WORLD"

The next part of the Sermon on the Mount is addressed directly to the disciples. It speaks of the position that the community of Jesus' disciples, which he would call the Church (Mt 16.18), should take in the world, and the role that it should play in personal and societal relationships:

> Ye are the salt of the earth; but if the salt have lost his savor, with what shall it be salted? It is thenceforth good for nothing, but to be cast out, and to be trodden under foot of men.
>
> Ye are the light of the world. A city that is set on an hill cannot be hid.
>
> Neither do men light a candle, and put it under a bushel, but on a candlestick, and it giveth light unto all that are in the house.
>
> Let your light so shine before men, that they may see your good works, and glorify your Father which is in heaven. (Mt 5.13–16)

In order to make his point clearer, Jesus, as in many other instances, uses images familiar to his hearers from the realm of everyday life.

1. "The Salt of the Earth"

In the time of Jesus, salt was used for two purposes: to impart taste to food and to preserve foodstuffs (primarily fish and meat). Besides this, salt was used with bread, and if bread was offered as a sacrifice, it was customary to salt it: "And every oblation of thy grain offering shalt thou season with salt; neither shalt thou suffer the salt of the covenant of thy God to be lacking from thy grain offering; with all thine offerings thou shalt offer salt" (Lev 2.13). Jesus himself also speaks of this ritual significance of salt: "For every one shall be salted with fire, and every sacrifice shall be salted with salt" (Mk 9.49).

Finally, salt was used for medicinal purposes, particularly at birth: after exiting the womb, a newborn would have its umbilical cord cut; then it was washed, and its skin rubbed with salt;[1] only after this would the baby be swaddled (Ezek 16.4). The use of salt for medicinal purposes is connected with the presence of sodium chloride in it, which has disinfectant properties. Even in the modern era, in the absence of other means, the heavily wounded have bandages soaked in saline solution placed on their wounds; this helps to prevent gangrene. Saline baths and saline solutions are also used for therapeutic purposes. Note, by the way, that when Jesus spoke of salt, he was speaking not of culinary salt in the form known to us today, but of organic salt, which is obtained from sea salt and possesses healing properties.

Such diverse use of salt in ancient times compels us to regard it as an extremely important product. Without salt food was tasteless and spoiled quickly; without salt it was impossible to offer sacrifices to God; a lack of

---

[1] The custom of rubbing a newborn's skin with salt is mentioned by St Jerome (*Commentary on Ezekiel* 4.16 [PL 25:127]): "The tender bodies of infants, while they still hold the warmth of the womb, and attest to the beginning of a laborious life by their first cry, are accustomed to be sprinkled with salt by the midwives, in order that they may be drier and (their skin) tightened." (Translation from James E. Latham, *The Religious Symbolism of Salt*, Théologie Historique 64 [Paris: Éditions Beauchesne, 1982], 120.)

The Sermon on the Mount, V. D. Polenov, 1890–1909

salt meant a shortage of an important medical supply. Under what circumstances could salt "lose its savor" and become useless? As is well known, with regard to its chemical composition, salt cannot cease to be salty.[2] Salt does not go bad, and under the right storage conditions it can be preserved for years. However, it loses its strength in the event that water gets into it in large quantities. Stores of salt that were hit by torrential rain would be destroyed.

Jesus uses this image in other instances as well, particularly when he speaks of the mutual relationship between the disciples: "Salt is good, but if the salt have lost its saltiness, with what will ye season it? Have salt in yourselves, and have peace one with another" (Mk 9.50). In Luke a different version of the same saying is given: "Salt is good, but if the salt have lost its savor, with what shall it be seasoned? It is neither fit for the land, nor yet for the dunghill; but men cast it out. He that hath ears to hear, let him hear" (Lk 14.34–35). Here yet another use of salt is mentioned—its use as a fertilizer. But spoiled salt cannot be used even for this purpose.

[2]See, in particular, Marianne Sawicki, *Crossing Galilee: Architectures of Contact in the Occupied Land of Jesus* (Harrisburg, PA: Trinity Press International, 2000), 165.

Early Christian writers interpreted Jesus' words both literally and figuratively. Origen spoke of how, just as salt protects meat from spoilage and allows it to be kept for a long time, "so also Christ's disciples, standing in the way of the stench that comes from the sins of idolatry and fornication, support and hold together this whole earthly realm."[3] In the words of John Chrysostom, it was as if Christ was saying to the disciples, "Not for your own life apart . . . but for the whole world, shall your account be. For not to two cities, nor to ten or twenty, nor to a single nation am I sending you, as I sent the prophets; but to earth, and sea, and the whole world." By saying "ye are the salt of the earth," Christ "signified all human nature to have 'lost its savor,' and to be decayed by our sins. For which cause, you see, He requires of them such virtues, as are most necessary and useful for the superintendence of the common sort."[4] Cyril of Alexandria believed that what Jesus called salt was the discernment that is filled with the apostolic word, "for without salt neither bread nor fish is edible. So too without the apostles' understanding and instruction, every soul is dull and unwholesome and unpleasant to God."[5]

What was the original meaning of Jesus' words concerning the salt of the earth? Multiple levels of meaning are found in this image. In the broadest sense one can say that Christianity gives flavor to human life, making it rich rather than insipid. If the kingdom of heaven, which Jesus brought to mankind, is a kind of special dimension of human life, then comparing it with salt allows one to better understand its properties and its value. Christians, according to Jesus' teaching, live "in the world" (Jn 16.33), but they are "not of the world" (Jn 15.19). Without mixing with the world, they fill its life with meaning; their presence in the world becomes an important factor of human wellbeing.

In the third century, in the era of the continuing persecution of Christians, the author of the anonymous *Epistle to Diognetus* speaks of the role

[3]Origen, *Fragments on Matthew* 91. English translation from *Matthew 1–13*, edited by Manlio Simonetti, Ancient Christian Commentary on Scripture New Testament 1a (Downers Grove, IL: InterVarsity, 2001), 92.

[4]John Chrysostom, *Homilies on Matthew* 15.10 (NPNF[1] 10:97)

[5]Cyril of Alexandria, *Fragments* 41. English translation from Simonetti, *Matthew 1–13*, 92.

that the Christian community played in the pagan world that surrounded it:

> For the Christians are distinguished from other men neither by coun-
> try, nor language, nor the customs which they observe. For they neither
> inhabit cities of their own, nor employ a peculiar form of speech, nor
> lead a life which is marked out by any singularity. . . . But, inhabiting
> Greek as well as barbarian cities, according as the lot of each of them
> has determined, and following the customs of the natives in respect
> to clothing, food, and the rest of their ordinary conduct, they display
> to us their wonderful and confessedly striking method of life. They
> dwell in their own countries, but simply as sojourners. As citizens, they
> share in all things with others, and yet endure all things as if foreigners.
> Every foreign land is to them as their native country, and every land of
> their birth as a land of strangers. They marry, as do all [others]; they
> beget children; but they do not destroy their offspring. They have a
> common table, but not a common bed. They are in the flesh, but they
> do not live after the flesh. They pass their days on earth, but they are
> citizens of heaven. They obey the prescribed laws, and at the same time
> surpass the laws by their lives. They love all men, and are persecuted
> by all. They are unknown and condemned; they are put to death, and
> restored to life. They are poor, yet make many rich; they are in lack
> of all things, and yet abound in all; they are dishonoured, and yet in
> their very dishonour are glorified. They are evil spoken of, and yet are
> justified; they are reviled, and bless; they are insulted, and repay the
> insult with honour; they do good, yet are punished as evil-doers. When
> punished, they rejoice as if quickened into life; they are assailed by the
> Jews as foreigners, and are persecuted by the Greeks; yet those who
> hate them are unable to assign any reason for their hatred. To sum up
> all in one word—what the soul is in the body, that are Christians in the
> world. . . . The soul is imprisoned in the body, yet preserves that very
> body; and Christians are confined in the world as in a prison, and yet
> they are the preservers of the world.[6]

[6]*Epistle to Diognetus* 5–6 (ANF 1:26–27).

*The Sermon
on the Mount,*
Fra Angelico,
1436–1443

The passage above clearly demonstrates how, two centuries after Jesus' death and resurrection, his followers were striving to live out what he had commanded. The paradoxical nature of his moral commandments did not trouble them. Neither were they troubled by the fact that they did not live in a world of their own: they were not divided from the world by a solid wall. Like other people, they married, but, unlike many others, they did not divorce and did not abandon or abort their children, but preserved a strong family way of life. They were subject to the same laws as other members of society, but the moral standard set for them was higher than the one that oriented civil law. While they were loyal citizens of their own state, they belonged to a different homeland, the kingdom of heaven; while they lived in cities, they had here "no continuing city, but [sought] one to come" (Heb 13.14). They were hated and persecuted, but nobody could say why; as a matter of fact, it was solely because they bore the name of Christ. Fulfilling his commandments, they did not answer evil with evil, and they patiently endured suffering.

In these words lies the answer to the critics of the morality of the gospel, who consider this morality impracticable and ill-suited to human society. These words also contain an important indication of the role that Christians are to play in the world. Like the soul in a body, they are to animate the life of the world. Like salt in food, they are called to make people's lives rich and filled with meaning, guarding human society from corruption and destruction by enmity, hate, conflicts, and vengeance. The presence of the Church in the world as a community of people who live by laws that are morally loftier than those prescribed in earthly legislation ought to transform the world from within, change it for the better, and raise humanity as a whole to a new level of being.

Notwithstanding the apparent difficulty of fulfilling Jesus' commandments and their seeming unsuitability to real life, we know the transformative effect that Christianity has had on all of human society. While Jesus lacked the characteristics of a social reformer, over the centuries, his teaching became the reason for deep, radical changes in the entire system of human interrelations—not only on the level of personal morality, but also on the societal level. Jesus did not call for the abolition of slavery, but it was precisely thanks to a Christian understanding of the innate equality of human beings that slavery was finally abolished. He did not call for a change of the political regime or for a reform of the legal code, but it was precisely thanks to Christianity that human society created the legal mechanisms that form the basis of the vital activity of many governments today. Jesus was not a fighter for social rights, but it is precisely on the basis of Christian anthropology that we now have the understanding of human rights that has allowed women and children to become full members of society and allowed the eradication of inequality and discrimination on ethnic and racial grounds, as well as the eradication of many other societal flaws that were characteristic of the ancient world, including of the era in which Jesus lived.

"The kingdom of Christ is not of this world," the philosopher reminds us. And he asks, "How can it be brought into the world?" The answer is seen in the influence that Christianity has exerted over the course of its history and continues to exert on the life and worldview of mankind:

The absolute revelation of the Gospel about the Kingdom of God cannot be expressed by any social and historical forms, which are always temporal and relative. . . . the Gospel revelation of the Kingdom of God brought about a change secretly, inwardly and imperceptibly, in all the departments of life and altered the very structure of the human soul, bringing forth new emotions. The Kingdom of God cometh not with observation [Lk 17.20]. . . . The gracious power of the Gospel revelation liberates men from the torments of fear, of pride, of love of power, and the insatiable lust for life. The solution of many vital and fundamental questions, however, is not made obvious in the Gospel, but is, as it were, veiled. It is left to man himself in his freedom to find a creative solution of the problems that continually confront him. The Gospel is concerned not so much with teaching us how to solve them as with healing and regenerating the texture of the human soul.[7]

In this sense we can say that Christianity became the salt of the earth and, over the course of centuries, proved its ability to "salt" the life of humanity by providing a new direction of growth for human morality as a whole. The Christian message continues to fulfill this role even today.

The apostle Paul wrote to the Christians of his time, "Let your speech be always with grace, seasoned with salt" (Col 4.6). Grace is the most important concept in Christian theology; in its broadest sense it refers to a divine gift or divine presence that accompanies a person's activity. Jesus' speech was "with grace" because God himself spoke with people through his lips. The speech of the apostles was with grace because God continued to teach people through them. And the Christian message that is proclaimed today in the churches should not be devoid of this gracious presence of God. For when the priest or bishop speaks in the service, God himself can touch his lips and through him transmit to people what they need to hear. Those who do not wish to listen to it are going against God himself.

[7]Berdyaev, *Destiny of Man*, 125.

2. "The Light of the World"

The images of light and a candle continue and elaborate on the theme that was uncovered with the use of the image of salt.

The theme of light is one of the central themes of Jesus' preaching as transmitted in the Gospel of John. In his conversation with Nicodemus, Jesus speaks of himself as the light that has come into the world, but "men loved darkness rather than light, because their deeds were evil" (Jn 3.19). Later, in the temple in Jerusalem, he would say to the Jews, "I am the light of the world; he that followeth me shall not walk in darkness, but shall have the light of life" (Jn 8.12).

Light is a symbol of paramount importance in many religious and philosophical traditions. In the New Testament, including the corpus of the Johannine writings, the term "light" is often applied to God. What light is Jesus speaking of when he exhorts his disciples: "Let your light so shine before men"? The word "light" here is understood figuratively: Jesus is speaking of the good works that should distinguish Christians from pagans. Christian morality should serve as an example for others: in this sense, Christians should be like a city on a hill.

It is significant that when he applies the image of light to his disciples, Jesus is speaking not of the natural light of the sun, but of the light of a lamp. In the Greek text the words used are *lychnos* and *lychnia*, which refer to a lamp and a stand for such a lamp respectively.[8] Lamps were used at night and were vessels with oil in which wicks were placed; before the lamp was lit, it was necessary to ensure that there was oil in it and adjust the wick (Mt 25.3–4, 7). A lit wick illuminated the room with a fairly dim light if there were not many lamps. Of course, lamps were never placed "under a bushel, or under a bed" (Mk 4.21): they were placed in visible

---

[8]It is possible that the translators of the King James Version chose the word "candle" in order to distinguish the word *lychnos* from the word *lampas*, which is used in Mt 25.3–7; however, in Greek there is a different word that means "candle"—*kēros* (this refers to a lit candle made of wax).

and elevated places from which they could illuminate the entire house. In Jesus' time, the home of a person who was not rich (and it was precisely such people that made up the majority of Jesus' listeners) consisted of one room, in which the entire family lived.

In the parable of the woman with the lost coin, Jesus uses the same image: she lights a lamp (*lychnos*) and begins to sweep the house until she finds the coin (Lk 15.8). The image of a lamp (*lampas*) plays an important role in the parable of the ten virgins (Mt 25.1–13).

In the same exhortation, Jesus uses the image of a city on a hill. As is known, ancient cities were very often built on elevated ground. This was not done for aesthetic reasons, but in order to protect the city's inhabitants from enemies. A city built on elevated ground and enclosed by high forti-fied walls was visible from everywhere, but was less vulnerable than a city located on low ground. However, it seems that in this particular instance Jesus had in view only one aspect of the whole rich semantic spectrum of the given image. A city standing on elevated ground "cannot be hid" from human eyes. In the same way, Jesus' followers are in the public eye, and people judge Jesus' teachings and Jesus himself based on them. Through their good works, they are called to reveal the heavenly Father, whom Jesus revealed in his own person and works.

Following a number of contemporary interpreters, we note that in the Sermon on the Mount Jesus is not calling the disciples to become the salt of the earth and the light of the world; rather, he is saying that they are already those things. "Ye shine as lights in the world," writes the apostle Paul, not in the imperative, but the indicative mood (Phil 2.15). In calling the disciples the salt of the earth and the light of the world, Jesus under-scores that this "belongs originally and essentially to their existence." This does not contradict the transition into the imperative in the words, "Let your light so shine before men, that they may see your good works." The disciples are not being called to become something different: they are to be themselves. They would not be Jesus' disciples if they were not the salt of the earth and the light of the world.[9]

[9]Karl Barth, *Church Doctrine*, vol. 4, *The Doctrine of Reconciliation*, pt. 3.2, trans. G. W. Bromiley, ed. T. F. Torrance (New York, NY: T&T Clark International, 2004), 763.

*The Parable of
the Ten Virgins,
Klavdy Lebedev,
19th century*

In what sense is the expression "good works" (*ta kala erga*) used here? We do not find an analogous expression in the Old Testament, but the phrase *ma'ăśîm tôḇîm* ("good works") is widely used in rabbinical literature,[10] where it is understood to refer to requirements from God that go beyond the prescribed law—above all, works of love and mercy.[11] In the New Testament this concept has a generalized meaning and refers to the Christian moral code as a whole, which is reflected particularly in the Sermon on the Mount. It includes but is not limited to works of love and mercy: all the qualities enumerated in the Beatitudes are meant to be demonstrated in concrete good works.

This is indicated by the use of this term in other New Testament sources, such as in the Epistle to the Hebrews: "And let us consider one another to provoke unto love and to good works" (Heb 10.24). We find in the writings of the apostle Peter a call that is textually close to Jesus' words in the Sermon on the Mount: "Dearly beloved, I beseech you . . . [have] your way of life honest among the Gentiles: that, whereas they speak against you as evildoers, they may by your good works, which they shall behold,

[10]Martin McNamara, "Some Targum Themes," in *Justification and Variegated Nomism*, ed. D. A. Carson, Peter T. O'Brien, and Mark A. Seifrid, vol. 1, *The Complexities of Second Temple Judaism* (Grand Rapids, MI: Baker Academic, 2001), 332–336.

[11]Luz, *Matthew 1–7*, 207.

glorify God in the day of visitation" (1 Pet 2.11–12). The apostle goes on to list qualities that can serve to explain the general concept of "good works": the followers of Christ are called to be obedient to every human authority, to respect everyone, to love the brethren, to fear God, to honor the king, and, above all, to patiently endure tribulation and suffering, thereby following in the footsteps of Christ. Servants ought to obey their masters, wives their husbands, and husbands love their wives. Christians are called to be of one mind, compassionate, brotherly, charitable, friendly, humble; they are not to return evil for evil or cursing for cursing (1 Pet 2.13–3.9).

To be the "salt of the earth" and the "light of the world" means to fulfill Jesus' commandments in real life, displaying a good example to others. As John Chrysostom explains:

> For God will have us profitable not to ourselves alone, but to all our neighbors as well. Now if thou givest, and abstainest from suing, thou hast sought thine own advantage only; but if thou give him some other thing, thou hast made him too better, and so sent him away. Of this nature is salt, which is what He would have them to be; seeing it both recruits itself, and keeps all other bodies with which it may associate: of this nature is light; for it shows objects both to a man's self and to all others. Forasmuch then as He hath set thee in the rank of these things, help thou likewise him who is sitting in darkness, and teach him that neither before did he take any thing by force: persuade him that he hath done no despite.[12]

The subsequent content of the Sermon on the Mount will be a deciphering of the meaning that Jesus has invested in the notion of "good works." In particular, this meaning includes refraining from anger (Mt 5.21–26), preserving chastity and matrimonial fidelity (Mt 5.22–32), refraining from swearing oaths (Mt 5.33–37), not resisting evil (Mt 5.38–42), loving one's enemies (Mt 5.43–47), almsgiving, prayer, and fasting (Mt 6.1–18), non-acquisitiveness (Matthew 6.19–21, 24–34), struggling to overcome one's own faults and tolerating the faults of others (Mt 7.1–5), and being able

---

[12]John Chrysostom, *Homilies on Matthew* 18.2 (NPNF[1] 10:125).

to treat others as one would have others treat oneself (Mt 7.12). Together, these good works reveal the perfection that the heavenly Father possesses, and which each Christian is called to possess in his or her own measure (Mt 6.48).

The Sermon on the Mount, Ivan Makarov, 1889

Chapter 4

"THE LAW AND THE PROPHETS"

T he law of Moses is not mentioned at all in the Beatitudes: the righteousness which Jesus calls for in the Beatitudes is in no way connected with the observance of the letter or the spirit of the Old Testament Law.[1] However, the part of the Sermon on the Mount that follows the Beatitudes is entirely dedicated to this topic, which is of the utmost importance—for all of the New Testament, and for the Gospel of Matthew in particular. It is Matthew who has most meticulously collected Jesus' words about the relationship between his teaching and the law of Moses.[2] It is also no coincidence that it is Matthew's Gospel that contains the Sermon on the Mount, which is distinguished from all other New Testament texts first and foremost by the fact that in it Jesus formulates the hermeneutic principles on which he constructs his interpretation of the Torah.[3] Without abolishing the Old Testament law, Jesus proposes a system of moral coordinates in light of which Old Testament morality takes on a different tone: henceforth, even the Ten Commandments of Moses are to be read in the light of the New Testament.[4]

[1]Roland Deines, "Not the Law but the Messiah: Law and Righteousness in the Gospel of Matthew—An Ongoing Debate," in *Built upon the Rock: Studies in the Gospel of Matthew*, ed. Daniel M. Gurtner and John Nolland (Grand Rapids, MI: Eerdmans, 2008), 73.

[2]On Jesus' attitude toward the law of Moses, see, in particular, Günther Bornkamm, Gerhard Barth, and Heinz Joachim Held, *Tradition and Interpretation in Matthew*, trans. Percy Scott, The New Testament Library (Philadelphia, PA: Westminster, 1963), 58–164; John P. Meier, *A Marginal Jew: Rethinking the Historical Jesus*, vol. 4, *Law and Love*, Anchor Yale Bible Reference Library (New Haven, CT: Yale University Press, 2009), 26–73.

[3]Betz, *Essays on the Sermon on the Mount*, 39.

[4]Cf. Oscar Cullmann, *Christ and Time: The Primitive Christian Conception of Time and History*, trans. Floyd V. Filson, rev. ed. (London: SCM Press, 1962), 226.

There is an opinion, fairly widespread among contemporary New Testament scholars, that Jesus observed Jewish customs and explained to his
Jewish disciples the true meaning of the Jewish law. Over time, however,
when the Church broke away from the synagogues and assumed an anti-
Jewish position, Christian authors put in Jesus' mouth criticism of the
Jewish law that was in fact not characteristic of him.[5] This opinion is based
on the same presumption of the unreliability of the gospel accounts, on
which many contemporary scholars build their arguments in defense of
the necessity of distinguishing the "historical Jesus" from the "Jesus of
faith" purportedly fabricated by the Church.

In our analysis we proceed from the presumption of the reliability of
what the evangelists tell us about Jesus. Apart from the canonical Gospels,
we do not have another reliable alternative source on Jesus' life and teaching. And therefore it is on the pages of the Gospels that we must search
for the answer to the question of how Jesus actually related to Jewish law:
was he merely one of many interpreters of the law of Moses, or did he
call for a reexamination of the regulations of the law? The most complete
answer is given by the section of the Sermon on the Mount to which we
now turn.

1. Jesus and the
Law of Moses

The section of the Sermon on the Mount dedicated to the law of Moses
begins with Jesus' solemn proclamation of the enduring value of the Old
Testament stipulations:

> Think not that I am come to destroy the law, or the prophets: I am not
> come to destroy, but to fulfill.

---

[5]See, for example, Bart D. Ehrman, *Misquoting Jesus: The Story behind Who Changed the
Bible and Why* (New York, NY: HarperCollins, 2005), 187–195.

Moses Coming down from Mt Sinai, engraving, Gustave Doré, 1860s

For verily I say unto you, till heaven and earth pass, one jot or one tittle shall in no wise pass from the law, till all be fulfilled.

Whosoever therefore shall break one of these least commandments, and shall teach men so, he shall be called the least in the kingdom of heaven; but whosoever shall do and teach them, the same shall be called great in the kingdom of heaven.

For I say unto you, that except your righteousness shall exceed the righteousness of the scribes and Pharisees, ye shall in no case enter into the kingdom of heaven. (Mt 5.17–20)

Although the passage above consists of four independent sayings, we must examine them as a whole, since all four speak of the same thing: of how Jesus and his preaching correlate with the Old Testament. Collectively, they serve as an introduction to the series of antitheses built around the refrain: "Ye have heard that it was said by them of old . . . but I say unto you . . ." Jesus is embarking on an analysis of the Old Testament regulations and, before contrasting his own teaching with that of the Old Testament, he speaks of the significance of the latter. He emphasizes that he has come not to destroy that which was created by his forebears, but to lead mankind to new spiritual and moral frontiers.

"Think Not That I Am Come to Destroy the Law, or the Prophets"

The words "think not" turn the focus from the disciples as the main audience of the Sermon on the Mount to the larger circle of Jesus' listeners. Note the analogous construction in another saying: "Think not that I am come to send peace on earth: I came not to send peace, but a sword" (Mt 10.34).

The terminological pair "the law and the prophets" refers to a significant portion of the Scriptures, which is known to us as the Old Testament. The term "the law" refers first of all to "the testimonies, and the statutes, and the judgments, which Moses spake unto the children of Israel" (Deut 4.45). In the broad sense, "the law" refers to the entirety of the regulations of religious worship, moral precepts, and civil laws that are contained in the Pentateuch.[6] "The prophets" is understood to refer to the books of Joshua and Judges, 1 and 2 Samuel, 1 and 2 Kings, and also all the books of the Prophets, with the exception of Daniel. Only these books were read at the worship assemblies in the synagogue (the other biblical books were not read, while the Psalms were sung as prayers).[7] Jesus' listeners held this collection of books in high regard, since it recorded the revelation received by the people of Israel directly from God through Moses and other messengers whom God had sent to them.

Besides the written Torah, there was also the oral Torah—the totality of the traditions and interpretations of the Torah in the oral tradition. In an

[6]Ernest C. Reisinger, *The Law and the Gospel* (Phillipsburg, NJ: Presbyterian & Reformed Pub. Co., 1997), 49–54; Brevard S. Childs, *Biblical Theology of the Old and New Testaments: Theological Reflection on the Christian Bible* (Minneapolis, MN: Fortress, 1993), 532.

[7]Meier, *Law and History*, 71.

era when oral tradition was the main means of transmitting information and the majority of people did not have access to written texts, interpretations were often confused in people's minds with the text itself and became inseparable from the text. In the synagogues, while listening to the rabbis, people absorbed the regulations of the law of Moses together with their interpretations. In the Jerusalem temple the interpretation of the law was undertaken by priests, in whose hands the authority to interpret specific regulations of the law was concentrated to a high degree.[8]

This important factor must be considered when examining Jesus' sayings concerning the law of Moses. He sometimes cites the regulations of the law literally, according to the written text, but sometimes he does so in paraphrase. His critique of the law of Moses sometimes concerns the regulations of the law as they were recorded in the written text, but sometimes he has in mind the interpretation of these regulations in the oral tradition—the "tradition of the elders" (Mt 15.2) that often became the object of his condemnation.

And so Jesus first and foremost defends himself from accusations that he is destroying the law: he came not to destroy (*katalyō*) it, but to fulfill (*plēroō*) it. The latter term can be understood to mean that Jesus intends to flesh out what was sketched in outline in the law. However, a more convincing interpretation proceeds from a more exact translation of this term, which means not only "fulfill" but also "complete": Jesus takes the law of Moses as the basis on which he will construct his own morality, as a starting point for his own teaching, which is called to renew and expand the Old Testament regulations. While "the law and the prophets" were addressed to a specific nation, Jesus' preaching is addressed to all of mankind: this alone demands a radical revision of the commandments of Moses and their enrichment and universalization.

It is in this sense that Irenaeus of Lyons understood Jesus' words. Disputing with the heretic Marcion (second century), who believed that Jesus abolished the Old Testament regulations and who therefore proposed throwing out the abovementioned verse from the Gospel,[9] Irenaeus said

---

[8]See Meier, *A Marginal Jew*, 4:27–30.
[9]See Tertullian, *Against Marcion* 5.14 (ANF 3:459–461).

that Christ "did not abrogate . . . but extended and fulfilled" the commandments of the law. Jesus' teaching does "not contain or imply an opposition
to and an overturning of the [precepts] of the past . . . but [they exhibit]
a fulfilling and an extension of them." The law, "since it was laid down for
those in bondage, used to instruct the soul by means of those corporeal
objects which were of an external nature, drawing it, as by a bond, to obey
its commandments, that man might learn to serve God. But the Word set
free the soul, and taught that through it the body should be willingly purified." All the natural laws, Irenaeus says, are common to Christians and
Jews: "They had in them indeed the beginning and origin; but in us they
have received growth and completion."[10]

Summarizing the views of ancient interpreters of the Sermon on the
Mount, Robert A. Guelich, the author of an important study dedicated to
the Sermon, emphasizes that, on the one hand, people saw in Jesus a successor to Moses and an interpreter of the law of Moses, who "fulfilled" it
by uncovering its true meaning. On the other hand, they note that Jesus
breaks with the law of Moses, because his moral requirements exceed
and even cast aside this law. In Guelich's opinion, both points of view are
based on the accentuation of one fragment of the Sermon on the Mount
(Mt 5.17–19) over another (Mt 5.21–48). He notes that for the Evangelist
Matthew, Jesus is not so much a new Moses as the one who has come to
fulfill the Old Testament prophetic expectation, announcing the kingdom
of heaven and making it a reality in human history.[11]

"Till Heaven and Earth Pass"

The significance of "the law and the prophets" is emphasized in the second
saying, in which Jesus says that the Old Testament retains its force for all
of time to come. He insists on the importance of the law up to the last "jot"
(*iōta*). In the Aramaic original of Jesus' speech, what is mentioned here is
obviously the letter *yod* (ʾ), the smallest letter in the Hebrew alphabet. By

---

[10]Irenaeus of Lyons, *Against Heresies* 4.13 (ANF 1:477–478).
[11]Guelich, *The Sermon on the Mount*, 28.

"tittle" (*keraia*) he is likely referring to an insignificant diacritical mark: such marks were used in both Hebrew and Greek writing.[12]

At first glance, this saying radically contradicts Jesus' way of life and his attitude toward the regulations of the law of Moses. Here he appears to demand literal and unconditional fulfillment of the smallest regulations of the law—which he himself did not do when, for example, he broke the Sabbath. Many scholars believe that the "historical Jesus" could not have uttered such exhortations, and that they are the work of the Evangelist Matthew.[13]

In addition to this, we find an analogous saying in the Gospel of Luke in Jesus' words to the covetous Pharisees who derided him: "Ye are they which justify yourselves before men; but God knoweth your hearts. For that which is highly esteemed among men is an abomination in the sight of God. The law and the prophets were until John. Since that time the kingdom of God is preached, and every man presseth into it. And it is easier for heaven and earth to pass, than one tittle of the law to fail" (Lk 16.15–17). Here the person of John the Baptist appears as a watershed between the Old and New Testaments. In addition, just as in the Sermon on the Mount, the law of Moses is spoken of as continuing to retain its significance to the end of history.

In the scholarly literature, the abovementioned saying is often treated as a reflection of one of two opposing tendencies in the early Church. On the one hand, it supposedly contains a more "liberal" understanding of the Torah, as presented by Stephen (Acts 7.48–53) and Paul (Gal 2.2–6, 11–16; Acts 15). On the other hand, the "strict Jewish Christian community" strove for absolute adherence to the Torah.[14] Such an interpretation proceeds from the idea, presented above, that Matthew wrote for a specific community, and that the interests of this community were reflected in his text.

---

[12]For more on the various interpretations of "jot" and "tittle," see, in particular, Meier, *Law and History*, 50–52. See also Turner, *Matthew*, 163.

[13]See, for example, E. P. Sanders, *Jesus and Judaism* (Philadelphia, PA: Fortress, 1985), 261.

[14]Eduard Schweizer, *The Good News according to Matthew*, trans. David E. Green (Atlanta, GA: John Knox, 1975), 104.

However, nothing prevents us from seeing in the given saying confirmation of the antinomianism that characterizes Jesus' own attitude to the law of Moses. On the one hand, he criticized literalism in the interpretation of its regulations and the ostentatious piety of the Pharisees, who considered themselves zealous for the law. On the other hand, he pointed out the enduring value of "the law and the prophets." He viewed his mission as being not the overthrow of the law of Moses, but its fulfillment.

Following this view, the Christian Church did not do away with the Old Testament, nor did it set aside a single part of this formidable collection of texts, but included the entire corpus of the Old Testament in its own Holy Scriptures. Only one-fifth of the modern Bible is made up of the New Testament; four-fifths of its volume is taken up by "the law and the prophets." The first generation of Christians did not have the Bible in its modern composition, and there was no other Scripture besides the Old Testament, which was also read in early Christian worship. After the appearance of the Gospels and the apostolic Epistles, this collection of texts was enlarged; the Gospels and the Epistles were recognized as holy books, but "one jot or one tittle" nevertheless did not pass away from the Old Testament.

In the hierarchy of the texts that make up the Christian Scriptures, the Gospels unquestionably took first place. The second place was taken by the Acts of the Apostles and the Epistles. In third place was the Old Testament. This is clearly illustrated by the divine services, in which the Gospel is read with special solemnity, and the other books of the New Testament in a less solemn way. Over the course of the year, during the divine services of the Orthodox Church, the entire New Testament is read through (with the exception of the book of Revelation). As for the books of the Old Testament, the Psalter is read in its entirety over the course of a week (during Great Lent, twice a week), and the Psalms make up the basis of the divine service; the books of Genesis, Exodus, Proverbs, and Isaiah are read through in their entirety (or almost in their entirety) in Great Lent; the other books of the Old Testament are read selectively.

The words "till heaven and earth pass" refer to the end of history. Jesus often said to his disciples that the world would come to an end: a whole series of his parables is dedicated to this, as well as one of his last discourses,

The Horsemen of
the Apocalypse,
V. M. Vasnetsov,
1887

delivered on the Mount of Olives (Mt 24.3–51). In this speech, in particular, he said, "Heaven and earth shall pass away, but my words shall not pass away" (Mt 24.35). What does this saying mean, and how does it relate to what Jesus says in the Sermon on the Mount about the meaning of the law and the prophets?

It seems that this saying is a direct parallel to the fragment of the Sermon on the Mount under discussion. In the Sermon on the Mount, Jesus says that "till (*heōs*) heaven and earth pass, one jot or one tittle shall in no wise pass from the law, till (*heōs*) all be fulfilled." The twice-used word *heōs* indicates that the two events will take place at the same time: the end of heaven and earth, and the fulfillment of the law. Thus the law continues to be in effect until the end of heaven and earth, but its effectiveness does not extend beyond this event. In contrast, Jesus' words "shall not pass away" even after heaven and earth pass away.

This, it seems to us, is the most substantial difference between the law of Moses and the law that Jesus teaches to his disciples. The law of Moses is of value exclusively from the perspective of earthly history: after the conclusion of this history it loses its relevance. The law established by Jesus is not restricted in time: it is addressed to earthly people, but has an absolute, timeless value. It unites time with eternity, history with meta-history. Here the border between the earthly existence of mankind and the kingdom of heaven is fully erased.

Herein lies the absolute novelty of Jesus' moral teaching. Perhaps it is precisely because of this that his teaching is taken to be something difficult to realize under the conditions of earthly reality: it is focused on values that possess a supracosmic, eternal, and meta-historical dimension.

"Whosoever . . . Shall Break One of These Least Commandments"

It is no coincidence that the kingdom of heaven is mentioned thrice in the third and fourth sayings in the passage we are examining. At first glance, these two sayings appear to contain an internal contradiction. One of them says, "Whosoever therefore shall break one of these least commandments, and shall teach men so, he shall be called the least in the kingdom of heaven: but whosoever shall do and teach them, the same shall be called great in the kingdom of heaven." The other, connected to the previous saying by the conjunction "for" and logically conceived of as its direct continuation, asserts that if the righteousness of Jesus' disciples does not exceed the righteousness of the scribes and Pharisees, they will not enter the kingdom of heaven. In the first case, what is being spoken of is the hierarchy within the kingdom of heaven: the first places in it will be taken by those who not only talk about the commandments, but also fulfill them; however, even those who do not fulfill all the commandments but simply talk about them will nevertheless not be excluded from this kingdom. In the second case, Jesus speaks of the full exclusion from the kingdom of heaven of those whose righteousness does not exceed that of the scribes and Pharisees.

How can we reconcile this apparent contradiction? First of all, we must say that, according to Jesus' teaching, a certain hierarchy exists in the kingdom of heaven: there are the greater and the lesser. This idea also exists in different passages in the Gospel of Matthew (Mt 11.11; 18.4; 20.23), and in parallel passages in the other two Synoptic Gospels, and also in the Gospel of John, where Jesus says, "In my Father's house are many mansions" (Jn 14.2). From this we can conclude that the doors of the kingdom of heaven are not closed, not only for those who fulfill all the commandments of the law of Moses, but also for those who fulfill *almost* all of them. In the saying we are discussing, Jesus allows for the breaking of "one of these least commandments," and, moreover, to "teach men so" (that is, to teach others to break this commandment). For such a person, entrance into the kingdom of heaven is not completely out of the question.

Furthermore, we must note that the concept of "righteousness" (Greek *dikaiosynē*, corresponding to Hebrew *ṣedeq*, *ṣədāqā*) includes various good works, such as almsgiving, prayer, and fasting. An entire section of the Sermon on the Mount that speaks of these good works (Mt 6.2–18) serves to emphasize their importance and at the same time warn people from emulating the Pharisees' ostentatious piety.[15]

Jesus' words concerning the righteousness of the scribes and the Pharisees, on the other hand, ought to be understood in the overall context of his polemics with this group of people, whom he treats with emphatic harshness. The Gospel of Matthew contains an entire series of rebukes, each of which begins with the words: "Woe unto you, scribes and Pharisees, hypocrites!" Here Jesus is first of all accusing the Pharisees of "shut[ting] up the kingdom of heaven against men": they themselves do not wish to enter into it and do not allow others to enter in. One of the main accusations is that the Pharisees and scribes observe the external regulations of the law while being completely indifferent to its inner content. In Jesus' words, the Pharisees "outwardly appear righteous unto men, but within . . . are full of hypocrisy and iniquity." Jesus' speech concludes with ominous words that recall the preaching of John the Baptist: "Ye serpents, ye generation of vipers, how can ye escape the damnation of hell?" (Mt 23.13–32).

In this way, the superficial righteousness of the Pharisees essentially differs from the righteousness of those who fulfill the entire law of Moses but break one of the least of its commandments. The righteousness of the Pharisees is false righteousness, hypocrisy, and pietism under the guise of righteousness. The Pharisees are like sepulchers that seem beautiful on the outside, but which are "within full of dead men's bones, and of all uncleanness" (Mt 23.27). Such false righteousness has no place in the kingdom of heaven.

The interpretation we have given is based on a literal reading of these two sayings of Jesus, one following the other, with consideration of the

[15]John P. Meier, *Matthew*, New Testament Message (Collegeville, MN: Liturgical Press, 1990), 56–57.

overall context of his teaching as it is presented in the Gospel of Matthew. Aside from this, in the patristic tradition we find another interpretation of the words about the "least in the kingdom of heaven." John Chrysostom, in particular, believed that Jesus was speaking of a person who would be cast into gehenna and torment. The term "kingdom of heaven," according to Chrysostom, is used here in a broad sense—referring not only to future bliss, but also to the universal judgment. At this judgment the one who breaks the commandment "will be at that time least, that is, cast out, last. And he that is last will surely then fall into hell."[16] Cyril of Alexandria is even more severe: in his words, "Whoever sets aside 'one of the least of the commandments' of the law is set aside by God as God's enemy and as an inventor of laws opposed to God."[17]

Without disputing this type of interpretation, we must, however, clarify that the expression "the kingdom of heaven," like the synonymous expression "the kingdom of God," is never and nowhere used in Jesus' speech to mean existence beyond the grave in general, encompassing both the bliss of the righteous and the torment of sinners. In the cases when Jesus speaks of recompense after death, the kingdom of heaven, or the kingdom of God, is contrasted with the fiery gehenna, and eternal life is contrasted with eternal torment. Here are just two examples: "And if thine eye offend thee, pluck it out: it is better for thee to enter into the kingdom of God with one eye, than having two eyes to be cast into hell fire" (Mk 9.47); "And these shall go away into everlasting punishment, but the righteous into life eternal" (Mt 25.46). One may adduce other examples that demonstrate that when speaking of the kingdom of heaven, Jesus always has in view being with God, even if this kingdom has its own hierarchy and many "mansions."

"Which Is the First Commandment of All?"

The topic of the relationship between the law of Moses and Jesus' teaching arises repeatedly on the pages of the Gospels. The following episode,

---

[16]John Chrysostom, *Homilies on Matthew* 16.5 (NPNF[1] 10:106).

[17]Cyril of Alexandria, *Fragments on Matthew* 48 (PG 72:376). English translation from Simonetti, *Matthew 1–13*, 98.

Jesus among the Scribes, Paolo Veronese, 1558

related by the three Synoptics, is important for understanding this topic. In Matthew and Luke this episode is told in an abbreviated variant (Mt 22.34–40; Lk 10.25–28). We find the fullest version of it in the shortest Gospel—that of Mark:

> And one of the scribes came, and . . . asked him, "Which is the first commandment of all?" And Jesus answered him, "The first of all the commandments is, 'Hear, O Israel: The Lord our God is one Lord, and thou shalt love the Lord thy God with all thy heart, and with all thy soul, and with all thy mind, and with all thy strength.' This is the first commandment. And the second is like, namely this, 'Thou shalt love thy neighbor as thyself.' There is no other commandment greater than these." And the scribe said unto him, "Well, Master, thou hast said the truth: for there is one God; and there is none other but he; and to love him with all the heart, and with all the understanding, and with all the soul, and with all the strength, and to love his neighbor as himself, is more than all whole burnt offerings and sacrifices." And when Jesus saw that he answered discreetly, he said unto him, "Thou art not far from the kingdom of God." And no man after that dared to ask him any question. (Mk 12.28–34)

As a rule, the Pharisees and teachers of the law appear in the Gospels as negative figures. In Matthew a teacher of the law asks Jesus a question to "tempt" him. He acts on behalf of an entire group of Pharisees that had resolved to send him to Jesus after Jesus had put the Sadducees to silence. In Luke the teacher of the law likewise "tempts" Jesus with his question. It is only in Mark that the teacher of the law comes across more as a positive figure and receives praise from Jesus for his wise answer.

Both the commandments that Jesus cites are taken from the Pentateuch of Moses. The first is in the part of the book of Deuteronomy in which the commandments and regulations of God, presented by Moses, are preceded by the repeated refrain "Hear, O Israel" (Deut 5.1; 6.3, 4; 9.1; 20.3; 27.9). The commandment is presented in this section in the following redaction: "Hear, O Israel: the LORD our God is one LORD; and thou shalt love the LORD thy God with all thine heart, and with all thy soul, and with all thy might" (Deut 6.4–5). It is in this redaction—with negligible changes (possibly brought about by the translation of Jesus' words from Aramaic to Greek)—that the first and most important commandment is cited by Jesus.

The second commandment is taken from the book of Leviticus: "Thou shalt love thy neighbor as thyself" (Lev 19.18). In the original Old Testament text, one's neighbors were thought of as being the members of one's tribe—members of the people of Israel. However, Jesus uses the concept of "neighbor" in his teaching in a broad sense, as referring to any member of the human race. The parable of the good Samaritan—which in the Gospel of Luke is a continuation of Jesus' dialogue with the teacher of the law—confirms that this was indeed the understanding of the term "neighbor" (Lk 10.30–37).

In the Old Testament the two abovementioned commandments are not connected to each other. In Jesus' words, in contrast, they are closely connected: the second flows from the first; the first is not conceivable without the second. In Matthew's version Jesus concludes his presentation of these commandments with the following words: "On these two commandments hang all the law and the prophets" (Mt 22.40).

Jesus draws out the very essence of the law from the multitude of Old Testament regulations, while the Pharisees and teachers of the law prided themselves on being experts in the law's many stipulations. All the rest, including the "least" commandments, which are spoken of in the Sermon on the Mount, are dependent on these foundational and fundamental spiritual and moral imperatives. Jesus often criticizes the Pharisees for being bogged down in petty formalism while omitting "the weightier matters of the law" (Mt 23.23). The weightiest—the quintessence of all the law and the prophets—are the two commandments cited above.

John Chrysostom speaks of the mutual relationship between the two commandments in the context of the relationship between Jesus and the Old Testament law:

> "And the second is like unto this, Thou shalt love thy neighbor as thyself."
>
> But wherefore "like unto this?" Because this makes the way for that, and by it is again established. . . .
>
> If therefore to love God is to love one's neighbor . . . but to love one's neighbor worketh a keeping of the commandments, with reason doth He say, "On these hang all the law and the prophets." . . .
>
> [B]eing asked the first commandment, He rehearses the second also, which is not much inferior to that (for though second, it is like that). . . . By this He shows Himself to be submissive both to the law and to the prophets.[18]

"Keep the Commandments"

Yet another example of Jesus' respect for the law of Moses is found in the part of his conversation with the rich young man in which he speaks about the commandments:

> And, behold, one came and said unto him, "Good Master, what good thing shall I do, that I may have eternal life?" And he said unto him, "Why callest thou me good? There is none good but one, that is, God; but if thou wilt enter into life, keep the commandments." He saith unto him, "Which?" Jesus said, "'Thou shalt do no murder,' 'Thou shalt not commit adultery,' 'Thou shalt not steal,' 'Thou shalt not bear false

---

[18]John Chrysostom, *Homilies on Matthew* 71.1 (NPNF[1] 10:431–432).

witness,' 'Honor thy father and thy mother': and, 'Thou shalt love thy neighbor as thyself.'" (Mt 19.16–19)

In answering the young man's question, Jesus does not cite all of the Ten Commandments of the law of Moses. Let us recall these commandments:

1. I am the LORD thy God, which have brought thee out of the land of Egypt, out of the house of bondage. Thou shalt have no other gods before me.
2. Thou shalt not make unto thee any graven image, or any likeness of any thing that is in heaven above, or that is in the earth beneath, or that is in the water under the earth: thou shalt not bow down thyself to them, nor serve them. . . .
3. Thou shalt not take the name of the LORD thy God in vain. . . .
4. Remember the sabbath day, to keep it holy. Six days shalt thou labor, and do all thy work: but the seventh day is the sabbath of the LORD thy God. . . .
5. Honor thy father and thy mother. . . .
6. Thou shalt not kill.
7. Thou shalt not commit adultery.
8. Thou shalt not steal.
9. Thou shalt not bear false witness against thy neighbor.
10. Thou shalt not covet thy neighbor's house, thou shalt not covet thy neighbor's wife, nor his manservant, nor his maidservant, nor his ox, nor his ass, nor any thing that is thy neighbor's. (Ex 20.2–7)

And so, of the Ten Commandments, Jesus, according to Matthew, cites the sixth, seventh, eighth, ninth, and fifth, adding to these the commandment that he considered one of the two most important in the law: to love one's neighbor. In Mark's redaction the commandments are given thus: "'Do not commit adultery,' 'Do not kill,' 'Do not steal,' 'Do not bear false witness,' 'Defraud not,' 'Honor thy father and mother.'" In Luke (Lk 18.20) the commandments are given in the same order as in Mark, with the omission

Christ and the Rich Young Ruler, Heinrich Hofmann, 1889

of the commandment "Defraud not." If we consider this commandment a short version of the tenth commandment in the law of Moses, we can assume that Jesus is referring to six of the Ten Commandments. In Mark and Luke the commandment to love one's neighbor is not mentioned in the given episode.

In the understanding of the ancient Jews, the Ten Commandments of the law of Moses were divided into two lists, corresponding to the two tablets on which they were inscribed (Ex 31.18; 32.15–19; 34.1–4, 28–29; Deut 4.13; 5.22): the first through fourth commandments, which speak of a person's attitude toward God, and the fifth through tenth commandments, which are dedicated to relationships between human beings. Jesus' answer to the rich young man may create the impression that he considered the fulfillment of the commandments from the second list to be sufficient for entering into eternal life.

The rest of the story, however, shows the opposite, as does the whole context of Jesus' moral teaching. While highly valuing the commandments of the Old Testament, Jesus offered his own followers a different way that was not reducible to the fulfillment of five or six of the Ten Commandments, nor of all ten. This is the way of spiritual perfection, to which he pointed the rich young man, and along which the young man did not wish to go (Mt 19.21–22; Mk 10.21–22; Lk 18.22–23). The way that Jesus offers does not abolish the law of Moses but leads a person significantly beyond it, as we shall see in the next section of the Sermon on the Mount.

As for specific commandments in the law of Moses, Jesus takes a differentiated approach. Some he simply cites; others, as we shall see, he fleshes out; and still others he completely reconceptualizes. The four sayings from the Sermon on the Mount that we have examined here, dedicated to the law and the prophets, are merely a prelude to the section of the Sermon in which moral precepts are presented in the form of antitheses. It is this section that most vividly and fully expresses Jesus' attitude toward "the law and the prophets."

2. "Ye Have Heard That It Was Said by Them of Old"

Of the multitude of moral topics discussed in the Old Testament, Jesus selects six: (1) murder and anger, (2) adultery and struggle with temptation, (3) divorce, (4) swearing oaths, (5) not resisting evil, and (6) love for one's enemies.

Contemporary scholars argue about who the author of the antitheses was—Jesus or a later redactor and compiler—or whether the antitheses were the result of the combined work of Jesus and a later redactor. In particular, Rudolf Bultmann considered only the first, second, and fourth antitheses to be original, that is, coming directly from Jesus; the rest (the third, fifth, and sixth) he considered derivative, that is, belonging to the author of the Gospel of Matthew.[19]

A discussion of the original and derivative nature of the antitheses seems to us as senseless and groundless as the attempts to define which of the Beatitudes "go back to Jesus" and which were supposedly thought up on his behalf by redactors. All these attempts are based on no more than the conjectures and speculations of scholars, each of whom interprets the text of the Gospels on the basis of some previously adopted paradigm. We

---

[19]Rudolf Bultmann, *The History of the Synoptic Tradition*, trans. John Marsh (Oxford: Blackwell, 1963), 135–136.

will be examining the antitheses in their entirety, as we have examined the Beatitudes, and understanding them as Jesus' direct speech, transmitted to us by one of his disciples.

Most of the antitheses begin with the words: "Ye have heard that it was said by them of old" (literally "to them of old"). The word "heard" (*ēkousate*) refers, first of all, to the oral tradition of passing on this information, as do the words "it was said" (*errethē*).[20] Although the first part of the quote is found in written texts, most of Jesus' listeners would most likely have become acquainted with it in oral

Moses, Valentin de Boulogne, 17th century

form during worship at the temple or synagogue. As we have said, besides the actual texts from the Scriptures, Jesus could have had in mind the oral tradition of commentaries on these texts, which were disseminated among the rabbis.[21] In this case, Jesus' criticism could be directed not so much at the regulations of the law of Moses as at their rabbinical interpretation: this is how the meaning of the antitheses is understood by certain scholars.[22] However, the text of the antitheses fairly persuasively demonstrates that Jesus' object of attention—or more precisely, the object of his new interpretation by means of substantial expansion and fleshing out—is the law of Moses itself, even if what he may sometimes have in mind is its rabbinical interpretation.

Who are "[those] of old" (*archaioi*) whom Jesus repeatedly mentions? These are the forebears of his listeners, to whom the law was given through Moses: to them "it was said" that to which Jesus contrasts his own commandments. However, Moses was not the creator of the Old Testament law: he was only an intermediary, a messenger of God.[23] The true author

---

[20]Morris, *Gospel according to Matthew*, 113–114.

[21]Meier, *Vision of Matthew*, 243.

[22]See, in particular, W. D. Davies, *The Setting of the Sermon on the Mount* (Cambridge: Cambridge University Press, 1964), 105 (in Davies' opinion, Jesus' teaching in the transmission of Matthew is an antithesis not to the written law of Moses, but to the oral tradition; at the same time, Davies proceeds from the old hypothesis that Matthew redacted and expanded on Mark).

[23]See Reisinger, *Law and the Gospel*, 139.

of the law, according to a literal reading of the text of the Old Testament, is God himself: it is he who, through Moses, gave the people the law, which therefore was considered to be above any criticism, expansion, or fleshing out. Jesus, being God, considered it his right to expand on the commandments that were given to "them of old."

In all of the six antitheses, the Old Testament commandment to which Jesus refers concerns specific human actions or behavioral norms (murder, lust, divorce, perjury, vengeance, and hatred toward one's enemies). In three cases Jesus contrasts one way of behavior to another, more perfect one, and in the other three cases he does not speak at all about a person's actions, but about his or her inner condition.

In two of the six antitheses Jesus does not discuss the content of the texts that he cites: the Old Testament regulation serves only as a starting point for him to present his own teaching. In the first antithesis, after citing the words concerning murder, Jesus immediately moves on to the topic of anger and insults. In the second antithesis, after citing the commandment on adultery, he speaks about lust and temptation.

In the last four antitheses Jesus does not simply correct but actually cancels out points of the Mosaic law. At the same time he does not refer to any other authority besides himself: he does not appeal to God or to any teachers preceding him. He simply announces, "But I say to you." Moreover, he does not consider it necessary to justify his requirements; he simply declares them.[24] Behind Jesus' preaching stands his own authority—the authority of God who became man and solemnly proclaimed the New Covenant between God and mankind.

3. Anger and Insults

The first antithesis concerns the Old Testament ordinance on murder. It consists of three parts: a commentary on one of the commandments of the law of Moses and two calls for reconciliation:

[24]See Luz, *Matthew 1–7*, 390.

Ye have heard that it was said by them of old, "Thou shalt not kill"; and whosoever shall kill shall be in danger of the judgment. But I say unto you, that whosoever is angry with his brother without a cause shall be in danger of the judgment; and whosoever shall say to his brother, "Raca," shall be in danger of the council; but whosoever shall say, "Thou fool," shall be in danger of hell fire.

Therefore if thou bring thy gift to the altar, and there rememberest that thy brother hath anything against thee, leave there thy gift before the altar, and go thy way; first be reconciled to thy brother, and then come and offer thy gift.

Agree with thine adversary quickly, while thou art on the way with him, lest at any time the adversary deliver thee to the judge, and the judge deliver thee to the officer, and thou be cast into prison. Verily I say unto thee, thou shalt by no means come out thence, till thou hast paid the last penny. (Mt 5.21–26)

The beginning of the first antithesis contains a direct quote from the Old Testament, the sixth commandment of the Mosaic law: "Thou shalt not kill" (Ex 20.13; Deut 5.17). However, the rest of the quote ("whosoever shall kill shall be in danger of the judgment") is absent from the Old Testament. To what text is Jesus referring? It is very likely that he is referring to a certain saying that existed among rabbis in oral or written form. The fact that the expression "be in danger of the judgment" is found twice in Jesus' speech, and is then rephrased twice ("be in danger of the council," "be in danger of hell fire"), speaks in favor of the possibility that Jesus is citing a certain saying, unknown to us, that had a fixed form and was widely known in his time.

In the Old Testament we encounter multiple references to the fact that a murderer was to be condemned to death (Ex 21.12, 15; Lev 24.17; Num 35.16–18). Based on this, we can assume that the words "be in danger of the judgment" refers not so much to the judicial process as such as to the death sentence as a result of the judicial process in the case of murder. Another interpretation is that Jesus is referring to the prescription of the Mosaic law, but simultaneously also to a practice that existed in his time, according to which a murderer became "in danger" of the judgment, that is, his case was liable to judicial investigation.

Further on in his speech Jesus does not mention murder at all. Instead he immediately proceeds to speak about that which can become the reason for murder: anger and insults. The general idea of the entire admonition is that it is not enough simply to punish a person for a crime; one must fight against the reasons for evil that are rooted in the soul. Murder is a result of a process that begins within a person (anger) and leads at first to an external manifestation in the form of insults, and then it can turn into physical violence. Jesus leaves aside the topic of punishment for murder as something that concerns the sphere of criminal justice (which in the Old Testament tradition was understood as being of divine origin). The idea that a murderer must be punished appears self-evident and does not require any commentary.

Jesus moves on from the legal sphere to the aspects of human daily life and relationships, which do not involve any judicial responsibility at all in the literal (but not figurative) sense. The images from the judicial sphere are used by Jesus metaphorically: it is obvious that a court of judgment (which was usually made up of twenty-three people) could not investigate cases of anger, while the Sanhedrin (here, "council": the higher court, composed of seventy-one people) could not be occupied with incidents connected with the use of insulting vocabulary. The court of judgment and the council here should be understood as harbingers of the divine judgment, to which the expression "hell fire" (lit. "fiery gehenna") refers. This is about a person's responsibility for his or her own feelings and words: he or she answers for them not before a human court, but before the court of God's justice.

The key word that is found four times in the passage under discussion is the word "brother" (*adelphos*). The entire realm of interpersonal relationships is described with the use of "familial" terminology: all people are imagined as belonging to one family, consisting of brothers. We encounter the very same insistent use of the term "brother" later on in the Sermon on the Mount in the passage about the beam and the speck (Mt 7.3–5), where this term would be used thrice, and then in the instruction on how to admonish a brother who has trespassed (Mt 18.15), where the word is used twice. To be angry at one's neighbor and insult him is forbidden, first and foremost because one's neighbor is one's brother. Following the Teacher, the apostle Peter would also use the term "brother" as a synonym for the term "neighbor" (Mt 18.21).

To what has already been said, we will add that the term "brother" in Jesus' usage possesses an inclusive (generalized) meaning, referring also to "sisters." According to a tradition going back to the Old Testament, all of Jesus' teachings were addressed as if to a male audience. At the same time, it was understood that they would automatically extend to women as well. To be convinced that the term "brother" held this very meaning for Jesus, one may recall how once, when he was talking with people within a house, "his mother and his brethren stood without, desiring to speak with him. Then one said unto him, 'Behold, thy mother and thy brethren stand without, desiring to speak with thee.' But he answered and said unto him that told him, 'Who is my mother? And who are my brethren?' And he stretched forth his hand toward his disciples, and said, 'Behold my mother and my brethren! For whosoever shall do the will of my Father which is in heaven, the same is my brother, and sister, and mother'" (Mt 12.46–50; Mk 3.31–35). Here we are not interested in the episode itself, but in the fact that the expression "mother and brethren" points to mother, brothers, and sisters.

The use of the term "brother" in the part of the Sermon on the Mount under discussion brings to mind the biblical story of two brothers—Cain and Abel (Gen 4.3–8). Cain killed Abel out of jealousy, and this crime was the first murder described in the Bible. In the book of the Wisdom of Solomon, anger is identified as the reason for this murder: "But when the unrighteous went away from her in his anger, he perished also in the fury wherewith he murdered his brother" (Wis 10.3). According to this, Cain went away from the Wisdom of God and committed a crime in his anger. It is notable that the one who perished is declared to be not Abel, who was slain by Cain, but Cain himself: his spiritual perdition was the curse that he received from God (Gen 4.11).

The Killing of Abel, Michiel Coxie, 16th century

Anger and wrath are present in another important biblical text—in the words that Jacob uttered on his deathbed, speaking of two of his sons: "Simeon and Levi are brethren; instruments of cruelty are in their habitations. O my soul, come not thou into their secret, unto their assembly, mine honor, be not thou united: for in their anger they slew a man, and in their selfwill they digged down a wall. Cursed be their anger, for it was fierce, and their wrath, for it was cruel" (Gen 49.5–7). Jacob is speaking here of the evil deed that the two brothers committed when they avenged the dishonoring of their sister. At the time, Jacob reproved them for this, but they disagreed with him (Gen 34.25–31). On his deathbed, Jacob recalls this evil deed and again reproves the two brothers and foretells the scattering of their descendants as punishment for their sin.

In the Old Testament the term "anger" (*orgē*) is usually used in two senses: with reference to God, and with reference to human beings.

God's anger is one of the key concepts of the Bible. It is encountered many times, especially in the accounts connected with the history of the people of Israel in the time of Moses. The anger of the Lord was kindled against Moses when he attempted to contradict God (Ex 4.14). The wrath of God caused the destruction of Pharaoh's army (Ex 15.7). God threatened those who broke his commandments with his wrath (Ex 22.24). God became angry at the people of Israel for their faithlessness and disobedience (Ex 32.10–12; Num 11.1). The wrath of the Lord struck the people of Israel with a "very great plague" (Num 11.33) and pestilence (Num 16.46–49). Miriam was afflicted with leprosy as a result of God's anger (Num 12.9–10). Because of God's anger, the people of Israel were compelled to wander in the wilderness for forty years, "until all the generation, that had done evil in the sight of the LORD, was consumed" (Num 32.13). The main reason for God's anger was the people's departure from the true faith and their worship of false gods:

Even all nations shall say, "Wherefore hath the LORD done thus unto this land? What meaneth the heat of this great anger?" Then men shall say, "Because they have forsaken the covenant of the LORD God of their fathers, which he made with them when he brought them forth out of the land of Egypt; for they went and served other gods, and worshipped them, gods whom they knew not, and whom he had not given unto them, and the anger of the LORD was kindled against this land, to bring upon it all the curses . . . and the LORD rooted them out of their land in anger, and in wrath, and in great indignation." (Deut 29.24–28)

We find a similar understanding of God's anger in the Psalter, the books of the Prophets, and other parts of the Old Testament. At the same time, it is emphasized that the anger of God is of a different nature than human anger: "I will not execute the fierceness of mine anger, I will not return to destroy Ephraim. For I am God, and not man" (Hos 11.9). The anger of a human being is more often than not motivated by a desire for revenge and is an emotional reaction to evil. The anger of God is motivated by God's desire to correct a person and save him or her, even if this correction comes in the form of a heavy punishment. In God anger and mercy are combined: "'In a little wrath I hid my face from thee for a moment; but with everlasting kindness will I have mercy on thee,' saith the LORD thy Redeemer" (Is 54.8). The anger of God lasts for a moment, while his favor lasts for life (Ps 29.6).

With reference to human beings, the concept of anger is used to describe the emotional state that may lead to injustice, insults, and murder. At the same time, there is righteous anger that is elicited by the evil deeds of others. Moses showed anger toward different persons on multiple occasions (Ex 11.8; Lev 10.16; Num 31.14) and toward the people of Israel as a whole (Ex 16.20; 32.19). The evangelists note manifestations of anger and jealousy for God from Jesus himself also (Mk 3.5; Jn 2.15–17).

Does Jesus forbid all anger or only anger without a cause in the Sermon on the Mount? Many ancient manuscripts of the Gospel of Matthew, the Codex Sinaiticus in particular, do not contain the Greek word for "without a cause" (*eikē*) in Mt 5.22. On this basis, modern critical editions of the New Testament give the following reading: "But I say unto you, that whosoever is angry with his brother shall be in danger of the judgment."[25] Of the ancient writers, Justin Martyr, Tertullian, Origen, and Augustine cite the short version of the text. The version with the addition is known to Cyprian of Carthage, John Chrysostom, and Cyril of Alexandria.[26]

One might assume that the addition "without a cause" was made in the original text of the Gospel fairly early and was a result of a correction by an editor, who was attempting to reduce the radicalism in this aspect of Jesus' moral teaching by doing so. Whatever the case, a literal reading of Jesus' words in either version leads first of all to the conclusion that anger is inadmissible as an unjust reaction to a neighbor's conduct, a reaction that leads to insulting one's neighbor. This, then, is about a very specific manifestation of anger.

It is in this sense that Jesus' words have been understood in the patristic tradition. Basil the Great speaks of irascibility as a passion that turns a person into a beast; at the same time, he allows the possibility of anger against the devil.[27] Gregory the Theologian writes of anger as a natural property of human beings, but insists on the necessity of controlling it: "Did not nature, one asks, give us anger? But also the controlling of anger. Who has given us reasoning? Who gives sight, or hands, or the stability of feet? God and nature gave them all, but only for a good end. I do not praise you for not using them well. . . . They are gifts from God, being moved by the guidance and rule of reason."[28] John Chrysostom points to positive examples of uses for anger. In particular, he believes that anger can help stop sinners from committing sinful deeds.[29] Interpreting Jesus' words on anger, Chrysostom (citing the version of the verse with the addition) writes:

[25]Nestle, Nestle, and Aland, *Novum Testamentum graece*, 10.

[26]Luz, *Matthew 1–7*, 238n41.

[27]Basil the Great, *Homily against Anger*. English translation from *On the Human Condition*, by Basil the Great, trans. Nonna Verna Harrison, Popular Patristics Series 30 (Crestwood, NY: St Vladimir's Seminary Press, 2005), 81–92.

[28]Gregory of Nazianzus, *Poems on Scripture* 25 [*On Anger*]. English translation from *Poems on Scripture*, by Gregory of Nazianzus, trans. Brian Dunkle, Popular Patristics Series 46 (Yonkers, NY: St Vladimir's Seminary Press, 2012), 107.

[29]John Chrysostom, *Commentary on the Psalms* 4.7 (PG 55:50–51).

So He speaks. Thus He hath not altogether taken the thing away: first, because it is not possible, being a man, to be freed from passions: we may indeed get the dominion over them, but to be altogether without them is out of the question.

Next, because this passion is even useful, if we know how to use it at the suitable time. . . . What then is the proper time for anger? When we are not avenging ourselves, but checking others in their lawless freaks, or forcing them to attend in their negligence.

And what is the unsuitable time? When we do so as avenging our-selves. . . . When we are contending for riches. . . . But most men do the contrary; becoming like wild beasts when they are injured themselves, but remiss and cowardly when they see despite done to another: both which are just opposite to the laws of the Gospel.

Being angry then is not a transgression, but being so unseasonably.[30]

Passing from the topic of anger to the topic of insults, Jesus uses two terms of insult, one of which has come down to us as it sounded originally, and the other in Greek translation. The term "raca" is of Aramaic origin, from the root *rwq*, "to be empty". The meaning of this word is usually conveyed by the words "empty, insignificant person." John Chrysostom believed that in Syriac (that is what he called Aramaic) this term was used to substitute for the pronoun "thou" when the use of the latter signified disrespect.[31]

The Greek term *mōros* (translated as "fool") literally means "dull" or "stupid." It is used in the Greek (Septuagint) translation of the Old Testament, especially in the following verse: "For the fool will speak foolishness [*mōros mōra lalēsei*], and his heart will think vain things: to practice law-lessness, to speak error against the Lord, to scatter hungry souls, and to make thirsty souls empty" (Is 32.6, OSB). Here *mōros* is understood not merely as referring to a stupid person, but to a lawless person, a blasphemer, an oppressor of others. We do not know which Hebrew or Aramaic word,

---

[30]John Chrysostom, *Homilies on Matthew* 16.9 (NPNF[1] 10:110).
[31]John Chrysostom, *Homilies on Matthew* 16.10 (NPNF[1] 10:110).

translated by the Greek word *mōros* in the vocative case (*mōre*), was used by Jesus in the given instance; however, from the overall context of the saying, it follows that this word was more insulting than the word "raca." It is this word that Jesus uses in the plural when he condemns the Pharisees: "Ye fools and blind [*mōroi kai typhloi*]" (Mt 23.17).

In the second part of the passage being discussed, Jesus speaks of reconciliation using an image from Jewish religious practice. The words "if thou bring thy gift to the altar" can be understood both literally and metaphorically: Jesus could be speaking about offering a sacrifice as well as about prayer—standing before God.[32]

Sacrifices retained their significance in temple worship in Jesus' time: as we recall, on the fortieth day after Jesus' birth, Joseph and Mary went to the temple "to offer a sacrifice according to that which is said in the law of the Lord, a pair of turtledoves, or two young pigeons" (Lk 2.24). The Gospels never mention Jesus himself or his disciples offering a sacrifice in the temple. At the same time, he commands the man healed of leprosy: "go, and show thyself to the priest, and offer for thy cleansing, according as Moses commanded" (Lk 5.14). Jesus did not abolish the practice of offering sacrifices, although he also agreed with the opinion of the scribe that loving God "with all the heart, and with all the understanding, and with all the soul, and with all the strength, and to love [one's] neighbor as [oneself], is more than all whole burnt offerings and sacrifices" (Mk 12.33).

In the Sermon on the Mount, Jesus insists that a person must not offer a sacrifice to God until he is reconciled with his neighbor. To God, what is valuable is not the sacrifice in itself, but the disposition of heart with which the sacrifice is offered and the good works toward one's neighbor that accompany the sacrifice. Even the Old Testament prophets spoke of this: "To what purpose is the multitude of your sacrifices unto me? . . .

---

[32]The earliest Church appears to have applied these words to corporate worship and the sacrifice of the Eucharist: "In accordance with the commandment of the Lord, gather together to break bread and give thanks, first confessing your failings, so that your sacrifice may be pure." *Didache* 14.1 (*On the Two Ways: Life or Death, Light or Darkness: Foundational Texts in the Tradition*, tr. Alistair Stewart, Popular Patristics Series 41 [Yonkers, NY: St Vladimir's Seminary Press, 2011], 42).—*Ed.*

I am full of the burnt offerings of rams, and the fat of fed beasts, and I delight not in the blood of bullocks, or of lambs, or of he-goats. . . . Wash yourselves, make yourselves clean; put away the evil of your doings from before mine eyes; cease to do evil; learn to do well" (Is 1.11, 16–17). Continuing, as it were, this theme in his preaching, which is entirely built on the development and interpretation of the key themes of Old Testament morality, Jesus makes reconciliation with one's brother a condition for a person's reconciliation with God and forgiveness of sins. The same idea is embedded in the words of the prayer that Jesus gives to his disciples: "And forgive us our debts, as we forgive our debtors" (Mt 6.12).

As he develops this theme, Jesus turns to images taken from the penal realm: one should agree with one's adversary while on the way with him, otherwise he might hand you over to the judge, and the judge hand you over to the officer. The officer (*hyperetēs*) here refers to a prison guard, and the prison (*phylakē*) refers to a debtor's prison, out of which a person cannot come until he hands over all he has, down to the last penny. The penal system in Israel involved several types of punishment. All of these are recounted in the words of the Persian king Artaxerxes that he addressed to Ezra, the leader of Israel: "And whosoever will not do the law of thy God, and the law of the king, let judgment be executed speedily upon him, whether it be unto death, or to banishment, or to confiscation of goods, or to imprisonment" (Ezra 7.26). In Jesus' time, only Romans possessed the right to pass the death sentence, while a Jewish judge could sentence a person to imprisonment. Imprisonment for debts was not practiced in the Jewish tradition, but this practice did exist in Roman law.

In Luke we find a similar saying of Jesus, pronounced "when there were gathered together an innumerable multitude of people, insomuch that they trode one upon another" (Lk 12.1). It corresponds almost word for word with what Jesus says in the Sermon on the Mount: "When thou goest with thine adversary to the magistrate, as thou art in the way, give diligence that thou mayest be delivered from him; lest he drag thee to the judge, and the judge deliver thee to the officer, and the officer cast thee into prison. I tell thee, thou shalt not depart thence, till thou hast paid the very last mite" (Lk 12.58–59). The two adversaries here are not simply on the same road: they are going "to the magistrate," obviously hoping that the magistrate will judge between them. The officer here in Luke is a *praktōr*, and the "penny" (*kodrantēn*, a Roman coin equal to two lepta) has become a "mite" (literally, a lepton).

In both cases—in both Matthew and Luke—we have a short parable, which Jesus uses, like other parables, to deliver a specific moral message using images from daily life. At the same time, the parable can be understood both literally and figuratively. If it is taken literally, Jesus is giving ordinary life advice: do not take an affair to court; find a compromise with your adversary. If the parable is interpreted figuratively, "beneath the surface of the commonsense compromise the perspective of the last judgment becomes visible."[33] The "way" is understood to mean earthly life: this is what is given to us in order to settle our debts with our neighbors, that is, to reconcile with them. If a person passes into the other life without being reconciled, there the judgment of God and severe punishment await.

Many interpreters, beginning with Origen, understand the parable in this latter way: "In this life, this way traveled by all, you do well to accept and not ignore the suggestions of the conscience. But if you are inconsiderate and negligent in this life, conscience itself, assuming the role of a prosecutor, will accuse you before the judge. Conscience will subject to the juryman's decision, and you will be handed over to incurable punishments."[34] A commentary attributed to John Chrysostom, but preserved only in Latin, says:

> The Lord hastens that we may hasten into friendship with our enemies as long as we live in this life . . . since he knows how dangerous it is if one of our enemies dies before we can make peace. . . . For if as long as you are on the road of this life you do not make peace with your adversary whom you harmed, but the two of you, still enemies through death, go before Christ the judge, your adversary will hand you over to Christ, arguing at his tribunal that you are guilty, and the judge will

[33]Luz, *Matthew 1–7*, 241.
[34]Origen, *Fragments on Matthew* 102. English translation from Simonetti, *Matthew 1–13*, 105.

hand you over to his servant, that is, the cruel angel of punishments, and he will send you to the prison of hell.[35]

---

4. Lust, Adultery, and Divorce

The next two antitheses of the Sermon on the Mount—the second and third—are dedicated to questions of family ethics. The second antithesis is Jesus' commentary on the seventh commandment in the law of Moses: "Thou shalt not commit adultery" (Ex 20.14; Deut 5.18). The third is dedicated to divorce. It seems helpful to examine both antitheses together, since they are connected to each other:

> Ye have heard that it was said by them of old, "Thou shalt not commit adultery." But I say unto you, that whosoever looketh on a woman to lust after her hath committed adultery with her already in his heart.
>
> And if thy right eye offend thee, pluck it out, and cast it from thee: for it is profitable for thee that one of thy members should perish, and not that thy whole body should be cast into hell. And if thy right hand offend thee, cut it off, and cast it from thee: for it is profitable for thee that one of thy members should perish, and not that thy whole body should be cast into hell.
>
> It hath been said, "Whosoever shall put away his wife, let him give her a writing of divorcement." But I say unto you, that whosoever shall put away his wife, saving for the cause of fornication [*porneias*], causeth her to commit adultery [*moicheuthēnai*]; and whosoever shall marry her that is divorced committeth adultery. (Mt 5.27–32)

[35]Pseudo-Chrysostom, *Commentary on Matthew* 12. English translation in *Incomplete Commentary on Matthew (Opus imperfectum)*, vol. 1, trans. James A. Kellerman, ed. Thomas C. Oden, Ancient Christian Texts (Downers Grove, IL: InterVarsity, 2010), 100. This commentary, earlier attributed to Chrysostom, is now considered the work of an unknown author of the early fifth century (Joop van Banning, ed., *Opus imperfectum in Matthaeum*, CCSL 87b [Turnhout: Brepols, 1988], v–xvi; Joop van Banning, "Il Padre Nostro nell'*Opus Imperfectum in Matthaeum*," *Gregorianum* 71, no. 2 [1990]: 293–313).

Adultery and Lust

Jesus Ben Sirach, Julius
Schnorr von Carolsfeld,
19th century

The term "adultery" in the biblical context refers first
and foremost to unfaithfulness to one's spouse.

In Greek, there are two terms used to refer to
adultery, each of which possesses different shades
of meaning: *moicheia* and *porneia*. The first refers
mainly to the violation of marital fidelity, the seduc-
tion of another's wife, that is, to "adultery" in the
direct sense of the word. The second term covers a
broader semantic spectrum: it can refer to fornication, prostitution, and
promiscuous behavior; it can also be used to refer to sexual relations before
marriage, incest, and other forms of sexual immorality (some of these are
listed in Leviticus 18.6–23). Speaking of the reason for which a man would
be allowed to divorce his wife, Jesus uses the second term (*porneia*), which
refers to a wanton act committed by a woman.

The instruction on chastity that Jesus gives, citing the seventh commandment of the law of Moses, seems at first glance fairly close to the
words of the tenth commandment: "Thou shalt not covet thy neighbor's
wife" (Ex 20.17; Deut 5.21). One can recall other biblical texts concerning
a chaste attitude toward women, particularly the words of Job: "I made a
covenant with mine eyes; why then should I think upon a maid?" (Job 31.1).
The book of the Wisdom of Sirach contains a whole series of instructions
on how a pious man should behave with women:

Gaze not on a maid, that thou fall not by those things that are precious
in her. . . .

Look not round about thee in the streets of the city, neither wander
thou in the solitary place thereof.

Turn away thine eye from a beautiful woman, and look not upon
another's beauty; for many have been deceived by the beauty of a
woman; for herewith love is kindled as a fire.

Sit not at all with another man's wife, nor sit down with her in thine
arms, and spend not thy money with her at the wine; lest thine heart

incline unto her, and so through thy desire thou fall into destruction. (Sir 9.5, 7–9)

King David was an example of a person whose fortunes in life were shattered by the sin of looking upon a woman lustfully. The life of this biblical king, the most successful king in the history of Israel, was for a long time on an ever-ascending trajectory: God blessed his works and labors, he won victory after victory, his kingdom flourished, and his wealth

The Death of Uriah, fresco, Michelangelo, 1500s

multiplied. Everything changed after he saw a w bathing oman while he was walking one day on the roof of his house, "and the woman was very beautiful to look upon." David, to whom everything was permitted since he possessed absolute power, "sent messengers, and took her; and she came in unto him, and he lay with her." The woman was in fact married, and David knew this. In order to get rid of her husband, Uriah the Hittite, he commanded that Uriah be placed at the most difficult position during a battle and that he be left without support. Uriah died in the battle, and his wife "mourned for her husband." But when her period of mourning was over, "David sent and fetched her to his house, and she became his wife, and bare him a son. But the thing that David had done displeased the LORD" (2 Sam 11.1–27). The penalty for this crime was the death of the son whom the wife of Uriah bore David, and David's own life was never again as successful as it had been before.

In ancient Israel, as in all patriarchal societies, women were not treated as fully equal participants in societal life: they remained at home and raised children while men worked, taught, argued with each other, listened to the instruction of teachers, and resolved social and other problems. It was assumed that if a woman had to know something, she would learn it from her husband, who would bring the news home.

Among the instructions that the Lord gave to Moses, there are also those that concern women. However, they are not addressed to women directly: "And the LORD spake unto Moses, saying, 'Speak unto the children of Israel, saying, if a woman have conceived seed, and born a man child, then she shall be unclean seven days'" (Lev 12.1–2). Moses relayed all the commandments that he received from the Lord exclusively to the sons of Israel, and they were in turn to relay to their wives that which the latter had to know.

Old Testament marital law was based on the notion that the wife was the property of the husband. The full text of the tenth commandment of the law of Moses reads thus: "Thou shalt not covet thy neighbor's house, thou shalt not covet thy neighbor's wife, [nor his field,] nor his manservant, nor his maidservant, nor his ox, nor his ass, [nor any of his cattle,] nor any thing that is thy neighbor's" (Ex 20.17; cf. Deut 5.21).[36] The wife here is mentioned in the same breath as the house, the servants, the ox, the cattle, the ass, and other property. Clearly, this commandment could not have a mirror-image equivalent applicable to married women, since the latter did not possess their own personal property: all property belonged to the husband, from whom the property would pass on to his sons by inheritance.

Concerning adultery, the law of Moses prescribes severe punishment for both guilty parties, men and women: "And the man that committeth adultery with another man's wife, even he that committeth adultery with his neighbor's wife, the adulterer and the adulteress shall surely be put to death" (Lev 20.10). This is about a specific situation: when the participants in adultery are a man and a married woman.

In many other cases, the law is much more harsh to women than to men. In particular, if a husband suspects his wife of infidelity, she is to be subjected to a humiliating trial by "the bitter water that causeth the curse" (Num 5.11–31). If a man, having entered into marriage, accuses his wife of not being a virgin, her parents are to "bring forth the tokens of the damsel's virginity" to the elders, that is, bring the bedsheets from her wedding night to them. If evidence of the wife's virginity before marriage is observed, the husband has to pay a monetary fine. If, on the other hand, it is proved that the wife lost her virginity before marriage, "they shall bring out the damsel

---

[36]The words enclosed in brackets are absent from the Masoretic text of the Bible, but are present in the Septuagint. In the Septuagint version, besides this, the first two prohibitions are given in reverse order, corresponding to Deut 5.21: "Neither shalt thou desire thy neighbor's wife, neither shalt thou covet thy neighbor's house."

to the door of her father's house, and the men of her city shall stone her with stones that she die, because she hath wrought folly in Israel" (Deut 22.13–21).

Double standards for men and women in marriage existed in many patriarchal societies. They are reflected in Greco-Roman law, which had a definite influence on Jewish tradition, and proceed from the idea, widespread in the ancient world, that a woman was entirely subject to a man. Marriage was understood as releasing a woman from the authority of her father and putting her under the authority of her husband. The honor of a man was based to a significant degree on the sexual purity of the women with whom he had familial relations: his mother, sisters, wife, and daughters. Purity was not expected of the man himself.[37]

The idea was widely accepted that women were morally inferior to men. This perception was shared by Philo of Alexandria and Flavius Josephus, who were Hellenized Jews living in the first century. In Philo's words, the Essenes avoided marriage because women were selfish and spent all their energy on seducing their husbands.[38] In Josephus we find the following interpretation of the regulations of the law of Moses: "But let not a single witness be credited, but three, or two at the least, and those such whose testimony is confirmed by their good lives. But let not the testimony of women be admitted, on account of the levity and boldness of their sex."[39] In this case Josephus draws on the biblical texts concerning the necessity of having two or three witnesses (Deut 17.6; 19.15–21), but adds to the texts a prohibition against calling upon women as witnesses.

In the ancient Jewish tradition, polygamy and bigamy were fairly widespread. Jacob had two wives (Gen 29), as did Lamech before him (Gen 4.19) and Elkanah after him (1 Sam 1.1), as well as a range of other individuals

---

[37]David Cohen, *Law, Sexuality, and Society: The Enforcement of Morals in Classical Athens* (Cambridge: Cambridge University Press, 1991), 140.

[38]Philo of Alexandria, *Apology for the Jews* 11.14–17. English translation from *The Works of Philo: Complete and Unabridged*, by Philo of Alexandria, trans. C. D. Yonge, new ed. (Peabody, MA: Hendrickson, 1993), 746.

[39]Flavius Josephus, *Antiquities of the Jews* 4.8.15. English translation from *The Works of Flavius Josephus*, by Flavius Josephus, trans. William Whiston (Auburn and Buffalo, NY: John E. Beardsley, 1895).

*Esau Sells His
Birthright,*
Matthias Stom,
17th century

mentioned in the Bible. The law of Moses provided for the possibility that a man could have two wives—one loved and the other unloved (Deut 21.15).

Besides having two or several wives, a man was allowed to have concubines from among his maidservants. There are many examples of this in the Bible. Abraham had a wife and several concubines, the number of which is not specified (Gen 25.1). Esau had three wives (Gen 26.34; 28.9). Jacob had two wives and two concubines: between them they bore Jacob twelve sons and one daughter (Gen 29.23–30.13). Of Gideon it is said that he had many wives, from whom he had seventy sons, and a concubine who bore him one more son (Judg 8.30–31). King David had many wives and concubines: first in Hebron, then in Jerusalem (2 Sam 5.13). King Solomon had a record number of wives and concubines, according to the Bible: 700 and 300 respectively (1 Kg 11.3).

In all the cases mentioned above, the men involved were rich and of high standing: patriarchs, kings, judges. Among the representatives of the middle class, polygamy was prevalent to a much smaller degree, while men of little means satisfied themselves with a single wife. Polygamy persisted among the Jews for a fairly long time. King Herod the Great, according to Josephus, had nine wives[40] (other witnesses place the number at ten).

[40]Flavius Josephus, *The Wars of the Jews* 1.28.4. English translation from Whiston, *Works of Flavius Josephus.*

In forbidding not only committing adultery with a woman, but also looking at one lustfully, Jesus, it may seem, is not saying anything fundamentally new in comparison with what has been said on this topic in the Old Testament. Moreover, he uses the same external form of the commandment that was used in the law of Moses, in which all the commandments were addressed to men.

Nevertheless, the actual tone in which Jesus gives his commandment regarding the inadmissibility of adultery, even in thought, contrasts very sharply with the overall tone of the instructions concerning spousal fidelity in the Old Testament. Using the hyperbolic images of the eye that must be plucked out and the hand that must be cut off, Jesus emphasizes the holiness of marriage, and it is in this that the central point of his instructions consists.[41] This starting point also determines his attitude toward divorce.

The Teaching on Divorce and Marriage

The norms concerning divorce are spelled out in the law of Moses in a fairly detailed manner:

> When a man hath taken a wife, and married her, and it come to pass that she find no favor in his eyes, because he hath found some uncleanness in her, then let him write her a bill of divorce, and give it in her hand, and send her out of his house. And when she is departed out of his house, she may go and be another man's wife. And if the latter husband hate her, and write her a bill of divorcement, and giveth it in her hand, and sendeth her out of his house, or if the latter husband die, which took her to be his wife, her former husband, which sent her away, may not take her again to be his wife, after that she is defiled; for that is an abomination before the LORD. (Deut 24.1–4)

This excerpt reflects the practice that was widespread in the Jewish tradition. Only the husband could initiate a divorce. If he decided to separate

---

[41]Craig S. Keener, *The Gospel of Matthew: A Socio-Rhetorical Commentary* (Grand Rapids, MI: Eerdmans, 2009), 192.

from his wife, he had to give her a written notice. In that case she could get married again.

The legislation concerning divorce was subject to multiple interpretations in the Jewish oral and written traditions.[42] In particular, the expression "he hath found some uncleanness in her" was variously interpreted. The meaning of this expression was disputed, including in the time of Jesus. We find a reference to this kind of dispute in the Mishnah, the code of the religious moral regulations of Orthodox Judaism, compiled at the turn of the second and third centuries:

> The School of Shammai says: A man may not divorce his wife unless he has found unchastity in her, for it is written, "Because he has found in her indecency in anything." And the School of Hillel says: [He may divorce her] even if she spoiled a dish for him, for it is written, "Because he has found in her indecency in anything." R. Akiba says: Even if he found another fairer than she, for it is written, "And it shall be if she found no favor in his eyes."[43]

The opinion of Rabbi Akiba could not have been known to Jesus, since this rabbi was active in the period after Jesus' death. As for the positions of the schools of Shammai and Hillel, they were most likely known to him. In the interpretation of the law of Moses that Matthew presents, Jesus is close to the school of Shammai: he considers the only permissible reason for divorce to be adultery on the part of the wife. However, he goes further, equating marriage to a divorced woman to adultery. By saying this, Jesus forbids second marriages for men.

He addresses this topic again in his dialogue with the Pharisees. Here is Matthew's version of the dialogue:

---

[42]See Phillip Sigal, *The Halakhah of Jesus of Nazareth according to the Gospel of Matthew*, Studies in Biblical Literature 18 (Atlanta, GA: Society of Biblical Literature, 2007), 105–143; Meier, *Marginal Jew*, 4:77–95.

[43]Mishnah, Gittin 9.10. English translation from *The Mishnah*, ed. and trans. Herbert Danby (Oxford: Oxford University Press, 1933), 321; also cited in Hays, *Moral Vision of the New Testament*, 353. See also Meier, *Marginal Jew*, 4:94–95.

The Pharisees also came unto him, tempting him, and saying unto him, "Is it lawful for a man to put away his wife for every cause?" And he answered and said unto them, "Have ye not read, that he which made them at the beginning made them male and female, and said, 'For this cause shall a man leave father and mother, and shall cleave to his wife: and the two shall be one flesh?' Wherefore they are no more two, but one flesh. What therefore God hath joined together, let not man put asunder." They say unto him, "Why did Moses then command to give a writing of divorcement, and to put her away?" He saith unto them, "Moses because of the hardness of your hearts allowed you to put away your wives; but from the beginning it was not so. And I say unto you, whosoever shall put away his wife, except it be for fornication, and shall marry another, committeth adultery; and whoever marrieth her who is put away doth commit adultery." (Mt 19.3–9)

The concluding sentence of the dialogue repeats what was said in the Sermon on the Mount nearly word for word. However, the beginning of the dialogue substantially broadens the topic. The Pharisees begin with a question that has a direct bearing on the dispute between the schools of Hillel and Shammai. Those who ask the question are clearly anticipating that Jesus would support the opinion of one camp, and then the other camp would declare him to be their enemy. Jesus, however, refers to the very origins of the question—to God's creation of the first married couple. Citing the first pages of the Bible word for word (Gen 1.27; 2.24), he says that God's original plan was such a union of two persons, in a marriage involving their union in "one flesh" and lifelong fidelity to each other. The marriage union is understood as being established by God himself: human beings do not have the right to put asunder that which God has joined together.[44]

---

[44]Certain scholars point to the closeness of Jesus' teaching on marriage and divorce to the similar teaching of the Essenes. See, in particular, Peter J. Tomson, *"If This Be from Heaven . . .": Jesus and the New Testament Authors in Their Relationship to Judaism*, Biblical Seminar 76 (Sheffield: Sheffield Academic Press, 2001), 150–151. See, however, Meier, *Marginal Jew*, 4:87–93 (the author demonstrates that the texts of the Qumran community contain a prohibition of polygamy, but not an unequivocal prohibition of divorce).

In the words cited above, Jesus formulates the view that lies at the basis of the Christian teaching that marriage is a God-given union.[45] The apostle Paul insists on the unity and indissolubility of marriage. He allows a second marriage for a wife only if her husband has died, and for a husband only if his wife has died:

> I say therefore to the unmarried and widows, it is good for them if they abide even as I. But if they cannot have self-control, let them marry; for it is better to marry than to burn. And unto the married I command, yet not I, but the Lord, let not the wife depart from her husband; but if she depart, let her remain unmarried, or be reconciled to her husband; and let not the husband put away his wife. . . . Art thou bound unto a wife? Seek not to be loosed. Art thou loosed from a wife? Seek not a wife. But if thou marry, thou hast not sinned. . . . The wife is bound by the law as long as her husband liveth; but if her husband be dead, she is at liberty to be married to whom she will, only in the Lord. (1 Cor 7.8–11, 27–28, 39)

The text above is interesting in that it is probably the earliest Christian document written on the topic of marriage and divorce. In it, men and women are presented as having equal rights and opportunities. This understanding reflects the very substantial development that the teaching on marriage and divorce underwent in the New Testament Church. Can we say that the rethinking of the roles of spouses in a marriage had already taken place in Jesus' preaching, or that this was a later development? It appears to us that it was Jesus who laid the foundation for this understanding of marriage in Christianity—an understanding that quite radically changes the whole perspective on the relationship between spouses and their obligations toward each other, in comparison with how these obligations are presented in the Mosaic legislation.

While in the Old Testament a wife is presented as the property of her husband, in Jesus' words, both husband and wife come across as having equal responsibility for preserving the integrity of the marriage. While in

---

[45]Francis J. Moloney, *"A Hard Saying": The Gospel and Culture* (Collegeville, MN: Liturgical Press, 2001), 43–44.

the Mosaic legislation, in all its possible interpretations, divorce is permitted at the initiative of the husband, who must give his wife a certificate of divorce, Jesus considers this legal norm to be a violation of the original divine plan. Divorce was allowed by Moses because of the hardness of the hearts of the people of Israel, but it contradicts the will of God that the marriage union be indissoluble. Not only does the husband have the right to count on his wife's fidelity, but the wife also has the right to count on her husband's fidelity as well.

This is confirmed in particular by the parallel account in Mark. In the beginning, it hardly differs at all from Matthew's account, except that the question posed by the Pharisees is not about what reason is acceptable for divorcing one's wife, but about the permissibility of divorce at all. In Mark's version Jesus answers the question with a question: "What did Moses command you?" The Pharisees quote the words concerning the certificate of divorce, and Jesus tells them the same thing that we have read in Matthew. However, Matthew and Mark differ significantly in their continuation of the story. In Matthew the disciples point out to Jesus that his teaching on marriage and divorce is excessively rigorous: "If the case of the man be so with his wife, it is not good to marry." In reply, Jesus expounds his understanding of celibacy (Mt 19.10–12). In Mark, on the other hand, the disciples, who have remained alone in the house with Jesus, ask him again about the reasons for divorce, and he replies: "Whosoever shall put away his wife, and marry another, committeth adultery against her. And if a woman shall put away her husband, and be married to another, she committeth adultery" (Mk 10.10–12).

Of interest to us here is the expression "committeth adultery against her" (*moichatai ep' autēn*). It refers to the violation of marital fidelity by a husband with respect to his wife. It is here that Jesus departs furthest from the Old Testament understanding of marriage and divorce: he talks about the husband's responsibility toward his wife. As in many other instances, when Jesus answers the Pharisees' question, he goes beyond the bounds of the problem posed to him, significantly expanding the very perspective from which the problem is to be examined. Starting out from a narrow legal dispute regarding the reasons for divorce, Jesus expounds a teaching based not on the prescriptions of the law, but on God's original plan for mankind.

In this way, Jesus recognizes a distinction in the Old Testament between what was established by God and is the manifestation of his will, and what was prescribed or allowed to the people by Moses due to their hard-heartedness. This hermeneutic approach can be applied to the Mosaic law as a whole. It cannot but shock modern people with its excessive strictness and even cruelty: it is enough to recall the extensive list of crimes and offenses punishable by death and the different means of carrying out the death sentence. It is significant, however, that Jesus criticizes the Mosaic law not for cruelty, but, on the contrary, for excessive laxity regarding certain questions, especially that of divorce. In this matter, Moses, in Jesus' opinion, had made concessions to the human inability (or unwillingness) to fully fulfill God's plan.

The difference between the versions of Mark and Matthew consists in the absence of the mention of the possibility of divorce because of fornication in Mark. Compare the two texts: "Whosoever shall put away his wife, and marry another, committeth adultery against her" (Mk 10.11); "Whosoever shall put away his wife, except it be for fornication, and shall marry another, committeth adultery" (Mt 19.9). The difference is clear. It is usually explained by the suggestion that Matthew has in this instance edited and added to Mark, inasmuch as for a Jewish audience, for whom Matthew's Gospel was intended, such an addition would have been important.[46] However, we should pay attention to the fact that in Matthew the quoted words are addressed to a broad audience, while in Mark they are part of an explanation that Jesus was giving to the disciples in the house.[47] It is possible that, while he was speaking with the people, Jesus pointed out the exception to the rule, while in his conversation with the disciples he considered this unnecessary.

---

[46]Bock, *Jesus according to Scripture*, 299–300.

[47]In Matthew, Jesus also gives a separate explanation to the disciples, but the content of this explanation differs: there Jesus speaks of eunuchs for the sake of the kingdom of heaven (Mt 19.10–12).

The Anointing of Jesus with Myrrh, miniature, 11th century

Jesus' attitude toward adultery and divorce may seem excessively rig-orist. However, he is viewing the whole system of human relationships not just through the eyes of a human being, but also through the eyes of God: in human society marriages break apart, but in the eyes of God they are inviolable.[48] In his preaching, Jesus always points to the absolute ideal.

Besides this, in Jesus' teaching, moral strictness is combined in a sur-prising way with leniency toward human weakness. He sets a high moral standard, but recognizes that not all are able to achieve it. He condemns sin, but does not condemn the sinner. This is demonstrated by his atti-tude toward people involved in adultery, fornication, and other sins. To the Pharisees he addresses the following words, which must have deeply angered them: "Verily I say unto you, that the publicans and the harlots go into the kingdom of God before you" (Mt 21.31). Sitting in the home of Simon the Pharisee, he allows the woman "which was a sinner" to anoint his feet with ointment (Lk 7.37).

The Mosaic legislation considered the problems of marriage and divorce almost exclusively within the legal realm, and therefore the regula-tions were mostly prohibitive in nature. Jesus does not take the subject of marriage and divorce completely out of this realm, but he turns his atten-tion foremost to the spiritual and moral aspects of marriage, speaking of

[48]Charles H. Talbert, *Reading the Sermon on the Mount: Character Formation and Decision Making in Matthew 5–7* (Grand Rapids, MI: Baker Academic, 2006), 82.

the danger not only of divorce and adultery, but also of the deviations from marital fidelity that belong exclusively to the mental or emotional realm of a person's life. It is in this realm that one must search for the solution to the problems that manifest themselves in concrete sinful actions.

From external regulations designed to protect society from infringements of the law and crimes, Jesus turns his attention to what goes on inside a person, to the heart. It is there that the source of crimes and sins is concealed. In Jesus' words, "out of the heart proceed evil thoughts, murders, adulteries, fornications, thefts, false witness, blasphemies" (Mt 15.19). In this list of sins we find both adulteries (*moicheiai*) and fornications (*porneiai*)—the same sins that are mentioned in the Sermon on the Mount.

Attention to a person's inner world, to the secrets of the soul and heart, is the most important aspect of Jesus' teaching on marriage, divorce, adultery, and lust. It is only at first glance that sins of a sexual nature appear to be sins of the flesh. The sources of these sins lie in the realm of the soul, in a person's heart. Jesus calls people not merely to avoid sinful actions but also to struggle with the thoughts and feelings that lead to them. This is the meaning of his words concerning the eye that must be plucked out and the hand that must be cut off. In another passage in Matthew, and also in Mark, we encounter the very same instruction again: to the eye and hand here the foot is added (Mt 18.8–9; Mk 9.43–48). We can assume that Jesus used these images repeatedly in referring to the difficulty of struggling with sinful desires: to tear the latter out of the heart is no less difficult and painful than to pluck out an eye or cut off a hand or a foot.

Jesus' words on this topic have a long history of interpretation in church tradition. Tertullian in particular writes, "[It is not possible] for a wife to be married whom you have not seen or desired. I grant it makes a wide difference whether a married man or an unmarried desire another woman. Every woman, (however), even to an unmarried man, is 'another,' so long as she belongs to some one else; nor yet is the means through which she becomes a married woman any other than that through which withal (she becomes) an adulteress. . . . Besides, what is the thing which takes place in all men and women to produce marriage and fornication? Commixture of the flesh, of course; the concupiscence whereof the Lord put on the same footing with fornication." Proceeding with this logic, Tertullian considers that "the best thing for a man is not to touch a woman." In his opinion, first marriages are allowed by God as an extreme indulgence; as for second and third marriages, they must be unequivocally forbidden.[49]

The Church has not accepted such an interpretation of Jesus' teaching. Jesus' moral strictness concerns those manifestations of human sexuality that violate marital fidelity and endanger marriage as a God-established union between a man and a woman. Neither Jesus nor the Church is at all opposed to a man's attraction to a woman as such if it is constrained within the bounds of a marriage union or leads to marriage. The body of a woman was originally created by God as a sacred vessel in which human life is conceived. A man's attitude towards it must be one of reverence and trembling, not carnality. In marriage spouses experience mutual attraction toward each other: the woman is naturally attracted to her husband (Gen 3.16), and the man experiences desire for the woman. Desire becomes sinful and dangerous when a man directs it at a woman who does not belong to him, or to whom he has no intention to be married. Herein lies the fundamental meaning of Jesus' words that "whosoever looketh on a woman to lust after her hath committed adultery with her already in his heart."

In interpreting these words, John Chrysostom describes various types of lust and different ways of looking upon women. That said, he is speaking either about the wives of others or about unknown women whom a man might meet on the street and stare at. "If thou desirest to look and find pleasure, look at thine own wife, and love her continually; no law forbids that," concludes Chrysostom. "But if thou art to be curious about the beauties that belong to another, thou art injuring both thy wife by letting thine eyes wander elsewhere, and her on whom thou hast looked, by touching her unlawfully."[50]

In this same commentary Chrysostom answers the question of why Jesus' instructions are addressed only to men. Saying nothing about the cultural context within which Jesus' instructions were delivered, Chrysostom insists that whatever was addressed to the men applies equally to the

---

[49]Tertullian, *On Exhortation to Chastity* 9 (ANF 4:55).
[50]John Chrysostom, *Homilies on Matthew* 17.2 (NPNF[1] 10:117).

The Holy Hierarch John Chrysostom, icon, 11th century

women as well. Using the expression of the apostle Paul (Eph 5.23: "The husband is the head of the wife, even as Christ is the head of the church"), Chrysostom asserts that "the laws which [Jesus] appoints are in every case common, although He seem to address Himself unto men only. For in discoursing with the head, He makes His admonition common to the whole body also. For woman and man He knows as one living creature, and nowhere distinguishes their kind."[51]

Chrysostom touches also on the relationship between Jesus' teaching and the Old Testament stipulation about divorce. In his words, in the Old Testament, "there was an ancient law made, that he who hated his wife, for whatever kind of cause, should not be forbidden to cast her out, and to bring home another instead of her" (thus Chrysostom understood this law in the same way as Hillel did). This law was given in order to avoid a greater sin—in order that the husbands who did not love their wives would not harm them: "I mean, had He made it necessary to keep in the house her even that was hated, the husband, hating, would have killed her. For such was the race of the Jews. For they who did not spare children, who slew prophets, and 'shed blood as water,' much more would they have showed no mercy to women." Chrysostom connects his interpretation of the commandment on divorce with Jesus' words about the impermissibility of anger: "But forasmuch as He had taken away all wrath, having forbidden not murder only, but even the mere feeling of anger, He with ease introduces this law likewise. With this view also He is ever bringing to mind the former words, to signify that His sayings are not contrary to them, but in agreement: that He is enforcing, not overthrowing them; perfecting, not doing them away."[52]

The theological understanding of marriage in the Christian tradition is based on the words from the book of Genesis, quoted by Jesus, that

[51]John Chrysostom, *Homilies on Matthew* 17.2 (NPNF[1] 10:117).
[52]John Chrysostom, *Homilies on Matthew* 17.4 (NPNF[1] 10:118–119).

The Wedding in
Cana of Galilee,
Paolo Veronese,
1562–1563

the "two shall be one flesh." On this basis the Church understands marriage to be a union between a man and a woman, entered into once, for life, and presupposing the faithfulness of the spouses to each other. Jesus' teaching remains not only an ideal in the Christian Church, but also the standard.

But if we are speaking of the implementation of this standard in practice, we may observe substantial differences between the Catholic and Orthodox traditions in particular. In the Catholic Church, divorce is practically forbidden; divorced spouses are not allowed to partake of the Eucharist; entering into a second marriage is possible only if the first marriage is annulled by ecclesiastical authorities (which happens extremely rarely and requires an ecclesiastical tribunal). In the Orthodox tradition, the principle of *oikonomia* (leniency, condescension) is widely applied, according to which divorce can be acknowledged as a fait accompli under certain conditions, and the divorced spouses (or one of them) allowed to enter into a second marriage, and under exceptional circumstances, into a third. At the same time, the procedure of a "church divorce" does not exist, nor does "un-crowning."[53] Divorce is considered a violation of the God-established order, but in certain cases it is acknowledged not merely to be permissible, but even necessary.[54]

---

[53]For more on the Orthodox understanding of marriage and the wedding service, see John Meyendorff, *Marriage: An Orthodox Perspective* (Crestwood, NY: St Vladimir's Seminary Press, 1975); *Glory and Honor: Orthodox Christian Resources on Marriage*, David C. Ford, Mary S. Ford, and Alfred K. Siewers, eds. (Yonkers, NY: St Vladimir's Seminary Press, 2016); Met. Hilarion Alfeyev, *Orthodox Christianity*, Vol. 5 (2019).—*Ed.*

[54]For example, if remaining in the marriage would threaten the life of the wife or children.

As for the Protestant world, there we find different approaches: from the extremely conservative (practically allowing neither divorce nor second marriages) to the extremely liberal (allowing not only divorce and second marriages, but also various alternatives to marriage in the form of cohabitation and gay union). That said, much is left to the discretion of the spouses themselves, or to their pastor. In the words of a Protestant scholar, "The inflexible divorce law in Catholicism appears to many to be the opposite of God's love and forgiveness. On the other hand, the absence of a practiced church divorce law in Protestantism means that the pastors are left to their own devices."[55]

Jesus' teaching on marriage and divorce remains the reference point that continues to be preserved at the center of the Christian understanding of marriage. At the same time, this teaching is one of the most difficult points to fulfill in the spiritual and moral program laid out in the Sermon on the Mount and in the other sermons of Jesus. This is demonstrated not only by the various deviations in practice from the standards set by Jesus, but also by the multitude of interpretations that have sprouted up around these standards in the theological and canonical tradition of the Christian churches.

5. Oaths and Lying

The fourth antithesis is dedicated to a topic that the modern reader may find fairly minor: oaths and perjury. The custom of swearing oaths and making promises continues in our time, but the attitude toward breaking a promise is usually quite tolerant in modern society, with the exception of those promises that are in the form of written contracts and whose

See Moscow Patriarchate, *The Basis of the Social Concept of the Russian Orthodox Church*, X.3, on line at https://mospat.ru/en/documents/social-concepts/kh/.

[55]Luz, *Matthew 1–7*, 258.

*The Sermon
on the Mount,*
Rudolf Yelin,
1912

violation by one party would entail legal or financial consequences. Swearing an oath in the name of God has fallen out of use in modern secular society, inasmuch as the very mention of the name of God has practically disappeared from the public sphere. Only in certain countries with Christian roots are such forms of oaths preserved, in particular swearing an oath on a Bible upon assuming the office of the head of state.

In antiquity the custom of swearing oaths was applied much more widely than in our time. The righteous people of the Old Testament used oaths (Gen 14.22; 21.24; 47.31) or demanded oaths from others (Josh 2.12). An oath was pronounced in a solemn setting, in the temple before the altar (1 Kg 8.31). The breaking of an oath was regarded as a serious sin that God would punish severely (Wis 14.25, 30–31). People swore by the Lord (1 Sam 28.10; 2 Sam 19.7; 1 Kg 2.8, 23), or by someone's life (Gen 42.15; 2 Sam 11.11). The law of Moses contains the following instructions concerning oaths and the necessity of fulfilling them:

> If a man vow a vow unto the LORD, or swear an oath to bind his soul
> with a bond; he shall not break his word, he shall do according to all
> that proceedeth out of his mouth. (Num 30.2)

When thou shalt vow a vow unto the LORD thy God, thou shalt not slack to pay it, for the LORD thy God will surely require it of thee; and it would be sin in thee. But if thou shalt forbear to vow, it shall be no sin in thee. That which is gone out of thy lips thou shalt keep and perform; even a freewill offering, according as thou hast vowed unto the LORD thy God. (Deut 23.21–23)

In the Sermon on the Mount Jesus does not quote any of the Old Testament texts word for word, but summarizes their content in the following words:

Again, ye have heard that it hath been said by them of old, "Thou shalt not forswear thyself, but shalt perform unto the Lord thine oaths." But I say unto you, swear not at all: neither by heaven, for it is God's throne; nor by the earth, for it is his footstool; neither by Jerusalem, for it is the city of the great King. Neither shalt thou swear by thy head, because thou canst not make one hair white or black. But let your communication be, "Yea, yea," "Nay, nay"; for whatsoever is more than these cometh of evil. (Mt 5.33–37)

We do not find direct parallels to this text in any of the Gospels. However, it is repeated in the Epistle of James almost word for word: "But above all things, my brethren, swear not, neither by heaven, neither by the earth, neither by any other oath: but let your yea be yea; and your nay, nay; lest ye fall into condemnation" (Jas 5.12).

"Swear Not at All"

Why did Jesus mention swearing by heaven, earth, and one's own head? By his time the custom of swearing by the Lord had fallen out of use, since the Jews had ceased to say the name of God so as not to break the second commandment of the law of Moses: "Thou shalt not take the name of the LORD thy God in vain, for the LORD will not hold him guiltless that taketh his name in vain" (Ex 20.7; Deut 5.11). Instead of the word "Lord" (Yahweh, Jehovah), the Jews in Jesus' time used euphemisms, such as the word "heaven" (hence the expressions "Father in heaven," "kingdom of heaven").

According to one interpretation of the second commandment, this commandment was directed against oaths in the name of God, while in the wider sense it was a prohibition against any false or unnecessary oaths.[56]

Disputes about the permissibility of oaths, the forms of oaths, and the degree of responsibility for breaking an oath took place in Jesus' time. This is obvious from Jesus' polemics with the Pharisees, who considered it impermissible to swear by the temple in Jerusalem or by its altar, but who swore by the gold of the temple and by that which was on the altar. Jesus harshly condemned them for hypocrisy: in his words, "Whoso therefore shall swear by the altar, sweareth by it, and by all things thereon. And whoso shall swear by the temple, sweareth by it, and by him that dwelleth therein. And he that shall swear by heaven, sweareth by the throne of God, and by him that sitteth thereon" (Mt 23.15–22). Jesus considered the use of such oaths one of the signs of "hypocrisy and iniquity" underneath an external appearance of righteousness (Mt 23.28). Jesus' words can also be understood to mean that the Pharisees considered the *breaking* of oaths impermissible if a person had sworn by Jerusalem or by the temple; if, on the other hand, he had sworn by the altar or the gift lying on the altar, then such an oath, from their point of view, was less binding.

The custom of completely refraining from swearing oaths, which Jesus calls for in the Sermon on the Mount, existed in his time among the Essenes. Josephus writes of the members of this movement: "Whatsoever they say also is firmer than an oath; but swearing is avoided by them, and they esteem it worse than perjury for they say that he who cannot be believed without [swearing by] God is already condemned."[57] At the same time, he points to the custom of giving a whole series of vows when entering the community:

> And before he is allowed to touch their common food, he is obliged to take tremendous oaths, that, in the first place, he will exercise piety towards God, and then that he will observe justice towards men, and that he will do no harm to any one, either of his own accord, or by

[56]Luz, *Matthew 1–7*, 263.
[57]Josephus, *Wars of the Jews* 2.8.6 (trans. Whiston).

the command of others; that he will always hate the wicked, and be assistant to the righteous; that he will ever show fidelity to all men, and especially to those in authority, because no one obtains the government without God's assistance; and that if he be in authority, he will at no time whatever abuse his authority, nor endeavor to outshine his subjects either in his garments, or any other finery; that he will be perpetually a lover of truth, and propose to himself to reprove those that tell lies; that he will keep his hands clear from theft, and his soul from unlawful gains; and that he will neither conceal any thing from those of his own sect, nor discover any of their doctrines to others, no, not though anyone should compel him so to do at the hazard of his life. Moreover, he swears to communicate their doctrines to no one any otherwise than as he received them himself; that he will abstain from robbery, and will equally preserve the books belonging to their sect, and the names of the angels [or messengers]. These are the oaths by which they secure their proselytes to themselves.[58]

Josephus calls these vows an "oath": a member of the community would be excluded if he broke them.[59] The distinction between oaths and vows was also drawn by the rabbis in Jesus' time: an oath was sworn in court to confirm the truth of one's testimony; a vow was offered to God and derived its assurance from the person's voluntary abstention from something.[60]

While in his polemics with the Pharisees Jesus emphasizes the custom of substituting a euphemism for the name of God, in the Sermon on the Mount he speaks of the impermissibility of oaths altogether, particularly oaths sworn by objects over which a person had no power. At the same time, he rephrases the words of the Lord from the book of the prophet Isaiah: "Heaven is my throne, and the earth is my footstool" (Is 66.1). A person must not swear by heaven or earth, because they do not belong to him: their Creator and Master is God.

---

[58]Josephus, *Wars of the Jews* 2.8.7 (trans. Whiston).

[59]Josephus, *Wars of the Jews* 2.8.8 (trans. Whiston).

[60]Joel B. Green, Scot McKnight, and I. Howard Marshall, eds., *Dictionary of Jesus and the Gospels: A Compendium of Contemporary Biblical Scholarship* (Downers Grove, IL: InterVarsity, 1992), 577–578.

Jerusalem, N. A. Yaroshenko, 1892

One cannot swear by Jerusalem because it is "the city of the great King," that is, it is the place where God dwells in his temple. Jesus calls the Jerusalem temple that which belongs to his Father (Lk 2.49), the house of his Father (Jn 2.16), and the house of God (Mt 12.4). Jerusalem is considered the "holy city" (Mt 4.5) precisely because it contains the temple—the place of God's special presence (2 Sam 7.5). God's own "dwelling place" is heaven (1 Kg 8.30, 39, 43, 49). However, the temple was built as a house for God, a place for him to abide in forever (1 Kg 8.13), to which his eyes are open (1 Kg 8.29), and to which people would stretch out their hands so that God would hear their prayer (1 Kg 8.38–39). The custom to pray facing Jerusalem was widespread in Jesus' time; it is preserved up to the present day in Orthodox Judaism.

Why can a man not swear by his own head, that is, by his own life or his own body? This is because he is born, lives, and dies not by his own will: the master of his life, as that of heaven and earth, is God. A man has no power over his own physical constitution: he lives in the body that he has received from God. This is the meaning of Jesus' words that nobody can change the color of his hair or add even a single cubit to his height (Mt 6.27). In our time, people not only dye their hair, but even undergo surgery in order to add a few inches to their height, change their appearance, or change their sex. The idea that each person is the master of his or her own life and the life of his or her potential offspring has led to the spread of suicide, euthanasia, and abortion. For Christians, however, Jesus' words continue to retain their significance, and the teaching of the Church on the impermissibility of such things derives from the worldview expressed by the Founder of the Church himself.

In the patristic tradition, Jesus' words about the impermissibility of oaths were interpreted in different ways. The widespread point of view was that swearing oaths was inadvisable due to the increased risk of oath-breaking. In the words of Gregory the Theologian, swearing oaths is forbidden to Christians because the breaking of an oath and the swearing of a false oath are terrible and intolerable things.[61] John Chrysostom believed that breaking one's oaths was "of the evil one," repugnant to God, while swearing is "an excess . . . something more, and added over and above."[62] On the other hand, Cyril of Alexandria believed that Christ forbade only swearing by the things that he had listed.[63] Furthermore, he refers to the words from the Epistle to the Hebrews: "For men verily swear by the greater, and an oath for confirmation is to them an end of all strife" (Heb 6.16).

The prohibition against swearing in the Christian tradition does not extend to the vows or oaths that a person makes when taking on a specific way of life or when entering holy orders. In particular, upon receiving baptism, a person rejects Satan and promises to be faithful to Christ. When a man and a woman get married, they promise to be faithful to each other: this promise is given in the church, before the priest, in the presence of witnesses. At the ordination of a deacon or a priest, an oath is pronounced before the cross and Gospel. At the ordination of a bishop, the oath is in the form of a detailed confession of faith and contains a promise to observe the canons of the Church.

In the Orthodox tradition, monastic tonsure includes the solemn pronouncement of several vows, which come down to three main ones: poverty, obedience, and chastity (celibacy). These vows are offered voluntarily; this is a necessary condition for the validity of the tonsure. Inasmuch as

---

[61]Gregory of Nazianzus, *Oration 4: First Invective against Julian* (PG 35:661, 664).

[62]John Chrysostom, *Homilies on Matthew* 17.5 (NPNF[1] 10:120).

[63]Cyril of Alexandria, *Fragments on Matthew* 63 (PG 72:380–381).

Taking the Veil,
M. V. Nesterov,
1898

these vows are made to God, no earthly authority, including that of the Church, can release a person from the duty of keeping them. The procedure of laicization of a monk, which is practiced in some churches, is not a blessing from the Church to undo monastic vows, but only an affirmation that the monk in question has violated his vows. This entails canonical consequences, including deposition from holy orders if he was a priest or a deacon, and prohibition of the former monk from entering into a church marriage if he decides to marry.

Monastic vows, in the Orthodox tradition, do not have an "expiration date." In some monastic orders of the Catholic Church, permanent vows are preceded by temporary ones. Thus, for example, Carthusians, after two years of their novitiate, give temporary vows for three years, and then renew them for another two years, and only after that do they give permanent vows, which must be kept for the rest of their lives. In the Protestant tradition, monasticism as such does not exist.

All these examples demonstrate that the Christian tradition has understood the fourth antithesis in the Sermon on the Mount not in the sense of a prohibition against any form of promise or vow, and not in the sense that promises ought not be made, so that they might not be broken later (although the latter interpretation, as we have seen, is encountered in some of the church fathers). There are situations in life or ministries that require a person to take on certain commitments, and promises and vows serve as evidence of this. The public nature of such a promise, made in the presence of witnesses, is intended to guarantee the fulfillment of the commitment that the person has made.

Lies Are from the Evil One

How should we understand this saying of Jesus: "But let your communication be, 'Yea, yea'; 'Nay, nay': for whatsoever is more than these cometh of evil"? It can apply to swearing, but it can also have an independent meaning. It is very likely that the conjunction *de* ("but"), which connects the saying to the preceding words concerning swearing, serves as a transition to the next topic,[64] as often happens in Jesus' speeches. In this case, the saying ought to be understood as a reminder of one's responsibility for one's own words, and a prohibition of lying, where one has one thing in one's mind or heart and another on one's tongue.

A direct prohibition of lying is found in the Old Testament: ". . . neither deal falsely, neither lie one to another" (Lev 19.11). The ninth commandment of the Mosaic law forbids bearing false witness against one's neighbor (Ex 20.16; Deut 5.20). Truth is of divine origin, while lies are from the devil. In Jesus' dialogues with the Jews, God is contrasted with the devil, and truth with lies, the father of which is the devil: "He was a murderer from the beginning, and abode not in the truth, because there is no truth in him. When he speaketh a lie, he speaketh of his own: for he is a liar, and the father of it" (Jn 8.44).

This is how we should understand the concluding part of Jesus' saying as well: "whatsoever is more than these cometh of evil" (or "the evil one"). The Greek word *ponēros*, meaning "evil," "wicked," applies to the devil. The devil acts through lies, tempting people with false promises and hopes

---

[64]The Greek particle *de* can be either adversative or copulative, i.e., it can indicate a contrast ("but") or it can simply join two clauses ("and").—*Ed.*

(Gen 3.13). Human beings should not be like the devil, using lies in their speech or accepting lying as a means to achieve their goals.

In the Christian tradition the prohibition against lying, like the prohibition against swearing, is interpreted in different ways. Answering the question of whether it is possible to lie for a good purpose, Basil the Great writes, "This is not condoned by the decree of the Lord, who said once and for all that lying is *from the devil* . . . making no distinctions between lies."[65] In the words of Abba Dorotheos, "no-one who lies is linked to God."[66] According to John Climacus, "A lie is the destruction of love, and a false oath is a denial of God."[67] That being said, in the ascetic literature, we encounter assertions that lying is permissible under specific circumstances. In the work of the same Climacus we find the paradoxical assertion: "When we are completely cleansed of lying, then we can resort to it, but only with fear and as occasion demands."[68]

Joshua Spares Rahab, engraving, Gustave Doré, 1860s

Under what circumstances could occasion demand the use of lying? In the Bible several such situations are described. Abraham passes Sarah off as his sister (Gen 8.13–19). Jacob lies to acquire his father's blessing for himself (Gen 29.15–30). In both of these instances, the Bible does not give any moral evaluation of these actions. However, in other instances, the Holy Scriptures in fact justify the actions of people who use lies and cunning to save lives. The story of the sojourn of the people of Israel in Egypt mentions the

[65]Basil the Great, *Shorter Responses* 76. English translation from *The Asketikon of St Basil the Great*, by Anna M. Silvas, Oxford Early Christian Studies (Oxford: Oxford University Press, 2005), 316. Italics in original.

[66]Dorotheos of Gaza, *Discourses* 9. English translation from *Discourses and Sayings*, by Dorotheos of Gaza, trans. Eric P. Wheeler, Cistercian Studies Series 33 (Kalamazoo, MI: Cistercian Publications, 1977), 156.

[67]John Climacus, *The Ladder of Divine Ascent* 12.2. English translation from *The Ladder of Divine Ascent*, by John Climacus, trans. Holy Transfiguration Monastery (Boston, MA: Holy Transfiguration Monastery, 2001), 94.

[68]John Climacus, *The Ladder of Divine Ascent* 12.12 (trans. Holy Transfiguration Monastery, 95).

midwives who saved the lives of the Hebrew children by deceiving Pharaoh: for this they received the blessing of God (Ex 1.17–20). Rahab the harlot saved the lives of the two young spies by concealing from the messengers of the king of Jericho the fact that the spies were in her house (Josh 2.1–6); her deed is cited as an example of faith and virtue (Heb 11.31; Jas 2.25). In a similar way, a maidservant saved the life of two of David's messengers: having hidden them in a well, she told Absalom's servants, who were pursuing them, that they had gone the other way (2 Sam 17.18–21).

The words from the Sermon on the Mount that we have examined cannot be understood as an unqualified prohibition of lying under all circumstances.[69] Jesus points to the main principle which ought to guide us in our lives: our words are not to be at variance with our thoughts or deeds. Lying is impermissible as an approach to life. If a person says "yes," it must mean "yes," and "no" must mean "no." This applies to the fulfillment of vows and promises as well.

---

6. Not Resisting
Evil with Violence

The fifth antithesis is a commentary on the following stipulations in the law of Moses: "Thou shalt give life for life, eye for eye, tooth for tooth, hand for hand, foot for foot, burning for burning, wound for wound, stripe for stripe" (Ex 21.23–25); "And if a man cause a blemish in his neighbour; as he hath done, so shall it be done to him: breach for breach, eye for eye, tooth for tooth; as he hath caused a blemish in a man, so shall it be done to him again" (Lev 24.19–20). Using these statements as a starting point, Jesus says:

---

[69]Both St John Chrysostom and St Gregory of Nyssa argue that deception can be used in a blameless or even praiseworthy way; see St John Chrysostom: *Six Books on the Priesthood* 1.8, tr. Graham Neville, Popular Patristics Series 1 [Crestwood, NY: St Vladimir's Seminary Press, 1977], 47–49, and St Gregory of Nyssa: Catechetical Discourse, 26, tr. Ignatius Green, Popular Patristics Series 60 (Yonkers, NY: St Vladimir's Seminary Press, 2019), 117–121. The later western tradition, however, was dominated by St Augustine's opinion, which condemned all lying categorically in *On Lying* and *Against Lying* (NPNF[1] 3:458–500).—*Ed.*

The Sermon on the Mount, Sebastiano Ricci, 1725

Ye have heard that it hath been said, "An eye for an eye, and a tooth for a tooth." But I say unto you, that ye resist not evil; but whosoever shall smite thee on thy right cheek, turn to him the other also. And if any man will sue thee at the law, and take away thy coat, let him have thy cloak also. And whosoever shall compel thee to go a mile, go with him two. Give to him that asketh thee, and from him that would borrow of thee turn not thou away. (Mt 5.38–42)

This passage consists of an utterance in which a general principle is postulated and five concrete examples that illustrate this principle's application. Of these examples, only one—and that only in the most straightforward literal interpretation—concerns the infliction of physical injury and belongs to the legal sphere; the second, too, belongs only to the legal sphere when interpreted literally; the next three do not have anything to do with it.[70]

On the whole, it can be said that the entire passage concentrates not so much on interpreting the law as on establishing new principles for how people should relate to each other in everyday life. Using a quote from the law as a starting point, Jesus leads his listeners to new horizons, proposing to them a new degree of moral perfection:

[70]See John Nolland, *The Gospel of Matthew: A Commentary on the Greek Text*, New International Greek Testament Commentary (Grand Rapids, MI: Eerdmans, 2005), 257.

Thus Moses led [the people] up from the level of iniquity and established [them] at the level of justice. "Do not strike your neighbor unjustly. If he strikes you, seek [vengeance] for yourself, but justly." But our Lord led [you] up from the level of justice and established [you] on the level of grace so that you would not seek [vengeance] from the one *who strikes you on your cheek.* But [instead], *turn the other to him.*[71]

The Law of Proportionate Retribution

The law of Moses was built on the principle of proportionate retribution for harm caused to a person: for material damage, a fine was levied corresponding to the damage inflicted; for bodily injury, a corresponding injury was inflicted on the offender; for murder, the death penalty was given (Ex 24.17–19). In the scholarly literature, this principle was named the "law of retribution" (Latin *lex talionis*, from the word *talis*, which means "of such kind"). The law of retribution existed in various forms in many ancient civilizations and can be traced back to one of the oldest human practices—blood vengeance.

In the law of Moses the principle of retribution was, among other things, limited: in return for putting out someone else's eye, a person could not be deprived of both eyes; neither could he lose several teeth for knocking out a single tooth.[72] The principle of proportionate retribution was important to prevent disproportionate revenge in the sociocultural context described in the Bible. There are more than a few examples of such revenge in the Old Testament. It is sufficient to recall the story of how Jacob's sons, Simeon and Levi, took revenge on the son of a local prince for dishonoring their sister: they persuaded all the men of the city to undergo circumcision, and

[71]Ephrem the Syrian, *Commentary on the Diatessaron* 6.14. English translation from *Saint Ephrem's Commentary on Tatian's Diatessaron: An English Translation of* Chester Beatty *Syriac MS 709 with Introduction and Notes*, by Carmel McCarthy, Journal of Semitic Studies Supplement 2 (Oxford: Oxford University Press, 1993), 116–117. Brackets and emphases in this English translation.

[72]See Christopher J. H. Wright, *Old Testament Ethics for the People of God* (Downers Grove, IL: IVP Academic, 2004), 335n8. For more on the interpretation of the principle of retribution in the Old Testament, the New Testament, and Talmudic Judaism, see Jacob Neusner, Bruce D. Chilton, and Baruch A. Levine, *Torah Revealed, Torah Fulfilled: Scriptural Laws in Formative Judaism and Earliest Christianity* (New York, NY: T&T Clark, 2008), 187–228.

Joseph's Brothers Empty Their Sacks of Bread and Money before Their Father Jacob, mosaic, 12th century

when the men were in pain, Simon and Levi attacked the city, killed the prince and his son with the sword, "slew all the males. . . . spoiled the city. . . . took their sheep, and their oxen, and their asses, and that which was in the city, and that which was in the field, and all their wealth, and all their little ones, and their wives took they captive" (Gen 34.1–29).

The infliction of bodily injury as punishment for a crime was widespread in the ancient world. It is practiced to this day in some countries with Sharia law. Sharia—like its source, Old Testament law—is built on the principle that the degree of punishment must correspond to the crime committed. In the civilized world, inflicting bodily injuries as a punishment is not practiced, but the idea that the punishment should be commensurate with the crime lies at the basis of any legislation, even in those countries where the most severe punishment is imprisonment: the more serious the crime, the longer the term of imprisonment, up to a life sentence.

While he quotes words relating to the legal sphere, Jesus does not comment on their literal meaning. Neither here nor in his other sermons does he dispute the right of state authorities to punish criminals in various ways, or oppose capital punishment, or call for the mitigation of criminal law. In requiring us to "render . . . unto Caesar the things which are Caesar's, and unto God the things that are God's" (Mt 22.21), Jesus draws a clear dividing line between earthly authority and heavenly authority, between earthly laws and the truth of eternal life that he has brought to mankind.

This truth is embedded in his teachings, including in the Sermon on the Mount, which does not contain any call to change the structure of society, but which is filled with calls to transform our inner world, to change the reference points for our values, our worldview, and our way of relating to other people.

It is important to remember that in the Sermon on the Mount Jesus was not addressing the judges of the people of Israel, but his own disciples. Jesus examines situations involving offended and offending parties from the perspective of the one offended, while the Old Testament law examined such situations from the perspective of the offender. By so doing he introduces a new and loftier standard of righteousness than the one characteristic of the Old Testament.[73]

Nonresistance to Evil

Why did Jesus command his listeners not to answer evil with evil? Because evil is not healed by evil: rooting out evil is possible only by opposing it with good. In the case of a conflict between two people, the moral victory, from the Christian point of view, is attained not by the one who succeeds in taking revenge on the offender, but by the one who prevents the conflict from continuing by making concessions, including by sacrificing his or her own interests. In the view of society, such a person may appear to have been defeated, but his personal victory over evil has a greater meaning for him than the personal interests that might have been put at a disadvantage in this situation.

The transformation of society begins with an internal change that takes place in a concrete person. In the long term, Jesus' moral teaching had an impact not only on individual people such as his followers and the members of the Church that he founded: it had an impact on the value system that lies at the basis of the legislation of all the countries whose history is connected with the Christian tradition. The ideals of humaneness and mercy, which are characteristic of the legal system of modern civilized states,

[73]James F. Davis, *Lex Talionis in Early Judaism and the Exhortation of Jesus in Matthew 5.38–42*, Journal for the Study of the New Testament, Supplement Series 281 (New York, NY: T&T Clark International, 2005), 4.

among other things, trace their roots to Christian moral teaching. The very idea of criminal punishment as a way to correct the offender, which lies at the basis of modern jurisprudence, was alien to the Old Testament, in which punishment was viewed primarily as vengeance (Deut 19.19), or as a way to deter others (Deut 13.11; 17.13; 19.20), or as a means to "put the evil away" from the midst of the people (Deut 13.5; 17.7, 12; 19.19; 21.21; 22.21–24; 24.7).

The Sermon on the Mount, engraving, Gustave Doré, 1860s

The world would be different today if Jesus had never delivered his Sermon on the Mount and his other sermons. Many centuries were needed for Christian moral ideals to be absorbed into the flesh and blood of human society. Many of these ideals, however, are viewed to this day as difficult to fulfill, especially if they are understood literally.

The words "resist not evil" (or "the evil one") have a verbal similarity with the Old Testament prescriptions according to which evil was to be purged from the midst of the people of Israel through proportionate retribution against the evildoer for the crime committed (Deut 19.15–21).[74] Beyond the external similarity, however, the profound difference in meaning is obvious. While it was precisely proportionate retribution that the Old Testament saw as the main way of fighting violence and injustice, Jesus proposes a different way that is directly antithetical: evil must be eradicated not with the help of evil, but with the help of good.

Jesus' abovementioned saying has a rich history of interpretation in the Christian tradition.[75] John Chrysostom notes:

> For this cause he hath also subjoined, "But I say unto you, that ye resist not the evil one." He did not say, "resist not your brother," but "the evil one," signifying that on his motion men dare so to act; and in this way

---

[74]See Willard M. Swartley, *Covenant of Peace: The Missing Piece in New Testament Theology and Ethics*, Studies in Peace and Scripture 9 (Grand Rapids, MI: Eerdmans, 2006), 60.

[75]See Dale C. Allison Jr., *The Sermon on the Mount: Inspiring the Moral Imagination*, Companions to the New Testament (New York, NY: Crossroad, 1999), 92–106.

relaxing and secretly removing most of our anger against the aggressor, by transferring the blame to another.

"What then?" it is said, "ought we not to resist the evil one?" Indeed we ought, but not in this way, but as He hath commanded, by giving one's self up to suffer wrongfully; for thus shalt thou prevail over him. For one fire is not quenched by another, but fire by water.[76]

Who is the "evil one" spoken of here? First of all, we must point out that for the word rendered "evil one" here, the Greek uses the same word *ponēros*, which in other places is used to refer to the devil (in this sense it was used two verses before this, at the end of the fourth antithesis). In the given instance, the evil one is not the devil; the idea of not resisting the devil must be immediately excluded, since it contradicts the Christian teaching regarding the necessity of resisting the devil (Jas 4.5; 1 Pet 5.9–10; Eph 6.11). What is being spoken of is also not some abstract evil, inasmuch as the word *ponēros* is used with a definite article, which points to a concrete bearer of evil, to a personification of evil. In the given instance, the "evil one" refers to any offender, any person who deliberately inflicts harm on others.

The advice that Jesus gives relates not to the legal sphere, but to the sphere of interpersonal relations. How literally should we understand his advice? Even ancient commentators noted that a slap is usually given to the left cheek, and not to the right: in order to strike the right cheek, one has to be left-handed. Some saw in this an indication that Jesus' words should not be understood in a literal sense.[77] However, in ancient Israel, it was a strike on the right cheek using the back of the right hand that was considered the most insulting (this custom is preserved to this day in some Middle Eastern societies).

We also note that in the parallel passage in Luke the saying is given in a somewhat different, condensed version: "And unto him that smiteth thee on the one cheek offer also the other; and him that taketh away thy cloak

---

[76]John Chrysostom, *Homilies on Matthew* 18.1 (NPNF[1] 10:124).

[77]Origen, *On First Principles* 4.3.3. English translation from *On First Principles*, by Origen, trans. G. W. Butterworth, ed. Tania M. Geist (Notre Dame, IN: Ave Maria Press, 2013), 389–391.

forbid not to take thy coat also. Give to every man that asketh of thee; and of him that taketh away thy goods ask them not again" (Lk 6.29–30). Here nothing is said of the right cheek; regarding the taking of one's cloak, nothing is said about it being the result of a legal procedure. In Matthew's version, on the contrary, the threat of the confiscation of one's personal property is regarded as the consequence of a legal procedure; it is not recommended to let matters get to this point. This recommendation echoes Jesus' words from earlier in the Sermon on the Mount: "Agree with thine adversary quickly, while thou art on the way with him; lest at any time the adversary deliver thee to the judge, and the judge deliver thee to the officer, and thou be cast into prison" (Mt 5.25). Rather than seeking legal protection for one's personal property, Jesus asks his disciples to simply give up their property.

While the first image (being struck on the right cheek) is about nonresistance to evil, and the second (one's clothing being taken away) is about voluntarily refusing to defend one's property rights, the third image is about the rendering of services: to the one who demands one service, it is necessary to render another as well. Jesus' words about how one has to go two miles with the person who wants to go one mile (*milion*),[78] which are not found in Luke's version, are dedicated precisely to this idea.[79]

At least four foundational principles of human communal life are disputed in this passage: the right to self-defense, the right to defend one's honor and dignity,[80] the right to defend one's property, and the principle that one need provide only the specific service asked of one.

---

[78] This refers to a Roman mile, which is about 4850 ft.

[79] "The first mile renders to Caesar the things that are Caesar's; the second mile . . . renders to God the things that are God's," notes T. W. Manson, bearing in mind that the principle introduced by Jesus surpasses the normal standards of universal human morality and brings interpersonal relationships into the religious plane. T. W. Manson, *The Sayings of Jesus: As Recorded in the Gospels according to St. Matthew and St. Luke; Arranged with Introduction and Commentary* (London: SCM, 1949), 160.

[80] See Jerome H. Neyrey, *Honor and Shame in the Gospel of Matthew* (Louisville, KY: Westminster John Knox, 1998), 203–208.

Christian Pacifism?

How literally should we understand Jesus' exhortation to not resist evil with force? Does it apply to Christians of all classes and professions? In particular, can a Christian serve in the army, defend his country with weapons in his hands, and kill people in order to save those close to him? At the turn of the the twentieth century, Leo Tolstoy vigorously preached radical pacifism. In his book *The Way of Life*,[81] Tolstoy quotes another pacifist, the American pastor Adin Ballou (1803–1890). The latter writes in his *Non-Resistant Catechism*:

> A Christian has not authority to take life, or inflict injury on injurious fellow man in any case whatsoever.
> Q. Could he not kill or maim another in self-defense?
> A. No.
> Q. Could he not enter a complaint before a magistrate with a view to get his injurer punished?
> A. No; for what he does through others he virtually does himself.
> Q. Can he not fight in the army or navy of his country against foreign enemies, or against domestic insurrectionists?
> A. Certainly not. He can take no part in war or military tactics. He cannot use deadly weapons. He cannot resist injury with injury, alone or in company, by himself or by others.[82]

The ideas of Ballou and Tolstoy are in many ways akin to anarchism, and both authors based their ideas on the teachings of Christ. In the twentieth century the Mennonite[83] theologian John Yoder preached radical pacifism (1927–1997). In his opinion, military service is contrary to Christianity, and the only correct answer to the military draft, for a Christian, is refusal:

> Many persons, when they hear of Christians whose conscience forbids their bearing arms, will argue against this position on the grounds that

---

[81]Leo Tolstoy, *Polnoe sobranie sochineniy* [Complete works], 90 vols. (Moscow: Gos. izd-vo khudozh. lit-ry, 1928–1958), 56:276. Translation by present translator.

[82]http://www.adinballou.org/catechism.shtml.

[83]The Mennonites are a Protestant denomination that arose in the 1530s, named after their founder, Menno Simons. According to Mennonite beliefs, Christians cannot take up arms.

it is quite unrealistic to expect nations to follow this example. This is a strange argument. In our teachings about moral purity and holiness in any other realm, we do not wait for the world to be ready to follow us before we follow Christ. We know clearly that to be called by Christ means being different from the world.

How then should our living the disarmed life depend on whether nations are ready to lay down their weapons? Jesus predicted that there would continue to be wars as long as this world lasts, just as he predicted that people's faith would grow cold and their morals loose. But this cannot be a reason for Christians to follow this world's ways, any more than the prevalence of theft or of waste is a model for Christians to follow.[84]

Refusal to serve in the army due to religious convictions is practiced in certain modern religious communities and sects. However, the overwhelming majority of Christians—Orthodox, Catholics, and Protestants—proceed from a different understanding of the Christian teaching. They perceive Jesus' calls in the Sermon on the Mount to make peace and not to resist evil with force as pertaining to the sphere of interpersonal relationships and not extending to the situation of war: in that situation, special conditions apply.

Nevertheless, many scholars who undertake to interpret the Gospel of Matthew incline toward a pacifist interpretation of Jesus' words in the Sermon on the Mount. Ulrich Luz sees in them an expression of "Christian passivity."[85] In his opinion, "the decisions in the major churches" regarding the acceptability of Christians serving in the army and participating in war "show how great the danger was that responsible participation in secular power meant that the proclamation of the reign of God was blurred and that for all practical purposes these commandments of Jesus that belong to it were abolished."[86] The American scholar Richard Hays, for his part, asserts, "[The] evidence, taken cumulatively, suggests that the New Testament writers did not see participation in the army as sinful a priori. . . . [T]here is nothing within the New Testament itself that explicitly excludes

[84] John H. Yoder, *He Came Preaching Peace* (Scottdale, PA: Herald, 1985), 26–27.
[85] Luz, *Matthew 1–7*, 276.
[86] Luz, *Matthew 1–7*, 281.

or forbids [military] careers."[87] At the same time, in his opinion, "the New Testament offers no basis forever declaring Christian participation in war 'just.' If that be true . . . the church's majority tradition, however venerable, must be rejected or corrected in light of the New Testament's teaching."[88]

The Example of Jesus

In order to understand how Jesus' teaching on nonresistance to evil can be applied in practice, we must look at his own example, and then at how this teaching is interpreted in the Christian tradition.

On the one hand, we see in Jesus an example of not resisting evil by force. The culmination of this nonresistance was his death on the cross. It is precisely the cross that has become the key proof that the commandment to not resist evil can be fulfilled:

> Indeed, what Jesus says to his disciples would all be pure Enthusiasm if we were to understand these statements to be a general ethical program, if we were to interpret the statement that evil will only be conquered by good as general secular wisdom for life in the world. That really would be an irresponsible imagining of laws which the world would never obey. Nonresistance as a principle for secular life is godless destruction of the order of the world which God graciously preserves. But it is not a programmatic thinker who is speaking here. Rather, the one speaking here about overcoming evil with suffering is he who himself was overcome by evil on the cross and who emerged from that defeat as the conqueror and victor. There is no other justification for this commandment of Jesus than his own cross.[89]

On the other hand, when we look at individual episodes from Jesus' life, we hardly see in him unconditional passivity before evil and aggression. While knowing that he had to die for mankind, he nevertheless made efforts to save his life. The beginning of his ministry is marked by an episode related by Luke: Jesus' words in the synagogue in Capernaum elicited the

[87]Hays, *Moral Vision of the New Testament*, 335.
[88]Hays, *Moral Vision of the New Testament*, 341.
[89]Bonhoeffer, *Discipleship*, 106.

Christ on the Cross, Peter Paul Rubens, 1627

rage of his listeners, who "rose up, and thrust him out of the city, and led him unto the brow of the hill whereon their city was built, that they might cast him down headlong. But he, passing through the midst of them, went his way" (Lk 4.28–30). The Gospel of John tells of an incident in which the Jews wanted to stone Jesus, but he asked them: "Many good works have I showed you from my Father; for which of those works do ye stone me?" (Jn 10.31–32). Then they attempted to seize him, but he "escaped out of their hand" (Jn 10.39).

In these episodes Jesus hardly comes across as a passive pacifist: he comes across as a man who does not resist evil with force, but at the same time does not capitulate in the face of evil but tries to prove that he is in the right. In two instances, he saves his own life, which is necessary because his time "is not yet come" (Jn 7.6); that is, he has not yet fulfilled to the end the mission foreordained for him.

The passion narrative gives us additional examples. The Gospel of Luke records the dialogue between Jesus and his disciples that took place not long before his arrest:

> And he said unto them, "When I sent you without purse, and bag, and shoes, lacked ye any thing?" And they said, "Nothing." Then said he unto them, "But now, he that hath a purse, let him take it, and likewise his bag; and he that hath no sword, let him sell his garment, and buy one. For I say unto you, that this that is written must yet be accomplished in me, 'And he was reckoned among the transgressors'; for the things concerning me have an end." And they said, "Lord, behold, here are two swords." And he said unto them, "It is enough." (Lk 22.35–38)

From this episode it follows that, anticipating Jesus' arrest, some of his disciples viewed armed resistance as a possible reaction to the coming events. The traditional interpretation of the Church understands the instruction to buy a sword as a metaphorical call to watchfulness. The answer of the disciples, as in many other instances, demonstrates that they did not understand the meaning of the Teacher's words. Nevertheless, we see that among the disciples two real swords appear, and Jesus does not forbid his disciples to carry them. One of these swords would later figure in the episode of the cutting off of the ear of the high priest's servant (Mt 26.51–54; Mk 14.47; Lk 22.49–50; Jn 18.10–11).

The Gospel of John tells of how when the high priest's servant struck Jesus on the cheek, Jesus said: "If I have spoken evil, bear witness of the evil; but if well, why smitest thou me?" (Jn 18.23). In response to the slap, not only did Jesus not turn the other cheek, but he even disputed the right of the high priest to strike him.[90]

Jesus' conduct in all the incidents mentioned above is difficult to identify with the unconditional pacifism that assumes complete passivity in the face of evil.

[90]See Neumann, *New Heart*, 110.

Eighteen Scenes from the Life of Christ, Netherlands, 15th century

The Christian Understanding of Nonresistance to Evil

The apostle Paul's Epistle to the Romans is an important commentary on Jesus' words from the Sermon on the Mount. Addressing the young Christian community founded in the heart of the empire in the immediate vicinity of the emperor and government authorities, Paul writes:

> Bless them which persecute you: bless, and curse not. . . . Recompense to no man evil for evil. Give thought to what is good in the sight of all men. If it be possible, as much as lieth in you, live peaceably with all men. Dearly beloved, avenge not yourselves, but rather give place unto God's wrath: for it is written, "'Vengeance is mine; I will repay,' saith the Lord." Therefore if thine enemy hunger, feed him; if he thirst, give him drink; for in so doing thou shalt heap coals of fire on his head. Be not overcome by evil, but overcome evil with good. (Rom 12.14, 17–21)

This exhortation displays similarities, in some places verbal, to Jesus' teaching presented in the Sermon on the Mount. However, Paul significantly clarifies Jesus' words: a person must not avenge himself, because God himself will avenge him. Continuing to develop his thoughts, Paul calls for obedience to higher authorities, "for there is no power but of God: the powers that be are ordained by God." He is speaking of earthly authorities, and resisting them would mean resisting what God has established.

The ruler "beareth not the sword in vain: for he is the minister of God, a revenger to execute wrath upon him that doeth evil." Therefore one must be subject to the authorities "not only for wrath, but also for conscience's sake" (Rom 13.1–5). In this way, according to Paul, the Christian's fulfillment of the fundamental moral principles derived from Jesus' teachings must be combined with loyalty to the civil authorities. Christian laws do not abolish earthly legislation, but complement it.

Regarding service in the army, different views existed among early Christian writers. Tertullian mentions Christian soldiers who served in the army of Marcus Aurelius.[91] Addressing the Roman rulers, Tertullian writes:

> We are but of yesterday, and we have filled every place among you—cities, islands, fortresses, towns, market-places, the very camp, tribes, companies, palace, senate, forum—we have left nothing to you but the temples of your gods. For what wars should we not be fit, not eager, even with unequal forces, we who so willingly yield ourselves to the sword?[92]

From these words, it follows that Christians in Tertullian's time served in the army (the term "camp" refers to military units). In later works, however, Tertullian changed his view on the permissibility of military service for Christians: "For albeit soldiers had come unto John, and had received the formula of their rule; albeit, likewise, a centurion had believed; still the Lord afterward, in disarming Peter, unbelted every soldier. No dress is lawful among us, if assigned to any unlawful action."[93] By the time these words were written, Tertullian had already left the Church and joined the sect of the Montanists.[94] A negative attitude to military service was also held by Origen, who wrote, "None fight better for the king than we do. We do not

---

[91]Tertullian, *To Scapula* 4 (ANF 3:107).

[92]Tertullian, *Apology* 37 (ANF 3:45).

[93]Tertullian, *On Idolatry* 19 (ANF 3:73).

[94]In Corpus Christianorum, Series Latina, Tertullian's work *On Idolatry* is placed in the volume *Opera montanistica* (CCSL 2:1099–1124). Montanism was a Christian sect of the second century, named after its founder, Montanus. The sect was distinguished by its extreme strictness in moral questions and its rejection of the ecclesiastical hierarchy and sacraments.

indeed fight under him, although he require it; but we fight on his behalf, forming a special army—an army of piety—by offering our prayers to God."[95]

The few instances of refusal to serve in the military that are known to us from the early Christian period were motivated by the fact that this service was connected to the cult of the emperor, who was worshipped and to whom sacrifices were offered by soldiers in the military. Christians refused to participate in these rites, and for this they were subjected to persecution: some Christian soldiers became martyrs for this reason.

The equestrian statue of Marcus Aurelius in the Capitoline Hill in Rome

During the reign of the emperor Constantine, the Church's attitude to military service became more positive. This was helped to no small degree by the Christianization of society, the government, and the army itself that began under his reign. Already in 314 the Council of Arles excommunicated Christians who refused military service in peacetime. At that time, the army was still primarily pagan. Toward the end of the fourth century, it became predominantly Christian, and after 416, when the Emperor Theodosius II decreed the exclusion of pagans from the army, it became completely Christian. At the beginning of the fifth century, Augustine formulated the theory of "just war." According to his teaching, every war is a calamity, but wars can be better or worse, just or unjust.[96]

It was approximately during this period that military service began to be considered a important labor of faith.[97] Over time, the words that Jesus said

[95]Origen, *Against Celsus* 8.73 (ANF 4:668).

[96]Augustine of Hippo, *City of God* 19.7 (NPNF[1] 2:405).

[97]A vivid example of this is Ambrose of Milan's praise of the army of emperor Gratian. In his parting words to the emperor when the latter went to war with the Goths, Ambrose affirmed that God would give the Christian army victory over the impious barbarians and thereby fulfill the Old Testament prophecy of the defeat of Gog (Ezek 39.3–16). See Ambrose of Milan, *Exposition of the Christian Faith* 2.16 (NPNF[2] 10:241–242). [But St Ambrose was no sycophant, and he serves as an important example that the Church did not succumb to the temptation to cow to imperial power. St Ambrose condemned Emperor Theodosius I's unjust use of violence to put down a riot in Thessalonica in 390. He insisted that the emperor do public penance for many

of himself, "Greater love hath no man than this, that a man lay down his life for his friends" (Jn 15.13), began to be applied to soldiers who had given their lives for the sake of others. In *The Life of Constantine the Philosopher*, we find the following episode from the dispute between St Cyril (also called Constantine), the Enlightener of the Slavs (ninth century), and the Muslims:

> [The Arabs asked,] "But if Christ is your God, why do you not do as He commands? For in the Gospels it is written: 'Pray for your enemies, do good to them that hate you and persecute you, and unto them that smite you turn your cheek!' [Mt 5.44; Lk 6.27]. You are not like that but, on the contrary, you sharpen weapons against those who treat you in such a manner."
>
> In answer to this the Philosopher said: "If the law contains two precepts, who appears to fulfill the law? He who keeps one precept, or both?"
>
> They answered: "Obviously he who keeps both."
>
> The Philosopher then said: "God said: 'Pray for them which despitefully use you' [Lk 6.27–29; Mt 5.39, 44]. And He also said: 'Greater love hath no man than this, that a man lay down his life for his friends' [Jn 15.13]. We do this for the sake of friends, lest their souls be captured together with their bodies."[98]

months before being admitted to the Eucharist, and Theodosius complied. See Sozomen, *Ecclesiastical History* 7.25 (NPNF² 2:393–94); Theodoret, *Ecclesiastical History* 5.17 (NPNF² 3:143–45); and St Ambrose' *Letter 51* to Emperor Theodosius (NPNF² 10:450–53), in which he also uses Old Testament imagery: here to compare the emperor's bloodshed to David's sin of murder (and, by implication, comparing his role as bishop to the prophet Nathaniel).—*Ed.*]

[98]Marvin Kantor and Richard S. White, trans., *The Vita of Constantine and the Vita of*

The works of early Christian writers compare the laws by which the Christian community lived with the laws of the pagan world. Arguing against Julian the Apostate, Gregory the Theologian says that the Christian law commands "neither to resist injury nor to go to law, nor to possess anything at all, nor to consider anything one's own, but to live in the other world, and to despise things present as though they were not; neither is it lawful for anyone to return evil for evil, but when they are smitten on the one cheek to turn the other also to the smiter, and to be stripped of the coat after the cloak."[99] The

St Mercurius Killing Julian the Apostate, Coptic icon

contrast between pagan laws and Christian morality arises from the fact that Christians are called to "live in the other world"; that is to say, while living among ordinary people and being subject to earthly laws, they are to live in accordance with other, higher moral precepts.

The moral rules that Jesus gives apply first of all within the Church— the community of his disciples. But a Christian cannot be such only among people like himself: he must embody Christian moral principles among people alien to these principles as well. This is why the conduct of Christians puzzled pagans and required an apology at each new stage of the Church's existence.

"Give to Him That Asketh Thee"

The fifth antithesis concludes with the following words: "Give to him that asketh thee, and from him that would borrow of thee turn not thou away." This commandment is repeated almost word for word in the Sermon on the Plain in the Gospel of Luke (Lk 6.30), where it is embedded in the teaching that corresponds with the sixth antithesis in the Sermon on the Mount. However, in Luke, the following words are added to the text that we read in

Methodius, Michigan Slavic Materials 13 (Ann Arbor, MI: Dept. of Slavic Languages and Literature, University of Michigan, 1976), 17.

[99]Gregory of Nazianzus, *Oration 4, Against Julian*. English translation from *Julian the Emperor, Containing Gregory Nazianzen's Two Invectives and Libanius' Monody, with Julian's Extant Theosophical Works*, trans. C. W. King (London: George Bell and Sons, 1888), 64.

Christ the All-Merciful, icon, 13th century

Matthew: "And if ye lend to them of whom ye hope to receive, what thank have ye? For sinners also lend to sinners, to receive as much again. But . . . lend, hoping for nothing again, and your reward shall be great. . . . Be ye therefore merciful, as your Father also is merciful" (Lk 6.34–36).

If we hold to the hypothesis that Matthew and Luke used a common source that Luke abbreviated, it is not fully clear why Matthew lacks the words that appear in Luke. It is also unclear why the ending of the above quote from Luke differs from the parallel text in Matthew: "Be ye therefore perfect, even as your Father which is in heaven is perfect" (Mt 5.48). The term "merciful" (*oiktirmōn*) differs from the term "perfect" (*teleios*) in meaning.

The words "give to him that asketh thee" are a general rule that can apply to any request. As for the words "from him that would borrow of thee turn not thou away," these apply to a more particular situation, which in the Sermon on the Mount is left without further clarification. In the Sermon on the Plain in Luke, we receive a clarification that demonstrates that here, too, Jesus is revising the fundamental principles of the Mosaic law. The law speaks of forgiveness, which consists of this: "Every creditor that lendeth anything unto his neighbor shall release it; he shall not exact it of his neighbor, or of his brother; because it is called the LORD's release." However, such forgiveness took place once in seven years and was not extended to foreigners (Deut 15.1–3). Jesus transforms a personal provision of the law into a universal principle.

7. Loving One's Enemies

The series of antitheses, in which Jesus contrasts his own teaching with the Old Testament prescriptions, concludes with the following words on loving one's enemies:

> Ye have heard that it hath been said, "Thou shalt love thy neighbor, and hate thine enemy." But I say unto you, love your enemies, bless them that curse you, do good to them that hate you, and pray for them which despitefully use you, and persecute you; that ye may be the children of your Father which is in heaven. For he maketh his sun to rise on the evil and on the good, and sendeth rain on the just and on the unjust.
>
> For if ye love them which love you, what reward have ye? Do not even the publicans the same? And if ye salute your brethren only,

what do ye more than others? Do not even the publicans do so? (Mt 5.43–47)

The saying to which Jesus refers is not found in the Old Testament. The closest equivalent is from the book of Leviticus: "Thou shalt not avenge, nor bear any grudge against the children of thy people, but thou shalt love thy neighbor as thyself" (Lev 19.18). The word "neighbor" (Hebrew *rēᵃʻ*) here is understood to refer to a compatriot, a representative of the people of Israel, who believes in one God: this exhortation in the book of Leviticus does not extend to foreigners and pagans. In the Sermon on the Mount Jesus takes up only the semantic core from this saying, "love thy neighbor"; all the rest he leaves aside. In other instances, however, he cites a fuller variant of this commandment: "Thou shalt love thy neighbor as thyself" (Mt 22.39; Mk 12.31).

This variant of the commandment is encountered in Jesus' conversation with the lawyer who, testing Jesus, asks, "Master, which is the great commandment in the law?" Jesus answers: "'Thou shalt love the Lord thy God with all thy heart, and with all thy soul, and with all thy mind.' This is the first and great commandment. And the second is like unto it, 'Thou shalt love thy neighbor as thyself.' On these two commandments hang all the law and the prophets" (Mt 22.35–40). In the parallel narrative in Mark, Jesus, having quoted the two fundamental commandments, says to the lawyer: "There is no other commandment greater than these" (Mk 12.28–34).

We find the same story in Luke, but here the lawyer's question is formulated differently: "Master, what shall I do to inherit eternal life?" Jesus answers the question with a question: "What is written in the law? How readest thou?" In Luke's version, the commandment to love God and one's neighbor is articulated by the lawyer himself. Jesus responds with the following words: "Thou hast answered right: this do, and thou shalt live." But the lawyer is not satisfied; he asks, "And who is my neighbor?" (Lk 10.25–29). In response, Jesus offers the parable of how a certain man fell into the hands of robbers, who stripped and beat him; the priest and Levite passing by did not help the man, but only the Samaritan, who saw him, took pity on him, bound up his wounds, and took him to an inn. Jesus concludes the parable with a question: "Which now of these three, think-est thou, was neighbor unto him that fell among the thieves?" The lawyer answers, "He that showed mercy on him." Jesus says to him, "Go, and do thou likewise" (Lk 10.30–37).

We must take all this material into account in order to understand the meaning that Jesus has invested into the commandment to love one's neighbor. First, he asserts that this is one of the two key commandments of the law of Moses: together, the commandments to love God and love one's neighbor make up the moral core of "the law and the prophets." Second, Jesus understands "neighbor" to refer not only to people of the same faith and tribe: one's neighbor is anyone who needs help, concern, and care.

In this way, starting out from the letter of the Old Testament, Jesus reveals its spirit, imbuing the commandment of the Mosaic law with com-pletely different content than that which was originally placed in it. The usual behavioral norm that emphasizes the necessity of solidarity between members of the same nation is transformed by Jesus into a fundamen-tal moral principle that ought to extend to all people regardless of their nationality and religion.

We do not find the words "hate thine enemy" as such in the Old Tes-tament. It is possible that the saying "Thou shalt love thy neighbor, and hate thine enemy" was used by Jewish rabbis and was familiar to those to whom Jesus was addressing the Sermon on the Mount. We find a similar instruction in the Qumran "Community Rule": "Love all the sons of light, each according to his lot in God's design, and hate all the sons of darkness, each according to his guilt in God's vengeance. . . . These are the rules of conduct for the Master in those times with respect to his loving and hat-ing. Everlasting hatred in a spirit of secrecy for the men of perdition!"[100] Nevertheless, this text cannot be considered a direct parallel to the saying that Jesus quotes.[101]

---

[100] 1QS 1.9–11; 9.21–22. English translation from *The Complete Dead Sea Scrolls in English*, by Geza Vermes, rev. ed. (New York, NY: Penguin, 2011), 99, 111.

[101] It has been proposed that Mt 5.17 and 5.43 came about in the context of "Jesus' encounter with Essene concepts" (Kurt Schubert, "The Sermon on the Mount and the Qumran Texts," in *The Scrolls and the New Testament*, ed. K. Stendahl [New York, NY: Harper & Brothers, 1957], 121), but we do not have evidence of such an encounter.

The Sermon on the Mount, P. V. Basin, 1843–1855

In its content, the expression, "Thou shalt love thy neighbor, and hate thine enemy," though lacking a direct analogue in the law of Moses, fully agrees with the general moral setting of the Old Testament, where the term "enemy" (Hebrew *ōyēḇ*) is used with two basic meanings: (a) the enemy of the people of Israel, that is, every nation that undertakes military action against Israel, or its potential adversary, in the broad sense of any other nation; (b) the personal enemy of a particular person. God's blessing is expressed through God delivering a person's enemies into his hands (Gen 14.20; 22.17; 24.60; 49.8). But this happens only if a person is faithful to God: "But if thou shalt indeed obey his voice, and do all that I speak; then I will be an enemy unto thine enemies, and an adversary unto thine adversaries" (Ex 23.22). The ancient Jews sincerely believed that if they observed Gods commandments, God would make their enemies his own enemies.

Very few texts in the Old Testament propose a humane attitude toward one's enemies (Ex 23.4–5; Prov 24.17–18; 25.21–22). In the overwhelming majority of cases when the Bible mentions enemies, this mention has a pronounced negative overtone. The psalms of King David are full of complaints against his enemies, prayers for victory over them, and even reproaches addressed to God for allowing the righteous to be overcome by their enemies. We will provide only a few examples from the beginning and end of the Psalter:

> O Lord, why are they multiplied that afflict me? Many rise up against me. Many say unto my soul: There is no salvation for him in his God. . . . Arise, O Lord, save me, O my God, for thou hast smitten all who without cause are mine enemies; the teeth of sinners hast thou broken. (Ps 3.2–3, 8)

Let all mine enemies be greatly put to shame and be troubled, let them be turned back, and speedily be greatly put to shame. (Ps 6.11)

Arise, O Lord, in thine anger, exalt thyself to the furthest boundaries of thine enemies. (Ps 7.7)

How long, O Lord, wilt thou utterly forget me? How long wilt thou turn thy face away from me? . . . How long shall mine enemy be exalted over me? Look upon me, hear me, O Lord my God; . . . Lest at any time mine enemy say: I have prevailed against him. They that afflict me will rejoice if I am shaken. (Ps 12.2–5)

. . . keep me, O Lord, as the apple of thine eye. In the shelter of thy wings wilt thou shelter me, from the face of the ungodly which have oppressed me. Mine enemies have surrounded my soul . . . (Ps 16.8–9)

Though I should walk in the midst of affliction, thou shalt quicken me; against the wrath of mine enemies hast thou stretched forth thy hands, and thy right hand hath saved me. (Ps 137.7)

For the enemy hath persecuted my soul; he hath humbled my life down to the earth. He hath sat me in darkness as those that have been long dead. . . . Rescue me from mine enemies, O Lord; unto thee have I fled for refuge. (Ps 142.3, 9)

Hatred of their enemies was not simply a characteristic of the ancient Hebrews: it was a part of their identity, their outlook on the world. One can only imagine the astonishment and indignation that the Pharisees and lawyers felt at Jesus' call to love your enemies, bless those who curse you, do good to those to hate you, and pray for those who offend and persecute you. This call overturned their fundamental attitude to life, radically diverged from the spirit and letter of the law of Moses, and required of them a re-evaluation of their own pattern of behavior in everyday life:

Loving one's enemies is not only an unbearable offense to the natural person. It demands more than the strength a natural person can muster, and it offends the natural concept of good and evil. But even more important, loving one's enemies appears to people living according to the law to be a sin against God's law itself. Separation from enemies and condemning them is what the law demands. But Jesus takes God's law into his hands and interprets it. To overcome enemies by loving them—that is God's will which is contained in the law.[102]

Aside from that, this call had a sociopolitical dimension: for the Pharisees, to reject the idea that other nations were enemies of their own nation and that pagans and foreigners were enemies of God, meant none other than to completely lose the ground under their feet, be deprived of one of the key components of their history, and lose their motivation to fight against Roman occupation. The fact that Jesus used foreigners and people of other faiths as examples in his speeches, be it the Samaritan (Lk 10.33), the Roman centurion (Mt 8.5–10; Lk 7.2–9), the pagan widow of Sarepta, or Naaman the Syrian, also a pagan (Lk 4.25–27), elicited irritation, anger, and hatred from his listeners from among the Pharisees and lawyers. In response to one such speech they nearly threw him off a mountain (Lk 4.29).

Through his commandment Jesus is first and foremost attempting to widen his listeners' framework of thinking, to make them understand that his teaching has universal scope. Jesus does not oppose love for one's enemies to love for one's neighbors; he broadens the concept of "neighbor" in *including* enemies in this concept. The one who loves only those who love him differs in no way from the tax collectors; the one who greets only his brothers differs in no way from the pagans; thus it is in the Sermon on the Mount. In the Sermon on the Plain the parallel passage reads somewhat differently: "For if ye love them which love you, what thank have ye? For sinners also love those that love them. And if ye do good to them which do good to you, what thank have ye? For sinners also do even the same" (Lk 6.32–33). In Matthew, Jesus contrasts the one who fulfills the commandment with tax collectors and pagans; in Luke the contrast is with sinners. The Matthean "if ye salute your brethren only," which has a fairly narrow

---

[102]Bonhoeffer, *Discipleship*, 108.

Christ Preaching, the Great Lavra, Mount Athos, Byzantine Empire, 13th century

sense, is replaced in Luke by the broader and more comprehensive "if ye do good to them which do good to you."

The basic idea in both cases can be conveyed in the following way: our attitude toward someone should not depend on his attitude toward us; love should not be merely mutual; good cannot be merely reciprocal. In displaying love and in doing good works, the Christian is called to take a proactive, not reactive, position: he should not simply react to the feelings and behavior of others, but should himself become a source of love and good.

This is the conduct that Jesus himself displayed. Thousands of people streamed to him, and he associated with them, healed their diseases, delved into their needs, and showed them love and mercy without expecting love in return or rewards for doing good. Not a single category of people was excluded from his attention and love, including the tax collectors and prostitutes. Even the Pharisees and lawyers were not deprived of his care: while he took a harsh and uncompromising stand against Pharisaism, condemning its most ugly manifestations, Jesus did not refuse to associate with Pharisees and lawyers, answer their questions, visit their homes, and recline at the same table with them. As for the commandment to pray for those who offend and persecute us, he fulfilled it literally when he prayed on the cross for those who were crucifying him: "Father, forgive them; for they know not what they do" (Lk 23.34).

In the New Testament "love" (*agapē*) is one of the fundamental terms that are key to understanding Jesus' entire worldview. The Christian understanding of love is revealed most fully in the corpus of John's writings—his Gospel and Epistles. The Sermon on the Mount, in contrast to the Fourth Gospel, does not contain a holistic theology of love. The Sermon on the Mount speaks of one of the manifestations of love: love for one's enemies. But it is one's ability to love one's enemies that turns out to be the main indicator of how fully one has absorbed the Christian teaching on love and to what degree one is ready to put it into practice.

The commandment to love one's enemies can be called the quintessence of all of Christian ethics: in it, as at a focal point, Jesus' other commandments are reflected. It is no coincidence that it is placed last in a series of antitheses in which his teaching is contrasted with the Old Testament regulations. It is the commandment to love one's enemies that most definitely updates the Old Testament ideas of love, of morality, and of the criteria on which the attitude of one person to another should be built. This commandment lays the foundation for the new world order that is clearly wholly unrealizable outside the community of Jesus' disciples.

Love is an inner feeling, the disposition of a person toward other people. It has not only a rational basis but also an emotional basis. For this reason it is very difficult for a person to *force* himself to love someone, or to *compel* himself to love his enemies. Love for one's enemies is not achieved through self-hypnosis; it cannot be the consequence of a *decision* to behave toward one's neighbors in one way and not another. Undoubtedly, acquiring love for one's enemies requires work on oneself, but this work alone is insufficient. The presence of an enabling environment is also necessary, in which a person can develop this quality in himself. The community of Jesus' disciples—the Church—is such an environment.

Jesus' moral exhortations in the Sermon on the Mount are sometimes perceived as a call to strict self-control, including control over one's words and emotions (Mt 5.21–26, 33–37) and behavior in the sexual sphere (Mt 5.27–30).[103] From our point of view, the modern term "self-control" can hardly serve to fully reflect the spiritual work that the Sermon on the Mount requires of a person. This work does not merely boil down to control over one's passions or behavior: above all, this work is directed at the eradication of the passions and the elimination of the reasons that lead to bad behavior. As for love for one's enemies, no amount of self-control can possibly achieve it: it requires help from above.

John Chrysostom calls loving one's enemies "the very summit of virtue" and praying for those who have wronged one "the pinnacle of self-command."[104] The patristic tradition understands the term translated here as "self-command" (*philosophia*) in the narrow sense as referring to Greek philosophy; in a broader sense, this term refers to wisdom, temperance, restraint, and other qualities that constitute a virtuous way of life, or to that way of life itself. In the given context Chrysostom's words can be understood as an allusion to ancient systems of philosophy, which are contrasted to the teachings of Jesus, which surpass them morally. The call to love one's neighbors, in the form that we find it in the Sermon on the Mount, is alien not only to the Old Testament mentality: it is also alien to the way of thinking of the ancient philosophers, in whose systems we do not find a similar call.[105] Then again, Jesus' entire spiritual and moral program quite radically diverges from ancient systems of philosophy, even if in some of those systems there are parallels to particular Christian moral precepts.

The call to pray for those who offend and persecute us was widely reflected in works of early Christian literature. In the Acts of the Apostles we read of Stephen, who, when he was being stoned, cried out, "Lord, lay not this sin to their charge" (Acts 7.60). In the *Didache* (composed at the end of the first century or in the first half of the second century) Chris-

---

[103]Stephen C. Barton, *Discipleship and Family Ties in Mark and Matthew*, Society for New Testament Studies Monograph Series 80 (Cambridge: Cambridge University Press, 1994), 214.

[104]John Chrysostom, *Homilies on Matthew* 18.4 (NPNF¹ 10:126).

[105]Donald Senior, *Matthew*, Abingdon New Testament Commentaries (Nashville, TN: Abingdon, 1998), 80.

Polycarp of Smyrna,
fresco, 14th century

tian teaching is summed up in the following words: "Bless those who curse you, and pray for your enemies, fast on behalf of those who persecute you. For what is the merit of loving those who love you? Do not even the gentiles do the same? But love those who hate you, and you shall have no enemy."[106]

Polycarp of Smyrna (second century) writes, "Pray for all the saints. Pray also for kings, and potentates, and princes, and for those that persecute and hate you, and for the enemies of the cross, that your fruit may be manifest to all, and that ye may be perfect in Him."[107] "Saints" here refers to the members of the Christian community, while "enemies of the cross" refers to the pagans, the persecutors of the Church, including the Roman authorities. The phrase "those that persecute and hate you" is probably an early Christian liturgical formula: similar formulas (for example, "for those that hate and offend us") have been preserved in the Orthodox worship services.

Aside from in the *Didache*, the commandment to love one's enemies is encountered in the works of a number of early Christian writers. Clement of Rome (second century) notes the pagans' reaction to the Christians' fulfillment or non-fulfillment of this commandment: "For, whenever they hear from us that God saith, 'No thank have ye, if ye love them which love you, but ye have thank, if ye love your enemies and them which hate you'— whenever they hear these words, they marvel at the surpassing measure of their goodness; but when they see, that not only do we not love those who hate, but that we love not even those who love, they laugh us to scorn."[108]

Justin Martyr (second century) quotes Jesus' words as follows: "If ye love them that love you, what new thing do ye? For even fornicators do this. But I say unto you, pray for your enemies, and love them that hate you, and bless them that curse you, and pray for them that despitefully use

---

[106]*Didache* 1.3 (PPS 41:35–36).
[107]Polycarp of Smyrna, *Epistle to the Philippians* 12 (ANF 1:36).
[108]2 Clement 13 (ANF 9:254).

you."[109] We note here the use of the word "fornicators" (*pornoi*) instead of the original "publicans" (as in Matthew) or "sinners" (as in Luke): Justin seems to want to accentuate Jesus' point as much as possible by drawing a parallel between love based solely on reciprocity on the one hand, and fornication on the other. What is also interesting here is the substitution of the Matthean "what do ye more [*ti perisson*] than others" with "what new thing [*ti kainon*] do ye": here is an implicit reference to the novelty of the commandment to love one's enemies in comparison with the teachings of Judaism and paganism, which Justin engages in polemics with in his writings.

Loving our enemies does not exclude but rather complements loving our friends, loved ones, and those who love us: it is something "more" and "new" that is added to the "usual" and "old" but does not do away with the latter. Here we see an obvious example of how Jesus "fulfills" (completes, fills in) the Old Testament without breaking or abolishing it (Mt 5.17). That a person is called to love those who love him and to do good to those who do good to him—this is, as it were, a matter of course, just as it goes without saying that it is forbidden to murder and commit adultery. But Jesus calls for righteousness that surpasses the righteousness of the Pharisees, and he does not simply regulate human relationships in their legal aspects, but opens to people the way into the kingdom of heaven (Mt 5.20), making them sons and daughters of the heavenly Father.

According to Jesus' teachings, God's love for a person does not depend on that person's behavior. Herein lies the meaning of his words that God "maketh his sun to rise on the evil and on the good, and sendeth rain on the just and on the unjust" (Mt 5.45), for "he is kind unto the unthankful and to the evil" (Lk 6.35). Like the father in the parable of the prodigal son, God loves both those who are faithful to him and those who stray from him (Lk 15.11–24). The degree of God's love for a person does not depend on the degree of that person's piety and the measure of his labors: this is spoken of in the parable of the laborers at the eleventh hour (Mt 20.1–16).

This approach introduces substantial adjustments to the Old Testament understanding of God, to whom the authors of the biblical books

---

[109]Justin Martyr, *First Apology* 15 (ANF 1:167).

ascribed the ability to repent of his actions toward people as a result of
their bad behavior (Gen 6.6–7; 1 Sam 15.35). God is presented in the Old
Testament as a just Judge: he commends righteousness and punishes sins.
The degree of punishment corresponds to the degree of a person's sinfulness: the idea of the law of just retribution ("an eye for an eye," "a tooth
for a tooth") carries over from the sphere of human relationships into the
sphere of the relationship between God and human beings.

Jesus does not completely do away with this "judicial" aspect of divine
justice: in particular, he speaks of the last judgment, at which a person will
receive the penalty for his sins (Mt 25.31–46). But the emphasis is shifted
toward the side of divine mercy. This has allowed certain Christian writers
to even dispute the idea that God is just. This idea is disputed with the most
polemic keenness by Isaac the Syrian, who says that there is no gradation
in the love of God, no "greater" or "lesser": the goodness and love of God
do not diminish as a result of people's evil acts.[110] God equally loves both
the righteous and sinners without differentiating between them: "He has
the same love toward us and the holy angels. And it is the very same love
for sinners as it is for the righteous. The incarnation is evidence of this."[111]
When God punishes a person, he does this out of love, and not out of
vengefulness, hatred, or rage.[112]

The idea of God's mercy and forgiveness is not alien to the Old Testament. When he revealed himself to Moses, God said of himself: "The
LORD, The LORD God, merciful and gracious, longsuffering, and abundant in goodness and truth, keeping mercy for thousands, forgiving iniquity and transgression and sin, and that will by no means clear the guilty,
visiting the iniquity of the fathers upon the children, and upon the children's children, unto the third and to the fourth generation" (Ex 34.6–7).
Here the theme of love for mankind, mercy, and forgiveness is in fact more
dominant than the theme of punishment. But this cannot be said of the

[110]Isaac the Syrian, *The Second Part* 38.5. English translation from *'The Second Part,' Chapters
IV–XLI*, by Isaac of Nineveh, trans. Sebastian Brock, Corpus scriptorum christianorum orientalium 555, Scriptores syri 225 (Louvain: Peeters, 1995), 161.

[111]Isaac the Syrian. *Chapters on Knowledge* 4.87. Translated by the present translator from
the Russian.

[112]Isaac the Syrian, *Ascetical Homilies* 48 (trans. Holy Transfiguration Monastery, 364).

entire Old Testament. We find a genuine and radical shift toward the idea of God as a source of love, mercy, and forgiveness only in the New Testament—in Jesus' preaching and in the teaching of the apostles based on his preaching.

Jesus' commandment to love one's enemies has a long and complex history of interpretation in the tradition of the Church. Christian writers have attempted to mitigate its sharpness in various ways, to make it more practically workable than it might appear. Origen drew attention to the fact that Jesus called us to love our neighbors "as ourselves," but excluded these words when speaking about loving our enemies. Based on the words in the Greek translation of the Song of Songs, "set ye in order charity in me" (Song 2.4),[113] Origen allegorically interprets these words to mean that love must have its own hierarchy. One must love Christ more than one's father, son, or daughter. As for love for other people, "we are commanded to love first our parents, then our children, and thirdly members of our household. But if there is a bad son and a good retainer, let the domestic take the son's place in our love. And so it shall come to pass that the charity of the saints is set in order". At the same time, while God must be loved "with thy whole heart and with thy whole soul and with thy whole strength and with thy whole mind," it is not required to love one's neighbor thus: he or she must be loved "as thyself." Concerning love for one's enemies, "the Divine Word . . . does not command impossibilities, and he does not say 'Love your enemies as yourselves,' but only, *Love your enemies*. It is enough for them that we love them and do not hate them."[114]

Such an interpretation was not supported in the later tradition. However, attempts to mitigate Jesus' commandment continued even after Origen, mainly by relegating the commandment exclusively to the sphere of personal morality. The enemies of God and opponents in war, in particular, were excluded from the commandment to love one's enemies. The words of St Philaret of Moscow, with which he concluded his sermon on love for

[113]In the Hebrew Masoretic text a completely different sentence is found here; most English translations follow the Hebrew and not the Greek Septuagint, which Origen used.

[114]Origen, *Homilies on the Song of Songs* 2.8. English translation from *The Song of Songs: Commentary and Homilies*, by Origen, trans. R. P. Lawson, Ancient Christian Writers 26 (Westminster, MD: Newman Press, 1957), 296.

Initial from a
medieval Latin
text of the
Song of Songs,
Winchester
Cathedral, 1100s

one's enemies, delivered between 1806 and 1808, became widely known: "Abhor the enemies of God, smite the enemies of the fatherland, love your enemies."[115] First, these words reflect the general principle that has always guided the Church in her attitude toward heretics, the godless, and blasphemers; second, they point to the situation in which the commandment to love one's enemies cannot be applied: the situation of war. Here another kind of logic comes into play; other rules come into effect.

If we pay close attention to Jesus' words, we see that the words "love your enemies" constitute a general principle, which is then made concrete in three other exhortations: "Bless them that curse you, do good to them that hate you, and pray for them which despitefully use you, and persecute you." All three calls obviously relate to the sphere of personal morality. At the same time, only one proposes concrete actions ("do good"), while the other two ("bless" and "pray for") speak more about a person's state of mind, his inner disposition. Here the situation of war is in no way touched upon, and to derive from these exhortations a basis for rejecting fighting with armed opponents would plainly be a forced argument. Here nothing is said about

[115]Philaret of Moscow, "Slovo v nedelyu 19 po Pyatidesyatnitse" [Homily on the 19th Sunday after Pentecost], in *Slova i rechi* [Homilies and speeches], vol. 1 (Moscow, 1873), 289.

*Christt
Pantocrator,*
mosaic,
11th century

the enemies of God, either—those who violate holy things and the truth, who blaspheme the name of God and bring harm to the Church.

One may see a contradiction between Philaret of Moscow's call to "abhor the enemies of God" and the words cited earlier of Isaac the Syrian on the person who has a "merciful heart" and who "offers up prayers with tears continually even for irrational beasts, for the enemies of the truth, and for those who harm him, that they be protected and receive mercy."[116] However, this is only a seeming contradiction. The Church has at all times treated heretics as enemies of God and enemies of the truth with maximal strictness, cutting them off from her own body, but at the same time never ceasing to pray for their repentance, enlightenment, and return to the bosom of the Church. The abhorrence of heresy, blasphemy, sacrilege, and other qualities and vices that make a person an enemy of the Church, does not prevent a Christian from praying for him and hoping for his salvation.

[116]Isaac the Syrian, *Ascetical Homilies* 71 (trans. Holy Transfiguration Monastery, 491).

Prayer is the universal answer to spite, hatred, and enmity. This was the answer that Jesus gave when he prayed for those who were crucifying him (Lk 23.34). The call to pray for those who abuse and persecute us is a very important aspect of the Christian teaching to love our enemies, which is often not given proper attention. This call goes beyond the bounds of personal morality: it extends not only to those who offend a person personally, but also to the persecutors of the Church. The verb "to persecute" (diōkō) and the words derived from it have a very concrete meaning in the Gospels: in most instances, it refers to the persecution of Jesus' disciples as a single community, to the persecution of the Church. We cannot but recall the concluding Beatitude: "Blessed are they which are persecuted [dediōgmenoi] for righteousness' sake. . . . Blessed are ye, when men shall revile you, and persecute [diōxōsin] you, and shall say all manner of evil against you falsely, for my sake" (Mt 5.10–11). How should the members of the Church treat their persecutors? First and foremost, they should pray for them.

In the twentieth century, St Silouan the Athonite, an outstanding ascetic, wrote about loving one's neighbors and praying for them. He divided people not into enemies and friends, but into those who knew God and those who did not.[117] In his notes, which were published after his death, he writes:

> The Lord wants us to love our fellow-man. . . . And if you . . . love your enemies, counting yourself the vilest of all, it is a sign of abundant grace of the Holy Spirit in you.
>
> He who has the Holy Spirit in him, to however slight a degree, sorrows day and night for all mankind. His heart is filled with pity for all God's creatures, more especially for those who do not know God, or who resist Him and therefore are bound for the fire of torment. For them, more than for himself, he prays day and night, that all may repent and know the Lord.

---

[117]Archimandrite Sophrony (Sakharov), *Saint Silouan the Athonite*, trans. Rosemary Edmonds (Crestwood, NY: St Vladimir's Seminary Press, 1999), 115.

*Venerable
Silouan the
Athonite, 1930s*

Christ prayed for them that were crucifying him: "Father, forgive them; for they know not what they do." Stephen the Martyr prayed for those who stoned him, that the Lord "lay not this sin to their charge." And we, if we wish to preserve grace, must pray for our enemies. If you do not feel pity for the sinner destined to suffer the pains of hellfire, it means that the grace of the Holy Spirit is not in you.[118]

The words of this twentieth-century Russian ascetic echo in many ways the words of the seventh-century Syrian saint. For both of them, prayer becomes the nurturing context in which love for one's enemies is nourished as a deep inner experience that allows one to see all people and the entire world in the light of love. Both writers belong to the monastic tradition—the tradition in which Jesus' commandments found their most literal application. It is precisely for this reason that monastics leave the world, in order not to be subject to the laws and standards of this world, but to live unhindered according to the commandments of the gospel. Imitating Jesus' way of life, they realize in practice that which seemed to many

[118]Archimandrite Sophrony, *Saint Silouan the Athonite*, 351–352.

to be unrealizable, proving, in the footsteps of Jesus, that the ideals that he outlined are not utopian, although they are difficult to achieve. At the same time, monks do not consider their way of life to be somehow exceptional: besides celibacy, poverty, obedience, and communal life, which is the distinguishing feature of the monastic tradition, in everything else they are called to fulfill the moral ideal that is addressed to the entire community of those who follow Jesus.

8. Christian Perfection

The series of the six antitheses concludes with a brief sentence: "Be ye therefore perfect, even as your Father which is in heaven is perfect" (Mt 5.48). The word "therefore" (*oun*) indicates that this sentence is aimed at summarizing that which was said earlier. What exactly does it summarize? The sixth antithesis, on loving one's enemies? Or the entire series of antitheses? Or everything said up to the present moment in the Sermon on the Mount, including the Beatitudes?

It seems that each of these interpretations is reasonable. As we will recall, however, the Gospel of Luke contains a similar exhortation: "Be ye therefore merciful, as your Father also is merciful" (Lk 6.36). In Luke this sentence concludes a series of exhortations on love and mercy. In Matthew, on the other hand, instead of the term "merciful," we find the term "perfect," which is all-encompassing in nature.

Perfection is not simply a quality: it is a totality of qualities. From the concept of Christian perfection we cannot exclude any of the qualities that are included in the moral program of the Sermon on the Mount. Consequently, the sentence "Be ye therefore perfect, even as your Father which is in heaven is perfect" can apply to all the qualities listed in the Sermon on the Mount.

Moreover, this sentence also summarizes what will be said later in the Sermon on the Mount and in the Gospel of Matthew as a whole. The word "perfect" is encountered in this Gospel one more time, in Jesus' conversation with the rich young man: "If thou wilt be perfect, go and sell what thou hast, and give to the poor, and thou shalt have treasure in heaven; and come and follow me" (Mt 19.21). As we recall, the rich young man tells Jesus that he has kept the main commandments of the law of Moses. And only after this does Jesus say these crucial words: "If thou wilt be perfect . . ." What follows these words no longer concerns righteousness, but perfection, the mark of which in the given case is a person's readiness to give up his earthly possessions. This readiness was not displayed by the rich young man.

The term *teleios* used in the Sermon on the Mount can mean, depending on the context, "finished," "complete," "mature," "whole," "perfect," "best," and "supreme." In the Septuagint this word is used to translate (in most cases) two Hebrew concepts—*šālēm* ("preserved," "intact") and *tāmîm* ("whole," "perfect"). Both terms indicate integrity and completeness: the first in a neutral sense, and the second in a religious sense. The term *šālēm* also can possess a religious meaning—in the expression *bə-lēb šālēm* ("with all one's heart," literally "with a whole heart").[119]

We do not know which exact Hebrew or Aramaic equivalent of the word *teleios* was used by Jesus (attempts to reconstruct the Aramaic original of his speech are hypothetical in nature). However, we cannot but notice a certain parallelism between the utterance of Jesus under discussion and the words often repeated in the Old Testament that were pronounced by Moses on behalf of God: "Ye shall be holy; for I am holy" (Lev 11.44, 45; 20.7). The apostle Peter refers to this utterance in his First Epistle, when he links the striving for holiness with the idea of God's fatherhood in relation to those who have believed in him:

As obedient children, not fashioning yourselves according to the former lusts in your ignorance, but as he which hath called you is holy, so be ye holy in all conduct, because it is written, "Be ye holy; for I am

[119]Koehler and Baumgartner, *Hebräisches und aramäisches Lexikon*, 4:1424.

Church Fathers,
miniature from
the *Izbornik
Sviatoslava,*
fragment

holy." And if ye call on the Father, who without respect of persons jud-geth according to every man's work, pass the time of your sojourning here in fear. (1 Pet 1.14–17)

On Jesus' lips, the Old Testament idea that people were to imitate God in his holiness is modified to a call to imitate God in his perfection. This call relates to all of the content of the Sermon on the Mount. The Sermon on the Mount is a guide to holiness and perfection, setting the basic param-eters for defining these concepts in the Christian perspective.

The further development of Jesus' teaching on perfection became the teaching of the church fathers. The reception of this teaching in the patris-tic tradition was influenced by the understanding of the term "perfect" in Greek philosophy, where this term was used foremost in relation to people who had achieved a state of inner beauty and nobility. To denote this state, Greek philosophy used the term *kalokagathia* ("beauty," "nobility," "per-fection"), which is derived from the combination of two adjectives: *kalos* ("beautiful," "wonderful," "good") and *agathos* ("good," "virtuous").

Sometimes the term *kalokagathia* is used in Eastern patristics as well.[120] However, the church fathers preferred the term *teleiōtēs* ("perfection," "completeness"), which has a direct connection with the Sermon on the Mount. It was used both in relation to God—the source of every perfection—and in relation to people. Perfection in a person was thought of as being a reflection of divine perfection, acquired through imitating Christ.

Gregory of Nyssa develops the teaching on perfection in two treatises: *The Life of Moses, or, Concerning Perfection in Virtue*, and *Epistle to Olympus* (also known as *On Perfection*). The first of these treatises is an allegorical interpretation of the story of Moses as described in the book of Exodus. In the preamble to the treatise, Gregory presents the teaching that perfection in virtue has no limit, since the source of good is God himself:

> The perfection [*teleiōtēs*] of everything which can be measured by the senses is marked off by certain definite boundaries. . . . But in the case of virtue we have learned from the Apostle that its one limit of perfection is the fact that it has no limit. . . . no Good has a limit in its own nature. . . . The Divine One is himself the Good (in the primary and proper sense of the word), whose very nature is goodness. . . . we hold the divine nature to be unlimited and infinite. Certainly whoever pursues true virtue participates in nothing other than God, because he is himself absolute virtue. . . . It is therefore undoubtedly impossible to attain perfection, since, as I have said, perfection is not marked off by limits: The one limit of virtue is the absence of a limit. How then would one arrive at the sought-for boundary when he can find no boundary?[121]

---

[120] As a synonym for "perfection" the term *kalokagathia* is used in particular by Ignatius of Antioch (*Epistle to the Ephesians* 14.1 [PPS 49:36, 37]), Clement of Alexandria (*The Instructor* 3.2 [PG 8:560A]), Origen (*Against Celsus* 3.51 [PG 11:988A]), and Gregory of Nazianzus (*Epistles* 126 [PG 37:221A]).

[121] Gregory of Nyssa, *The Life of Moses* 5–8. English translation from *The Life of Moses*, trans. Abraham J. Malherbe and Everett Ferguson, Classics of Western Spirituality (New York, NY: Paulist Press, 1978), 30–31.

Gregory of Nyssa did not consider the Jesus' words from the Sermon on the Mount, "Be ye therefore perfect, even as your Father which is in heaven is perfect," to be impossible to fulfill. According to his teaching, it is impossible to achieve the fullness of perfection, because such fullness is possessed by God alone. But a person can acquire perfection to the degree that he is able to achieve it. At the same time, at each stage, he must strive to acquire even more.[122] It is true that at the end of his treatise, having presented the story of Moses, Gregory says that his life "did ascend the highest mount of perfection."[123] However, these words ought to be understood figuratively, inasmuch as the life of Moses is examined not as a chain of historical events, nor as a description of the qualities of a real historical personage, but as an allegorical indication of the qualities that a perfect Christian ought to possess.

In *Epistle to Olympus*, or *On Perfection*, Gregory approaches the theme of perfection from another angle, systematically examining what the apostle Paul says about Christ. Gregory's basic idea is that the qualities of a genuine Christian would be those that Christ possessed as a human being. The name "Christ" indicates both Christ's divine and human qualities. Consequently, "it is necessary for the Christian life to illustrate all the interpretative terms signifying Christ, some through imitation, others through worship."[124]

* * *

At this stage of our study of the Sermon on the Mount, we may return to the question of how realistic its calls to spiritual perfection are. As we said in the beginning of this volume, there are different answers to this question: some commentators consider the Sermon on the Mount to be a guide to action; others see in it a description of a manifestly unattainable ideal; yet others speak of the "eschatological ethics" contained in it.

---

[122]Gregory of Nyssa, *The Life of Moses* 9–10 (trans. Malherbe and Ferguson, 31).

[123]Gregory of Nyssa, *The Life of Moses* 319 (trans. Malherbe and Ferguson, 137).

[124]Gregory of Nyssa, *On Perfection* 4. English translation from *Ascetical Works*, by Gregory of Nyssa, trans. Virginia Woods Callahan, Fathers of the Church 58 (Washington, DC: Catholic University of America Press, 1967), 99.

The following exhortation may serve as the key to understanding the meaning of the Sermon on the Mount as a whole: "Be ye therefore perfect, even as your Father which is in heaven is perfect." This exhortation shows that the ideal for human beings should be God himself and his absolute perfection. Jesus does not at all propose any other ideal, whether lesser or intermediate. He oriented himself to this ideal in his words and actions, concerning which he spoke directly to the Jews: "The Son can do nothing of himself, but what he seeth the Father do; for what things soever he doeth, these also doeth the Son likewise" (Jn 5.19). And he desired that people orient themselves to the same absolute ideal.

The Sermon on the Mount is not built within the frame of reference according to which people are accustomed to living and acting: rather, it projects the reality in which God lives and acts onto human society. Consequently, the Sermon on the Mount is not so much a description of human life as it is a verbal icon of the invisible God. Only by examining the Sermon on the Mount from this perspective can a person discern in it not just a code of disparate rules of conduct, but the genuine and unique revelation of God through Jesus Christ—the Son of God and the Son of Man.

One modern American theologian, an author of popular books about Christianity, writes:

> For years I had thought of the Sermon on the Mount as a blueprint for human behavior that no one could possibly follow. Reading it again, I found that Jesus gave these words not to cumber us, but to tell us what *God* is like. The character of God is the urtext of the Sermon on the Mount. Why should we love our enemies? Because our clement Father causes his sun to rise on the evil and the good. Why be perfect? Because God is perfect. Why store up treasures in heaven? Because the Father lives there and will lavishly reward us. Why live without fear and worry? Because the same God who clothes the lilies and the grass of the field has promised to take care of us. . . . Jesus [proclaimed] the Sermon on the Mount. . . . to impart to us God's Ideal toward which we should never stop striving.[125]

[125]Philip Yancey, *The Jesus I Never Knew* (Grand Rapids, MI: Zondervan, 1995), 143–144.

The Sermon on the Mount, icon, 19th century

We do not know whether the author of these lines read the works of Gregory of Nyssa, but his idea of God as an absolute ideal of perfection is in harmony with what this fourth-century saint said. The call to perfection is the vector that shows a person the direction of his or her spiritual path. The end of this path is God himself—the eternal and unattainable ideal, revealed to humanity in the person of his only begotten Son.

Chapter 5

ALMSGIVING AND PRAYER

---

1. True and False Righteousness

The next part of the Sermon on the Mount is dedicated to works of piety and includes sections on almsgiving, prayer, and fasting. In these three sections, a comparison with hypocrites is repeated as a refrain: the expression "as the hypocrites," used three times, refers to the practice of the Pharisees. It is in the context of this strong criticism of Pharisaism that Jesus develops his teaching on almsgiving, prayer, and fasting. The thrice-used refrain, "Verily I say unto you," underscores Jesus' uncompromising attitude toward the Pharisees, who *already*—this is also said thrice—"have their reward," that is to say, they are deprived of heavenly reward for their works.

The word "hypocrite" (*hypokritēs*) is found multiple times in the Gospel of Matthew, often in connection with the "scribes and Pharisees." In chapter 23 alone we find the following formula seven times: "Woe unto you, scribes and Pharisees, hypocrites!" (Mt 23.13, 14, 15, 23, 25, 27, 29). To this are added other epithets addressed to the Pharisees: "blind guides" (Mt 23.24), "fools and blind" (Mt 23.17, 19), "serpents . . . generation of vipers" (Mt 23.33). Jesus denounces the Pharisees because

... they bind burdens heavy and grievous to be borne, and lay them on men's shoulders, but they themselves will not move them with one of their fingers. But all their works they do to be seen by men: they make broad their phylacteries, and enlarge the borders of their garments, and love the uppermost rooms at feasts, and the chief seats in the synagogues, and greetings in the markets, and to be called by men, "Rabbi, Rabbi." (Mt 23.4–7)

In Jesus' words, the Pharisees "for a pretense make long prayers" (Mt 23.14) and give a tenth of their mint, anise, and cumin, but at the same time "have omitted the weightier matters of the law, judgment, mercy, and faith" (Mt 23.23), and "make clean the outside of the cup and of the platter, but within they are full of extortion and excess" (Mt 23.25).

The Gospel of Matthew, like the other Gospels, is full of accounts of the polemics between Jesus and the Pharisees. Evidently, the Pharisees were his main opponents: he constantly rebuked and derided them. What was it about them that outraged Jesus most of all? It was the fact that their piety was for show and merely external; it was not accompanied by the inner cultivation of the self that Jesus placed at the center of his moral teaching. He was outraged by the Pharisees' small-mindedness and their inability and unwillingness to distinguish that which was essential from that which was secondary in the law of Moses. They obsessed over the study of the law, argued about the interpretation of rules, imposed their interpretation on others, and demanded adherence to their instructions. As a result, their entire religious practice boiled down to a collection of trivial directives, the fulfillment of which, according to the Pharisees, brought a person closer to God. According to the teaching of Jesus, on the other hand, such piety only served to distance a person from God and placed obstacles on their path to God: in his words, the Pharisees closed off the kingdom of heaven to others, as they did not go in themselves and did not allow in those who wanted to enter (Mt 23.13).

Jesus' condemnation of the Pharisees was not absolute. He condemned their practice first and foremost: they "say, and do not do" (Mt 23.3). It is in this context that one must understand the words from the Sermon on

*The Pharisee and
the Publican,*
James Tissot,
1886–1894

the Mount with which Jesus criticizes the behavior and customs of the Pharisees. While in the preceding section of the Sermon he was commenting on the law of Moses itself and bringing it to its fullness with his own interpretation, now he turns directly to the Pharisees' interpretation of the precepts of the law. His tone becomes harsher, as would always happen when he was speaking with or about the Pharisees.

The part of the Sermon on the Mount that we are examining begins in the Textus Receptus,[1] and in the translations made from the Textus Receptus, with the following words:

[1] The Textus Receptus (Latin for "received text") is the Greek text of the New Testament that is reflected in the edition published by Erasmus of Rotterdam in 1516 and in subsequent scholarly editions of the sixteenth and seventeenth centuries.

Take heed that ye do not give your alms before men, to be seen by them; otherwise ye have no reward from your Father who is in heaven. (Mt 6.1)

However, in most ancient manuscripts, the text begins with the following words: "Take heed that ye do not your righteousness before men."[2] Almsgiving appears only in the second verse. The consonance of the Greek words for "righteousness" (*dikaiosynē*) and "almsgiving" (*eleēmosynē*) led later copyists to correct the opening sentence in order to bring its meaning more in line with what follows.

However, if the first sentence were about "almsgiving," it would have introduced only the section dedicated to this topic. If, on the other hand, it is about "righteousness," the sentence should be understood as a preamble to the entire part of the Sermon on the Mount covering almsgiving, prayer, and fasting. It is not only the use of the word "righteousness" in the majority of ancient manuscripts but also the very construction of the sentence that argues in favor of such an interpretation: the expression "to be seen by them" is equally applicable to the sections on almsgiving, prayer, and fasting; the same applies to the words "otherwise ye have no reward of your Father which is in heaven." These words precede the thrice-used phrase "they have their reward," which is applicable to all three topics. It is the topic of ostentatious righteousness that links the three sections on almsgiving, prayer, and fasting into a single whole.

One more link in the chain that also applies to the three themes is the following refrain: "And thy Father which seeth in secret himself shall reward thee openly" (Mt 6.4; 6.6; 6.18). In the majority of ancient manuscripts, in all three instances the text reads thus: "And thy Father which seeth in secret himself shall reward thee." The expression "openly" (*en tō phanerō*) is absent. In later manuscripts it appears as a result of semantic correction, as an antonym to the words "in secret" (*en tō kryptō* in 6.4 and 6.6, *en tō kryphaiō* in 6.18). Both of these later readings entered the Textus Receptus.

---

[2]Nestle, Nestle, and Aland, *Novum Testamentum Graece*, 12.

Earlier in the Sermon on the Mount, Jesus said, "Let your light so shine before men, *that they may see your good works*, and glorify your Father which is in heaven" (Mt 5.16, emphasis added). The words "Take heed that ye do not your righteousness before men, *to be seen by them*" may appear to contradict what was said before. In both cases, however, Jesus' words must be understood in context. In the first instance he is speaking of the calling of the Christian community to be a witness to the outside world: this witness is to be realized not so much through words as through works and through the entire way of life and behavior that the Sermon on the Mount discloses. In the second instance Jesus is speaking of ostentatious piety, which is deprived of internal, spiritual substance and oriented exclusively toward producing an external effect.

We note that all three sections—on righteousness and almsgiving (Mt 6.1–4), prayer (Mt 6.5–8), and fasting (Mt 6.16–18)—consist of material unique to the Gospel of Matthew, without any parallels in the other Gospels. In Luke we find in an abridged form only the Lord's Prayer, which Jesus presents in response to the disciples' request to teach them to pray (Lk 11.1–4), while in Mark we find the words on forgiveness (Mk 11.25–26) that correspond to Matthew's commentary on this prayer (Mt 6.14–15). As we have already said, the Lord's Prayer in Matthew is the compositional center of the Sermon on the Mount. With regard to the section on almsgiving, prayer, and fasting, the prayer fulfills the same function, being at the center of this section and linking together that which precedes it and that which follows it.

2. Almsgiving

The section on almsgiving begins with a caricature of the Pharisees' behavior:

Therefore when thou givest thine alms, do not sound a trumpet before thee, as the hypocrites do in the synagogues and in the streets, that they may have glory by men. Verily I say unto you, they have their reward. But when thou doest alms, let not thy left hand know what thy right hand doeth, that thine alms may be in secret; and thy Father which seeth in secret himself shall reward thee openly. (Mt 6.2–4)

In this passage, Jesus does not give detailed instructions concerning almsgiving: he does not specify to whom, when, and how much one ought to give. He touches only on one aspect of this virtue: it must not be done for show. One must give alms not in order to obtain praise from others, but in order to receive a heavenly reward.

The idea of a reward from God for works of charity is not new: it is encountered in the Old Testament. In Proverbs this idea is expressed in the following way: "He that hath pity upon the poor lendeth unto the LORD; and that which he hath given, he will repay him again" (Prov 19.17). In the same book the one who is charitable toward the poor is called "happy" (or "blessed") (Prov 14.21). In Ezekiel almsgiving is in the list of good works that make up human righteousness: "But if a man be just, and do that which is lawful and right, . . . hath restored to the debtor his pledge, . . . hath given his bread to the hungry, and hath covered the naked with a garment; . . . hath not given forth upon usury, neither hath taken any increase, . . . hath walked in my statutes, and hath kept my judgments, to deal truly; he is just, he shall surely live, saith the Lord GOD" (Ezek 18.5–9).

Detailed instructions concerning almsgiving are found in the law of Moses: "Thou shalt open thine hand wide unto thy brother, to thy poor, and to thy needy, in thy land" (Deut 15.11); "Thou shalt not oppress a hired servant that is poor and needy, whether he be of thy brethren, or of thy strangers that are in thy land within thy gates" (Deut 24.14). The concrete expression of these principles, however, indicates that the topic is not so much about giving as it is about lending: "If there be among you a poor man of one of thy brethren within any of thy gates in thy land which the LORD thy God giveth thee, thou shalt not harden thine heart, nor shut thine hand from thy poor brother; but thou shalt open thine hand wide unto him, and shalt surely lend him sufficient for his need, in that which he wanteth" (Deut 15.7–8). When lending money to the poor, one was

*The Good
Samaritan,*
Rembrandt, 1638

not to impose interest (Ex 22.25). This rule extended also to strangers and
sojourners: "Take thou no usury of him, or increase. . . . Thou shalt not
give him thy money with interest, nor lend him thy food for profit" (Lev
25.35–37). Certain provisions of the law concern "the stranger," "the father-
less," and "the widow": these were to receive the remainder of the grain
harvest, olive harvest, and grape harvest (Deut 24.19–22). They, as well as
the Levites, were entitled to receive a tithe of the entire agricultural harvest
(Deut 14.28–29).

The custom of giving a tithe was preserved among the Pharisees in
Jesus' time. This is referenced in the prayer of the Pharisee in Jesus' parable
of the publican and the Pharisee: "God, I thank thee, that I am not as other
men are, extortioners, unjust, adulterers, or even as this publican. I fast
twice in the week, I give tithes of all that I possess" (Lk 18.11–12).

In those days a significant portion of the population of Palestine
lived below the poverty line. There were poor people everywhere. This is

indicated by Jesus' words, "For ye have the poor always with you" (Mt 26.11; Mk 14.7; Jn 12.8), which is a paraphrase of the words from Deuteronomy, "For the poor shall never cease out of the land" (Deut 15.11). Among the poor there were many who were blind, paralyzed, or disabled. In Israel the disabled did not have any social safety net: the majority of them were cared for by relatives, but many were forced to beg and panhandle. The Jerusalem temple was the center for a massive concentration of beggars, where they occupied different spaces.[3] Beggars also gathered near other holy places, near synagogues; they asked for alms on the streets, squares, and crossroads, and at the gates of rich people. The images of the rich man, dressed in purple and fine linen, and of Lazarus, lying by the rich man's gates and dreaming of eating the crumbs from his table, were likely drawn from daily life (Lk 16.19–21).

Jesus considered care for the poor to be a natural quality of a pious person. This is indirectly indicated by the account of the dinner in Bethany, where a woman poured precious ointment on Jesus' feet. Seeing this, some of those present—according to Matthew, "his disciples" (Mt 26.8)—"had indignation within themselves, and said, 'Why was this waste of the ointment made? For it might have been sold for more than three hundred pence, and have been given to the poor'" (Mk 14.3–5). In John's version the idea of selling the ointment for three hundred denarii was voiced by Judas Iscariot: "This he said, not that he cared for the poor; but because he was a thief, and had the moneybag, and took out what was put in it" (Jn 12.4–6). Judas' words testify to the fact that the donations that Jesus' disciples collected and placed into a common bag were used for giving alms, among other things. Jesus' answer in Mark's version is characteristic: "For ye have the poor with you always, and *whenever ye wish ye may do them good*; but me ye have not always" (Mk 14.7, emphasis ours).

As he considered works of charity and care for the poor to be important elements of religious practice, Jesus condemned the Pharisees for their charitable works done for show, which for them were mingled with

---

[3]See Joachim Jeremias, *Jerusalem in the Time of Jesus: An Investigation into Economic and Social Conditions during the New Testament Period*, trans. F. H. Cave and C. H. Cave (Philadelphia, PA: Fortress, 1969), 117–118.

greed: in Jesus' words, the Pharisees "devour widows' houses" (Mt 23.14), are characterized by love of money, and serve both God and mammon, but at the time they "justify [themselves] before men" (Lk 16.13–15). The alms that they give on the streets and in the synagogues are given to conceal their love of money and their greed.

Describing the habits of the Pharisees, Jesus uses the metaphorical expression "sound a trumpet before thee, as the hypocrites do in the synagogues and in the streets." This expression could refer in particular to the widespread custom of announcing in the synagogue the name of a donor and the amount donated.[4]

When he says that alms must be given in secret, Jesus uses a different metaphor: the right hand must not know what the left hand is doing. The meaning of this expression is that a person, having done a good deed, must forget about it as soon as possible, neither announcing it nor taking pride in it. Clement of Alexandria says, "'If thou doest alms,' it is said, 'let no one know it.'"[5] John Chrysostom paraphrases the metaphor thus: "'If it can be,' saith He, 'for thyself not to know it, let this be the object of thine endeavor; that, if it were possible, it may be concealed from the very hands that minister.'"[6]

---

3. Prayer

The teaching on prayer in the Sermon on the Mount consists of three parts: a criticism of various elements of the practice of the Pharisees and the gentiles, the text of the Lord's Prayer, and a brief explanation of one of the verses of this text. Let us consider the first part, which in its structure and vocabulary is close to the previously examined excerpt on almsgiving:

> And when thou prayest, thou shalt not be as the hypocrites are: for they love to pray standing in the synagogues and in the corners of the

[4]Schweizer, *Good News according to Matthew*, 143.
[5]Clement of Alexandria, *Stromata* 4.22 (ANF 2:434).
[6]John Chrysostom, *Homilies on Matthew* 19.2 (NPNF[1] 10:131).

streets, that they may be seen by men. Verily I say unto you, they have their reward. But thou, when thou prayest, enter into thy closet, and when thou hast shut thy door, pray to thy Father which is in secret; and thy Father which seeth in secret shall reward thee openly.

But when ye pray, use not vain repetitions, as the gentiles do. For they think that they shall be heard for their much speaking. Be not ye therefore like unto them. For your Father knoweth what things ye have need of, before ye ask him. (Mt 6.5–8)

What stands out here is the transition to the second person singular: when speaking of prayer, Jesus moves twice from the collective (plural) "ye" to the more intimate (singular) "thou." This device is encountered in Jesus' speech in other places: "Take heed that ye do not your alms before men. . . . Therefore when thou doest thine alms, do not sound a trumpet before thee" (Mt 6.1–2); "Judge not, that ye be not judged. . . . And why beholdest thou the speck that is in thy brother's eye . . . ?" (Mt 7.1–3); "Woe unto you, scribes and Pharisees, hypocrites! For ye make clean the outside of the cup and of the platter. . . . Thou blind Pharisee, cleanse first that which is within the cup and platter, that the outside of them may be clean also" (Mt 23.25–26).

The transition from the plural to the singular in these different situations serves different goals; however, it seems that in all cases this device is directed at highlighting the idea and focusing the listener's special attention on it, compelling the listener to feel that Jesus' words are addressed to him or her personally. In the passage in the Sermon on the Mount under discussion, the unexpected transition to "thou" additionally gives Jesus' speech greater warmth and trustworthiness.

It is difficult for a modern person to understand the spirit of Jesus' criticism of the Pharisees, inasmuch as the custom of praying ostentatiously in the way described in the Sermon on the Mount has long fallen out of use. People prefer to pray alone; many are embarrassed to pray in front of others and feel awkward if they find themselves in a group of people praying. This has to do with the idea that the whole realm of religion is deeply intimate, private, and personal, that a person's religion must in no way manifest itself in the public sphere, in communal life. The modern person is used to comfort and convenience; he is used to living in a separate apartment, or at least having a separate room, the door of which he can shut behind himself at any time when he wishes to do so.

In Jesus' time matters stood differently. The majority of his listeners belonged to the class of people that did not necessarily possess their own separate rooms: as a rule, families lived together, not divided by partitions between members of the family. A person's entire life took place in full view of others: relatives, acquaintances, friends, bystanders. In small towns and villages (and it was in such places or on their outskirts that Jesus preached) all the inhabitants knew each other and everything about each other: it was impossible to hide from other people's eyes. And, conversely, if a person wished to be noticed, there was a lot more opportunity for that than in our time. It was enough to simply go out onto the street and do something in front of other people—for example, stop and pray, or give alms so that others could notice—and others would immediately notice.

Jesus mentions two ways of praying that are characteristic of the Pharisees' piety: on the streets and in the synagogues. Prayer in the middle of the street could indeed be surprising, but why would prayer in the synagogue be inappropriate? We do not know precisely what concrete examples Jesus had in mind, but it is evident that certain Pharisees used prayer in the synagogues as a way to demonstrate their piety or erudition. As he regularly visited the synagogues, Jesus could not help but pay attention to how the Pharisees prayed: it is possible that even the prayer of the Pharisee in the parable of the publican and the Pharisee was not made up, but overheard in the temple. This is all the more likely since praying silently, in the mind only, was not customary: everyone prayed aloud, even if the prayer was personal and there were other people around.

Jesus contrasts ostentatious public prayer with prayer in a secluded place. In describing the room in which one was supposed to pray, the Greek text of the New Testament uses the word *tameion*, which refers to a utility closet or storage room. Each house would have had a small storage room.[7]

[7]Luz, *Matthew 1–7*, 301.

*The Pharisees
and the
Sadducees Come
to Tempt Jesus,*
James Tissot,
1886–1894

However, the image of a room possesses a deeper meaning here: what matters is not the particular space, but simply that a person ought to pray far away from the gaze of others, and that prayer ought to be motivated by a thirst for communication with God, rather than a desire to exhibit oneself in front of other people. In subsequent tradition, an allegorical interpretation of this text became widespread: one ought to understand "closet" as referring to a person's heart or mind, while the closed door refers to protecting the mind from extraneous thoughts and concentrating on the words of the prayer. In the words of Hilary of Poitiers (fourth century), Christ calls us to "enter the secret places, not of a house, but of the room of our heart," "enclosed within the privacy of our mind."[8] Augustine of Hippo writes, "Outside are all temporal and visible things, which make their way through the door, i.e. through the fleshly sense into our thoughts, and clamorously interrupt those who are praying by a crowd of vain phantoms. Hence the door is to be shut, i.e. the fleshly sense is to be resisted, so that spiritual prayer may be directed to the Father, which is done in the inmost heart, where prayer is offered to the Father which is in secret."[9]

[8]Hilary of Poitiers, *Commentary on Matthew* 5.1. English translation from *Commentary on Matthew*, by Hilary of Poitiers, trans. D. H. Williams, Fathers of the Church 125 (Washington, DC: Catholic University of America Press, 2012), 74.
[9]Augustine of Hippo, *Our Lord's Sermon on the Mount* 2.3.11 (NPNF[1] 6:37).

Besides the Pharisees' custom of praying for show, another target of Jesus' criticism was verbose prayer, which was characteristic of the gentiles. It is not entirely clear what specific practice is in view here and where Jesus would have encountered it. It is possible that he is referring to examples of gentile prayers that are given in the Old Testament. One such example was widely known—the prayer of the 450 priests of Baal, which is vividly described in 1 Kings:

> And they took the bullock which was given them, and they dressed it, and called on the name of Baal from morning even until noon, saying, "O Baal, hear us." But there was no voice, nor any that answered. And they leaped upon the altar which was made. And it came to pass at noon that Elijah mocked them and said, "Cry aloud, for he is a god. Either he is talking, or he is pursuing, or he is in a journey, or perhaps he sleepeth, and must be awaked." And they cried aloud, and cut themselves after their manner with knives and lancets, till the blood gushed out upon them. And it came to pass, when midday was past, and they prophesied until the time of the offering of the evening sacrifice, that there was neither voice, nor any to answer, nor any that regarded. (1 Kg 18.26–29)

The verb *battalogeō*, translated as "use vain repetitions," is found nowhere else in the New Testament; besides this verse, only one instance of its use is known in Greek literature. The meaning of this verb can be conveyed by the words "heap up empty phrases," "use a lot of meaningless words," "speak stammeringly," or "say the same thing over and over again."[10] The meaning of the verb is partially clarified by the use of the noun *polylogia* ("many words").

Interpreting Jesus' words about prayer presents a certain difficulty and can give rise to many questions, especially when one compares what he says to the practice of most Christian communities. If he objects to public prayer, why does the Church insist so much on the necessity of participating in public worship? If God knows everything that we need, why ask

[10]Barclay M. Newman and Philip C. Stine, *A Handbook on the Gospel of Matthew*, UBS Helps for Translators (New York, NY: United Bible Societies, 1992), 166.

anything of him? If Jesus criticizes excessive wordiness in prayer, why are Christian services (especially Orthodox ones) so long?

First and foremost, Jesus is not arguing against public prayer as such. The fact that he went to the Jerusalem temple once or several times a year is evidence of his respect for public prayer. His harsh criticism is directed at a specific aspect of the behavior of the Pharisees in places where people gathered for prayer, not at communal prayer itself. If he were against such prayer, he would not have said to his disciples, "Again I say unto you, that if two of you shall agree on earth concerning any thing that they shall ask, it shall be done for them by my Father which is in heaven. For where two or three are gathered together in my name, there am I in the midst of them" (Mt 18.19–20).

Aside from this, nowhere does Jesus oppose prolonged prayer—neither in the Sermon on the Mount, nor anywhere else. The admonition to not use vain repetitions in prayer does not at all mean that prayer cannot be prolonged. Jesus himself sometimes spent entire nights in prayer. This is evinced in particular in the account of the storm at sea. Having dismissed the people and the disciples in the evening, that is, one must assume, before sunset, he went up a mountain to pray alone. He returned to his disciples only "in the fourth watch of the night," that is, in the morning, not long before sunrise (Mt 14.22–25). Before choosing the twelve apostles, he also went up a mountain and "continued all night in prayer to God" (Lk 6.12).

The habit of withdrawing from people for solitary prayer was typical of Jesus (Mt 14.23; Mk 6.46; Lk 5.16; Lk 6.12; Jn 6.15; Jn 8.1). However, as is clear from the Gospels, he could also pray in the presence of his disciples (Lk 10.21; Jn 17.1–26), and even in the presence of the multitudes, interrupting a speech he was addressing to them in order to pray (Mt 11.25–26; Jn 12.27–28). Prayer was for him such a natural form of self-expression that he could address God at any given moment. Sometimes people heard not only his prayer, but God's response also (Jn 12.28).

The admonition to "use not vain repetitions" in prayer can apply not just to the external form of a prayer, but also to its internal content,[11] especially

---

[11]Cf. Keener, *Gospel of Matthew*, 212.

if it is examined in light of the reminder that God knows everything a person needs beforehand. The greatest value in prayer is not in some earthly blessing that a person can receive through prayer, but prayer itself, standing before God, feeling the presence of God. The Danish existentialist philosopher Søren Kierkegaard (1813–1855) describes the experience of a praying person in this way:

Søren Kierkegaard

> There was something that was very much on his mind, a matter that was so important for him to have God understand properly; he was afraid that he might have forgotten something in his prayer—alas, and if he had forgotten it, he was afraid that God would not have remembered it on his own: therefore, he wanted to gather his thoughts and pray truly fervently. And then, if he in fact prayed truly fervently, what happened to him? Something strange and wonderful happened to him: gradually, as he became more and more fervent in prayer, he had less and less to say, and finally he became entirely silent. He became silent. Indeed, he became what is, if possible, even more the opposite of talking than silence: he became a listener. He had thought that to pray was to talk; he learned that to pray is not only to keep silent, but to listen. And that is how it is: to pray is not to listen to oneself speak, but is to come to keep silent, and to continue keeping silent, to wait, until the person who prays hears God.[12]

To listen to God, to feel the Father in him, to sense his presence in one's life—this is the true goal of prayer. This is eloquently illustrated by the Lord's Prayer, in which petitions concerning earthly needs and wants are practically absent (with the exception of the petition for daily bread, if one understands this bread to be material food), but which is wholly focused on the realities of the spiritual life: the name of God, the kingdom of God, the will of God, the remission of sins, and deliverance from the power of

---

[12]Søren Kierkegaard, *The Lily of the Field and the Bird of the Air*, trans. Bruce H. Kirmmse (Princeton, NJ: Princeton University Press, 2016), 19–20.

the devil. This succinct prayer is a concrete example of how a follower of Jesus is called to pray, not saying anything excessive, but turning in thought to the heavenly Father, abandoning earthly cares, and ascending in mind to the heights of divine silence.

Chapter 6

THE LORD'S PRAYER

The disciples often saw Jesus praying[1] and could not help but sense his closeness to God. They also wanted to participate in this special relationship with God, and so one day, when Jesus had finished praying, one of them asked him, "Lord, teach us to pray, as John also taught his disciples." In reply, Jesus dictated to them the text of the Lord's Prayer (Lk 11.1–2). As we have said, however, in the most ancient manuscripts of Luke, the prayer is given in a somewhat condensed form.

In Matthew we find the Lord's Prayer within the Sermon on the Mount, where it appears without the disciples' request and in a fuller form. Here are both versions of the prayer (we give Luke's version according to the critical edition of the New Testament):[2]

Mt 6.9–13	Lk 11.2–4
Our Father who art in heaven,	Father!
Hallowed be thy name.	Hallowed be thy name.
Thy kingdom come.	Thy kingdom come.
Thy will be done on earth, as it is in heaven.	
Give us this day our daily bread.	Give us day by day our daily bread.
And forgive us our debts,	And forgive us our sins;
as we forgive our debtors.	for we also forgive every one that is indebted to us.
And lead us not into temptation,	And lead us not into temptation.
but deliver us from evil.	

[1]All four evangelists speak of Jesus praying, but we find the most mentions of this in Luke—twelve times in total (Lk 3.21; 5.16; 6.12; 9.18, 28–29; 10.21; 11.1; 22.32, 41, 44–45; 23.34, 46). For more detail, see Geir Otto Holmås, *Prayer and Vindication in Luke-Acts: The Theme of Prayer within the Context of the Legitimating and Edifying Objective of the Lukan Narrative*, Library of New Testament Studies 433 (New York, NY: T&T Clark, 2011), 77–114.

[2]Nestle, Nestle, and Aland, *Novum Testamentum graece*, 181.

In the scholarly literature there are different theories regarding the origin of the Lord's prayer. Some scholars who hold to the idea of the primacy
of the Gospel of Mark believe that Matthew composed the prayer on the
basis of separate verses in Mark: namely, the words "Our Father" are taken
from Mk 14.36 ("Abba, Father"); "who art in heaven" from Mk 11.25 ("your
Father . . . which is in heaven"); "thy kingdom come" from Mk 9.1 ("there be
some of them that stand here, which shall not taste of death, till they have
seen the kingdom of God come with power"); "thy will be done" from Mk
14.36 ("nevertheless not what I will, but what thou wilt"); "forgive us our
debts" from Mk 11.25 ("And when ye stand praying, forgive, if ye have anything against anyone"); and "lead us not into temptation" from Mk 14.38
("Watch ye and pray, lest ye enter into temptation"). Based on these verses
from Mark, with the addition of two verses taken from his own material
("hallowed be thy name" from Mt 4.10 and "give us this day our daily bread"
from Mt 7.9), Matthew composed the prayer for liturgical use in his own
community, while Luke condensed this prayer later on.[3]

Such an extravagant theory of the prayer's origin is used to explain
why it is absent from the Gospel of Mark. Other scholars, proceeding
from different conceptions of the interdependence of the three Synoptic Gospels, propose other theories. Researchers who proceed from the
"two-source hypothesis" basically converge on the opinion that the most
ancient and authentic version (going back to Q and, through it, to Jesus
himself) is the version of Luke,[4] to which Matthew added two petitions.
The authenticity of Luke's version and its greater correspondence to the
language of Jesus, in the opinion of these authors, is supported by the fact
that Jesus used the word "Father" in the prayer, which is documented in

---

[3]M. D. Goulder, "The Composition of the Lord's Prayer," *Journal of Theological Studies* 14
(1963): 35–45.

[4]See, in particular, Strecker, *Sermon on the Mount*, 107; W. D. Davies and Dale C. Allison, *A
Critical and Exegetical Commentary on the Gospel according to Saint Matthew*, vol. 1, *Introduc-
tion and Commentary on Matthew I–VII* (Edinburgh: T&T Clark, 1988), 592; Keener, *Gospel of
Matthew*, 214. However, some researchers believe that the original form of the prayer did not
survive, and both of the versions that have come down to us reflect later developments (Douglas
E. Oakman, "The Lord's Prayer in Social Perspective," in *Authenticating the Words of Jesus*, ed.
Bruce Chilton and Craig A. Evans [Boston, MA: Brill, 2002], 151–152).

Jesus Christ's Sermon on the Mount, Church of the Resurrection in Akhmatovo village in Tver Oblast, fresco

the New Testament thrice in its original Aramaic form, "Abba" (Mk 14.36; Rom 8.15; Gal 4.6).[5]

It is possible that the difference between Matthew's and Luke's versions is due to different versions of the Lord's Prayer being used in different Christian communities. At the same time, Luke's version is not found in any liturgical document, while Matthew's version has entered all the known sources that reflect the liturgical practice of the ancient Church, including the *Didache*[6] (where the prayer is given according to Matthew's version). This fact speaks in favor of the significantly greater prevalence of Matthew's version already in the first century. As a result, Matthew's version, through harmonizing corrections, completely displaced Luke's original version even from the manuscript tradition of the Gospel of Luke.

Most theories of the origin of the Lord's Prayer that have been proposed by modern scholars are the fruit of speculations and conjectures. They are not only not based on the data of the Gospels of Matthew and Luke themselves, but even blatantly ignore them. If we follow the two

---

[5]Joseph A. Fitzmyer, *The Gospel according to Luke: Introduction, Translation and Notes*, vol. 2, *Luke X–XXIV*, Anchor Bible 28A (Garden City, NY: Doubleday, 1985), 897.

[6]*Didache* 8.2 (PPS 41:39).

versions of the prayer's origin that are contained in these Gospels, then their harmonization leads us to the following conclusion: Jesus dictated the Lord's Prayer to his disciples twice—once as part of the Sermon on the Mount, and at another time in reply to their request to teach them to pray. There is nothing unbelievable in the possibility that things happened exactly how the evangelists describe it, and not in the way scholars have fantasized—by having Matthew compose the prayer from scraps cut out from Mark, or by having him add petitions to Luke's version.

Moreover, Jesus could have repeated this prayer in other situations as well, and the disciples could very well have begun to use it in their practice of prayer even in his lifetime. It would be strange, even, if the disciples, having heard this prayer from Jesus' lips on at least two occasions, including once in response to their direct request, proceeded to immediately forget it and not use it. Jesus himself could have said this prayer together with his disciples, and its preservation in the early Church's prayer practice was a direct continuation of the practice that developed in the community of his disciples.

This prayer beginning with the words "Our Father" received the name of the Lord's Prayer in the Christian tradition. From the Church's point of view, this is the only prayer contained in the liturgical books that was not composed by men, but was dictated by God to men. In this respect, it is unique. In some sense, it serves as a model for many other prayers that people have composed.

The question of which language Jesus used originally to pronounce this prayer, Hebrew or Aramaic, remains unresolved. He spoke with his disciples in Aramaic, while Hebrew was the language of the Psalms and prayers. In favor of an Aramaic original stands the fact that two of its opening verses are textually quite close to the Kaddish, an Aramaic prayer that has come down to us. It is not known when the Kaddish appeared, but it was presumably composed before the destruction of the Jerusalem temple in AD 70. This prayer, which was read at the conclusion of the part of the service containing the preaching, includes these words: "May his great name be exalted and sanctified in the world which he created according to his will. May he establish his kingdom during your lifetime and during your days, and during the lifetime of all the House of Israel, speedily and very soon." In the opinion of a number of scholars, the beginning of the Lord's Prayer is a generalization of the Kaddish;[7] the parallel is too close to be coincidental.[8] At the same time, they note that petitions concerning God's name and kingdom are often found next to each other in other Jewish prayers as well.[9]

The external similarity between individual petitions of the Lord's Prayer and Jewish prayers of Jesus' time notwithstanding, the Lord's Prayer sharply contrasts with the majority of these prayers in its simplicity and brevity. Rudolf Bultmann compares the "ornate, emotional, often liturgically beautiful, but often over-loaded, forms of address in Jewish prayer" with the "stark simplicity" of the Lord's Prayer. This prayer, in his words, "stands out above Jewish prayers not only in its simple address but in its direct simplicity throughout. . . . God is near; He hears and understands the requests which come thronging to Him, as a father understands the requests of his own child."[10]

The Lord's Prayer contains key concepts of Christian theology: the heavenly Father, the name of God, the kingdom of God, the will of God, heaven and earth, daily bread, the remission of debts (sins), temptation, the evil one. Each of these concepts has its prehistory in the Old Testament; each is filled with multifaceted meaning in Jesus' speech; each has a rich history of interpretation in the ensuing Christian tradition. Among the interpreters within this tradition are the teachers of the early Church (Tertullian, Cyprian of Carthage, Origen), the Eastern church fathers (Ephrem the Syrian, Cyril of Jerusalem, Gregory of Nyssa, John Chrysostom, Cyril of Alexandria, Maximus the Confessor), the Western fathers (Ambrose,

---

[7]See, in particular, Paul Fiebig, *Das Vaterunser: Ursprung, Sinn und Bedeutung des christlichen Hauptgebetes* (Gütersloh: C. Bertelsmann, 1927), 34–36; Joachim Jeremias, *Abba: Studien zur neutestamentlichen Theologie und Zeitgeschichte* (Göttingen: Vandenhoeck & Ruprecht, 1966), 152–171; Norman Metzler, "The Lord's Prayer: Second Thoughts on the First Petition," in *Authenticating the Words of Jesus*, ed. Chilton and Evans, 193–195.

[8]Norman Perrin, *Jesus and the Language of the Kingdom: Symbol and Metaphor in New Testament Interpretation* (London: SCM, 1976), 47.

[9]Luz, *Matthew 1–7*, 316.

[10]Rudolf Bultmann, *Theology of the New Testament*, trans. Kendrick Grobel, vol. 1 (Waco, TX: Baylor University Press, 2007), 23–24.

Jerome, Augustine, John Cassian), and writers of the following centuries, right up to our contemporaries.[11]

Many modern scholars divide the Lord's Prayer into two halves, each of which includes three petitions.[12] In the first three petitions, following the appeal to the heavenly Father, the persons praying focus on God, who is addressed using "thou":

> Hallowed by *thy* name.
> *Thy* kingdom come.
> *Thy* will be done on earth, as it is in heaven.

In the following petitions the attention of the persons praying switches, as it were, to themselves, and they speak of their own needs:

> Give *us* this day our daily bread.
> And forgive us *our* debts, as *we* forgive *our* debtors.
> And lead *us* not into temptation, but deliver *us* from evil.

The two halves of the prayer are sometimes called "divine" (corresponding to the words "as it is in heaven") and "human" (corresponding to the words "on earth"). At the same time, the internal unity of the prayer is emphasized, which allows us to say that in both halves both God and man are present, both heaven and earth: the human "we" and the divine "thou," the heavenly "thy" and the human "our" interact in the prayer, forming a "dialectical relationship, like two sides of the same coin, which can be distinguished but not separated."[13]

[11]For a brief overview, see Kenneth W. Stevenson, *The Lord's Prayer: A Text in Tradition* (Minneapolis, MN: Fortress, 2004), 43–102 (the patristic period), 103–150 (medieval authors), 151–186 (the Renaissance and Reformation), 187–219 (later interpretations).

[12]The first half of the prayer is called the "Thou-petitions," and the second "we-petitions." See, for example, Birger Gerhardsson, "The Matthean Version of the Lord's Prayer (Matt 6:9b–13): Some Observations," in *The New Testament Age: Essays in Honor of Bo Reicke*, ed. William C. Weinrich, vol. 1 (Macon, GA: Mercer University Press, 1984), 209–217; J. Samuel Subramanian, "The Lord's Prayer in the Gospel of Matthew," in *Resourcing New Testament Studies: Literary, Historical, and Theological Essays in Honor of David L. Dungan*, ed. Allan J. McNicol, David B. Peabody, and J. Samuel Subramanian (New York, NY: T&T Clark International, 2009), 116–122.

[13]John Dominic Crossan, *The Greatest Prayer: Rediscovering the Revolutionary Message of the Lord's Prayer* (New York, NY: HarperOne, 2010), 47–49.

1. "Our Father Who Art in Heaven"

The Lord's Prayer has come down to us only in Greek translation, and any reconstruction of it, whether it be Hebrew or Aramaic, is of a hypothetical nature. However, on the basis of the thrice-used Aramaic word "Abba" (*'abbā*) in the New Testament, we may assume that it was with this word that Jesus began the prayer. In the Garden of Gethsemane he would pray the following words: "Abba, Father, all things are possible unto thee; take away this cup from me: nevertheless not what I will, but what thou wilt" (Mk 14.36). The word "Abba" is translated into Greek as *pater* ("father" in the vocative case). It was originally used in family life: a child would call his father by this name; the same word was applied to the elderly. The use of this word in a prayer addressed to God is unusual,[14] although the appeal itself to God as Father was not unprecedented.

In the Hebrew Old Testament, God is called "Father" fifteen times in total (Deut 32.6; 2 Sam 7.14; 1 Chr 17.13; 22.10; 28.6; Ps 67.6; 88.27; Is 63.16; 64.8; Jer 3.4, 19; 31.9; Mal 1.6; 2.10).[15] We find a few more instances of the use of the name "Father" applied to God in the deuterocanonical books (Tob 13.4; Wis 14.3; Sir 23.1, 4; 3 Macc 6.2, 6). The name "Father" in relation to God is used multiple times by Philo of Alexandria and seven times by Josephus.[16]

Origen, an outstanding expert on the Holy Scriptures, conducted a special inquiry into the use of the word "Father" in relation to God in the Old Testament. He shares his conclusions with the reader on the pages of his treatise, *On Prayer*:

---

[14]Werner Georg Kümmel, *Theology of the New Testament according to Its Major Witnesses: Jesus—Paul—John*, trans. John E. Steely (Nashville, TN: Abingdon, 1973), 40.

[15]Taeseong Roh, *Die* familia dei *in den synoptischen Evangelien: eine redaktions- und sozialgeschichtliche Untersuchung zu einem urchristlichen Bildfeld*, Novum testamentum et orbis antiquus 37 (Fribourg: Universitätsverlag; Göttingen: Vandenhoeck & Ruprecht, 2001), 3.

[16]Isabel Ann Massey, *Interpreting the Sermon on the Mount in the Light of Jewish Tradition as Evidenced in the Palestinian Targums of the Pentateuch: Selected Themes*, Studies in the Bible and Early Christianity 25 (Lewiston, NY: E. Mellen, 1991), 18–20.

A careful examination of what is called the Old Testament is worthwhile, in order to discern whether anybody is to be found in it addressing their prayer to God as Father. For although I have made such an examination to the best of my ability I have yet to find any. This is not to say that God is not said to be a father, or that those who are accounted as believers are not called sons of God, but that boldness of speech in prayer which is revealed by the Savior in addressing God as "Father" I have yet to find. . . . And so, even if God is termed "father," and those begotten by the word through their faith in him are called "sons," nonetheless a firm and abiding sonship is not to be discerned among the ancient people.[17]

Tertullian believed that the name of God the Father was not known before the coming of Christ into the world: "Even Moses, who had asked it of God himself, heard of a different name (Ex 3.14–15). But to us it is revealed in the Son, for now we know that Son is the new name of the Father. 'I have come,' he said, 'in the name of the Father' (Jn 5.43). And again: 'Father, glorify your name' (Jn 12.28). And, more openly: 'I have made your name known to people' (Jn 17.6)."[18]

In the New Testament, on the contrary, calling God "Father" becomes fundamental: in this respect the New Testament sharply contrasts with the Old. In the Gospels God is called "Father" 174 times: 109 in John, 44 in Matthew, 17 in Luke, and 4 in Mark. In the Gospel of Matthew the highest concentration of the use of the name "Father" as a reference to God occurs in the Sermon on the Mount: here it is found seventeen times.[19]

The genuine novelty of the opening words of the Lord's Prayer consists, perhaps, not so much in the very fact of the use of the name "Father" in relation to God, as much as in the content that Jesus invested in this name. He called God first of all his *own* Father: the expression "my Father" is often

[17]Origen, *On Prayer* 22.1–2. English translation from *On the Lord's Prayer: Tertullian, Cyprian, Origen*, trans. Alistair Stewart-Sykes, Popular Patristics Series 29 (Crestwood, NY: St Vladimir's Seminary Press, 2004), 160.

[18]Tertullian, *On Prayer* 3 (*Tertullian, Cyprian & Origen: On the Lord's Prayer*, trans. Alistair Stewart-Sykes, Popular Patristics Series 29 [Crestwood, NY: St Vladimir's Seminary Press, 2004], 42–43).

[19]Pennington, *Heaven and Earth*, 230.

encountered in his speech. This use of words shocked his listeners among the Pharisees: they wanted to kill him "because he not only had broken the sabbath, but said also that God was his Father, making himself equal with God" (Jn 5.18). That said, Jesus did not limit himself to using this expression when he spoke of *his* relationship with God: he believed that his listeners could also call God *their* Father. In the Sermon on the Mount alone, the expression "your Father" is encountered nine times (Mt 5.16, 45, 48; 6.1, 8, 14, 15, 32; 7.11), and "thy Father" another three times (Mt 6.4, 6).

Here it is appropriate to recall that in the thinking of the apostle Paul, when people pray to God as their Abba-Father, the Holy Spirit prays in them:

> For as many as are led by the Spirit of God, they are the sons of God. For ye have not received the spirit of bondage again to fear; but ye have received the Spirit of adoption, whereby we cry, "Abba, Father." The Spirit itself beareth witness with our spirit, that we are the children of God; and if children, then heirs; heirs of God, and joint-heirs with Christ, if so be that we suffer with him, that we may be also glorified together. (Rom 8.14–17)

Earlier, when we were examining the seventh Beatitude, we already spoke of the concept of God's adoption of human beings—one of the important points of Paul's theology. Developing this concept in the Epistle to the Galatians, the apostle addresses the meaning of the prayer "Abba, Father" and asserts that God's adoption of human beings is the direct result of the redemption accomplished by God the Son. The apostle compares the Old Testament idea of God with childhood, and the New Testament idea of God with maturity. The right to address God as Father, which people have received thanks to Jesus Christ, is evidence of humanity's entrance into maturity:

> Now I say, that the heir, as long as he is a child, differeth nothing from a servant, though he be lord of all; but is under tutors and governors until the time appointed of the father. Even so we, when we were children, were in bondage under the elements of the world: but when the fullness

of the time was come, God sent forth his Son, born of a woman, born under the law, to redeem them that were under the law, that we might receive the adoption of sons. (Gal 4.1–5)

God's fatherhood in relation to human beings has a unique character. Emphasizing this, Jesus said, "And call no man your father upon the earth: for one is your Father, which is in heaven" (Mt 23.9). It is in this perspective that one should understand the opening words of the Lord's Prayer. Nobody on earth, not a single earthly father can realize fatherhood in the way and to the degree that God realizes it in relation to all of the human race and each human being. The fatherhood of God does not have an analogy at the human level.

Is God's fatherhood in relation to human beings universal, or does it extend only to a specific category of persons? The answer to this question is not as simple as it might seem. A contemporary researcher writes:

> A cardinal tenet of nineteenth-century liberalism was belief in the fatherhood of God. Many people today still believe that Jesus taught a universal fatherhood of God and the accompanying doctrine of the brotherhood of mankind. . . . Yet upon closer examination it becomes clear that Jesus did not teach a doctrine of the universal fatherhood of God. His references to God as "your Father" must be understood in light of the fact that Jesus was not teaching the crowds but his disciples (Mt 5:1–2). Similarly, the Lord's Prayer was not given as a general prayer that all people everywhere should pray. Rather, it was a prayer given to his disciples (Lk 11:1–2).
>
> Jesus did not teach a universal fatherhood of God. Never did he base this relationship with God as Father on something that could apply to everyone, such as God's being Creator of all things. Quite the contrary, Jesus even described some people as having the devil as their father (Jn 8:44; compare Mt 12:34). It was only through faith in him that this relationship with God was possible.[20]

---

[20]Robert H. Stein, *Jesus the Messiah: A Survey of the Life of Christ* (Downers Grove, IL: InterVarsity, 1996), 133.

We can agree with these words only partially. On the one hand, nowhere and never did Jesus teach that God's love for human beings or his fatherhood in relation to them was of a selective nature. In the absolute sense, God is Father for all people, inasmuch as he created each person and cares for each one: there is no person who is excluded from this care. On the other hand, the genuine children of God are those who have believed in his only begotten Son. The fatherhood of God is realized and actualized in the people who believe in Jesus as the Son of God and keep his commandments. In other words, God's fatherhood is realized to the fullest degree in the community of Jesus' disciples.

Christ in Majesty,
icon, 15th century

The right to be called a son of the heavenly Father can be compared with the right to an inheritance. All the children of a single father have a formal right to the inheritance; however, not all will receive it, but only those who fulfill the will of the father and whom the father mentions in his last will. And even if a son, as in the parable from the Gospel of Luke, receives the inheritance, it does not mean that he will be able to manage it properly. Having betrayed his father and squandered the inheritance he received, the prodigal son lost the right to be called a son. This right was reinstated only after he repented and returned to his father (Lk 15.11–24).

As applied to God, the word "Father" is deprived of the characteristic of gender.[21] It is not a coincidence that in the Old Testament God is not only called "Father," but also compared to a mother: "Can a woman forget her sucking child, that she should not have compassion on the son of her womb? Yea, they may forget, yet will I not forget thee" (Is 49.15); "As one whom his mother comforteth, so will I comfort you" (Is 66.3).

In our time, people have a very different experience with fathers and fatherhood. Many children grow up without a father or see their father only from time to time; the connection between generations is often

---

[21]Cf. Stein, *Jesus the Messiah*, 134.

disrupted because of family problems, conflicts, and divorces. Therefore, each person invests the concept of "father" with his or her own content. The fatherhood of God is of a different nature than earthly fatherhood and earthly motherhood: a person can learn about this only through the personal experience of communicating with God.

According to Tertullian, in confessing God as Father, the Christian simultaneously prays to the Son, while confessing the Church as Mother:

> It begins with bearing witness to God and with the reward of faith when we say: "Father, you who are in the heavens." For we are praying to God and confessing the faith of which this mode of address is an indication.... However, when we say "Father" we are also naming God in a form of address which demonstrates both devotion and power. Moreover the Son is invoked in the Father, for he says: "I and the Father are one" (Jn 10.30). Nor is the mother, the church, neglected, since the mother is found within the Father and the Son, for the name of Father and Son find their meaning in her. Therefore under one term and with one name we honor God along with those who are his, both recalling God's commandment and scorning those who have forgotten the Father.[22]

The pronoun "our," added to the word "Father" in Matthew's version, emphasizes the communal, collective character of this prayer. According to Cyprian of Carthage (third century), the Lord's Prayer is pronounced on behalf of the entire community as a single family of the followers of Jesus:

> Before all else, the teacher of peace and master of unity desires that we should not make our prayer individually and alone, as whoever prays by himself prays only for himself. We do not say: "My father, who are in the heavens," nor "Give me my bread this day." Nor does anybody request that his debt be pardoned for himself alone, nor ask that he alone be not led into temptation and delivered from the evil one. Our prayer is common and collective, and when we pray we pray not for one

---

[22]Tertullian, *On Prayer* 2 (PPS 29:42–43).

but for all people, because we are all one people together. The God of peace and master of concord, who taught that we should be united, wanted one to pray in this manner for all, as he himself bore all in one.[23]

The Eucharist, mosaic in the Cathedral of the Archangel Michael in St Michael's Golden-Domed Monastery (Kiev), 1108–1113

In the opinion of John Chrysostom, the Lord's Prayer abolishes the notion of social inequality and teaches us to love all our neighbors, regardless of their status, position, and place in society:

He teaches, moreover, to make our prayer common, in behalf of our brethren also. For He saith not, "my Father, who art in Heaven," but, "our Father," offering up his supplications for the body in common, and nowhere looking to his own, but everywhere to his neighbor's good. And by this He at once takes away hatred, and quells pride, and casts out envy, and brings in the mother of all good things, even charity, and exterminates the inequality of human things, and shows how far the equality reaches between the king and the poor man, if at least in those things which are greatest and most indispensable, we are all of us fellows.[24]

It is no coincidence that the Lord's Prayer is included in the divine services, including in the Eucharist, in which the community's union with God is expressed most fully. In the Orthodox Church, without this prayer, not a single service could be done: besides the liturgy, where the prayer is said by all the people with especial solemnity immediately before communion, it is also included in the services of matins, vespers, the hours, midnight office, and compline. The conciliar nature of the prayer does not prevent believers from reading it in their home prayer rule. A Christian, even when he addresses God on his own after closing the door to his room, prays as a member of the church community: he feels himself to be a part

[23]Cyprian of Carthage, *On the Lord's Prayer* 8 (PPS 29:69).
[24]John Chrysostom, *Homilies on Matthew* 19.6 (NPNF[1] 10:134).

The Apocalypse,
Albert Goodwin,
1903

of the single body of the Church, connected by invisible threads to all the other parts.

The expression "who art in heaven" merits separate consideration. The beginning of the Lord's Prayer is the vocative of the phrase "our heavenly Father" (*ho patēr hēmōn ho ouranios*, or *ho patēr hēmōn ho en tois ouranois*), which is encountered multiple times in Jesus' direct speech. In the Gospel of Matthew the phrase "heavenly Father" (always with the possessive pronoun "your" or "my") is encountered twenty times in total.[25]

The generally accepted opinion in scholarly literature on the New Testament is that the word "heaven" was used in Jesus' time as a synonym for the name of God, and Jesus' use of such expressions as "the kingdom of heaven" was linked to the pious tradition of avoiding direct mentions of God.[26] This tradition, as it is supposed, was motivated by unwillingness to violate the second commandment of the law of Moses: "Thou shalt not take the name of the LORD thy God in vain" (Ex 20.7; Deut 5.11). It is preserved in Judaism to this day: not only in Hebrew, but in other languages also, Jews prefer to avoid the word "God," substituting for it the words "the Most High," "heaven," or "the Name."

---

[25]For comparison, in Mark the expression "Father which is in heaven" is used only once (Mk 11.25), and in Luke "heavenly Father" is used once (Lk 11.13). See Gustaf Dalman, *Die Worte Jesu*, 2nd ed., Bd. 1, *Einleitung und wichtige Begriffe* (Leipzig: J. C. Hinrichs, 1930), 155.

[26]See Albright and Mann, *Matthew*, 49; David Hill, ed., *The Gospel of Matthew*, New Century Bible (London: Oliphants, 1972), 90; Francis Wright Beare, *The Gospel according to Matthew: A Commentary* (Oxford: Blackwell, 1981), 33; Manson, *Sayings of Jesus*, 152.

That being said, the concept of "heaven" in the Gospels is by no means reducible to a simple substitute for the term "God," but has its own independent meaning. As scholars have shown,[27] this concept occupies an exceptional place in the Gospel of Matthew: the word *ouranos* (heaven) is encountered in it eighty-two times, but significantly more rarely in the other Gospels (eighteen times in Mark, thirty-two in Luke, eighteen in John). The term "heaven" is encountered in Revelation no less often than in the Gospel of Matthew (fifty-five times, versus eighty-two, while the entire text of Revelation is almost half as long). Thus, the greatest frequency of the use of the concept of "heaven" is found in the books that open and close the New Testament.

Of the eighty-two mentions of heaven in the Gospel of Matthew, in fifty-five instances the plural form is used: *ouranoi* (heavens). In classical Greek the use of the word "heaven" in the plural is not typical, in contrast with Hebrew and Aramaic, where the term "heaven" is plural (Hebrew *šāmayim*, Aramaic *šmayyā*). The use of the term "heavens" in the Greek text of the Gospels is a typical Semiticism.

Such frequent use of the word "heaven" in the New Testament is a continuation of the Old Testament tradition.[28] In the Old Testament the term "heaven" (or "heavens") is encountered 458 times in total and covers a very wide semantic spectrum. It is present in the very first verse of the Bible, which includes three nouns in total: God, heaven, and earth (Gen 1.1). Heaven is what God called the firmament that divided water from water (Gen 1.7–8). Later on the word "heaven" is encountered in connection with various meteorological phenomena (rain, snow, frost, dew, wind, clouds), celestial bodies (stars, sun, moon), and birds. A few times the expression "heavens of heavens" (Ps 148.4) is encountered, as well as "the heaven and the heaven of heavens" (Deut 10.14; 1 Kg 8.27; 2 Chr 2.6; 6.18; Neh 9.6).

In the Old Testament heaven is understood to be the place where God dwells. From this idea, in particular, is derived the custom of raising one's eyes to heaven during prayer. The Old Testament writers knew that God was present not only in heaven; the idea of his omnipresence is quite

---

[27]Pennington, *Heaven and Earth*, 2–3.
[28]Pennington, *Heaven and Earth*, 39–45.

clearly expressed in many texts, including in the words of the psalm: "If I go up into heaven, thou art there; if I go down into hades, thou art present there" (Ps 138.8). And nonetheless the voice of God is never heard to come from under the earth, from the lower regions: to communicate with people, God uses heaven. From there he speaks with the sons of Israel (Ex 20.22), from there his voice calls out (Gen 21.17; Deut 4.36), from there he looks upon people (Ps 14.2), there is his throne established (Ps 10.4; 102.19; Is 66.1). God is "in the height of heaven," and nonetheless "thick clouds are a covering to him," and he "walketh in the circuit of heaven" (Job 22.12–14).

The idea of heaven as the dwelling place of God is developed with particular force in the words of the prayer that King Solomon uttered before the dedication of the newly built Jerusalem temple:

> But will God indeed dwell on the earth? Behold, *the heaven and heaven of heavens cannot contain thee,* how much less this house that I have built [to thy name]? Yet have thou respect unto the prayer of thy servant, and to his supplication. . . . And hearken thou to the supplication of thy servant, and of thy people Israel, when they shall pray toward this place, and *hear thou in heaven thy dwelling place*: and when thou hearest, forgive. . . . When thy people Israel be smitten down before the enemy, because they have sinned against thee, and shall turn again to thee, and confess thy name, and pray, and make supplication unto thee in this house: then *hear thou in heaven,* and forgive the sin of thy people Israel. . . . When heaven is shut up, and there is no rain, because they have sinned against thee; if they pray toward this place, and confess thy name, and turn from their sin, when thou afflictest them, then *hear thou in heaven.* . . . Whatsoever prayer and supplication be made by any man, or by all thy people Israel, which shall know every man the plague of his own heart, and spread forth his hands toward this house, then *hear thou in heaven thy dwelling place,* and forgive. . . . Moreover concerning a stranger, that is not of thy people Israel, but cometh out of a far country for thy name's sake . . . when he shall come and pray toward this house, *hear thou in heaven thy dwelling place,* and

do according to all that the stranger calleth to thee for. (1 Kg 8.27–43)[29]

The Prophet Nathan Anointing Solomon King, Constantinople, Byzantine Empire, 10th century

Translating the Old Testament wording into a paradigm familiar to us, we could say that the word "heaven" was used in two main senses—for denoting the material heaven stretched out over the earth (i.e., the sky and outer space beyond it), and for denoting the spiritual space in which God dwells. However, the Old Testament person did not make this distinction between the material and spiritual, which is characteristic of philosophical thinking. The material and spiritual heaven, in such a person's consciousness, merged into one phenomenon, and the spiritual reality of the higher plane of existence was glimpsed through material clouds.

In a similar way, God, too, was imagined not as a purely spiritual being, but as an entity with material, bodily characteristics. The biblical God has eyes (Deut 11.11; 2 Chr 16.9; Job 24.23; 34.21; Ps 10.4; 33.16; 65.7; Prov 15.3; 22.12), ears and a face (Ps 33.16–17), hands (2 Sam 24.14; 1 Chr 21.13) and feet (1 Chr 28.2; Ps 109.1; Is 60.13; 66.1). He walks (Gen 3.8), rests (Gen 2.2), remembers (Gen 8.1; 19.29; 30.22) and forgets (Ps 9.32–33), hates (Ps 11.5; Is 61.8; Jer 44.4; Am 5.21; Zech 8.17), turns away (2 Kg 17.20; Ezek 23.18), grieves and repents (Gen 6.6), sleeps and wakes up (Ps 43.24).

The intertwining of the spiritual and the material in the ideas of God and heaven, which is characteristic of the Old Testament, is preserved also in New Testament word usage, including in Jesus' direct speech. The same term is used to denote both the material heaven and heaven as a spiritual reality. We will provide only a few of the most striking examples from the Gospel of Matthew:

> When it is evening, ye say, "It will be fair weather: for the *sky* [lit. "heaven"] is red." And in the morning, "It will be foul weather to day:

[29]Emphasis added.

Monument to the apostle
Peter in the ruins of the
ancient city Capernaum
(Israel)

for the *sky* [lit. "heaven"] is red and lowring." O ye hypocrites, ye can discern the face of the *sky* [lit. "heaven"]; but can ye not discern the signs of the times? (Mt 16.2–3)

Blessed art thou, Simon Bar Jonah, for flesh and blood hath not revealed it unto thee, but my Father which is in *heaven*. And I say also unto thee, that thou art Peter, and upon this rock I will build my church; and the gates of hell shall not prevail against it. And I will give unto thee the keys of the kingdom of heaven: and whatsoever thou shalt bind on earth shall be bound in *heaven*, and whatsoever thou shalt loose on earth shall be loosed in *heaven*. (Mt 16.17–19)

Take heed that ye despise not one of these little ones; for I say unto you, that in *heaven* their angels do always behold the face of my Father which is in *heaven*. (Mt 18.10)

Immediately after the tribulation of those days shall the sun be darkened, and the moon shall not give her light, and the stars shall fall from *heaven*, and the powers of the *heavens* shall be shaken: and then shall appear the sign of the Son of man in *heaven*: and then shall all the tribes of the earth mourn, and they shall see the Son of man coming in the clouds of *heaven* with power and great glory. And he shall send his angels with a great sound of a trumpet, and they shall gather together his elect from the four winds, from one end of *heaven* to the other. (Mt 24.29–31)[30]

In many instances, to refer to the material heaven (i.e., the sky), the term *ouranos* is used in the singular, while to refer to the spiritual reality, the plural is used. However, this is not necessarily always the pattern: in many cases in the New Testament the word "heaven" in the singular refers to the place where God dwells. Sometimes the term is used alternately

[30]Emphasis added in all quotations.

in the singular or plural: "Our Father who art in *heaven* [lit. 'in the *heavens*].... Thy will be done on earth, as it is in *heaven*" (Mt 6.9–10).

In the Gospel narratives, as in the Old Testament, heaven is the place from which people hear the voice of God. When Jesus, after being baptized by John, came out of the water, "Lo, the heavens were opened unto him, and he saw the Spirit of God descending like a dove, and lighting upon him. And lo, a voice *from heaven*, saying, 'This is my beloved Son, in whom I am well pleased'" (Mt 3.16–17; Mk 1.11; Lk 3.22). At the moment of the transfiguration the same words are heard out of a cloud, that is, from heaven once again (Mt 17.5; Mk 9.7; Lk 9.35).

The Apocalypse: The Seven Trumpets, woodcut, Albrecht Dürer, 1592–1593

In another instance, when Jesus interrupted his speech to the Jews in order to turn to God in prayer, the Father's reply came from heaven (Jn 12.28).

According to the Gospels, heaven is the dwelling place not only of the Father, but also of the Son. Jesus said of himself that he "came down from heaven" (Jn 3.13; 6.38). He called himself the bread "which cometh down from heaven, and giveth life unto the world" (Jn 6.33, 50–51, 58). To the high priest at the council he said, "Hereafter shall ye see the Son of Man sitting on the right hand of power, and coming in the clouds of heaven" (Mt 26.64; Mk 14.62). At the conclusion of his earthly mission, Jesus ascended to heaven before the eyes of his disciples (Lk 24.51; Acts 1.9) and sat at the right hand of God (Mk 16.19). And while the disciples were still looking at the sky, two angels appeared to them and said, "Ye men of Galilee, why stand ye gazing up into heaven? This same Jesus, which is taken up from you into heaven, shall so come in like manner as ye have seen him go into heaven" (Acts 1.10–11).

The Baptism of the Lord, fresco in Sretensky Monastery (Moscow), 1707

The Transfiguration of the Lord, icon, Novgorod, 15th century

The extremely rich semantics of the concepts of "heaven" and "the heavens" should be taken into account when considering the Lord's Prayer as well as other gospel texts that speak of the heavenly Father, the kingdom of heaven, and the Son who came down from heaven. We should not see this choice of words to be merely an archaism requiring a metaphorical interpretation. The spiritual and the material are not completely separate even in the life of modern people. They may be separate in philosophical discourse, but in practice the phenomena of the spiritual life remain, as before, tied to material objects and events.

The writers of the ancient Church made a sharp distinction between the material heaven and the "heaven" that metaphorically expresses spiritual reality. They emphasized that a literal understanding of the words "who art in heaven" leads to the idea that God has a physical body, but such an idea contradicts the biblical teaching about God:

The Transfiguration, Raphael, 1519–1520

When the Father of the saints is said to be "in the heavens," it is not to be supposed that he is circumscribed by corporeal shape, and that so he dwells "in the heavens," for if the heavens contain him it follows that God would be less than the heavens, whereas the ineffable power of his divinity entails our belief that all things are contained and held together by him. . . . To link these points with "Our Father, who are in the heavens" was, I think, necessary for the sake of removing the degraded conception of God held by those who think that he is "in the heavens" in a spatial sense, and lest anybody say that God is in a material space. For it follows on from this that he is corporeal, from which derisive doctrines follow, namely that he is divisible and material and corruptible, for every body is divisible and material and corruptible.[31]

The modern idea of how the universe works is strikingly different from how ancient people imagined the world worked. Today every school-child knows that the earth revolves around the sun, that the solar system is only one part of our galaxy, which, in its turn, makes up a small part of the universe. Yet heaven remains an important element of human life. In the heavens we daily behold sunrises and sunsets, and see distant stars. Even today the heavens remind people of the greatness of the Creator of the universe.

Icon of the Savior "the Unsleeping Eye," 16th century

Moreover, heaven continues to remain an image of the spiritual space in which human beings communicate with God, and God with human beings. Raising his eyes to heaven in prayer, a person directs his thoughts to God. At the same time he remembers that God is Spirit (Jn 4.24) and that God's existence is not connected with any space in the material world whatsoever. God dwells in the spiritual world, which exists parallel to the material world.

Contact with this spiritual world takes place through communion with God, through prayer. While being of a different nature from the material world, God is at the same time present in it. Immeasurably distant from man in his nature, God is at the same time immeasurably close to him: he sees and hears him when the latter, raising his eyes to heaven, turns to him in prayer.

[31]Origen, *On Prayer* 23.1, 3 (PPS 29:162–163).

2. "Hallowed
Be Thy Name"

The meaning of the first petition of the Lord's Prayer cannot be understood without taking into account the biblical theology of names.[32] In the Bible there is the idea that God cannot be named, that his name is inaccessible to human beings (Gen 32.29; Judg 13.17–18). At the same time, in the Old Testament, God is constantly referred to by various names. Altogether there are more than a hundred of these names. Among them are such names as "God" (*'Ĕlōhîm*),[33] "my Lord" (*'Ǎḏōnay*),[34] "Most High God" (*'Ēl Šadday*, literally "the one who is on the mountain"),[35] and "Sabbaoth" (*Ṣǝḇā'ôṯ*, "[the Lord] of Hosts").

The most characteristic name of God in the Bible is *Yahwē* (Yahweh, Jehovah): this is the personal name of God, which he himself revealed to mankind.[36] The cult of this holy name occupies an exceptional place in the Bible. The book of Exodus connects the revelation of this name with Moses, whom God chose to lead the people of Israel out of Egypt into the promised land:

> And Moses said unto God, "Behold, when I come unto the children of Israel, and shall say unto them, 'The God of your fathers hath sent me unto you'; and they shall say to me, 'What is his name?' What shall I say unto them?" And God said unto Moses, "I AM THAT I AM": and he said, "Thus shalt thou say unto the children of Israel, 'I AM [*Yahwē*] hath sent me unto you.'" And God said moreover unto Moses, "Thus

---

[32]For more detail on this, see Metropolitan Hilarion (Alfeyev), *Orthodox Christianity* vol. 2, 67–74. In the present section we briefly summarize the conclusions made in this book.

[33]Literally "gods" (*pluralis majestatis*).

[34]Literally "my lords" (*pluralis majestatis*).

[35]Koehler and Baumgartner, *Hebräisches und aramäisches Lexikon*, 4:1320–1321. This interpretation remains conjectural (ibid.).

[36]The name *Yahwē* is encountered in the Old Testament about 6,700 times. In comparison, the name *'Ĕlōhîm* is encountered about 2,500 times, while the name *'Ǎḏōnay* is encountered about 450 times. See Floyd H. Barackman, *Practical Christian Theology: Examining the Great Doctrines of the Faith*, 3rd ed. (Grand Rapids, MI: Kregel, 1998), 65.

*Moses Striking
the Rock,*
Nicolas Poussin,
1649

shalt thou say unto the children of Israel, 'The LORD [*Yahwē*] God of your fathers, the God of Abraham, the God of Isaac, and the God of Jacob, hath sent me unto you: this is my name forever, and this is my memorial unto all generations.'" (Ex 3.13–15)

Although the meaning of the name Yahweh remains hidden and the name itself does not describe God, it is this name that was accepted in the Jewish tradition as the personal name of God: all other names of God are understood to be interpretations of the sacred name of Yahweh. Appearing to Moses on Mount Sinai, God "proclaims the name of Yahweh":

The LORD, the LORD (*Yahwē Yahwē*) God, merciful and gracious, longsuffering, and abundant in goodness and truth, keeping mercy for thousands, forgiving iniquity and transgression and sin, and that will by no means clear the guilty, visiting the iniquity of the fathers upon the children, and upon the children's children, unto the third and to the fourth generation. (Ex 34.6–7)

In this account, God's proclamation of the name of Yahweh, that is, his personal name, is the highest moment of revelation. All the other names that come after the name Yahweh—"God merciful and gracious," "longsuffering," and the rest—are merely interpretations of this name, adding, as it were, overtones to its basic sound.

The Old Testament religious cult is permeated with fear before the name of Yahweh. The Jerusalem temple is the temple of the name of God. Evidence for this is found in the account in the book of 1 Kings, which is dedicated to the building of the temple by King Solomon. The king begins his speech with the following words: "It was in the heart of David my father to build an house for the *name of the LORD* God of Israel. And the LORD said unto David my father, 'Whereas it was in thine heart to build an house *unto my name*, thou didst well that it was in thine heart. Nevertheless thou shalt not build the house; but thy son that shall come forth out of thy loins, he shall build the house *unto my name*'" (1 Kg 8.17–19).[37] He then utters a prayer, the text of which we have given earlier: in this prayer the name of God is mentioned multiple times as a synonym for God himself (1 Kg 8.23–53).

The entire life of the temple is focused on the worship of the name of God: the temple is called by the name of the Lord; the name of the Lord dwells in the temple; people come to the temple, having heard of the name of the Lord; the name of the Lord is confessed in the temple. The sacred name of Yahweh defines the entire liturgical order of the temple. Even after the first temple was destroyed and the second temple was built in its place after the return of the Jews from the Babylonian captivity, the temple is still understood as before to be the place in which the name of God dwells (1 Esd 6.12). By this time the Jews had ceased, out of reverence, to pronounce the name of Yahweh, substituting other names for it instead. Only once a year, on the Day of Atonement, was the high priest to enter into the sanctuary in order—with fear and tremblingto —pronounce this holy name in a whisper.

The cult of the name of God occupies a central place in the Psalter, where the name of the Lord is said to be great, glorious, holy, and awesome, and where it is an object of love, praise, glorification, reverential worship, hope, and fear:

O Lord, our Lord, how wonderful is thy name in all the earth! (Ps 8.2)

[37]Emphasis added.

O magnify the Lord with me, and let us exalt his name forever. (Ps 33.4)

I will give praise unto thee forever . . . and I will wait on thy name, for it is good before thy saints (Ps 51.11).

O God, in thy name save me. (Ps 53.3)

Sing unto God, chant unto his name; prepare ye the way for him that rideth upon the setting of the sun. Lord is his name; yea, rejoice before him. (Ps 67.5)

His name shall be blessed unto the ages, before the sun doth his name continue. And in him shall be blessed all the tribes of the earth, all the nations shall call him blessed. Blessed is the Lord. . . . And blessed is the name of his glory . . . (Ps 71.17–19)

The beggar and the poor man shall praise thy name. (Ps 73.21)

We will confess thee, O God, we will confess thee, and we will call upon thy name. (Ps 74.2)

In Judea God is known, his name is great in Israel. (Ps 75.2)

Help us, O God our Savior, for the sake of the glory of thy name. (Ps 78.9)

All the nations whom thou hast made shall come and shall worship before thee, O Lord, and shall glorify thy name. (Ps 85.9)

Holy and terrible is his name. (Ps 110.9)

I will exalt thee, O my God, my king, and I will bless thy name forever, yea, forever and ever. (Ps 144.1)

The name of God is found in all the prophetic books. One of the passages from the prophet Isaiah begins with these words: "Behold, the name of the LORD cometh from far." And then the Lord is presented as an anthropomorphic being, with lips, a tongue, a neck, and breath: ". . . burning with his anger, and the burden thereof is heavy; his lips are full of indignation, and his tongue as a devouring fire, and his breath, as an overflowing stream, shall reach to the midst of the neck . . ." (Is 30.27–28). The "name of the LORD" at the beginning of the passage is practically synonymous with the Lord himself.

The Prophet Isaiah, Ugolino di Nerio, early 14th century

The quotations above show with what reverence the Old Testament treated the name of God. This name was reverently worshipped; before it people trembled; it was feared; people hoped in it; it was praised in song; it was loved. The name of Yahweh was understood to be the highest revelation of the glory of God and to be the meeting point between God and man. The other names of God mentioned in the Bible were also treated with reverence, but they were understood foremost as interpretations of the name of Yahweh, which stood at the center of the God-revealed religion.

It is necessary to take into account all this Old Testament context in order to understand the meaning that Jesus invested in the words "Hallowed be thy name." In his dialogues with his disciples and the people, Jesus speaks time and again of the name of his Father. As we have seen, already in the Old Testament God was sometimes called "Father," but it is in the New Testament that God is spoken of *primarily* as Father.

In Jesus' dialogues with the Jews, which are reflected in the Gospel of John, words such as these are encountered: "I am come in my Father's *name*" (Jn 5.43); "the works that I do in my Father's *name*, they bear witness of me" (Jn 10.25). This same Gospel describes Jesus' dialogue with the Jews and Greeks, during the course of which he speaks of his impending death and turns to the Father with the prayer, "Father, glorify *thy name*," to which a voice from heaven replies, "I have both glorified it, and will glorify it again" (Jn 12.27–28). In the prayer that he utters at the conclusion of the Last Supper, addressed to the Father, Jesus says:

> I have manifested *thy name* unto the men which thou gavest me out of the world. Thine they were, and thou gavest them me, and they have kept thy word. . . . Holy Father, keep through *thine own name* those whom thou hast given me, that they may be one, as we are. . . . And the glory which thou gavest me I have given them, that they may be one, even as we are one. . . . O righteous Father, the world hath not known

thee, but I have known thee, and these have known that thou hast sent me. And I have declared unto them *thy name*, and will declare it: that the love wherewith thou hast loved me may be in them, and I in them. (Jn 17.6, 11, 22, 25–26)[38]

In this prayer, Jesus takes stock of his earthly mission, as it were, and speaks to the Father about what he considers to be most important. And the main result of his mission is formulated in the following words: "I have manifested thy name unto [them]." These words can be understood to mean that Jesus revealed to his disciples the meaning of the name of God—the meaning that hitherto had been hidden from them. However, taking into account the synonymity of the concepts of "God" and "the name of God" in the biblical tradition, we can understand Jesus' words to mean that he has revealed to his disciples God himself.

In the Christian community, God—whom Jesus has revealed to it—continues to be glorified in the name of God, just as in the Old Testament. This is why the Lord's Prayer begins with the words "Hallowed [or 'sanctified,' *hagiasthētō*] be thy name." It is possible that this petition is connected with the verse from the book of the prophet Isaiah: "they shall sanctify my name" (Is 29.23).[39] In the Septuagint this verse is conveyed with the words *hagiasousin to onoma mou* (literally, "they will sanctify my name"). By analogy with this verse, the second petition in the Lord's Prayer can have this meaning as well: "Let thy name be sanctified." Grammatically, the verb *hagiasthētō*, which is translated as "Hallowed be," is the impersonal form of the imperative mood of the verb *hagiazō* ("sanctify") in the passive voice. In this form, the verb, which is related to the word *hagios* ("holy"), could mean "let . . . be holy," "let . . . be sanctified."

The name of God has holiness in and of itself: human prayer cannot add to its holiness. Gregory of Nyssa poses the rhetorical question: "Now even if I did not say that, would it be at all possible that God's name should not be holy?"[40] The following answer is usually given: the

---

[38]Emphasis added.

[39]Craig A. Evans, *Matthew*, New Cambridge Bible Commentary (Cambridge: Cambridge University Press, 2012), 146.

expression "Hallowed be" should be understood in the sense that the name of God should be hallowed, or glorified, in human beings, in the Christian community. In the words of Cyprian of Carthage, "We say this not wishing that God should be made holy by our prayers, but asking the Lord that his name should be hallowed in us."[41] John Chrysostom says, "For 'hallowed' is *glorified*. For His own glory He hath complete, and ever continuing the same, but He commands him who prays to seek that He may be glorified also by our life."[42]

The name of God has gracious power in and of itself. Although the petition "Hallowed be thy name" is expressed in the impersonal form, it implies the involvement of concrete persons: by pronouncing this petition, the Christian community prays that the power of the name of God may be extended to all of its members, fill their lives with the sense of God's presence, and give them the strength necessary to walk on the path to righteousness and perfection that has been outlined by Jesus in the Gospels.

3. "Thy Kingdom Come"

The theme of the kingdom of God, or the kingdom of heaven, occupies a central place in all the Gospels. On the lips of Jesus this expression has a multifaceted meaning. He calls the posthumous existence of a person who has been made worthy to dwell with God for his good works the "kingdom of God": in this sense, the kingdom of God is synonymous with "eternal life" as understood in contrast to "eternal torment." But the kingdom of God is not merely the reality of existence beyond the grave. It is also the new dimension of life that becomes accessible to a person living on earth when he discovers God for himself through Jesus Christ.

---

[40] Gregory of Nyssa, *The Lord's Prayer* 3 (trans. Graef, 48).

[41] Cyprian of Carthage, *On the Lord's Prayer* 12 (PPS 29:73).

[42] John Chrysostom, *Homilies on Matthew* 19.7 (NPNF[1] 10:134).

The Gospel of Luke contains a short dialogue between Jesus and the Pharisees concerning the kingdom of God: "And when he was asked by the Pharisees when the kingdom of God should come, he answered them and said, 'The kingdom of God cometh not with observation. Neither shall they say, "Lo here!" Or, "Lo there!" For, behold, the kingdom of God is within you'" (Lk 17.20–21). These words indicate that the kingdom of God cannot be tied to any place in space nor to any point in time. Moreover, the kingdom of God does not come "with observation," and this means that it cannot be equated with the second coming of Christ, of which the apostle Peter says, "But the day of the Lord will come as a thief in the night, in which the heavens shall pass away with a great noise, and the elements shall melt with fervent heat, the earth also and the works that are therein shall be burned up" (2 Pet 3.10). The second coming will be an observable event: "For as the lightning cometh out of the east, and shineth even unto the west, so shall also the coming of the Son of man be" (Mt 24.27). In contrast, the kingdom of God comes without noise, without fire, without the brilliance of lightning.

The coming of the kingdom of God is an event that is exclusively internal: it is the meeting of a human being with God, the revelation of God to the human being. It takes place in the heart and can be imperceptible to bystanders. The book of 1 Kings describes God's appearance to the prophet Elijah, to whom the Lord says, "Go out tomorrow and stand on the mountain before the Lord; and behold, the Lord will pass by, and before the Lord, a great and powerful wind will be rending the mountains and shattering the rocks; but the Lord will not be in the wind. After the wind, an earthquake, but the Lord will not be in the earthquake. After the earthquake, there will be a fire, but the Lord will be in the fire. After the fire, there will be a sound of a gentle breeze, and the Lord will be there" (1 Kg 19.11–12, OSB). This account is often understood in the Christian tradition as a foreshadowing of the meeting with God that takes place in a person's heart thanks to prayer.

In light of the above, the words of the Lord's Prayer, "Thy kingdom come," should not at all be understood as a request for the approach of the second coming of Christ. In the ancient Church the idea existed that the second coming was to happen in the lifetime of the first generation of Christians. Revelation, which according to its contents is a liturgical book, concludes with the following words: "He which testifieth these things saith, 'Surely I come quickly.' Amen. Even so, come, Lord Jesus" (Rev 22.20). The idea that Jesus was to come "quickly" was a consequence of the literal interpretation of his words: "Ye shall not have gone over the cities of Israel, till the Son of man be come" (Mt 10.23).

In accordance with these eschatological sentiments, Tertullian writes:

> "May your Kingdom come" likewise pertains to the same matter as "let your will be done," namely among ourselves. . . . Therefore, if the open manifestation of the Lord's Kingdom pertains to the will of God and to our expectation, how could anyone ask for an extension of this world, when the Kingdom of God, for whose coming we pray, is directed toward the consummation of this world. We should seek to reign the sooner and not to be enslaved the longer.[43]

Over time, however, the term "parousia" (*parousia*) came to be understood not only as referring to the coming of Jesus in glory, but also to his constant presence in the Church and in the heart of each believer. Already Origen spoke of the kingdom of God as being a person's internal condition:

> If, according to the word of our Lord and Savior, the Kingdom of God does not come with observable signs, and people will not say "Here it is!" or "There it is," but the Kingdom of God is within us (Lk 17.20–21), then it is clear that whoever prays for the coming of the Kingdom of God is praying most blessedly for the springing up and the bearing of fruit and the perfection of the Kingdom within himself. . . . I think that the meaning of "the Kingdom of God" is the happy settlement of our governing faculty, and the ordering of wise reflections. . . . But every sinner is tyrannized by the ruler of this present age.[44]

---

[43]Tertullian, *On Prayer* 5 (PPS 29:45–46).
[44]Origen, *On Prayer* 25.1 (PPS 29:169).

Often the two dimensions (the kingdom of God as the second coming of Christ and the kingdom of God as the internal condition of the believer) are combined in a single interpretation:

> Just as we desire that his name be hallowed among us, we ask that the Kingdom of God be made known to us. . . . It is indeed possible, beloved brothers, that Christ himself is that Kingdom whose coming we daily desire, whose coming we desire soon to see. For since he is himself the resurrection, because we shall rise in him, so we may understand that he is himself the Kingdom of God, because in him we are to reign.[45]

The kingdom of God is opposed to an earthly kingdom. When a person prays for the coming of the kingdom of God, he places himself within a framework that contrasts sharply with the one accepted in earthly reality. In this context the words from the Lord's Prayer take on a definite political subtext. One contemporary writer reflects:

> It is the poor who inherit the kingdom of God, because the rich and powerful are too proud to enter. They have been issued invitations, but they do not turn up. Jesus was well aware of the dynamics of this process. It comes out in Jesus' pithy sentence recorded in Luke: "The Law and the Prophets were in effect until John came; since then, the good news of the [kingdom] . . . of God is proclaimed and everyone tries to enter it by force" (16.16 NRSV). What does this mean? Jesus is not speaking against the Law or the Prophets (16.17), but he is signaling a change. Before John and himself, rulers owned the "kingdom." They owned the land, often owned slaves, and kept everybody in their places. The laws of the elite defended the kingdom. But now the crowds just walk in, past the guards. The rabble are storming through the gates and pushing their way into God's kingdom. You don't need tickets![46]

As we have said earlier, in commanding people to render "unto Caesar the things which are Caesar's, and unto God the things that are

---

[45]Cyprian of Carthage, *On the Lord's Prayer* 13 (PPS 29:74).

[46]Alan Storkey, *Jesus and Politics: Confronting the Powers* (Grand Rapids, MI: Baker Academic, 2005), 122.

The Tribute Money,
Titian, 1516

God's" (Mt 22.21), Jesus drew a clear dividing line between earthly and heavenly dominion. He never encroached on earthly dominion, nor did he dispute its authority. Jesus' message in itself was devoid of a political component, and he did not set before himself or his disciples any political goals. And nonetheless the teachings that he preached entered into a permanent conflict with earthly norms, because they oriented people toward different values. In saying "My kingdom is not of this world" (Jn 18.36), Jesus emphasized that the kingdom of which he spoke was alien to the world and any worldly power.

Jesus' teaching does not pluck a person out of everyday life, nor does it place him in opposition to the authorities, to society, or to the state. Contrary to the opinion of certain scholars, who believe that "Jesus and his movement were engaged not simply in resistance but in a more serious revolt of some sort against the established order in Palestine,"[47] Jesus was neither a revolutionary nor a social reformer. He did not call for the overthrow of the Roman authorities nor for any other reorganization of society:

> Christianity is not revolutionary in the outward sense of the word. It has entered into the world not as a revolutionary social force, calling for a violent altering of the order of life. It is impossible even to call Christianity a force of social reform. The nature of Christianity is altogether inexpressible in the social categories of this world. Christianity has come into the world, as the good news about salvation and about the Kingdom of God, which is not of this world. . . . A social revolution is all contrary to the words of Christ. Social revolution seeks first of all that which is "to be added unto you" [Mt 6.33], and not the Kingdom of God; the makers of social revolution do not seek a perfection, like to

[47]Richard A. Horsley, *Jesus and the Spiral of Violence: Popular Jewish Resistance in Roman Palestine* (San Francisco, CA: Harper & Row, 1987), 321.

the perfection of the Heavenly Father; they want to gain all the entire world and by this corrupt therein their soul; the social revolution seeks for an order of life, which will come in perceptible form, about which can be said, that lo here it is, or lo there it is [Lk 17.21]; the kingdom, to which the social revolution strives, is of this world. . . . A genuinely new, more perfect and better life comes from within, and not from without, it comes from a spiritual rebirth, and not from a mere change of social conditions, of social means.[48]

According to John Chrysostom, the essence of the transformation of the social order that Christ calls for consists in that "even before heaven, He hath bidden us make the earth a heaven and do and say all things, even while we are continuing in it, as having our way of life there [i.e., in heaven]."[49] The words of this fourth-century church father resonate with the above passage from the twentieth-century Russian philosopher in that both writers see the goal of Christ's teaching to be not the reorganization of the earthly world order, but the filling of human life with new meaning.

It is impossible to turn the earth into paradise through social reforms. But earthly life can become "the kingdom of God come with power" (Mk 9.1) for those who live on earth according to different laws, which morally surpass earthly laws. Only by following these laws established by Christ can a person make earth into heaven. And only then can the kingdom of heaven come everywhere—not only in heaven, but also on earth.

---

[48]Nicolas Berdyaev, "Tsarstvo Bozhie i tsarstvo kesarya" [The kingdom of God and the kingdom of Caesar], in *Izbrannye filosofskie sochineniya 1920-x gg.* [Selected philosophical works of the 1920s] (Moscow: DirectMEDIA, 2015), 17–18. English translation from Nicolas Berdyaev, "The Kingdom of God and the Kingdom of Caesar," trans. Stephen Janos, Berdyaev Online Bibliotek Library, 2001, http://www.berdyaev.com/berdiaev/berd_lib/1925_303.html.

[49]John Chrysostom, *Homilies on Matthew* 19.7 (NPNF[1] 10:135).

4. "Thy Will Be Done on Earth, as It Is In Heaven"

The will of God is one of the most important concepts in biblical theology. According to the Bible, the will of God was the reason for the creation of the universe, the sun and the moon, the stars and the sky: "for he spake, and they came to be; he commanded, and they were created" (Ps 148.3–5). In accordance with the will of God, by the hands of God was man created (Ps 118.73). The fall of Adam and Eve (Gen 3.1–7) was a violation of the will of God and the reason that they were cast out of paradise (Gen 3.24). Nevertheless, their descendents preserved the awareness that the will of God was to act in the world. This awareness was renewed in each new generation. The kings of Israel strove to fulfill the will of God. They accompanied important decisions with the words "If . . . it be of the LORD our God" (1 Chr 13.2). The expectation of the coming Messiah was the expectation that "the will of the LORD shall prosper in his hand" (Is 53.10).

The Son of God became the Son of Man in fulfillment of the will of the Father: "For God so loved the world, that he gave his only begotten Son, that whosoever believeth in him should not perish, but have everlasting life" (Jn 3.16). Jesus said of himself, "For I came down from heaven, not to do mine own will, but the will of him that sent me" (Jn 6.38). Obedience to the will of the Father was the main driving force of the earthly mission of the Son of God. In fulfilling this obedience, he voluntarily endured suffering and death.

Before the fall of Adam and Eve, the will of man coincided with the will of God. After the fall, human will often was in conflict with God's will. The first-created humans did not have sinful inclinations: their free will was in obedience to the will of God and in harmony with it. But after mankind ate of tree of the knowledge of good and evil, that is, became familiar with evil and sin through experience, their free will ended up facing a perpetual choice between good and evil.

The Fall of Man, Hendrik Goltzius, 1616

Being fully human, Jesus Christ also possessed a fully human will. However, his human will did not come into conflict with the will of God the Father. In the words of Maximus the Confessor (seventh century): "Because the same Person was wholly God with the humanity, and wholly human with the Godhead. The same Person, as man, subjected human nature in Himself, and through Himself, to God the Father, showing Himself as the flawless image and pattern for us to imitate."[50]

The most striking example of the combination in Jesus of two wills—the divine and the human—is found in his prayer in the Garden of Gethsemane. According to Matthew, Jesus at first addresses God with these words: "O my Father, if it be possible, let this cup pass from me: nevertheless not as I will, but as thou wilt" (Mt 26.39). For a second and third time he entreats the Father: "O my Father, if this cup may not pass away from me, except I drink it, thy will be done" (Mt 26.42, 44). In Mark the following version of the prayer is given: "Abba, Father, all things are possible unto thee; take away this cup from me; nevertheless not what I will, but what thou wilt" (Mk 14.36). Luke gives Jesus' prayer in this form: "Father, if thou

---

[50]Maximus the Confessor, *Disputation with Pyrrhus*. English translation from *The Disputation with Pyrrhus of our Father among the Saints Maximus the Confessor*, by Maximus the Confessor, trans. Joseph P. Farrell (South Canaan, PA: St. Tikhon's Seminary Press, 1990), 27.

be willing, remove this cup from me; nevertheless not my will, but thine, be done" (Lk 22.42). All four versions of the prayer given by the Evangelists testify that as a human being, Jesus was afraid of death and wanted to avoid it, but he placed obedience to the will of the Father above his own human will. In addition, in one of the versions (Mt 26.42) we hear a word-for-word reproduction of the words from the Lord's Prayer. This coincidence cannot be accidental: "Jesus is the only biblical figure recorded as having prayed this way.... The last great prayer of his earthly ministry was clearly putting into practice the teaching he gave his disciples."[51]

The petition that Jesus included in the Lord's Prayer concerning the will of God is intended to teach people to submit to it. This will is accomplished in heaven, that is, in the angelic world, where nobody opposes it. The Christian prays also that it may be accomplished on earth, in human society. This does not contradict that fact that each person has his own will and that while praying to God he may ask for what he wants, just as Jesus himself asked that, if it were possible, the cup of suffering might pass from him. But, like Jesus, the one who believes in him must submit his own will to the will of God: laying aside his own desires while praying to God, he must humbly await God's answer and accept it as it is. The First Epistle of John says, "If we ask any thing according to his will, he heareth us" (1 Jn 5.14). From this we can conclude that if a person asks in prayer for something *not* according to divine will, God may not even hear such a prayer.

Jesus does not call his disciples to passively wait for the fulfillment of the will of God: he calls them to be coworkers with God in fulfilling his will. Herein lies the cardinal difference between the Christian approach to life and the worldview that is reflected in the widespread saying, "Everything is the will of God." God does not will "everything": God wills good, but he does not will evil and sin. By committing a sin, a person goes against the will of God and enters into conflict with his will. All the events of human history are divided into two categories: those that take place *according to*

---

[51]Gerald Bray, *Yours is the Kingdom: A Systematic Theology of the Lord's Prayer* (Nottingham, UK: Inter-Varsity Press, 2007), 74.

Olive Tree in the Garden of Gethsemane, V. D. Polenov, 1882

the will of God, and those that happen *against* the will of God. God permits the latter but does not bless or approve of it.

When a person prays for the fulfillment of God's will "on earth, as it is in heaven," he is asking for good to triumph over evil in the conditions of earthly life, that the good divine will prevail over the evil human will. At the same time, he is praying that he himself might become God's coworker. In a collection of orations by an anonymous writer at the beginning of the fifth century, ascribed to John Chrysostom, it is noted that the first three petitions of the Lord's Prayer are not addressed to God directly: they employ the impersonal form ("hallowed be thy name," "thy kingdom come," "thy will be done"). This indicates that the fulfillment of these petitions is a mutual work, "because mankind needs God and God needs mankind in order to do righteousness. For just as a person cannot do good unless he has the help of God, so neither can God work a good deed in a person unless the individual wants it."[52]

In the words "on earth, as it is in heaven," terminology characteristic of the Bible is used, beginning with its very first line. A detailed analysis of the use of the terminological pair "heaven" and "earth" in the Old Testament[53] shows that it is encountered no fewer than 185 times in total. Sometimes heaven and earth are united into one thematic pair, connected by the conjunction "and": "In the beginning God created the heaven and the earth" (Gen 1.1); "Thus the heavens and the earth were finished" (Gen 2.1); "The heavens and the earth shall shake" (Joel 3.16). Sometimes earth is juxtaposed with heaven within a single sentence; for example: "For what God is there in heaven or in earth, that can do according to thy works, and according to thy might?" (Deut 3.24); "The LORD he is God in heaven above, and upon the earth beneath" (Deut 4.39); "Thou shalt not make thee any graven image, or any likeness of any thing that is in heaven above, or that is in the earth beneath, or that is in the waters beneath the earth" (Deut 5.8); "For what have I in heaven? And besides thee, what have I desired upon earth?" (Ps 72.25); "Let the heavens be glad and let the earth rejoice" (Ps 95.11). In some cases "heaven" is not mentioned as part of a pair with "earth," but with another concept that has a similar function: the depths (Ps 106.26) or hades (Ps 138.8).

Jesus' direct speech, as it is reflected on the pages of the New Testament, fully absorbed the tradition of simultaneously using the concepts of "heaven" and "earth" as a terminological pair:

> Till heaven and earth pass, one jot or one tittle shall in no wise pass from the law. (Mt 5.18; Mk 13.31; Lk 16.17)

> Swear not at all: neither by heaven, for it is God's throne, nor by the earth, for it is his footstool. (Mt 5.34–35)

---

[52]Pseudo-Chrysostom, *Commentary on Matthew* 14. English translation from *Incomplete Commentary on Matthew*, trans. Kellerman, 1:123–124.

[53]Pennington, *Heaven and Earth*, 163–165.

Lay not up for yourselves treasures upon earth, where moth and rust doth corrupt, and where thieves break through and steal; but lay up for yourselves treasures in heaven, where neither moth nor rust doth corrupt, and where thieves do not break through nor steal. (Mt 6.19–20)

I thank thee, O Father, Lord of heaven and earth. (Mt 11.25; Lk 10.21)

Whatsoever thou shalt bind on earth shall be bound in heaven, and whatsoever thou shalt loose on earth shall be loosed in heaven. (Mt 16.19)

Heaven and earth shall pass away, but my words shall not pass away. (Mt 24.35; Lk 21.33)

Among such stands the petition from the Lord's Prayer: "Thy will be done on earth, as it is in heaven."

The terminological pair of "heaven" and "earth" fully expresses the peculiar properties of the religious worldview reflected in the Bible. This worldview is based on the idea that there are two polar principles, or two dimensions, in the world—the higher and the lower. God is present in both: he reigns both in heaven and on earth. At the same time, in heaven he reigns unhindered, but earth is the arena of the struggle between good and evil. On earth some people are faithful to God, while others are not; some "walk in his ways" (Deut 8.6; 10.12; 11.22; 19.9; 26.17; 28.9; 1 Kg 2.3; Ps 118.3; 127.1), while others "leave the paths of uprightness, to walk in the ways of darkness" (Prov 2.13).

The coming of the Son of God to earth radically changed the relationship between the two opposing principles. This relationship, as it might seem on the basis of certain passages of the Old Testament, formed as a result of a sort of consensus between God and the devil. In the opening chapters of the book of Job, God is presented observing what is happening on earth, while the devil acts within the limits granted to him by God (Job 1.6–19, 2.1–7). The long dispute between Job and friends takes place while God is completely silent; the devil also does not manifest himself in any way in this dispute. At the end of the book, God unexpectedly appears on the scene, answering Job out of the whirlwind (Job 38.1). However, he does

The Vehamor Gospel,
7th–9th century

not become a part of the action: he only reminds Job of his unlimited power and of the insurmountable distance dividing mankind from God and earth from heaven.

With the coming of the Son of God into the world, this distance disappears. Now heaven itself has descended to earth, and God himself, in the person of Jesus, enters into hand-to-hand combat with the devil: instead of being an external, albeit sympathetic, observer, he becomes an active participant. In this context, the words concerning the fulfillment of God's will on earth as in heaven take on a special meaning. These words were not spoken from heaven: Jesus pronounced them on earth, in the circle of his disciples. And he himself becomes the guarantor and conduit of God's will on earth.

In order that the will of God might be realized, only one thing is required of human beings—consent. This consent makes human beings like the angels and like Christ himself:

> We who pray while still on earth, being mindful that in heaven the will of God is done by all the inhabitants of the heavens, should pray that in like manner the will of God should be done on earth by us as it is by them. This will come about when we do nothing contrary to his will. And when the will of God as it is in heaven is upheld by us who are on the earth then we shall be made like those who are in heaven, bearing, like them, the image of the heavenly one (1 Cor 15.41), inheriting the Kingdom of the heavens while those who follow us on earth pray that they may in turn become like us who are in heaven.[54]

Certain commentators see the expression "on earth, as it is in heaven" as pertaining to the spiritual and bodily composition of a human being:

> For since we are in possession of a body from the earth and a spirit from heaven we are ourselves both earth and heaven, and we pray therefore that the will of God be done in both, that is both in our body and in our

[54]Origen, *On Prayer* 26.1 (PPS 29:172).

spirit. For there is strife between the flesh and the spirit, a daily contest as they clash with one another so that we do not the things we desire. While the spirit seeks the things that are heavenly and godly, the flesh lusts after the things which are earthly and worldly; and therefore we ask that reconciliation be brought about between the two through the help and assistance of God, and so, while the will of God is undertaken both in the spirit and in the flesh, the soul which is reborn through him may be saved.[55]

5. "Give Us This Day Our Daily Bread"

The expression "daily bread" has firmly entered the modern lexicon with the meaning of everyday food that is necessary for life. In many languages the Greek *epiousios* in the expression "daily bread" is translated with a word equivalent to "daily" (Latin *panis quotidianus*, French *pain quotidien*).

However, the exact meaning of this word has been the subject of disputes over the course of multiple centuries. In classical Greek this word did not exist at all. The Aramaic word that is conveyed using this word is unknown, and all attempts to reconstruct it are hypothetical in nature.[56] The combination of the prefix *epi* (on, above) with the noun *ousia* (essence, existence, substance, property) can be understood in several ways. If we take *ousia* to mean "substance" (as in wealth and possessions) or "property"—the word is used in this sense in, for example, the story of the woman who had "spent all her living upon physicians" (Lk 8.43)—then *epiousios* can be understood to mean "necessary for existence." If, however, the term *ousia* is taken to mean "essence," as it was understood in Greek patristic thought, then a literal translation of *epiousios* would be "above-essential," or "supersubstantial."

[55]Cyprian of Carthage, *On the Lord's Prayer* 16 (PPS 29:76).
[56]See Matthew Black, *An Aramaic Approach to the Gospels and Acts*, 2nd ed. (Oxford: Clarendon Press, 1954), 149–153.

Based on the closeness in meaning between the term in question to the expression *hē epiousa*, which means "the coming day," it may be possible to translate the petition from the Lord's Prayer thus: "Give us this day our bread of tomorrow." The term is also close to the concept of *epi tēn ousan* [*hēmeran*], which means "for the present day." Finally, the interpretation of the term may be connected with the concept *to epion*, which means "future": in this case "our daily bread" would be "our future bread."[57]

The multiplicity of interpretations for the term rendered "daily" is reflected in the patristic tradition. "What is '*daily bread*'? That for one day," asserts John Chrysostom.[58] Gregory of Nyssa interprets "daily bread" as "things necessary for the day," or "bodily requirements," emphasizing that we should ask of God only what is most necessary, and only for a single day.[59]

On the other hand, already in the third century the interpretation had become widespread that "daily bread" referred to the bread of the Eucharist, that is, the Body of Christ, administered to believers in the Eucharist. This interpretation derives from the custom of saying the Lord's Prayer at the eucharistic liturgy before communion. This is most extensively discussed by Origen:

> Since some assume that we are being charged to pray for corporeal bread, we should set forth the truth concerning the supersubstantial bread in order to refute their false opinions. . . . [T]he nourishing word is varied and diverse, for not all are able to receive sustenance from the solidity and strength of divine doctrines, he desires to supply nourishment fitting for the training of those who are nearer perfection as he says: "The bread which I shall give is my flesh, which I shall give on behalf of the life of the world" (Jn 6.51). . . . That is the true food, the flesh of Christ, which, being word, became flesh, in accordance with the statement: "And the Word was made flesh" (Jn 1.14).He "dwells among us" whenever we eat and drink him. . . . [Therefore,] let us, in

---

[57]Luz, *Matthew 1–7*, 320–321.
[58]John Chrysostom, *Homilies on Matthew* 19.8 (NPNF[1] 10:135).
[59]Gregory of Nyssa, *The Lord's Prayer* 5 (trans. Graef, 69–70).

fidelity to the teaching of our Savior, rightly believing and rightly living, ask the Father for the living bread, which is the same as the supersubstantial bread.[60]

Origen then enters into a detailed analysis of the origin of the word *epiousios*. He notes that this word "is not employed by any of the Greeks or of the wise, nor is it in colloquial use among the common people. Rather, it seems to have been invented by the evangelists." It is formed from the term "being" (*ousia*), which is used to designate the first principle of the entire material world. This first principle, in Origen's opinion, is of a spiritual nature. Therefore, similar to how material bread turns into the substance of the body through digestion, in the same way heavenly bread "gives a share in its own power" to the one who eats of it. From all this the writer concludes: "The 'supersubstantial' bread, therefore, is that which corresponds most closely to the rational nature, and is related to its essence, bringing about health and well-being and strength in the soul and, since the word of God is immortal, communicating its own immortality to anyone who eats it."[61]

The Savior Enthroned,
icon, Palekh, 19th century

Cyprian of Carthage also interprets this petition from the Lord's Prayer in a eucharistic key:

For Christ is the bread of life (Jn 6.48), and thus he is not the bread of anybody but ourselves. And in the same way that we say "Our Father," since he is the Father of those who have knowledge and belief, so we refer to "our" bread, since Christ is the bread of those who participate in his body. Moreover we ask that this bread should be given to us daily lest we who are in Christ, and receive his eucharist daily as the food of salvation, should be prevented by the interposition of some terrible sin and so be separated from the Body of Christ, inhibited from and not receiving the heavenly bread. . . . This he himself taught when he

[60]Origen, *On Prayer* 27.1, 4, 6 (PPS 29:175, 177, 178).
[61]Origen, *On Prayer* 27.9 (PPS 29:181).

said: "I am the bread of life which came down from heaven. If anyone
should eat of my bread he shall live forever. And the bread which I shall
give is my flesh for the life of the world" (Jn 6.51). Thus, when he says
that anyone who eats of his bread will live forever, so making it clear
that those who participate in his body and receive the eucharist, communicating by right, are those who live.[62]

Tertullian unites both interpretations. In his thinking, Christ calls for
us to pray for both the eucharistic bread of life as well as everyday, material bread.

For Christ is our bread, because Christ is life and bread is life. . . . [H]is
body is accounted bread: "This is my body" (Mt 26.26; 1Cor 11.24).
. . . Therefore, when we ask for our daily bread, we are asking that we
should perpetually be in Christ and that we should not be separated
from his body. Although, that clause is open to a carnal interpretation.
. . . [The Lord says], "Would a father take away bread from his children
and hand it over to dogs" (Mt 15.26).And again: "Would he hand his
son a stone when he asks for bread?" (Mt 7.9)[63]

In order to understand the original meaning of Jesus' words, it seems
to us that it is necessary to concentrate not so much on the meaning of
the multivalent and ambiguous term "*epiousios*" as on the meaning of the
concept of "bread" itself.

The term "bread" is first used at the beginning of the Bible in God's
words to Adam after the latter's fall: "In the sweat of thy face shalt thou eat
bread" (Gen 3.19). Later, bread is mentioned in the story of how Melchizedek, the king of Salem, brought out bread and wine to bless Abraham (Gen
14.18). Abraham served bread to the three travellers who came to him (Gen
18.5). Bread (or grain) plays an important role in the story of Joseph and his
brothers: when Joseph, who had stored up a lot of grain, became second
only to Pharaoh while all the surrounding lands were suffering famine, his
brothers came to him for grain (Gen 42.1–5). Before bringing the people

[62]Cyprian of Carthage, *On the Lord's Prayer* 18 (PPS 29:78).
[63]Tertullian, *On Prayer* 6 (PPS 29:46–47).

The Meeting of Abraham and Melchizedek, Dieric Bouts, 1464

of Israel out of Egypt, God established the feast of Passover, ordering the people to remove everything leavened from their homes and to eat only unleavened bread for seven days (Ex 12.15–20). In the wilderness, when the people ran short of bread, God sent them "bread from heaven"; the people called this bread "manna" (Ex 16.2–31).

In the Bible, bread is a universal symbol of food. The quality of the bread and the mood in which someone eats bread symbolize the quality of a person's life. In sorrows, tears become bread for a person (Ps 41.1; 79.6), but when God favors his works, he eats bread with joy (Eccl 9.7). Wicked and evil people "eat the bread of wickedness" (Prov 4.17), while the virtuous and hardworking wife "eateth not the bread of idleness" (Prov 31.27).

Bread was part of Old Testament worship. The showbread was to be always set on a special table in the tabernacle (Ex 25.23–40), and then in the temple (1 Kg 7.48; 2 Chr 13.11): on this table the bread was placed while hot, as an offering to the Lord (1 Sam 21.6). The book of Leviticus contains a detailed description of how the showbread was to be baked and preserved: there had to be twelve loaves, according to the number of tribes of Israel; they were to be laid on the table every Sabbath, while the bread remaining from the previous Sabbath had to be eaten by the priests "in the holy place; for it is most holy unto him of the offerings of the LORD" (Lev 24.5–9). The same book contains instructions concerning the "meat [i.e., grain] offering": it consisted of flour that a person would bring to the priests, and they would burn it on the altar (Lev 2.1–13). The first sheaf of the harvest was brought as a sacrifice to the Lord, and the grain offering together with it (Lev 23.10–13).

The entirety of this long prehistory has a direct bearing on Jesus and his ministry, as well as on his teaching concerning "daily bread" and "bread from heaven." Bread is mentioned multiple times in all four Gospels. In the wilderness Jesus, while being tempted by the devil, refuses to turn stones into bread, responding to the temptation with these words from the Old Testament: "Man shall not live by bread alone, but by every word that proceedeth out of the mouth of God" (Mt 4.4). In reply to the accusation that he was breaking the Sabbath, Jesus reminds the Pharisees of the story of David, who ate the consecrated showbread, which was not to be eaten by anyone except the priests (Mt 12.1–4; Mk 2.23–28; Lk 6.1–5). Twice he performs a miracle involving bread—once by multiplying five loaves and two fishes and feeding five thousand people with them, not counting women and children (Mt 14.15–21; Mk 6.35–44; Lk 9.12–17; Jn 6.5–13), and at another time feeding four thousand people in a similar way with seven loaves and a few fishes (Mt 15.32–38; Mk 8.1–9).

The Gospel of John contains Jesus' conversation with the Jews in the synagogue in Capernaum. In this conversation he says of himself:

The synagogue
in Capernaum

I am the bread of life. He that cometh to me shall never hunger; and he that believeth on me shall never thirst. . . . I am that bread of life. Your fathers did eat manna in the wilderness, and are dead. This is the bread which cometh down from heaven, that a man may eat thereof, and not die. I am the living bread which came down from heaven. If any man eat of this bread, he shall live forever; and the bread that I will give is my flesh, which I will give for the life of the world. . . . Verily, verily, I say unto you, except ye eat the flesh of the Son of man, and drink his blood, ye have no life in you. (Jn 6.35, 48–51, 53)

This conversation was the prologue to an event that John does not record, but which is reflected in the three Synoptic Gospels. They tell of how at the Last Supper Jesus took bread and, having blessed it, broke it and, distributing it to the disciples, said: "Take, eat; this is my body." Then, having taken the cup with the wine, he gave it to them with the words: "Drink ye all of it; for this is my blood of the new testament, which is shed for many for the remission of sins" (Mt 26.26–28; Mk 14.22–24; Lk 22.19–20). It is this that Jesus was speaking of to the Jews in that conversation, the meaning of which even many of his disciples failed to understand at the time (Jn 6.60).

The Last Supper was the event that began the reckoning of eucharistic time in the life of the Christian Church. This time continues even now, inasmuch as the Eucharist is celebrated in every church community according to Jesus' commandment, "This do in remembrance of me" (Lk 22.19). After he died and rose again, it was the Eucharist, celebrated in homes (for a long time, Christians did not have their own churches), that became the event that time and again made the disciples participants in the Last Supper and reunited them to Jesus, who had ascended into heaven but had not left them. And each time the Eucharist was celebrated, they believed that Jesus was present among them and that his body—the same body that had suffered and died on the cross—was being received by them in the appearance of bread, together with his blood, which was poured out for the remission of the sins of the whole world, and was being received by them in the appearance of wine.

When interpreting the Lord's Prayer, we must take into account the eucharistic context in which the early Church understood this prayer. From the very beginning this prayer became a part of the Eucharist, and in this context the words "Give us this day our daily bread" could mean only one thing: a request to commune of the bread that came down from heaven—that "supersubstantial" bread, which is the Body of Christ broken in the Eucharist. The words of the Lord's Prayer are imbued with this meaning each time they are heard in the liturgy.

If, on the other hand, the Lord's Prayer is read outside of a liturgical context, for example, before a meal (as is the custom for Orthodox Christians), then "daily bread" is understood to refer to regular earthly food, which every person and every family need. Daily bread can be understood in an extended sense to refer to all that is necessary for a person to live. That being said, one's list of daily needs, as Gregory of Nyssa reminds us, should not include articles of luxury.[64]

Later on in the Sermon on the Mount we will hear Jesus' exhortations not vworry about food, drink, or clothing (Mt 6.25–32) and not to worry about tomorrow (Mt 6.34). The words of the Lord's Prayer concerning daily bread do not contradict these exhortations. The person who is praying is not asking for bread for tomorrow: he or she is asking for bread for today (this is why the attempts to define daily bread as "for tomorrow"

---

[64]Gregory of Nyssa, *The Lord's Prayer* 5 (trans. Graef, 63).

The Gathering of Manna, Tintoretto, 16th century

or "for the future" appear unpersuasive to us). In the words of Cyprian of Carthage, "Anyone who has begun to be a disciple of Christ, renouncing all things according to the demand of his master, needs to ask for his daily food, and not to extend the desires for which he prays into the future. . . . It would be a contradictory and negative thing were we, who ask that the Kingdom of God come quickly, to seek to live a long time in this present age."[65]

Here we cannot help but recall a detail from the story of how God fed the people of Israel with manna. Manna fell on the earth every morning, and the people could gather as much of it as they wanted. However, they were forbidden to keep it for the next day, except for the Sabbath, for which reserves of manna were stored up on the eve (Ex 16.19–22). The person who places his hope in God does not worry about tomorrow in the sense that he does not fear the future. He believes that God will not

[65]Cyprian of Carthage, *On the Lord's Prayer* 19 (PPS 29:79).

abandon him, and asks God for daily sustenance for himself and for his family.

In one of the accounts in the *Sayings of the Desert Fathers*, the story is told of how an elder and his disciple were walking along the seashore. The disciple wished to drink and told his elder about this. The elder prayed and said, "Drink from the sea." The disciple drank his fill of the water, which through the prayers of the elder had become fresh, but then he decided to store up water for the rest of the way. The elder asked, "Why did you pour [some into the vessel]?" The disciple answered, "Forgive me, in case I get thirsty later on." Then the elder said, "God is here and God is everywhere."[66]

This story, like the biblical account of the manna that came down from heaven each day, may seem to some to be a pious legend. Many people in our time do not believe at all in the possibility of miracles, saying, like Ernest Renan or Leo Tolstoy, "Miracles do not happen."[67]

Nevertheless, the miracle of the changing of the bread and wine into the Body and Blood of Christ is performed daily in the Church. One may believe it or not believe it, but it is impossible to deny the fact that is obvious to each person who comes into contact with the life of the Church: people who commune of this bread and this wine change and become better than they were before; their lives take on a new dimension. This daily miracle of personal transformation is observed by thousands of priests. Like doctors who prescribe the correct medicines and then observe their healing effect on the patient, priests offer people the medicine of the "bread which came down from heaven" and see the beneficial effect that this bread has on them.

---

[66] *Sayings of the Desert Fathers*, Bessarion 1. English translation from *Give Me a Word: The Alphabetical Sayings of the Desert Fathers*, trans. John Wortley, Popular Patristics Series 52 (Yonkers, NY: St Vladimir's Seminary Press, 2014), 77–78.

[67] "There has been hitherto no miracle proved" (Ernest Renan, *The Life of Christ*, trans. Charles Edwin Wilbour [New York, NY: Carleton, 1864], 44). Concerning the healing of the paralytic at the Sheep Gate: "The whole passage, generally regarded as the story of a miracle, proves only that there can be no miracles, and that the man is ill who waits for and expects miracles" (Leo Tolstoy, *The Four Gospels Harmonized and Translated*, vol. 2 [Croydon: The Brotherhood Pub. Co., 1896], 35).

A person cannot live without food, without daily bread. But "man shall not live by bread alone." A person needs spiritual food to no lesser degree than he needs material bread. The miracle of the transformation of regular earthly bread, baked by human hands, into the Body of Christ—this is only part of what takes place in the Church. The other part is the miracle of the inner transfiguration of a person, which takes place when a person meets God, communicates with Jesus through prayer, and unites with him by partaking of the heavenly bread.

6. "And Forgive Us Our Debts, as We Forgive Our Debtors"

The next petition in the Lord's Prayer has a direct bearing on a person's way of life, since it makes the forgiveness that a person receives from God directly dependent on whether the individual forgives his or her own debtors. Many of Jesus' instructions are dedicated to this topic, including the part of the Sermon on the Mount that follows immediately after the Lord's Prayer and which is a commentary on the verse in question:

> For if ye forgive men their trespasses, your heavenly Father will also forgive you; but if ye forgive not men their trespasses, neither will your Father forgive your trespasses. (Mt 6.14–15)

It seems proper to examine this verse of the prayer together with the commentary above.

First of all, let us turn our attention to the terms used. In the Lord's Prayer as it is recorded in Matthew, Jesus speaks of "debts" (*opheilēmata*). In the parallel text in Luke the term "sins" (*hamartiai*) is used. In the commentary on the prayer that is in Matthew, as well as in the parallel commentary in Mark (Mk 11.25), the term "trespasses" (*paraptōmata*) is used. Clearly, these three terms are understood to be synonymous, although each of them has its own particular meaning. The term *opheilēma* is

*Before
Confession,
A. I. Korzukhin,
1877*

used primarily in the financial sphere and means "debt," "indebtedness." The term *hamartia*, translated as "sin," originally referred to "missing the mark"; it can be translated as "mistake," "deviation," "failure." Finally, the term *paraptōma* means "error," "mistake,."

The word "debt," which is used in the version of the Lord's Prayer that is included in the Sermon on the Mount, brings to mind the parable of the two debtors (Mt 18.23–35). In this parable Jesus speaks about a man whose enormous debt was forgiven by his lord, but the servant in turn did not want to forgive the much smaller debt of his own debtor. The lord in the parable says to his servant, "Shouldest not thou also have had compassion on thy fellowservant, even as I had pity on thee?" (Mt 18.33). The parable serves as a reminder that God treats people leniently, forgiving them their debts, mistakes, missteps, and sins; consequently, people should also treat each other with the same leniency.

One must be able to forgive if one wishes to obtain forgiveness from God: this idea was firmly assimilated by the early Church. In the first half of the second century, Polycarp of Smyrna wrote to the Christian community in Philippi: "If then we entreat the Lord to forgive us, we ought also ourselves to forgive; for we are before the eyes of our Lord and God, and 'we must all appear at the judgment-seat of Christ, and must every one give an account of himself.'"[68] In the third century, Cyprian of Carthage said:

---

[68]Polycarp of Smyrna, *Epistle to the Philippians* 6 (ANF 1:34).

Philippi

Therefore he says that God is faithful in forgiving sins, for he faithfully keeps the promise that he has made that the Father's mercy and pardon would come to us who make our prayers on account of our debts and sins. The Savior added and affixed a clear rule, binding us by an assured condition and pledge, that just as we ask that our debts should be pardoned, following this we ourselves pardon those who are in debt to us. We know that we cannot obtain that for which we ask on account of our sins unless we ourselves do the same for those who have sinned against us. . . . On the day of judgment no excuse will remain to you, should you be judged in accordance with the sentence you have passed, and you will suffer whatever you have meted out.[69]

Do the words of the Lord's Prayer about forgiveness mean that a follower of Jesus must close his eyes to the sins of his neighbor, refraining from attempting to reason with him or to stop him from falling into even greater sins? Such a conclusion does not follow from the overall context of Jesus' teaching about forgiveness. On the one hand, to Peter's perplexed question, "Lord, how often shall my brother sin against me, and I forgive him? Till seven times?" Jesus replies, "I say not unto thee, until seven times: but, until seventy times seven" (Mt 18.21–22). By saying this he emphasizes

[69]Cyprian of Carthage, *Treatise on the Lord's Prayer* 22–23 (PPS 29:82).

that mercy and patience should not have limits: one has to forgive as many times as a person might sin. On the other hand, we find in Jesus' words the following instructions:

> Moreover if thy brother shall trespass against thee, go and tell him his fault between thee and him alone. If he shall hear thee, thou hast gained thy brother. But if he will not hear thee, then take with thee one or two more, that in the mouth of two or three witnesses every word may be established. And if he shall neglect to hear them, tell it unto the church. But if he neglect to hear the church, let him be unto thee as a gentile and a publican. (Mt 18.15–17)

While the answer to Peter speaks only of forgiveness and says nothing about the possibility of correcting a sinner, the passage above contains quite concrete instructions on how to correct sin in another person. The key word in this passage is the word "Church," which in the entire corpus of the Four Gospels is encountered only one other time—in Jesus' words to Peter: "Thou art Peter, and upon this rock I will build my Church; and the gates of hell shall not prevail against it" (Mt 16.18). While in this instance Jesus is speaking of the Church in its universal dimension, in the previous case, he is speaking of a local church community. It is the word "church," understood as referring to a specific church community, that indicates the context in which it is possible to correct one's neighbor.

So, when he answers Peter's question of how many times one is to forgive one's debtor, Jesus speaks of forgiving one's debtor but nothing about correcting him. This is connected with the fact that to correct someone else is a thankless and, as a rule, fruitless task. A husband cannot correct and change his wife for the better through admonishments or proofs of his own rightness, nor can a wife her husband, nor a friend his friend, nor a neighbor his neighbor. Correction must begin from one's own self; this is what the entire Sermon on the Mount is about. Its point is directed at a concrete person, the listener, whom Jesus is asking to examine *his own*, and not someone else's, value system, and to begin to live in a new way. If he does this, then those around him could also begin to change for the

The Apostle Peter with Keys, icon, 6th century

better—not as a result of admonishments, but because they see the "good works" of the one who follows Jesus' example in his way of life.

But when Jesus speaks of the church community, the community has a mechanism of collective action, its own means of forgiveness and punishment. It is necessary to begin with a one-on-one conversation. If this does

Mary Magdalene in Penitence, El Greco, circa 1589

not help, two or three witnesses must be called. If this also does not work, then the whole church community must be engaged to resolve the question. If, then, the person "neglect to hear the church," it is necessary to sever ties with him. Jesus consequently allows the possibility also of fully severing relations with a "debtor" and the possibility of excluding him from the church community ("let him be unto thee as gentile").

These are precisely the mechanisms established in the Church for the admonishment of a heretic or schismatic: first he must be called to the local bishop, then handed over to an ecclesiastical court, and then, if he perseveres in heresy or schism, excommunicated from the Church. If he is a bishop, then the ecclesiastical court judging him would be made up of bishops. Excommunication from the Church is the extreme and highest degree of punishment. How long the excommunication stays in effect depends exclusively on the one who is excommunicated: if he repents, he can be reinstated as a member of the community.

From the earliest period of the Church's existence, repentance was understood as a necessary condition for the forgiveness of sins. In the Lord's Prayer, nothing is said about repentance: one had to forgive a debtor not because he asked for it, but because he is a debtor. In Peter's question about how many times we are to forgive someone who has sinned against us, and also in Jesus' answer, nothing is said about whether the person in question has asked for forgiveness either. Augustine of Hippo emphasizes that we must forgive all sins and not only those for which someone has asked our forgiveness.[70]

However, the right to forgive belongs not only to individual members of the Church, but also to the entire church community. From the very first years of the Church's existence, the practice of confessing one's sins existed. This was spoken of already in the Acts of the Apostles: "And many that believed came, and confessed, and showed their deeds" (Acts 19.18). In

[70]Augustine of Hippo, *Our Lord's Sermon on the Mount* 2.8.29 (NPNF[1] 6:43).

Confession,
K. V. Lebedev,
19th–early 20th
century

the First Epistle of John we read, "If we confess [*homologōmen*] our sins, he is faithful and just to forgive us our sins, and to cleanse us from all unrighteousness" (1 Jn 1.9). The apostle James writes, "Confess your faults one to another, and pray one for another, that ye may be healed" (Jas 5.16).

Here what is being spoken of is not just a private conversation in which one Christian might acknowledge to another that he had committed an offense: what is most likely being spoken of is an act of a liturgical nature that would take place at a gathering of the community: "one to another" means "in the church," at a gathering. This is supported by these words from the *Didache*: "You shall confess your transgressions in the assembly [or 'church,' *ekklēsia*]."[71] In another passage in the *Didache*, the confession of sins is directly connected with the Eucharist: "In accordance with the [commandment] of the Lord, gather together to break bread and give thanks, first confessing your failings, so that your sacrifice may be pure."[72]

[71]*Didache* 4.14 (PPS 41:38).
[72]*Didache* 14.1 (PPS 41:42).

From this early Christian practice developed the sacrament of repentance, or confession, which existed in various forms, including in the form of a public acknowledgement of sins in front of the entire community or in front of a few priests. Later on only one form of confession was preserved: confession in front of a priest, in private. In Christian literature we encounter multiple indications that asking God for forgiveness in prayer is not enough: one must confess one's sins in front of a priest. Here are just a few examples:

> For, if we have done this and revealed our sins not only to God but also to those who can heal our wounds and our sins, our sins will be blotted out by him who says, "I shall blot out your transgressions like a cloud, and like a mist your sins" [Is 44.22].[73]

> Should one who wishes to confess his sins confess them to all, whoever they may be, or only to certain ones? . . . It is necessary that sins be confessed to those entrusted with *the stewardship of the mysteries of God*.[74]

> "The Father hath given all judgement unto the Son" [Jn 5.22]. But I see that the Son has placed it all in their hands [i.e. of priests]. . . . The priests of the Jews had authority to cure leprosy of the body, or rather, not to cure it, but only to certify the cure. . . . But our priests have received authority not over leprosy of the body but over uncleanness of the soul, and not just to certify its cure, but actually to cure it.[75]

> Are you a sinner? Enter into the Church, say, "I have sinned," and you dissolve the sin.[76]

[73]Origen, *Homilies on Luke* 17.8. English translation from *Homilies on Luke; Fragments on Luke*, by Origen, trans. Joseph T. Lienhard, Fathers of the Church 94 (Washington, DC: Catholic University of America Press, 1996), 74.

[74]Basil the Great, *Shorter Responses* 288. English translation from *The Asketikon of St Basil the Great*, by Anna M. Silvas, Oxford Early Christian Studies (Oxford: Oxford University Press, 2005), 431. Emphasis in original.

[75]John Chrysostom, *On the Priesthood* 3.5–6. English translation in *Six Books on the Priesthood*, by John Chrysostom, trans. Graham Neville, Popular Patristics Series 1 (Crestwood, NY: St Vladimir's Seminary Press, 1977), 72–74.

[76]John Chrysostom, *Homilies on Repentance* 3. English translation from *On Repentance and*

There are those who consider it sufficient for their salvation to confess their sins to God alone. . . . But invite thou a priest and confess thy hidden things to him. . . . For thy wounds, instead of God, use a priest as an intermediary, and open to him thy ways, and he will give thee a pledge of reconciliation.[77]

The sacrament of confession became an important addition to the prayer for forgiveness of sins that a Christian should offer daily. It is interesting that the Lord's Prayer is included in the order of confession. And if at the reading of this prayer at the Eucharist, the main stress is on the words concerning daily bread, then when this prayer is read before confession, the main stress falls on the words "and forgive us our debts." This forgiveness has a concrete, visible form in confession: after the sins are named, the priest forgives and absolves the penitent of all his sins in the name of God.

---

7. "And Lead Us Not into Temptation, but Deliver Us from Evil"

The last petition of the Lord's Prayer places before us a whole series of exegetical questions. What is temptation? Can God be a source of temptation and lead people into it? What is the "evil" (or "evil one") spoken of here—the devil, or evil in general? If God leads people into temptation, then what is the connection with the request to be delivered from evil?

The Greek term *peirasmos* can be translated as "temptation" or "testing." In the Bible we find a few different forms of temptation. People can be tested by God or tempted by the devil. God tests Abraham in order to

---

Almsgiving, by John Chrysostom, translated by Gus George Christo, Fathers of the Church 96 (Washington, DC: Catholic University of America, 1998), 30.

[77] Augustine of Hippo, *On the Visitation of the Sick* 2.4 (PL 40:1154–1155). (Translated by the present translator.)

prove his faith when he asks Abraham to sacrifice his son (Gen 22.1–2). God tests his people "in the furnace of affliction" (Is 48.10); he tests the "hearts and reins" of people (Ps 7.10; Jer 11.20); he tests "all the inward parts of the belly" of each person (Prov 20.27). On the other hand, the devil tempts Adam and Eve by convincing them to eat the forbidden fruit (Gen 3.1–6); the devil tempts Jesus three times in the wilderness (Mt 4.1–11). At the same time, however, the devil cannot act without God's consent: before he tempts Job, he asks God for permission (Job 1.6–12; 2.1–6).

In the Gospel of Matthew, including in the Sermon on the Mount, the term *peirasmos* (temptation) is encountered only three times. We first encounter it in the story of Jesus' temptation by the devil (Mt 4.1). Next, it is used in the Lord's Prayer. Finally, it is used for the third time in the Garden of Gethsemane, when Jesus addresses his disciples: "Watch and pray, that ye enter not into temptation. The spirit indeed is willing, but the flesh is weak" (Mt 26.41). These words were uttered at a critical moment—when, before his arrest, Jesus was praying to the Father that, if it were possible, the cup of suffering might pass from him. The disciples, however, were sleeping at that time, "for their eyes were heavy" (Mt 26.43). When he exhorts them to watch and pray, Jesus reminds them of the weakness of the flesh, which is one of the reasons that a person falls into temptation.

Of the other instances when the term "temptation" is used in the New Testament, we ought to take note of the First Epistle of Peter, where he speaks of the persecution of Christians: "Beloved, think it not strange concerning the fiery trial which is to try you, as though some strange thing happened unto you; but rejoice, inasmuch as ye are partakers of Christ's sufferings, that, when his glory shall be revealed, ye may be glad also with exceeding joy" (1 Pet 4.12–13). Here he is saying that temptation (trial) is sent, presumably by God himself, to test their faith. On the other hand, the same apostle Peter writes, "The Lord knoweth how to deliver the godly out of temptations, and to reserve the unjust unto the day of judgment to be punished" (2 Pet 2.9). The apostle James completely excludes the possibility of temptation coming from God: "Let no man say when he is tempted, I am tempted of God: for God cannot be tempted with evil, neither tempteth he any man; but every man is tempted, when he is drawn away of his own lust, and enticed" (Jas 1.13–14).

The apostle Paul refers to Satan as the source of temptation in the First Epistle to the Corinthians (1 Cor 7.5). In another passage in the same epistle he writes, "There hath no temptation taken you but such as is common to man, but God is faithful, who will not suffer you to be tempted above what ye are able, but will with the temptation also make a way to escape, that ye may be able to bear it" (1 Cor 10.13). The idea that God proportions temptation in accordance with a person's capability undergoes further development in the patristic tradition.

The Agony in the Garden of Gethsemane, or The Prayer for the Chalice, El Greco, circa 1608

The Epistle to the Hebrews develops the idea that Christ had to be "made like unto his brethren, that he might be a merciful and faithful high priest in things pertaining to God, to make reconciliation for the sins of the people. For in that he himself hath suffered being tempted, he is able to succor them that are tempted" (Heb 2.17–18). Here temptation is understood to refer not so much to the devil's temptation of Jesus in the wilderness, as to his suffering and death on the cross. Thanks to the redeeming work of Christ, "we have not a high priest which cannot be touched with the feeling of our infirmities, but was in all points tempted like as we are, yet without sin" (Heb 4.15).

In light of the biblical understanding of the term "temptation," the petition, "And lead us not into temptation," may be understood in two ways: as a request for God not to subject a person to trials beyond his strength, or as a request to be protected from diabolical temptations. In the writings of the church fathers we find both interpretations. According to Cyprian of Carthage, temptation comes from the devil, but only has as much power as God permits:

Three Temptations of Christ (detail), Sandro Botticelli, 1480–1482

We are shown in this clause that the adversary can do nothing against us unless God allows it beforehand. Thus all our fear and our devotion and our heedfulness should be directed toward God, so that when we are in temptation he allow no power to the evil one apart from that which he grants. . . . For two reasons is power granted against us: for punishment when we sin and for glory when we are proved. This is what we see in the case of Job, for God makes this clear when he says: "Look, everything that he has I give into your hands. But be sure that you do not touch the man himself" (Job 1.12).[78]

On the other hand, Basil the Great says that "a certain providential ordering is granted to us through affliction, that the amount of torment

---

[78]Cyprian of Carthage, *Treatise on the Lord's Prayer* 25–26 (PPS 29:84–85).

brought upon each to prove him is proportionate to the faith present in him."[79]

The theme of trials and temptations is reflected in ascetical literature. In *On the Freedom of the Mind*, Macarius of Egypt (fifth century) says:

> By God's providence, the testing of souls by various sorrows is permitted, in order that the souls that sincerely love the Lord may be made undoubtedly manifest. . . . For malice always has the same trick: to cast us into despondency in times of sorrow, in order to deprive us of our hope in the Lord.

Saint Macarius of Egypt, fresco, 16th century

> But God never allows the soul that hopes in him to grow exhausted in temptations or reach despair before that point. . . . And the evil one grieves the soul not to the degree to which he desires, but to the degree that God allows him. . . . It is known to God to what degree each soul must be exposed to temptation.[80]

Isaac the Syrian talks about both kinds of temptation: when God tests a person and when the devil tempts a person. The first case is an experience necessary for knowing God, and the second is what a Christian should fear and try to escape. Isaac was asked the following question: How do Christ's constant calls to endure temptation and suffering (Mt 10.28, 39) reconcile with his words "Watch and pray, that ye enter not into temptation" (Mt 26.41)? Isaac answers in the following way:

> Pray, He says, that you enter not into temptations of your faith. Pray that through your mind's self-esteem you enter not into temptation with the demon of blasphemy and pride. Pray that you enter not by

---

[79]Basil the Great, *Homily Explaining That God Is Not the Cause of Evil* 1. English translation from *On the Human Condition*, by Basil the Great, trans. Nonna Verna Harrison, Popular Patristics Series 30 (Crestwood, NY: St Vladimir's Seminary Press, 2005), 65.

[80]Macarius of Egypt, *On the Freedom of the Mind* 13 (PG 34:945). (Translated by present translator.) Compare with Macarius of Egypt, *Homilies* 55.1–3, 55.2 (Collection 1), in Heinz Berthold, ed., *Makarios/Symeon: Reden und Briefe; Die Sammlung I des Vaticanus Graecus 694 B*, vol. 1 (Berlin: Akademie-Verlag, 1973), 164–166.

Saint Isaac the Syrian, fresco, 16th century

God's permission into the manifest temptation of the devil because of the evil thoughts which you have entertained in your mind and on account of which you suffer temptation. Pray that the angel of your chastity may not withdraw from you, that you be not warred upon by the fiery war of sin, and be separated from him. Pray that you enter not into a temptation of vexation with someone. Pray that you enter not into temptations of soul through doubts and provocations by which the soul is violently drawn into great conflict.

Howbeit, prepare yourself with all your soul to receive bodily temptations. . . . For without trials God's providence is not seen, and you cannot obtain boldness before God, nor learn the wisdom of the Spirit, nor can divine longing be established in you. . . . And again, pray that you enter not into the fearsome temptation of the devil by reason of your arrogance, but because you love God, and you wish that His power might help you and through you vanquish His enemies. Pray that you enter not into such trials because of the wickedness of your thoughts and works, but rather in order that your love of God may be tested, and that His strength be glorified in your patience.[81]

---

[81]Isaac the Syrian, *Ascetical Homilies* 3 (trans. Holy Transfiguration Monastery, 137–138).

The petition "but deliver us from evil" can be understood in two ways, depending on what the term "evil" means. The Greek phrase *apo tou ponērou* can be translated as both "from the evil one" and "from evil." In Greek the genitive case of masculine and neuter nouns is the same: consequently, the expression could be derived from the masculine noun *ho ponēros* (the evil one, the wicked one, the devil) as well as from the neuter noun *to ponēron* (evil). In the first case evil is personified, while in the second it is impersonal in nature. In modern translations of the prayer, both variants are used; for example, some English translations read "deliver us from the evil one," while others read "deliver us from evil."

Meanwhile, the word "evil" is found in the Gospel of Matthew more than once. We heard earlier it in the words, ". . . for whatsoever is more than these cometh of evil" (Mt 5.37). It is true that there the genitive case is also used, which suggests the possibility of a double interpretation. However, in his explanation of the parable of the sower, Jesus uses the word in the nominative case (*ponēros*): "When any one heareth the word of the kingdom, and understandeth it not, then cometh the wicked one [or 'the evil one'], and catcheth away that which was sown in his heart" (Mt 13.19). Here a specific figure is in view: in the parallel passages in the Synoptics where this parable is recorded, he is called "Satan" (Mk 4.15) and "the devil" (Lk 8.12). It is in this sense that the petition "but deliver us from evil" is understood by the majority of church fathers: "The evil is the demon opposing us, from whom we pray to be set free"[82]; "[Jesus] here calls the devil 'the wicked one,' commanding us to wage against him a war that knows no truce."[83]

Let us point out one interesting compositional peculiarity of the Lord's Prayer. Its first word in the original is "Father," addressed to God, and its last word is "evil," which recalls the devil. A person's life takes place between two poles: God, who is the source of all good, and the devil, the source of evil. The choice between good and evil, between God and the devil, between

---

[82]Cyril of Jerusalem, *Mystagogical Catecheses* 5.18. English translation from *Lectures on the Christian Sacraments: Greek Original and English Translation*, by Cyril of Jerusalem, trans. Maxwell E. Johnson, Popular Patristics Series 57 (Yonkers, NY: St Vladimir's Seminary Press, 2017), 133.

[83]John Chrysostom, *Homilies on Matthew* 19.10 (NPNF[1] 10:136).

life and death, is made daily and is reflected in an individual's actions, his way of life and conduct, his thoughts and feelings. God reminded the people of Israel of this choice even in the time of Moses: "I have set before you life and death, blessing and cursing: therefore choose life, that both thou and thy seed may live" (Deut 30.18).

Jesus, the new Moses, gave people concrete advice to help them choose the way to God, goodness, truth, and life, and not to deviate onto the "way of unrighteousness" (Ps 118.29, 104), not to succumb to the temptations of the devil. The Sermon on the Mount serves as a compass that shows us the right direction. The Lord's Prayer, in its turn, is a condensed version of the Sermon on the Mount, a "summary of heavenly doctrine," in which "is nothing whatever with regard to our pleading and our prayer omitted, nothing not contained."[84] This prayer, like the Sermon on the Mount as a whole, contains the guiding line that helps a person not to lose his way, fall into temptation, or fall prey to the evil one.

8. The Concluding Doxology

In the Textus Receptus and translations based on it, the Lord's Prayer concludes with these words: "For thine is the kingdom, and the power, and the glory, forever. Amen" (Mt 6.13). This sentence is absent from the majority of the ancient and most authoritative manuscripts of the Gospel, on the basis of which it has been excluded from modern critical editions of the New Testament.[85] The appearance of this sentence in certain manuscripts, as well as its inclusion in the commentaries of the church fathers, is assumed to be connected with the liturgical use of the Lord's Prayer.

In the Christian divine services each prayer concluded with a doxology, and already from a very early period a doxology was added to the Lord's Prayer. We have the first witness to this in the *Didache*, where to the prayer

[84]Cyprian of Carthage, *On the Lord's Prayer* 9 (PPS 29:70).
[85]Nestle, Nestle, and Aland, *Novum Testamentum graece*, 13.

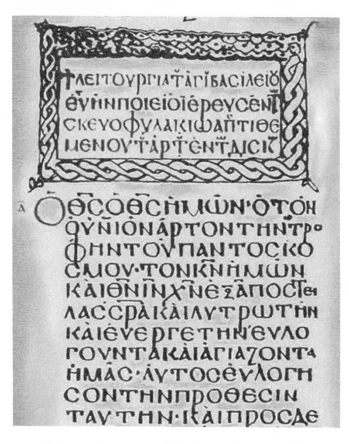

The Barberini
Euchologion

are added the words "for Thine is the power and the glory forever."[86] In the
writings of Cyril of Jerusalem this doxology is absent, but the word "Amen"
(which is absent in the *Didache*) is added to the text of the prayer.[87] In the
writings of Gregory of Nyssa the Lord's Prayer is quoted without the concluding doxology; however, the commentary itself concludes with these
words: "But let us rise and say to God, *Lead us not into temptation*—that
is to say, into the evils of the world—*but deliver us from evil* which holds
sway in this world; from which may we be delivered by the grace of Christ,
for His is the power and glory with the Father and the Holy Spirit, now

---

[86]*Didache* 8.2 (ANF 7:379).

[87]Cyril of Jerusalem, *Mystagogical Catecheses* 5.18. English translation in *Lectures on the
Christian Sacraments*, trans. Johnson, 133.

and always, and forever and ever. Amen."[88] This ending is evidence that Gregory was familiar with the liturgical practice of adding a concluding doxology to the Lord's Prayer, but that he did not consider the doxology a part of the prayer. In contrast, Gregory's younger contemporary, John Chrysostom, saw the doxology as a part of the prayer. In his commentary it takes the form in which it would enter the Textus Receptus and the translations based on the latter: ". . . for Thine is the kingdom, and the power, and the glory, forever. Amen."[89]

Subsequently, in the West the doxology retained the form in which it is cited by Chrysostom. In this same form it entered many manuscripts of the New Testament. In the East, however, it acquired a Trinitarian character: "For thine is the kingdom and the power and the glory, of the Father and of the Son and of the Holy Spirit, now and ever and unto the ages of ages. Amen." The doxology is encountered in this form in all known Greek liturgical manuscripts, beginning with the Barberini Euchologion (end of the eighth century).[90]

This shows that, in the Orthodox Church, the Lord's Prayer, which is addressed to God the Father, is understood to relate also to the other two Persons of the Holy Trinity—the Son and the Holy Spirit. That being said, in the current practice of the Orthodox Church, the concluding doxology is pronounced only by the priest. In the absence of a priest, for example, when a believer reads the Lord's Prayer at home, the concluding doxology is left unsaid, and the prayer concludes with the words "but deliver us from evil."

[88]Gregory of Nyssa, *The Lord's Prayer* 5 (trans. Graef, 84). Emphasis in the original.

[89]John Chrysostom, *Homilies on Matthew* 19.10 (NPNF[1] 10:136).

[90]Robert F. Taft, *A History of the Liturgy of St. John Chrysostom*, vol. 5, *The Precommunion Rites*, Orientalia Christiana analecta 261 (Rome: Pontificio Istituto Orientale, 2000), 151–152.

Chapter 7

FASTING

The section on fasting connects thematically to the sections on alms-giving and prayer. Again we hear criticism of the hypocrites who make fasting a means to publicly demonstrate their own righteousness:

> Moreover when ye fast, be not, as the hypocrites, of a sad countenance: for they disfigure their faces, that they may appear unto men to fast. Verily I say unto you, they have their reward. But thou, when thou fast-est, anoint thine head, and wash thy face, that thou appear not unto men to fast, but unto thy Father which is in secret; and thy Father, which seeth in secret, shall reward thee openly. (Mt 6.16–18)

In this teaching Jesus does not dispute the practice of fasting itself. He is arguing only against an understanding of fasting that places the empha-sis on the external, conspicuous form of the practice while ignoring its internal content.

In the Old Testament the word "fasting" (ṣôm) signified complete absti-nence from food and drink during daylight hours—from sunrise to sunset: it has this meaning in the expression "fasted that day until evening" (Judg 20.26). A fast could last for as long as anywhere from one day to an entire week (1 Sam 31.13; 2 Sam 12.16–20), and even longer in exceptional cases. On the Day of Atonement (Lev 16.29–31) and on certain other days, a fast was prescribed for the entire people of Israel. They fasted as a sign of repentance (Joel 1.14, 2.15–17) or mourning (1 Sam 31.13; 2 Sam 1.12; Esth 4.3), they fasted in order to prevent punishment from God and other tribu-lations (Esth 4.16; Jer 36.9; Jon 3.5–9), and they fasted before major battles (Judg 20.26; 1 Sam 7.16; 14.24; 2 Chr 20.3). Fasts could be undertaken communally or individually: Moses fasted "forty days and forty nights;

The Prophet Daniel, icon, 16th century

he did neither eat bread, nor drink water" (Ex 34.28; Deut 9.9, 18); King David fasted for seven days as a sign of his repentance (2 Sam 12.16–20); the prophet Daniel fasted when praying (Dan 9.3).

In addition to abstinence from food, certain other external signs accompanied the practice of fasting: a person who was fasting could rend his garments, put on sackcloth, sleep in sackcloth, go about with a sorrowful countenance (1 Kg 21.27), and sprinkle ashes on his head (Neh 9.1).

Alongside the practice of fasting by complete abstinence from food and drink, there existed the practice of abstaining from certain types of food for an extended period of time: for example, Daniel abstained from "pleasant bread," meat, and wine over the course of three weeks (Dan 10.3). The Nazarites did not drink wine or eat other products made from the vine for the entire period of their vow (Num 6.1–12).

The prophets warned against formalism with regard to fasting and against considering fasting to be a sufficient means for pleasing God: fasting should not be reduced merely to abstinence from food and to ritual actions; it should be accompanied by good works toward one's neighbors. In the Book of Isaiah the people ask God, "Wherefore have we fasted . . . and thou seest not? Wherefore have we afflicted our soul, and thou takest no knowledge?" To this God replies:

> Behold, in the day of your fast ye find pleasure, and exact all your labors. Behold, ye fast for strife and debate, and to smite with the fist of wickedness; ye shall not fast as ye do this day, to make your voice to be heard on high. Is it such a fast that I have chosen? A day for a man to afflict his soul? Is it to bow down his head as a bulrush, and to spread sackcloth and ashes under him? Wilt thou call this a fast, and an acceptable day to the LORD? Is not this the fast that I have chosen? To loose the bands of wickedness, to undo the heavy burdens, and to let the oppressed go free, and that ye break every yoke? Is it not to deal thy bread to the hungry, and that thou bring the poor that are cast out to thy house? When thou seest the naked, that thou cover him; and that thou hide not thyself from thine own flesh? (Is 58.3–7)

In the parable of the publican and the Pharisee, Jesus mentions the practice of observing two fast days a week as one of the elements of outward Pharisaical piety (Lk 18.12). This Jewish practice is reflected in the *Didache*, which says, "Your fasts should not be with the hypocrites for they fast on the fifth and the second of the week, yet you fast on the fourth and on the preparation (Friday)."[1] The second and fifth days of the week were understood to correspond to Monday and Thursday (the days were

[1]*Didache* 8.1 (PPS 41:39).

Ravenna mosaic
on the parable of
the publican and
the Pharisee,
6th century

counted from Sunday, which was the first day); the fourth and sixth days
corresponded to Wednesday and Friday. The fast on Monday and Thursday is also mentioned in Jewish sources.[2]

After Jesus' death and resurrection, his disciples went to the temple and
synagogues and observed various Jewish customs for a period of time. However, they soon stopped doing so. A new approach to religious life demanded
a new form of piety. Already in the first generation of Christians circumcision was abolished, while the major Jewish feasts, Passover (Pascha) and
Pentecost, were completely reinterpreted and received new meaning.

As for days of fasting, as the *Didache* attests, these were established
on Wednesdays and Fridays in the early stages of the Church's existence.
The celebration of Pascha was preceded by one or several days of fasting.
Hippolytus of Rome in particular mentions a two-day fast before Pascha.[3]
Irenaeus of Lyons writes, "For some think that they should fast one day,
others two, yet others more; some, moreover, count their day as consisting
of forty hours day and night."[4] A lengthier fast was prescribed for those

[2]Fitzmyer, *Luke X–XXIV*, 1187.
[3]Hippolytus of Rome, *On the Apostolic Tradition* 33 [Dix 29]. In *On the Apostolic Tradition*,
by Hippolytus of Rome, 2nd ed., trans. Alistair Stewart, Popular Patristics Series 54 (Yonkers,
NY: St Vladimir's Seminary Press, 2015), 186.
[4]Irenaeus of Lyons, *Epistle to Victor, Bishop of Rome*. Cited by Eusebius in *Ecclesiastical
History* 5.24.12 (NPNF[2] 1:243).

preparing to receive baptism.[5] Over time the fast preceding Pascha grew to forty days, although in the fifth century there was still significant variation as to how the fast was understood in different Christian communities. According to the historian Socrates Scholasticus (fifth century), in Rome the fast was observed for three weeks before Pascha, aside from Saturdays and Sundays. In other churches the fast was for six or seven weeks, although it was everywhere considered to last forty days. There was also variation in the dietary rules: some did not eat at all until the ninth hour, some ate only bread, some abstained from animal products, some allowed themselves fish, and some allowed themselves fish and fowl.[6]

Over the centuries the practice of Great Lent in the Christian East became unified, but under the influence of the monastic tradition three more lengthy fasts were added: the Nativity Fast, the Dormition Fast, and the Apostles' Fast. Wednesdays and Fridays continued to be days of fasting throughout the course of the year: Wednesdays in remembrance of Judas' betrayal and Jesus' arrest, and Fridays in remembrance of the crucifixion. Certain weeks in the year are exceptions, during which fasting is forbidden altogether (they are called "fast-free weeks").

The practice of refraining from eating and drinking from sunrise to sunset has not been preserved in the Christian Church (it has been preserved only in Islam). The strictest monastic rules prescribe complete abstinence from food on certain days of Great Lent, but at the same time none of them suggests refraining from water. On the whole, fasting is understood not as complete abstinence from food, but as abstinence from specific types of food—meat, dairy products, alcohol, and, on certain days, fish as well. In addition, following the prophet Isaiah, Christian sources maintain that bodily abstinence during a fast is merely a means to an end. The main goal of fasting is to help a person in his or her spiritual ascent to God, to lighten the flesh in order that it may better serve the spirit.

To what we have said about fasting in this chapter, we may add the observations that we made when examining Jesus' answer to John the Baptist's disciples regarding the reasons that the disciples of Jesus did not

[5]Justin Martyr, *First Apology* 61 (ANF 1:183).
[6]Socrates Scholasticus, *Ecclesiastical History* 5.22 (NPNF² 2:131).

The Fight between Carnival and Lent, Pieter Bruegel the Elder, 1559

fast (Mt 9.14–17; Mk 2.18–22; Lk 5.33–39).[7] This answer is sometimes interpreted to mean that Jesus had a negative or scornful attitude toward fasting as such and did not himself fast. We, however, have seen that this is not the case. Jesus' answer only mentions that his disciples did not fast; it does not say that Jesus himself did not fast.

As we recall, before going out to preach, Jesus fasted for forty days and forty nights (Mt 4.2). Indirect evidence of the possibility that Jesus fasted while his disciples did not fast lies in the story of the healing of the demon-possessed boy. Answering his disciples' question as to why they were not able to heal him, Jesus says, among other things, "This kind goeth not out but by prayer and fasting" (Mt 17.21).

[7]See Metropolitan Hilarion Alfeyev, *Jesus Christ*, 1:497–500.

Chapter 8

EARTHLY AND HEAVENLY WEALTH

In the next part of the Sermon on the Mount, Jesus focuses on the topic of earthly wealth. As in the six antitheses, in which Jesus contrasted his teaching with the Old Testament regulations, antithetical constructions are actively used in this section of the Sermon: treasures in heaven and treasures on earth are contrasted with each other (Mt 6.19–20), as are light and darkness (Mt 6.23), God and mammon (Mt 6.24), seeking the kingdom of God and worrying about tomorrow (Mt 6.33–34). Practically all of this part of the Sermon on the Mount has parallels in the Gospel of Luke: we will indicate these as we proceed, along with the differences between the texts.

Jesus considered wealth to be a hindrance to attaining the kingdom of heaven (Mt 19.23–24; Mk 10.23–25). He emphasized that "a man's life consisteth not in the abundance of the things which he possesseth" (Lk 12.15). He criticized the rich in his parables (Mt 13.22; Mk 4.19; Lk 12.16–21; 8.14), contrasting them with the poor. In the parable of the rich man and Lazarus, the former goes to a place of torment after his death, while the latter goes to Abraham's bosom. In reply to the tormented rich man's request for mercy, Abraham says, "Son, remember that thou in thy lifetime receivedst thy good things, and likewise Lazarus evil things; but now he is comforted, and thou art tormented" (Lk 16.19–31). Jesus treats the theme of wealth and poverty in the same spirit in the Sermon on the Plain: "Blessed be ye poor: for yours is the kingdom of God. . . . But woe unto you that are rich! For ye have received your consolation" (Lk 6.20, 24).

The Sermon on the Mount, mosaic, Ravenna, 6th century

Condemning covetousness and avarice (Lk 12.15; 16.13–14), Jesus exhorted the rich to give away their possessions. To the rich young man he says, "If thou wilt be perfect, go and sell what thou hast, and give to the poor, and thou shalt have treasure in heaven" (Mt 19.21; Mk 10.21; Lk 18.22). Here we encounter the same idea of heavenly reward that is also in the Sermon on the Mount.

Almsgiving and giving money to the poor constitute one of the ways to salvation. The publican Zacchaeus, gladdened by Jesus' visit, promises him: "Behold, Lord, the half of my goods I give to the poor; and if I have taken any thing from any man by false accusation, I restore him fourfold." In reply to this sincere outburst, Jesus says to Zacchaeus, "This day is salvation come to this house" (Lk 19.8–9). Jesus advises the rich Pharisee who had invited him to his home:

> When thou makest a dinner or a supper, call not thy friends, nor thy brethren, neither thy kinsmen, nor thy rich neighbors; lest they also invite thee again, and a recompense be made thee. But when thou makest a feast, call the poor, the maimed, the lame, the blind, and thou shalt be blessed; for they cannot recompense thee. For thou shalt be recompensed at the resurrection of the just. (Lk 14.12–14)

*Jesus Addressing
Zacchaeus,*
mosaic,
St Mark's
Basilica, Venice,
13th century

It is in this context that we ought to understand the sections of the Sermon on the Mount that discuss the topics of earthly treasures, serving mammon, and worrying about tomorrow.

1. Treasure on Earth and in Heaven

The first section of the part of the Sermon on the Mount under discussion is dedicated to earthly and heavenly treasures:

> Lay not up for yourselves treasures upon earth, where moth and rust doth corrupt, and where thieves break through and steal. But lay up for yourselves treasures in heaven, where neither moth nor rust doth corrupt, and where thieves do not break through nor steal. For where your treasure is, there will your heart be also. (Mt 6.19–21)

In Luke we read a version, which is different in the beginning, but almost identical at the end: "Sell what ye have, and give alms. Provide yourselves bags[1] which grow not old, a treasure in the heavens that faileth not, where no thief approacheth, neither moth corrupteth. For where your treasure is, there will your heart be also" (Lk 12.33–34).

[1]The Greek *ballantion* means "bag," "purse."

Of key importance here is the threefold repetition of the word "treasure" (*thēsauros*). What does "treasures in heaven" refer to in this case? The answer may be found in two short parables from a series of parables delivered by Jesus from the boat:

> Again, the kingdom of heaven is like unto treasure hid in a field, which, when a man hath found, he hideth, and for joy thereof goeth and selleth all that he hath, and buyeth that field. Again, the kingdom of heaven is like unto a merchant man, seeking goodly pearls, who, when he had found one pearl of great price, went and sold all that he had, and bought it. (Mt 13.44–46)

The treasures in heaven are none other than the kingdom of heaven. It is more valuable than all earthly riches: "for joy thereof" one can renounce everything else. The behavior of the protagonists of both parables seems inexplicable from the point of view of normal human logic. But the entire Sermon on the Mount, beginning with the Beatitudes, is intended to refute this logic. Instead of it another logic is introduced, which is built not on calculation but on the spontaneous movement of the heart.

As for the treasures on earth, these are understood to be material wealth in general, as well as any material goods in particular. The possession of wealth can pose a threat to a person's life. But it poses an even greater threat to eternal life.

Jesus' words on rust and moths resonated with his disciples. One of them, James, the brother of the Lord, develops these same ideas in his epistle using similar images:

> Come now, ye rich men, weep and howl for your miseries that shall come upon you. Your riches are corrupted, and your garments are motheaten. Your gold and silver is cankered, and the rust of them shall be a witness against you, and shall eat your flesh as it were fire. Ye have heaped treasure together for the last days. (Jas 5.1–3)

Here the term "treasure" refers to earthly wealth that becomes cause for a person's condemnation at the Last Judgment.

It is likely that the apostle Paul was familiar with Jesus' words about treasure in heaven. In the First Epistle to Timothy, he uses expressions that are close in meaning:

> Charge them that are rich in this world, that they be not highminded, nor trust in uncertain riches, but in the living God, who giveth us richly all things to enjoy; that they do good, that they be rich in good works, ready to distribute, willing to communicate; laying up in store for themselves a good foundation against the time to come, that they may lay hold on eternal life. (1 Tim 6.17–19)

Here the laying up of treasures for eternal life is understood to refer to good works. It is from this perspective that the theme of wealth would be examined in the later ascetic tradition. Jesus' call for the complete rejection of wealth would, as in Paul, be modified into a call for the wealthy to share with the poor. In the second century, Clement of Rome exhorted the Christians of Corinth: "Let the rich man provide for the wants of the poor; and let the poor man bless God, because He hath given him one by whom his need may be supplied."[2]

At the turn of the third century, Clement of Alexandria wrote an entire treatise on the topic, *Who Is the Rich Man That Shall Be Saved?* This treatise can be considered the first Christian apology for wealth. It begins by examining Jesus' words: "It is easier for a camel to go through the eye of a needle, than for a rich man to enter into the kingdom of God" (Mt 19.24). Contrary to the seemingly categorical nature of these words, Clement believes that "the inheritance of the kingdom of heaven is not quite cut off from [the rich] if they obey the commandments."[3] Moreover, how can a person fulfill the commandments concerning charitable giving if he does not possess the means for it? How can he feed the poor, give drink to the thirsty, clothe the naked, or give shelter to the homeless, if he himself possesses nothing? Clement gives examples from the Gospels demonstrating that Jesus did not require everyone to give away all of their wealth. In particular, Zacchaeus promised to give half of his possessions to the poor,

---

[2]Clement of Rome, *First Epistle to the Corinthians* 38 (ANF 9:240).
[3]Clement of Alexandria, *Who Is the Rich Man That Shall Be Saved?* 3 (ANF 2:591).

and this turned out to be sufficient for salvation (Lk 19.8–9).[4] Clement comes to the following conclusions:

> Riches, then, which benefit also our neighbours, are not to be thrown away. For they are possessions, inasmuch as they are possessed, and goods, inasmuch as they are useful and provided by God for the use of men; and they lie to our hand, and are put under our power, as material and instruments which are for good use to those who know the instrument. If you use it skilfully, it is skilful; if you are deficient in skill, it is affected by your want of skill, being itself destitute of blame. Such an instrument is wealth. Are you able to make a right use of it? It is subservient to righteousness. Does one make a wrong use of it? It is, on the other hand, a minister of wrong. For its nature is to be subservient, not to rule. . . . So let no man destroy wealth, rather than the passions of the soul, which are incompatible with the better use of wealth. So that, becoming virtuous and good, he may be able to make a good use of these riches. The renunciation, then, and selling of all possessions, is to be understood as spoken of the passions of the soul.[5]

Here we have an example of an interpretation in which the radicalism of Jesus' call to reject wealth has been significantly softened and partially allegorized. The author of the treatise considers it possible to understand the call to reject wealth in a metaphorical way—as a call to struggle with the passions. And he demonstrates that wealth is not bad in itself: it becomes dangerous when a person subjugates himself to it. On the contrary, if someone uses wealth for almsgiving and good works, then wealth not only does not do him harm, but on the contrary opens to him the way to salvation.

The subsequent exegetical tradition continues in the same vein. The call to not lay up treasures on earth is treated foremost as an exhortation to not become a slave to wealth:

---

[4]Clement of Alexandria, *Who Is the Rich Man That Shall Be Saved?* 13 (ANF 2:594–595).
[5]Clement of Alexandria, *Who Is the Rich Man That Shall Be Saved?* 14 (ANF 2:595).

The Sermon on the Mount, Evangeliary miniature, 11th century

"Where the man's treasure is, there is his heart also". ... thou wilt undergo no small harm, in being nailed to the things below, and in becoming a slave instead of a freeman, and casting thyself out of the heavenly things, and having no power to think on anything that is high, but all about money, usuries and loans, and gains, and ignoble traffickings. What could be more wretched than this? For in truth such a one will be worse off than any slave, bringing upon himself a most grievous tyranny, and giving up the chiefest thing of all, even the nobility and the liberty of man. For however much any one may discourse unto thee, thou wilt not be able to hear any of those things which concern thee, whilst thy mind is nailed down to money; but bound like a dog to a tomb, by the tyranny of riches, more grievously than by any chain, barking at all that come near thee, thou hast this one employment continually, to keep for others what thou hast laid up.[6]

[6]John Chrysostom, *Homilies on Matthew* 20.3 (NPNF[1] 10:142–143).

While he cautions against enslavement to wealth, at the same time,
John Chrysostom not only does not condemn those who possess wealth,
but on the contrary demonstrates (following Clement of Alexandria) that
wealth in itself is a boon, not an evil, and exhorts the rich to help the
poor:

> And these things I say, not because riches are a sin: the sin is in not
> distributing them to the poor. . . . For God made nothing evil but all
> things very good [cf. Gen 1.31]; so that riches too are good; i.e. if they
> do not master their owners; if the wants of our neighbors be done away
> by them. For neither is that light good which instead of dissipating
> darkness rather makes it intense: nor should I call that wealth, which
> instead of doing away poverty rather increases it. For the rich man
> seeks not to take from others but to help others: but he that seeks to
> receive from others is no longer rich, but is emphatically poor. So that
> it is not riches that are an evil, but the needy mind which turns wealth
> into poverty.[7]

2. The Light of the Body

At first glance, the next section of the Sermon on the Mount has no connection with the preceding section and looks like an interpolation, especially if we take into account the fact that after this Jesus returns again to
the topic of earthly wealth:

> The light of the body is the eye. If therefore thine eye be clear, thy whole
> body shall be full of light. But if thine eye be evil, thy whole body shall
> be full of darkness. If therefore the light that is in thee be darkness, how
> great is that darkness! (Mt 6.22–23)

---

[7]John Chrysostom, *Homilies on 1 Corinthians* 13.8 (NPNF[1] 12:76).

In the parallel passage in Luke, the phrasing is slightly changed: "Take heed therefore that the light which is in thee be not darkness. If thy whole body therefore be full of light, having no part dark, the whole shall be full of light, as when the bright shining of a candle doth give thee light" (Lk 11.35–36). While in Matthew's version the saying is constructed around two pairs of contrasts—clear and evil, light and dark—in Luke's version the contrast is absent. While in Matthew Jesus speaks of the eye and the body, in Luke he speaks only about the body. The saying about the light that is darkness, which concludes the teaching in Matthew, is in Luke the starting point.

The use of the adjective *haplous* to mean "clear" is unusual: it literally means "simple." Key in both instances is the word "eye," as are the terms "light" and "darkness," which are rich in meaning in the biblical tradition.

The image of the eye is used to refer to sight in the sense of the ability to distinguish light from darkness. If a person loses this ability, he becomes blind. Blindness can be physical as well as spiritual, and Jesus speaks of this in his conversation with the Pharisees after the healing of the blind man: "For judgment I am come into this world, that they which see not might see, and that they which see might be made blind." These words confused the Pharisees, who asked, "Are we blind also?" Jesus answered, "If ye were blind, ye should have no sin. But now ye say, 'We see.' Therefore your sin remaineth" (Jn 9.39–41).

Here, as in the Sermon on the Mount, Jesus is speaking of a person's ability to differentiate between good and evil, to distinguish true treasures from false treasures. Considering the link with the preceding passage on treasures in heaven and on earth, as well as the link with the subsequent words about God and mammon, it is possible to say that spiritual blindness is the absence or loss of the ability to make the right choice. And conversely, the possession of spiritual sight refers to the presence of an inner voice that helps a person to recognize true and abiding treasure, which is not vulnerable to the passage of time, which cannot be harmed by moth and rust, and which cannot be taken away or stolen.

The use of the image of an "evil eye" goes back to the Old Testament, which speaks of the eye that is unmerciful to the poor (Deut 15.9), the eye that grudges alms (Tob 4.7), and the wicked eye that envies bread (Sir 14.10). As for the image of the "clear eye," it should be examined in the overall context of Jesus' teaching about the inner purity, or simplicity, which is supposed to characterize his disciples (the expression *ophthalmos haplous* literally means "simple eye").

Christian commentators often understand the word "eye" as a reference to the mind, heart, or conscience. Blessed Augustine writes, "This passage we are to understand in such a way as to learn from it that all our works are pure and well-pleasing in the sight of God, when they are done with a single heart."[8] In the words of John Chrysostom, "just what the eye is to the body, the same is the mind to the soul. . . . as therefore in the body this is our aim, namely, to keep the eye sound, so also the mind in the soul."[9]

The use of the concepts of "light" and "darkness" deserves particular attention. The juxtaposition of these concepts is found throughout the entire Bible. The book of Genesis begins with God creating light, seeing that "it was good," and separating it from the darkness (Gen 1.2–4). In this way, from the very start, light is equated with good and becomes the universal symbol of good. Moreover, light is the symbol of God, of his glory and his presence: "The Lord is my light and my savior" (Ps 26.1); "in thy light shall we see light" (Ps 35.10); "O send out thy light and thy truth" (Ps 42.3); "come ye, and let us walk in the light of the LORD" (Is 2.5); "the LORD shall be unto thee an everlasting light" (Is 60.19).

Darkness, on the contrary, is the universal symbol of evil and the absence of God. Sheol (hades) is thought of as "the land of darkness and the shadow of death; a land of darkness, as darkness itself; and of the shadow of death, without any order, and where the light is as darkness" (Job 10.21–22). Darkness and light are contrasted as two polar opposites—one evil, one good: "When I looked for good, then evil came unto me; and when I waited for light, there came darkness" (Job 30.25); "Let that day be darkness; let not God regard it from above, neither let the light shine upon it" (Job 3.4); "But the path of the just is as the shining light, that shineth more and more unto

---

[8] Augustine of Hippo, *Our Lord's Sermon on the Mount* 2.13 (NPNF[1] 6:48).
[9] John Chrysostom, *Homilies on Matthew* 20.3 (NPNF[1] 10:143).

The Creation of Light, mosaic, 13th century

the perfect day. The way of the wicked is as darkness: they know not at what they stumble" (Prov 4.18–19); "Arise, shine, for thy light is come, and the glory of the LORD is risen upon thee. For, behold, the darkness shall cover the earth, and gross darkness the people: but the LORD shall arise upon thee, and his glory shall be seen upon thee" (Is 60.1–2).

At the same time, it is emphasized that darkness cannot triumph over light or hide a person from the face of God: "If I say, surely the darkness shall cover me, even the night shall be light about me. Yea, the darkness hideth not from thee; but the night shineth as the day. The darkness and the light are both alike to thee" (Ps 138.11–2). Moreover, both light and darkness are called to bless the Lord (Dan 3.71).

The symbolism of light has a special meaning in the writings of John. But in the Synoptic Gospels, too, especially in Matthew, this symbolism is also present, including in the Sermon on the Mount (Mt 5.14–16). Jesus contrasts the "children of light" with the "children of this world" (Lk 16.8). The expression "children of light" is not encountered in the Old Testament, but it is encountered in the Qumran manuscripts, where the members of the Essene community call themselves this; in these same manuscripts the "sons of light" are often contrasted with the "sons of darkness."[10] We find similar phrasing used by the apostle Paul: "Ye are all the children of light,

[10]See Green, McKnight, and Marshall, *Dictionary of Jesus and the Gospels*, 401.

and the children of the day. We are not of the night, nor of darkness" (1 Thess 5.5).

The meaning of the words, "If therefore the light that is in thee be darkness, how great is that darkness," can be conveyed in this way: if the relationship between light and darkness has been violated in a person, if he has lost the proper system of coordinates, he is no longer capable of distinguishing good from evil, of making the right choice between earthly and heavenly riches, between God and mammon. Thus the image of the light of the body becomes the link between the passages that precede and follow it.

It is no coincidence that John Chrysostom resorts to the image of darkness when interpreting Jesus' words about wealth. This image helps him to paint a vivid picture of people who have darkened their minds with earthly riches:

> And as they that are in darkness see nothing distinct, but if they look at a rope, they suppose it to be a serpent, if at mountains and ravines, they are dead with fear, so these also: what is not alarming to them that have sight, that they regard with suspicion. Thus among other things they tremble at poverty: or rather not at poverty only, but even at any trifling loss. Yea, and if they should lose some little matter, those who are in want of necessary food do not so grieve and bewail themselves as they. At least many of the rich have come even to the noose [i.e., hanged themselves], not enduring such ill fortune.[11]

---

[11]John Chrysostom, *Homilies on Matthew* 20.4 (NPNF[1] 10:144).

3. God and Mammon

The following words continue the series of teachings dedicated to the topic of earthly and heavenly riches:

> No man can serve two masters: for either he will hate the one, and love the other; or else he will hold to the one, and despise the other. Ye cannot serve God and mammon. (Mt 6.24)

In the parallel passage in Luke, only the word "servant" is added: "No servant [*oiketēs*] can serve two masters . . ." (Lk 16.13). The rest of the text is identical. Both evangelists use the verb *douleuein* ("to serve"), which refers to the work of a slave (from *doulos*, "slave").

Slavery was a widespread institution in the ancient world. Slavery had existed in Israel from as early as the time of Abraham. Slaves were foreigners who had been taken into captivity (Deut 21.10) or bought from neighboring tribes (Lev 25.44). A person might become a slave because of poverty (Lev 25.39) or because of debt (2 Kg 4.1). Slaves were bought with money (Gen 17.12); they were also treated as the property (lit. "money") of their master (Ex 21.20–21). The legal status of slaves in Israel was regulated by the law, which introduced some limitations to the power that their masters had over them (Ex 21.1–11, 21, 26–27; Lev 25.39–55).

Jesus did not challenge slavery, just as he did not challenge other social institutions that existed in his time. The early Church also did not challenge this institution. The apostle Paul exhorted slaves to be obedient to their masters "with fear and trembling," "with good will doing service, as to the Lord, and not to men" (Eph 6.5–7). He believed that each person was to remain in the station in which he was called, but advised slaves to obtain their freedom if possible (1 Cor 7.20–24). At the same time, he emphasized that in the Church there is neither slave nor free, but all are one "in Christ Jesus" (Gal 3.28).

The Worship of Mammon,
Evelyn De Morgan, 1909

In speaking of the person who serves two masters, Jesus used an image that was well known to his listeners. At the same time, his instruction was completely free of any social focus. The image of the servant with two masters was intended only to demonstrate the impossibility of simultaneously serving two ideals—the heavenly and the earthly. Each excludes the other; reconciling God and mammon is impossible.

The word *mamōnas* (mammon), which is incomprehensible to a Greek reader, is used not only in Matthew but also in Luke, from whom one would have expected a translation. Moreover, in Luke this term is used thrice: in the passage parallel to the passage in the Sermon currently under discussion, and also in the parable preceding that passage, about the unrighteous steward. The parable concludes with the following words: "Make for yourselves friends of the mammon of unrighteousness, that, when ye fail, they may receive you into everlasting habitations. . . . If therefore ye have not been faithful in the unrighteous mammon, who will commit to your trust true riches?" (Lk 16.9, 11).

Why did both evangelists use an obscure Semitism? It seems that there could be two reasons for this. First, they wanted to present Jesus' sayings in a form that was maximally close to how they originally sounded. Second, it is possible that they did not find a suitable Greek equivalent.

The term used is conveyed either by the Hebrew *māmôn* or, more likely, the Aramaic *māmōnā*, which is usually translated as "wealth," "property," or "money."[12] This word is not encountered in the Old Testament, but it is encountered in the Qumran manuscripts both in Hebrew[13] as well as in Aramaic.[14] It is possible that this word was widely used in Jesus' time and

[12]On the etymology of this word, see A. M. Honeyman, "The Etymology of Mammon," *Archivum linguisticum* 4 (1952): 60–65.

[13]David J. A. Clines, ed., *The Dictionary of Classical Hebrew*, 9 vols. (Sheffield: Sheffield Academic, 1993–2016), 5:330.

[14]Edward M. Cook, *Dictionary of Qumran Aramaic* (Winona Lake, IN: Eisenbrauns, 2015), 141; Fitzmyer, *Luke X–XXIV*, 1109.

*The Miserly
Knight*, K. E.
Makovsky, 1890s

had a specific meaning that was still known to the authors of the Gospel
narratives. Augustine of Hippo believed that the word originated from the
Punic language.[15] John Chrysostom uses this term when he returns again
to the assertion that what is bad is not wealth itself, but enslavement to
wealth:

> "How then," saith one, "did Abraham, how did Job obtain a good report?"
> Tell me not of them that are rich, but of them that serve riches. Since
> Job also was rich, but he served not mammon, but possessed it and
> ruled over it, and was a master, not a slave. Therefore he so possessed all

---

[15] Augustine of Hippo, *Our Lord's Sermon on the Mount* 2.14 (NPNF[1] 6:49); *Sermons* 63.2
[=113.2] (NPNF[1] 6:450). The Punic language belonged to the Semitic family of languages and
was a variety of Phoenician. Punic was spoken in North Africa, especially in Carthage, and also
in some other places along the Mediterranean coast.

those things, as if he had been the steward of another man's goods; not only not extorting from others, but even giving up his own to them that were in need. And what is more, when he had them they were no joy to him: so he also declared, saying, "If I did so much as rejoice when my wealth waxed great" [Job 31.25]: wherefore neither did he grieve when it was gone. But they that are rich are not now such as he was, but are rather in a worse condition than any slave, paying as it were tribute to some grievous tyrant.[16]

In the Sermon on the Mount, Jesus used an image familiar to his listeners, that of the work of a slave, to refer to spiritual slavery, which comes about when a person becomes a captive and slave to his own possessions. Following Jesus, the church fathers deemed that wealth carries spiritual danger, but only if one is enslaved to it, giving all one's strength and soul to preserve and multiply one's earthly wealth. As we have already said, according to the teaching of the fathers, wealth can be useful if it is shared with other people. But it becomes a hindrance on the path to God if it turns into a goal in itself and an object of worth in itself. A person's life loses its meaning if its main goal is the maintenance of his or her material assets and properties.

Besides material wealth, there are also other types of wealth that can become a hindrance to the attainment of the kingdom of heaven. The priest Alexander Elchaninov, who served in the Russian emigration in the 1920s and the beginning of the 1930s, refers to this:

> We must not think that there is only one kind of wealth—money. One can be rich in youth, possess the assets of talent, of gifts, the capital of health. These riches too are obstacles to salvation. Material wealth enslaves us, sharpening self-interest, corroding the heart, overwhelming us with anxiety and fear; like an insatiable demon, it demands sacrifice. Instead of serving us, it makes us serve it. Cannot the same be said of the treasures of health, strength, youth, beauty, talent? Do not they likewise confirm us in our pride and constrain the heart, leading it away from God?

[16]John Chrysostom, *Homilies on Matthew* 21.2 (NPNF[1] 10:147).

Yes, truly: "Blessed are the poor" in the world's goods. How easily they gain evangelical lightness of spirit and freedom of earthly fetters; but blessed also are those who are without health and youth (for "he who suffers in the flesh ceases to sin"). Blessed the ugly, the ungifted, the unlucky—they are free of the chief enemy, pride—for they have nothing to be proud of.[17]

4. Worrying about Tomorrow

The next section of the Sermon on the Mount, in which Jesus cautions against excessive worry, directly continues the discussion of mammon:

Therefore I say unto you, take no thought for your life, what ye shall eat, or what ye shall drink, nor yet for your body, what ye shall put on. Is not the life more than food, and the body than raiment? Behold the fowls of the air: for they sow not, neither do they reap, nor gather into barns; yet your heavenly Father feedeth them. Are ye not much better than they? Which of you by taking thought can add one cubit unto his stature?

And why take ye thought for raiment? Consider the lilies of the field, how they grow; they toil not, neither do they spin. And yet I say unto you, that even Solomon in all his glory was not arrayed like one of these. Wherefore, if God so clothe the grass of the field, which today is, and tomorrow is cast into the oven, shall he not much more clothe you, O ye of little faith?

Therefore take no thought, saying, "What shall we eat?" or, "What shall we drink?" or, "With what shall we be clothed?" (for after all these things do the Gentiles seek). For your heavenly Father knoweth that ye have need of all these things. But seek ye first the kingdom of God,

[17]Alexander Elchaninov, *Zapisi* [Notes] (Moscow, 1992), 36–37. English translation from *A Treasury of Russian Spirituality*, ed. G. P. Fedotov (New York, NY: Sheed & Ward, 1948), 439–440.

Martha, medieval
manuscript

and his righteousness; and all these things shall be added unto you.

Take therefore no thought for the morrow: for the morrow shall take thought for the things of itself. Sufficient unto the day is the evil thereof. (Mt 6.25–34)

The key word in the passage above is the verb *merimnaō*, which means "to worry," "to be anxious," "to fret." This verb is used six times in the text, giving the passage its compositional integrity. It is appropriate here to recall the use of the same verb in the words that Jesus addressed to the woman with many cares: "Martha, Martha, thou art anxious [*merimnas*] and troubled about many things, but one thing is needful" (Lk 10.41–42).

A person's earthly life is described in the above passage from the Sermon on the Mount with the help of a selection of repeated words ("life," "body," "eat," "drink," "clothe," "seek," "morrow"), while the reality of another world is indicated by the expressions "kingdom of God" and "your heavenly Father." The contrast between the earthly and the heavenly is strengthened with the help of vivid images: the birds of the air, the lilies of the field, Solomon in all his glory. As a result, the listener (or the reader) receives a vibrant, rich, memorable message about the priorities in life.

Jesus' words, "Take no thought for your life [literally, "soul," *psychē*], what ye shall eat, or what ye shall drink," do not mean that the soul has need of food or drink: the Greek word for "soul" here is used to mean "life." We find a similar choice of words elsewhere: "For whosoever will save his life [*tēn psychēn*] shall lose it: and whosoever will lose his life [*tēn psychēn*] for my sake shall find it" (Mt 16.25). "Is not the life [*hē psychē*] more than meat, and the body than raiment?"—these words mean that a person's life cannot be reduced to food and drink; there are other, loftier things of value in it.

In the Gospel of Matthew the term *psychē* ("soul," or sometimes "life") is used sixteen times, and *sōma* ("body") fourteen times (seven times in the

*Poppies
in a Field,*
Mary Cassatt,
19th century

Sermon on the Mount).[18] The soul and the body constitute a dichotomy often encountered on the pages of the New Testament. In many instances, when the body and the soul are mentioned as a pair, they are contrasted with each other, and the body's subordination to the soul is emphasized. However, in the above passage from the Sermon on the Mount, the body and the soul (as "life") are presented as two components of human nature, in relation to which food and clothing occupy a subordinate position.

Occupying the central place in this passage is the comparison of human activity with natural phenomena: hard work and worry are contrasted with the image of the life of the birds of the air, whom the heavenly Father feeds. The beauty of the lilies of the field is contrasted with the "glory" of King Solomon: no human workmanship can be compared with the beauty and variety of God's creations, including those that people consider weeds, which they tear out by the roots and burn.

The concluding lines of the passage summarize its content. Note the use of the word *kakia*, which literally means "evil," "vice." Note also the usage by a number of early Christian writers of the following version of one of the verses in the passage: "Seek what is great, and the little things shall be added."[19]

[18]Jaime Clark-Soles, *Death and the Afterlife in the New Testament* (New York, NY: T&T Clark, 2006), 161–163.

[19]Clement of Alexandria, *Stromata* 1.24 (ANF 2:336); Origen, *On Prayer* 14.1 (PPS 29:143). Origen adds the following: "And ask for heavenly things and mundane things shall be added to you."

We find a similar exhortation in Luke—not in the Sermon on the Plain, but in another sermon addressed to the disciples and delivered in the presence of thousands of people (Lk 12.22–31). In Luke the given exhortation follows the parable of the rich man who had built barns to store his accumulated grain (Lk 12.16–21). With the exception of the use of the word "ravens" (in place of "fowls of the air"), Luke's version is textually very close to that in the Sermon on the Mount. However, they differ in their concluding lines. Instead of a repeated call to not worry about tomorrow, here we find completely different words addressed to the disciples: "Fear not, little flock; for it is your Father's good pleasure to give you the kingdom" (Lk 12.32). These words emphasize that the addressees of the exhortation are Jesus' disciples—the "little flock" that would subsequently become the Church (the term *poimnion*, meaning "flock," would be used to refer to the "flock" of a bishop or a priest).

In the Sermon on the Mount Jesus' exhortation directly follows from the discussion of God and mammon. The words "Therefore I say unto you" serve as the link. However, these words connect the exhortation with all the preceding text of the Sermon on the Mount as well, beginning from the Beatitudes, in which the thesis of the incompatibility of the earthly and the heavenly is asserted and emphasized, and the entire scale of earthly values turns out to be inverted. Only within the overall context of the Sermon on the Mount does this passage acquire its meaning.

The reference to Solomon is not a coincidence. Solomon entered the history of the people of Israel not only as a king whose court was distinguished by singular wealth and grandeur (1 Kg 4.21–28; 10.4–5, 21–23), but also as the author of the book of Ecclesiastes, which is close in its mentality to the passage from the Sermon on the Mount that we are discussing. The leitmotif of this book, which stands apart in the entire corpus of the Old Testament, consists in the words with which it begins and ends: "Vanity of vanities; all is vanity" (Eccl 1.2, 12.8). The refrain is repeated multiple times: "all is vanity and vexation of spirit" (Eccl 1.14; 2.11, 17, 26; 4.4, 16; 6.9); "this also is vanity" (Eccl 2.1, 15, 19).

One of the themes of the book is man's labor. The author of the book describes various occupations, but each of them is nothing but "vanity and

The Visit of the Queen of Sheba to King Solomon, Edward Poynter, 1890

a great evil" (Eccl 2.21), or "vanity . . . a sore travail" (Eccl 4.8), or "vanity and . . . an evil disease" (Eccl 6.2). No matter how much a person labors, he or she cannot change the course of history or influence the life of nature:

> What profit hath a man of all his labor which he taketh under the sun? One generation passeth away, and another generation cometh; but the earth abideth forever. The sun also ariseth, and the sun goeth down, and hasteth to his place where he arose. The wind goeth toward the south, and turneth about unto the north; it whirleth about continually, and the wind returneth again according to his circuits. All the rivers run into the sea; yet the sea is not full; unto the place from whence the rivers come, thither they return again. All things are full of labor; man cannot utter it; the eye is not satisfied with seeing, nor the ear filled with hearing. The thing that hath been, it is that which shall be; and that which is done is that which shall be done, and there is no new thing under the sun. . . . I have seen all the works that are done under the sun; and, behold, all is vanity and vexation of spirit. . . . What profit hath he that worketh in that wherein he laboreth? I have seen the travail, which God hath given to the sons of men to be exercised in it. (Eccl 1.3–9, 14; 3.9–10)

Other themes of the book of Ecclesiastes are wealth, glory, and earthly diversions. None of these can satisfy a person:

> I made me great works; I built houses; I planted vineyards; I made gardens and orchards, and I planted trees in them of all kind of fruits: . . . I gathered also silver and gold, and the peculiar treasure of kings and of the provinces: I got men singers and women singers, and the delights of the sons of men, as musical instruments, and that of all sorts. So I was great, and increased more than all that were before me in Jerusalem. . . . And whatsoever mine eyes desired I kept not from them, I withheld not my heart from any joy. . . . Then I looked on all the works that my hands had wrought . . . and, behold, all was vanity and vexation of spirit, and there was no profit under the sun. (Eccl 2.4–11)

> He that loveth silver shall not be satisfied with silver; nor he that loveth abundance with increase. This is also vanity. When goods increase, they are increased that eat them; and what good is there to the owners thereof, saving the beholding of them with their eyes? . . . There is a sore evil which I have seen under the sun, namely, riches kept for the owners thereof to their hurt. But those riches perish by evil travail; and he begetteth a son, and there is nothing in his hand. As he came forth of his mother's womb, naked shall he return to go as he came, and shall take nothing of his labor, which he may carry away in his hand. And this also is a sore evil, that in all points as he came, so shall he go: and what profit hath he that hath labored for the wind? (Eccl 5.10–11, 13–16)

A literal reading of the book of Ecclesiastes may lead to the idea that the author of the book is promoting laziness and inaction. This, however, is a deceptive impression. In another book, attributed to the same Solomon, we find a condemnation of laziness: "Go to the ant, thou sluggard; consider her ways, and be wise: which having no guide, overseer, or ruler, provideth her food in the summer, and gathereth her food in the harvest. How long wilt thou sleep, O sluggard? When wilt thou arise out of thy sleep?" (Prov 6.6–9). Likewise, the book of Ecclesiastes does not at all contain an exhortation to passivity: it merely shows that every human labor has relative and not absolute value.

It is of this that Jesus speaks in the Sermon on the Mount, only with different words. A literal reading of the passage under discussion from the Sermon on the Mount raises a whole series of questions. How can a person not worry at all about the next day or not think about food and clothing? Doesn't simple everyday experience suggest that if a person does not take care of himself, nobody will take care of him? Even the birds of the air, although they do not sow or reap, obtain food for themselves and their chicks: shouldn't a person do the same? We

King Solomon in Old Age,
engraving, Gustave Doré,
1866

must look for the answer in the semantic content of the word translated as "travail," which in the book of Ecclesiastes is used to mean "vanity," "useless labor." Correspondingly, the verb translated as "take thought for," which Jesus repeatedly uses, means not simply "take care of," but "worry," "be anxious."

Between the two texts—Ecclesiastes and the Sermon on the Mount— there is much in common, but there is also a very substantial difference. The book of Ecclesiastes does not lead us out of the circle of weighty reflections on the vanity of the earthly world, the labors and achievements of a person, his wealth, and even his wisdom. The author of the book does not find an alternative to vanity, and all the action of the book takes place "under the sun." The Sermon on the Mount gives a clear alternative and a clear reference point: the kingdom of heaven. It is precisely in the light of the reality that is called the kingdom of heaven that material wealth loses its significance, as do the labors and achievements that one person or other might take pride in. They are nothing before the majesty of this kingdom.

As in the Beatitudes, the kingdom of heaven is contrasted with earthly kingdoms, the symbol of which is Solomon "in all his glory." Jesus does not forbid people to work or to take care of providing for themselves and their children: he is cautioning against being enslaved to labor, against turning labor into a goal in itself. The ideal of a person who is wholly absorbed in his professional interests and devotedly gives all his strength and health to earthly labor without entering into the spiritual sphere is alien to the Sermon on the Mount. The Sermon paints a picture of a different ideal: that of a person who lives on earth but is not swallowed up by vanity and the many cares of earthly affairs; who instead seeks "the kingdom of God, and his righteousness."

Herein lies the affinity between the given passage from the Sermon on the Mount and what Jesus said about being a slave to wealth. A person should not be enslaved by anything, neither material wealth nor care about the next day, which "shall take thought for the things of itself." Jesus calls us to concentrate on *today*, and to not worry because of tomorrow. Recall that in the Lord's Prayer he commands us to ask for bread only for today, and not for tomorrow.

Neither is it a coincidence that the words "you of little faith" are used here. A person can, and must, labor, but he must remember that his labor is beneficial only if he does not forget about God and his kingdom, which exists in parallel with the kingdom of earth. Faith in God, trust in him, and readiness to obey his will must dominate in a person's life.

Here again one may recall Solomon. In the Psalter the following words are attributed to him: "Except the Lord build the house, in vain do they labor that build it. Except the Lord guard the city, in vain doth he watch that guardeth her" (Ps 126.1). These words do not mean that houses should not be built, or that cities should not be guarded. They merely remind us of the futility and vanity of every labor that is not blessed by God and which God does not support.

The segment of the Sermon on the Mount that we are discussing received an original interpretation in Søren Kierkegaard's work *The Lily of the Field and the Bird of the Air*. He treats the words "seek ye first the kingdom of God" as a call to prayer. To truly pray means to enter into silence, a silence like the one possessed by the birds of the air and the lilies of the field:

Cupolas and Swallows, K. F. Yuon, 1921

The bird *keeps silent and waits*: it knows, or rather it fully and firmly believes, that everything takes place at its appointed time. Therefore the bird waits, but it knows that it is not granted to it to know the hour or the day; therefore it keeps silent. "It will surely take place at the appointed time," the bird says. Or no, the bird does not say this, but keeps silent. But its silence speaks, and its silence says that it believes it, and because it believes it, it keeps silent and waits. Then, when the moment comes, the silent bird understands that this is the moment; it makes use of it and is never put to shame. This is also how it is with the lily, it keeps silent and waits. It does not ask impatiently, "When is spring coming?" because it knows that it will come at the appointed time; it knows that it would not benefit in any way whatever if it were permitted to determine the seasons of the year. It does not say, "When will we get rain?" or "When will we have sunshine?" or "Now we have had too much rain," or "Now it is too hot." It does not ask in advance how the summer will be this year, how long or short; no, it keeps silent and waits—that is how simple it is, but nonetheless it is never deceived.[20]

[20]Kierkegaard, *Lily of the Field*, 23–24.

The bird, the philosopher continues, is not kept from suffering, but it endures suffering silently. In so doing, it "frees itself from what makes the suffering more burdensome: from the misunderstood sympathy of others; frees itself from what makes the suffering last longer: from all the talk of suffering; frees itself from what makes the suffering into something worse than suffering: from the sin of impatience and sadness."[21] The lily is also silent: "Even though it stands and suffers while it withers, it keeps silent. ... It cannot dissemble and can do nothing about the fact that its color changes and that it thereby betrays something we of course know from this pallid change of color: that it is suffering; but it remains silent."[22]

Kierkegaard concludes that human beings should learn from the bird and the lily how to stand in prayer before God: "For when just two of us talk together, even more so when we are ten or more, it is so easily forgotten that you and I, that we two, or that we ten, are before God. But the lily, who is the teacher, is profound. It does not involve itself with you at all; it keeps silent, and by keeping silent it wants to signify to you that you are before God."[23]

The existentialist philosopher speaks of essentially the same thing that the authors of the biblical books did when they used the expression "walked with God" (Gen 5.22, 24). This expression has a multifaceted meaning. While it emphasizes the righteousness and purity of a particular person (Gen 6.9), it indicates at the same time the source of all righteousness— God. If a person does not forget about the presence of God, if God is his first priority, if faith in God defines his system of values, then everything else naturally falls into place around this core. Such a person is involved in earthly acquisition, but it does not possess him: he does not become its slave, because he feels himself to be the slave of God.

According to the Old Testament view, an abundance of earthly blessings is the reward for faith and righteousness. This same idea is present in the Sermon on the Mount, only in a somewhat modified form: seek first

---

[21]Kierkegaard, *Lily of the Field*, 26.
[22]Kierkegaard, *Lily of the Field*, 27–28.
[23]Kierkegaard, *Lily of the Field*, 30–31.

The Sermon on the Mount, Henrik Olrik, 1880

the kingdom of God and his righteousness, and everything necessary for life "shall be added unto you."

* * *

Over the centuries, worldly wisdom has labored to work out the principles by which any given object, ability, or phenomenon can be converted into money. Already in ancient times people had learned to turn food, household items, livestock, land, real estate, each other (through the selling of slaves), and labor into money. Every new generation has thought up new ways of earning money, perfected the financial mechanisms invented earlier, and created new ones.

Jesus Christ taught people a different art: the conversion of earthly goods to a wealth that does not remain on earth but has its existence in eternal life. It is precisely in this life that he called people to invest their resources, possessions, talents, and abilities. He reminded them that there were valuable things in their lives that could be neither bought or sold, which nothing could repair if they were damaged. The soul is one of these valuable things: "For what is a man profited, if he shall gain the whole world, and lose his own soul? Or what shall a man give in exchange for his soul?" (Mt 16.26).

In one of Jesus' parables, the rich man who had an abundant harvest in the field asks himself, "What shall I do, because I have no room to store my fruits?" And he says, "This will I do: I will pull down my barns, and build greater; and there will I store all my fruits and my goods. And I will say to my soul, 'Soul, thou hast much goods laid up for many years; take thine ease, eat, drink, and be merry.'" And although this man says this to himself, God unexpectedly answers him: "Thou fool, this night thy soul shall be required of thee. Then whose shall those things be, which thou hast provided?" Jesus concludes the parable with these words: "So is he that layeth up treasure for himself, and is not rich toward God" (Lk 12.16–21).

This parable serves as a clear illustration of what Jesus says about wealth in the Sermon on the Mount. The value system that he proposes would perhaps not have any meaning if there were not a factor in people's lives that cannot be escaped for any amount of money: death. People can argue about the existence of God, of the world beyond the grave, of posthumous retribution; but the fact that the life of every person ends in death is not a matter of dispute. It is in light of this indisputable and universal fact that Jesus' spiritual and moral teaching acquires the particular value that it has retained regardless of changing epochs, political regimes, and worldviews. And it is precisely the inevitability of death that forces many to ponder the questions to which Jesus gives an answer.

In his speech he constantly dealt with such concepts as the kingdom of heaven, treasures in heaven, and eternal life. Even then, for most people, these concepts were unclear, while today they seem to many to be distant, outdated, or abstract. The specifics of life demand that more and more sacrifices be brought to the altar of mammon. But even if a person does not recognize the eternal dimension in his own life, this dimension does not disappear from it; if he does not believe in life beyond the grave, his life will nevertheless continue after biological death; and if he does not believe in retribution, he will get it all the same—whether here or there.

The quiet voice of Jesus, which we hear from the pages of the Gospels, reminds us of the eternal dimension that can come into one's life if one seriously ponders its meaning in light of inescapable death. That is when the old words about the kingdom of heaven and about treasures in heaven

The Angel of Great Counsel, Jesus Christ, fresco, Holy Mother of God Peribleptos Church, Ohrid, Macedonia, 1295

can resound in a new way in one's heart. That is when one will be able to feel the strength of these words, which are capable not only of opening to one the gates to eternal blessedness, but also of filling one's earthly life with meaning and giving it the absolute value that is impossible to acquire with money.

Chapter 9

HUMAN JUDGMENT
AND
DIVINE JUDGMENT

In the next part of the Sermon on the Mount Jesus turns again to the topic of interpersonal relationships and sets out the principles by which his followers are to judge each other:

> Judge not, that ye be not judged. For with what judgment ye judge, ye shall be judged, and with what measure ye measure, it shall be measured to you again. And why beholdest thou the speck that is in thy brother's eye, but considerest not the beam that is in thine own eye? Or how wilt thou say to thy brother, "Let me pull out the speck out of thine eye"; and, behold, a beam is in thine own eye? Thou hypocrite, first cast out the beam out of thine own eye; and then shalt thou see clearly to cast out the speck out of thy brother's eye. (Mt 7.1–5)

The text is carefully constructed and has a compositional integrity that allows one to remember it easily. In the first sentences, words with a common root are used multiple times: "judge," "judged," "judgment"; "measure," "measured." The next few sentences are bound together by the threefold repetition of the words "mote," "beam," and "thy brother," and the sixfold repetition of the word "eye." The transition from the second person plural to the second person singular from one part of the passage to the next is used to emphasize the presence of a concrete audience in the lesson: the listener is to recognize himself in the instruction presented to him. Finally, the word "hypocrite" in the last sentence is used as an evaluation. As we recall, when this word is used in Jesus' direct speech, most of the time it refers to the Pharisees. One can suppose that here, too, the practice of the Pharisees serves as a clear example of how a follower of Jesus should not act.

This text has many parallels in the two other Synoptic Gospels. In Mark one of the teachings of Jesus delivered from the boat contains the following fragment: "Take heed what ye hear: with what measure ye measure, it shall be measured to you, and unto you that hear shall more be given. For he that hath, to him shall be given, and he that hath not, from him shall be taken even that which he hath" (Mk 4.24–25). The latter sentence of the given fragment is also present in Matthew, twice: in the sermon given from the boat (Mt 13.12) and, with slight modifications, in the parable of the talents (Mt 25.29).

In Luke we read an expanded version of this teaching that includes some fragments that we find in other places in Matthew:

> "Judge not, and ye shall not be judged; condemn not, and ye shall not be condemned; forgive, and ye shall be forgiven; give, and it shall be given unto you: good measure, pressed down, and shaken together, and running over, shall men give into your bosom. For with the same measure that ye measure it shall be measured to you again." And he spake a parable unto them, "Can the blind lead the blind? Shall they not both fall into the ditch? The disciple is not above his master: but every one that is perfect shall be as his master. And why beholdest thou the speck that is in thy brother's eye, but perceivest not the beam that is in thine own eye? Either how canst thou say to thy brother, 'Brother, let me pull out the speck that is in thine eye,' when thou thyself beholdest not the beam that is in thine own eye? Thou hypocrite, cast out first the beam out of thine own eye, and then shalt thou see clearly to pull out the speck that is in thy brother's eye." (Lk 6.37–42)

The fragment of the Sermon on the Mount that we are discussing corresponds to the beginning and end of this passage from Luke. The first command is expanded: a person is called not only not to judge, but also not to condemn, and to forgive. The "measure" of which Jesus speaks in the Sermon on the Mount is deciphered in Luke with the help of four attributes: it is good, pressed down, shaken together, and running over (this is understood to refer to grain, which is poured out for the buyer in the market). In Matthew, the words "if the blind lead the blind, both shall fall into the ditch" is applied to the Pharisees (Mt 15.14), and in Matthew, the phrase "the disciple is not above his master" is inserted into the instruction of the twelve apostles after they were chosen (Mt 10.24). The three concluding sentences in the passage from Luke are almost identical to the words from the Sermon on the Mount.

Scholars explain the different readings and variations between Matthew and Luke by the possibility that they were working from the same primary source but were using it differently. For our part, we could assume that Jesus often repeated the same images and formulas ("the disciple is not above his master," "if the blind lead the blind," "with the same measure") in different contexts. The use of the same verbal refrains was a characteristic feature of Jesus' speech, and we have no reason to suspect the presence of a redactor in all cases when the same formula is found in two or three Gospels in various situations.

The words "judge not" reflect Jesus' stance in life: he did not condemn anyone—not tax collectors, nor the sinful woman (Lk 7.37–48), nor the woman accused of adultery (Jn 8.3–11). Of his mission on earth, Jesus said, "For God sent not his Son into the world to condemn the world; but that the world through him might be saved" (Jn 3.17). The only category of persons who elicited a tone of condemnation in Jesus' speech was the Pharisees: Jesus publicly condemned their mores, way of acting, and way of thinking.

Jesus' conscious refusal to condemn sinners does not mean that he condoned sin. On the contrary, he very clearly calls a spade a spade, and in many of his exhortations he warns his listeners against committing various sins. But he distinguishes the sin from the sinner and views his task to be not condemning people, as the Pharisees did (Lk 18.11), but saving them, delivering them from slavery to sin, and opening to them the way to the kingdom of heaven.

The Last Judgment, icon, 16th century

His refusal to condemn does not do away with the prospect of the Last Judgment, which Jesus repeatedly mentioned. For every evil deed a person will receive retribution, and for good works, a reward: this conclusion follows from Jesus' words about the Last Judgment (Mt 25.31–46). The words "that ye be not judged" point to the same prospect. Jesus establishes a direct interdependence between how a person judges others and how God will judge that person. We have seen an analogous interdependence in the following words: "For if ye forgive men their trespasses, your heavenly Father will also forgive you; but if ye forgive not men their trespasses, neither will your Father forgive your trespasses" (Mt 6.14–15).

The criteria by which a person judges others will be applied to that same person at the Last Judgment. The Apostle Paul speaks of this, almost repeating the same formula from Jesus' speech word for word: "Therefore thou art inexcusable, O man, whosoever thou art that judgest: for wherein thou judgest another, thou condemnest thyself; for thou that judgest doest the same things. But we are sure that the judgment of God is according to truth against them which commit such things. And thinkest thou this, O man, that judgest them which do such things, and doest the same, that thou shalt escape the judgment of God?" (Rom 2.1–3). This passage testifies that this saying of Jesus was widely circulated among early Christians even before it was recorded in the Synoptic Gospels.

The words "that ye be not judged" can be understood to mean that other people will judge a person the same way he or she judges others. Such an interpretation is partly facilitated by the passive form of the verbs used: "ye shall *be judged*" (*krithēsesthe*), "it shall *be measured* to you again" (*metrēthēsetai hymin*). Such an interpretation links this saying of Jesus with what he said earlier in the Sermon on the Mount: "Let your light so shine before men, that they may see your good works, and glorify your Father which is in heaven" (Mt 5.16). The disciples and followers of Jesus do not live in isolation from the world around them: they live in the world and are called to be the "light of the world" (Mt 5.15). Consequently, they have to hold themselves, rather than those around them, to a high moral standard.

This is made clear by the images of the beam and mote. With the help of these images, Jesus draws attention to a widespread phenomenon: a person's ability to see the shortcomings of others and inability to see his own faults and sins. The images of the beam and speck also point to different degrees of sinfulness: very often a person notices insubstantial shortcomings in others, while refusing to see in himself the grievous sins that separate him from God.

In the context of Jesus' polemics with the Pharisees, the images of the beam and speck fulfill the same function as the images of the camel and gnat in the following words: "Ye blind guides, which strain at a gnat, and swallow a camel" (Mt 23.24). It is no coincidence that in Luke the words on the beam and speck precede the rhetorical question, "Can the blind lead the blind?" Jesus called the Pharisees blind guides who were incapable of distinguishing what was important from what was secondary. John Chrysostom says that it was precisely the Pharisees that Jesus had in view in this part of the Sermon on the Mount:

> In this place, then, as it seems at least to me, He doth not simply command us not to judge any of men's sins, neither doth He simply forbid the doing of such a thing, but to them that are full of innumerable ills, and are trampling upon other men for trifles. And I think that certain Jews too are here hinted at, for that while they were bitter accusing their neighbors for small faults, and such as came to nothing, they were themselves insensibly committing deadly sins.[1]

It is necessary to keep in mind that besides having the authority to teach, the Pharisees also had the authority to judge: most of the high court (Great Sanhedrin) and local courts (Lesser Sanhedrins) were made up of Pharisees. Jesus was not denying the judicial authority of the Pharisees: he was disputing the criteria according to which the Pharisees carried out their judgment. Addressing the Pharisees, Jesus said, "Judge not according to the appearance, but judge righteous judgment" (Jn 7.24). These words can be viewed as a clarification of what was said in the Sermon on the Mount. While in the Sermon on the Mount the words "judge not" are in the form of a universal prohibition, extending to Jesus' disciples as well as to his opponents (both could have been present among his listeners), in the dialogue with the Pharisees Jesus merely points to the error of the Pharisees' approach to the exercise of their judicial powers.

The expression "judge righteous judgment" is an allusion to the judiciary institution established by the law of Moses: "Judges and officers shalt thou make thee in all thy gates, which the LORD thy God giveth thee, throughout thy tribes: and they shall judge the people with just judgment" (Deut 16.18). Addressing the people of Israel, Moses said, "And I charged

---

[1]John Chrysostom, *Commentary on Matthew* 23.1 (NPNF[1] 10:157).

The Last Judgment, icon, 12th century

your judges at that time, saying, 'Hear the causes between your brethren, and judge righteously between every man and his brother, and the stranger that is with him. Ye shall not respect persons in judgment; but ye shall hear the small as well as the great; ye shall not be afraid of the face of man; for the judgment is God's'" (Deut 1.16–17). For quite a long time, judges possessed not only legislative power, but executive power as well: it was they who governed the Hebrew state after the death of Joshua the son of Nun up until the choosing of the first king of Israel (the book of Judges is dedicated to this period in the life of the people of Israel).

We repeat: Jesus was not challenging the judicial institution, just as he was not challenging the other social institutions that existed in his time and had been inherited from the past. People need courts so that when justice is violated, it can be restored, and when a crime is committed, the perpetrator can be punished. But, first of all, a court must be headed by those who possess the authority to do so; second, a court must be "righteous," that is, fair and unbiased; third—and this is key—not even the most perfect judicial system can force a person to give up sinful actions and reform his thinking. One must start a reform with oneself: this is why it is necessary to take out the beam from one's own eye before undertaking to remove the speck from the eye of one's brother.

Here, as elsewhere, Jesus is speaking primarily of a person's daily life. The relationship between a criminal and a judge in the context of the judicial process remains beyond the scope of the Sermon on the Mount: Jesus does not consider it necessary to speak of it, just as he did not consider it necessary to dwell on the literal meaning of the commandment "do not kill." The attention of the listener is perpetually guided beyond the judicial and legal sphere—into the sphere of interpersonal relationships. It is this sphere that is the space in which Jesus' commandments acquire concrete meaning. He draws the attention of his listeners not so much to the merits and shortcomings of human judgment as to the judgment of God, which will ultimately put everything in its place. In light of this judgment, relationships between human beings take on a special quality that allows one to see every other person as a brother and to not judge him, but rather strive first and foremost to eradicate one's own shortcomings and vices.

Chapter 10

"GIVE NOT THAT WHICH IS HOLY UNTO THE DOGS"

W e have come to a passage whose exact meaning has remained a mystery for many centuries:

> Give not that which is holy unto the dogs, neither cast ye your pearls before swine, lest they trample them under their feet, and turn again and rend you. (Mt 7.6)

This passage, it seems, stands in isolation from what comes before and after it within the Sermon on the Mount. The saying has the form of a proverb, the significance of which is difficult to understand in our time, inasmuch as we can only hypothetically reconstruct the context in which is was originally said.[1]

In order to understand the meaning of this saying and the range of associations that it could have evoked in the minds of Jesus' listeners, it is necessary to turn to the Old Testament and see in what sense swine, dogs, holy things, and pearls were spoken of there.

Swine are considered an unclean animal in the Jewish tradition: the law of Moses prohibits the eating of pork and touching pig carcasses (Lev 11.7; Deut 14.8). In Isaiah the "rebellious people" is the one that "sacrificeth in gardens, and burneth incense upon altars of brick, which remain among the graves, and lodge in the monuments, which eat swine's flesh, and broth of abominable things is in their vessels" (Is 65.2–4). When the

---

[1]Guelich, *Sermon on the Mount*, 354.

Lord comes with fire and sword in order to judge all flesh, "they that sanctify themselves, and purify themselves in the gardens behind one tree in
the midst, eating swine's flesh, and the abomination, and the mouse, shall
be consumed together" (Is 66.15–17).

Dogs were also considered unclean and despised animals. In the Old
Testament dogs were not mentioned in connection with domestic animals
or sheepdogs that watched herds. As a rule, the dogs that were mentioned
referred to feral dogs that were ready to pounce on people and tear them
apart. In Psalm 21, understood in the Christian tradition as a prophecy of
the suffering Messiah, it says, "For many dogs have encircled me, the con-
gregations of evil-doers hath surrounded me; they have pierced my hands
and my feet" (Ps 21.17). Of the lawless the psalmist says, "They shall return
at evening, and shall hunger like dogs, and shall go round about the city"
(Ps 58.7, 15). Dogs drink human blood (1 Kg 22.38; Ps 67.24) and eat human
corpses (1 Kg 14.11; 16.4; 21.23; 2 Kg 9.10, 36). The comparison of a person
to a dog was seen as a great insult (1 Sam 17.43; Josh 56.10–11).

The term "holy things" (Heb. *qodeš*) in the Old Testament was used
especially with reference to sacrificial meat. Of the ram that was brought
as a sacrifice at the consecration of priests it is said: "And Aaron and his
sons shall eat the flesh of the ram, and the bread that is in the basket, by
the door of the tabernacle of the congregation. And they shall eat those
things wherewith the atonement was made, to consecrate and to sanctify them; but a stranger shall not eat thereof, because they are holy" (Ex
29.32–34). However, the term "holy thing" had a wider application as well:
the remnant of the grain offering (Lev 2.3, 10; 7.12), the sin offering and
guilt offering (Lev 6.17, 25, 29; 7.1, 6), the altar (Ex 29.37; 30.10; 40.10) and
its accessories (Ex 30.29), and the anointing oil for consecrating priests (Ex
30.31–32), as well as other objects dedicated to God, were all called holy
things. The golden plate with the inscription "holiness to the Lord" was
made for priests to wear (Ex 39.30–31).

Pearls were perceived in the Old Testament as a symbol of the most
valuable thing a person could possess. As the book of Job puts it, "But
where shall wisdom be found? . . . Man knoweth not the price of it. . . . the

*The Ark of
the Covenant,*
mosaic,
9th century

price of wisdom is above pearls" (Job 28.12, 13, 18). Isaac the Syrian, who was familiar with the craft of pearl-divers from his youth, testifies to this:

> If the diver found a pearl in every oyster, then everyone would quickly become rich! And if he brought one up the moment he dived, without the waves beating against him, without any sharks encountering him, without having to hold his breath until he almost expires, without being deprived of the clear air which is granted to everyone, and having to descend to the abyss—(if all this were the case), pearls would come more thick and fast than lightning flashes![2]

The literal meaning of the saying from the Sermon on the Mount that we are discussing assumes that the holy things refer to sacrificial meat: thus was it evidently understood by Jesus' listeners. The words "neither cast ye your pearls before swine" are an extension of the words about holy things and dogs. The words "lest they trample them under their feet, and turn again and rend you" should be understood to relate not so much to swine as to dogs: dogs are more likely to attack and tear a person to pieces than swine, but one needs to protect holy things from both the one and the other.

[2]Isaac the Syrian, *The Second Part: Chapter 34* 4 (trans. Brock, 148).

Jesus' words had already begun to be understood in a broad sense in the first generation of Christians, who extended them to the main Christian holy thing—the Eucharist. We see this understanding in the *Didache*: "Let nobody eat or drink from your Eucharist but those baptized into the name of the Lord. For concerning this the Lord has said: 'Do not give the holy to the dogs.'"[3] Athanasius the Great writes, "And so we will not cast our pearl, the most pure Mysteries, before people who are like swine. . . . Pay heed too, deacon; do not give to the unworthy the porphyry of the most pure Body, so that this may not fall under your responsibility—not according to civil laws, but according to the word of the Lord."[4] John Chrysostom interprets these words from the Sermon on the Mount in the same spirit: "For the mysteries we too therefore celebrate with closed doors, and keep out the uninitiated, not for any weakness of which we have convicted our rites, but because the many are as yet imperfectly prepared for them."[5]

In the quote above Chrysostom is referring to the liturgical custom of closing the doors of the church after the beginning of the Eucharist. This custom, from which the contemporary liturgy has retained the exclamation "The doors, the doors! In wisdom, let us attend," was only part of the protective system built by the early Christians around the Eucharist and other sacraments (mysteries). At the basis of this system, which was called the *disciplina arcana* ("the secret discipline") or *disciplina arcani* ("the discipline of the secret"), lay the idea that the meaning of the sacrament of the Eucharist was inaccessible to those who had not undergone catechesis and received baptism. In the fourth century Cyril of Jerusalem conducted a series of lectures for catechumens, expounding to them the basic principles of the faith, but he began to speak of the Eucharist only after all his listeners had received baptism, explaining that they had hitherto been unprepared to apprehend the teaching on the sacraments.[6]

[3] *Didache* 9.5 (PPS 41:40).
[4] Athanasius the Great, *Fragments on Matthew* 18 (PG 27:1380). Translated by present translator.
[5] John Chrysostom, *Homilies on Matthew* 23.3 (NPNF[1] 10:160).
[6] Cyril of Jerusalem, *Mystagogical Catecheses* 1.1 (PPS 57:85).

Thus in the ancient Church the abovementioned passage from the Sermon on the Mount was understood first of all as a call to protect the Eucharist from outsiders.

But another interpretation existed as well: "swine" and "dogs" were understood to refer to various kinds of false prophets, heretics, and apostates. This interpretation can be traced to the words of the apostle Peter:

> But there were false prophets also among the people, even as there shall be false teachers among you, who secretly shall bring in damnable heresies, even denying the Lord that bought them, and bring upon themselves swift destruction. . . . But these, as natural brute beasts, made to be taken and destroyed, speak evil of the things that they understand not, and shall utterly perish in their own corruption. . . . For when they speak great swelling words of vanity, they allure through the lusts of the flesh, through much wantonness, those that were clean escaped from them who live in error. . . . For if after they have escaped the pollutions of the world through the knowledge of the Lord and Savior Jesus Christ, they are again entangled therein, and overcome, the latter end is worse with them than the beginning. For it had been better for them not to have known the way of righteousness, than, after they have known it, to turn from the holy commandment delivered unto them. But it is happened unto them according to the true proverb, "The dog is turned to his own vomit again; and the sow that was washed to her wallowing in the mire." (2 Pet 2.1, 12, 18, 20–22)

The simultaneous use of the images of the dog and swine here is not a coincidence: it is likely that Peter had in mind Jesus' saying, which was well-known to him, from the Sermon on the Mount. In other cases these images are used separately. The apostle Paul wrote of false teachers in the first century: "Beware of dogs, beware of evil workers" (Phil 3.2). In the next generation Ignatius of Antioch used the same image: "For some are in the habit of carrying about the name [of Jesus Christ] in wicked guile, while yet they practise things unworthy of God, whom ye must flee as ye would wild beasts. For they are ravening dogs, who bite secretly."[7] The Epistle of

---

[7]Ignatius of Antioch, *Epistle to the Ephesians* 7.1 (PPS 49:33).

Barnabas mentioned swine: "Do not associate . . . with such people who are like pigs."[8] Athanasius the Great said that one must not open the mysteries of the faith to such people, lest they "turn and tear you apart, having produced schisms and heresies."[9]

Gregory the Theologian used both images, that of dogs and swine. Here the image of swine is used to refer to persons who alter the true doctrine and become apostates from the Christian faith:

> We all become pious by simply condemning the impiety of others; and we claim the services of ungodly judges, and fling that which is holy to the dogs, and cast pearls before swine, by publishing divine things in the hearing of profane souls. . . . But what is to be said of those who. . . . rush headlong against every form of doctrine in swinish fashion, and trample under foot the fair pearls of the truth? What again of those who . . . listen to all kinds of doctrines and teachers. . . . and, after being deluged and trodden down by all kinds of doctrine, and having rung the changes on a long succession of teachers . . . they become equally disgusted with all forms of doctrine, and assume the wretched character of deriding and despising our faith as unstable and unsound. . . . Accordingly, to impress the truth upon a soul when it is still fresh, like wax not yet subjected to the seal, is an easier task than inscribing pious doctrine on the top of inscriptions—I mean wrong doctrines and dogmas.[10]

In the fifth century Isidore of Pelusium compared those who at first "came from heresy to true doctrine" but then "gave themselves over to their former perversity again" with dogs.[11] Hilary of Poitiers (sixth century) understood "dogs" to refer to pagans, and "swine" to heretics.[12]

---

[8]Barnabas 10.3 (PPS 41:72).

[9]Athanasius the Great, *Fragments on Matthew* 18 (PG 27:1380). Translated by present translator.

[10]Gregory of Nazianzus, *Orations* 2 (NPNF² 7:204–227).

[11]Isidore of Pelusium, *Letters* 143 (PG 78:280). Translated by present translator.

[12]Hilary of Poitiers, *Commentary on Matthew* 6.1. English translation from *Commentary on Matthew*, by Hilary of Poitiers, trans. D. H. Williams, Fathers of the Church 125 (Washington, D.C.: Catholic University of America Press, 2012), 85.

The Church's response to heretics and schismatics was from the very beginning as harsh as Jesus' response to the Pharisees. "A man that is a heretic after the first and second admonition reject": this principle, articulated by the apostle Paul (Tit 3.10) and based on Mt 18.15–17, has been applied in practice throughout all the centuries of the Church's existence.

In our time this saying of Jesus is usually understood as a call not to share what is holy and dear to us with people who are unable to appreciate it in the proper way. Even with the best intentions, excessive openness can lead to the very people to whom you have opened yourself becoming your enemies. It is necessary not just to send a signal but to also think about how this signal may be received by those to whom it is addressed. Even talking about God should be done "not before every audience, nor at all times, nor on all points; but on certain occasions, and before certain persons, and within certain limits."[13] Considering the audience's possible reaction is no less important for a preacher than correctly composing a speech or clearly articulating a thought.

[13]Gregory of Nazianzus, *Orations* 27.3 (NPNF[2] 7:285).

Chapter 11

"ASK, AND IT SHALL BE GIVEN YOU"

In the next segment of the Sermon on the Mount Jesus returns to the topic of prayer. He had already touched on this topic earlier in the Sermon on the Mount when he gave his disciples the Lord's Prayer; however, while the emphasis there had been on how the disciples were to pray, here the focal point is the result of prayer, God's answer to it:

> Ask, and it shall be given you; seek, and ye shall find; knock, and it shall be opened unto you: for every one that asketh receiveth; and he that seeketh findeth; and to him that knocketh it shall be opened.
>
> Or what man is there of you, whom if his son ask bread, will he give him a stone? Or if he ask a fish, will he give him a serpent?
>
> If ye then, being evil, know how to give good gifts unto your children, how much more shall your Father which is in heaven give good things to them that ask him? (Mt 7.7–11)

This passage consists of three interrelated sayings: the first presents a general principle, the second offers an example from daily life, and the third is a conclusion proceeding from both the general principle and the example. All three sayings are connected by the verbs "give" and "ask."

We find an analogous passage in Luke. In it the first part matches the version in Matthew. The second part differs slightly: "If a son shall ask bread of any of you that is a father, will he give him a stone? Or if he ask a fish, will he for a fish give him a serpent? Or if he shall ask an egg, will he offer him a scorpion?" The third part again matches practically perfectly

Jesus Christ Teaching the Disciples How to Pray, fresco, 14th century

with the text in Matthew, with the exception of the words "good things," which are substituted with "the Holy Spirit" in Luke (Lk 11.9–13).

In Luke's version the given passage is embedded in the teaching on prayer, which is preceded by a request from one of the disciples: "Lord, teach us to pray." Jesus pronounces the Lord's Prayer in reply. This is followed by unique material from Luke, which we do not encounter in any other Gospel:

> And he said unto them, "Which of you shall have a friend, and shall go unto him at midnight, and say unto him, 'Friend, lend me three loaves,

for a friend of mine in his journey is come to me, and I have nothing to set before him'? And he from within shall answer and say, 'Trouble me not. The door is now shut, and my children are with me in bed; I cannot rise and give thee.' I say unto you, though he will not rise and give him, because he is his friend, yet because of his importunity he will rise and give him as many as he needeth." (Lk 11.5–8)

It is in the Gospel of Luke that Jesus' teaching on prayer is most fully articulated. Alongside the above excerpt, in this Gospel we also find "a parable unto them to this end, that men ought always to pray, and not to lose heart." The parable speaks of a widow who has been pestering a judge with a petition to defend her from her adversary. The judge, "which feared not God, neither regarded man," did not wish to get around to addressing her request for a long time, but in the end he said, "Though I fear not God, nor regard man, yet because this widow troubleth me, I will avenge her, lest by her continual coming she weary me." The parable concludes with these words: "Hear what the unjust judge saith. And shall not God avenge his own elect, which cry day and night unto him, though he bear long with them? I tell you that he will avenge them speedily" (Lk 18.1–8).

In both of these passages from the Gospel of Luke, the same idea can be clearly traced: even if God "bears long" with fulfilling a person's request, he will fulfill it "because of his importunity." In other words, we are called not to simply turn to God with a one-time request; we must "pester" God with our persistent requests until they are fulfilled.

The passages on prayer from the Gospel of Luke are consonant with the Sermon on the Mount, in which we also find the image of a person who persistently strives to fulfill his goal. This image is created with the help of the threefold "ask, seek, knock" and the threefold "receive, find, open." The same logic of "proof by contradiction" is used as in the passages from the Gospel of Luke. While the latter gives the examples of a person who pesters his friend at midnight and a widow who pesters a judge, in the Sermon on the Mount the one who prays is compared to children who receive good things from their father.

The expression "being evil" may appear offensive. However, in the over-all context of Jesus' way of speaking, it does not have such an overtone. It is more likely that "evil" as an attribute of human nature is being contrasted here with "good" as a divine attribute. Jesus considered the term "good" to be proper to God alone (Mt 19.17). Not a single person can be considered good, since good in human beings is intermingled with evil. A person can be evil toward other people, but in relating to his own children, good comes to the fore. The earthly love of a father for his own children is a reflection of the love of the heavenly Father toward all people. That is why human beings have a right to pester their Father in prayer as well.

To what has been said about prayer in Matthew and Luke, we should add some of Jesus' sayings from the Gospel of John:

> And whatsoever ye shall ask in my name, that will I do, that the Father may be glorified in the Son. If ye shall ask any thing in my name, I will do it. (Jn 14.13–14)

> If ye abide in me, and my words abide in you, ye shall ask what ye will, and it shall be done unto you. (Jn 15.7)

> Verily, verily, I say unto you, whatsoever ye shall ask the Father in my name, he will give it you. Hitherto have ye asked nothing in my name: ask, and ye shall receive, that your joy may be full. (Jn 16.23–24)

All three sayings are part of the Jesus' last instruction to his disciples. All of them are connected by the verb "ask," just like the abovementioned passages from Matthew and Luke. In two of the three sayings, God the Father is mentioned. Thrice it is said that a request addressed to the Father must be "in Jesus' name." The request, according to one of the sayings, will be fulfilled by the Father; according to another saying, it will be fulfilled by Jesus himself.

It is evident that Jesus was not simply promising his disciples that the Father would pay attention to their requests: he himself was acting as guar-antor that their requests would be fulfilled. This is also spoken of in the following words from the Gospel of Matthew: "Again I say unto you, that if two of you shall agree on earth as touching any thing that they shall ask, it shall be done for them by my Father who is in heaven. For where two or three are gathered together in my name, there am I in the midst of them" (Mt 18.19–20). Jesus promises his disciples that he will be among them, and that the Father will grant them what they ask, if they gather "in his name" and ask "as touching any thing." These words found their direct continuation in the Christian practice of gathering for prayer, first and foremost in gathering for the Eucharist.

We can formulate certain conditions under which a Christian's prayer to God the Father would be heard. First, the prayer should be accompanied by firm faith that God hears it. Second, the prayer should be persistent and, if necessary, sustained. Third, it should be offered in Jesus' name. Fourth, regardless of whether a Christian prays alone or together with others, he or she should pray not as an isolated individual, but as a member of the united community of Jesus' disciples. This sense of community will give the Christian assurance that what has been promised to the entire community will certainly extend to him or her as well.

In what situations may a prayer remain unheard and a request remain unfulfilled? The search for the answer to this question had already begun in the first generation of Christians, since the experience of prayer shows that God does not always give a person that which he or she requests. In his Catholic Epistle, the apostle James, addressing people mired in enmity and strife, says, "Ye desire, and have not. . . . because ye ask not. Ye ask, and receive not, because ye ask amiss, that ye may spend it upon your lusts" (Jas 4.2–3). Here the receiving of what one has asked of God directly depends on what goal a person has in making the request. If he or she asks "amiss" (or "wrongly," *kakōs*) the request can remain unfulfilled.

The First Epistle of John says, "And whatsoever we ask, we receive from him, because we keep his commandments, and do those things that are pleasing in his sight" (1 Jn 3.22). In the same epistle we read: "And this is the confidence that we have in him, that, if we ask any thing according to his will, he heareth us. And if we know that he hear us, whatsoever we ask, we know that we have the petitions that we desired from him" (1 Jn 5.14–15). In these passages God's fulfillment of requests made in prayer is correlated with observing his commandments, doing works pleasing to him, and asking that which is according to his will.

One of the mandates of the Shepherd of Hermas provides a detailed commentary on Jesus' words in the Sermon on the Mount:

> Put away doubting from you and do not hesitate to ask of the Lord, saying to yourself, "How can I ask of the Lord and receive from Him, seeing I have sinned so much against Him?" Do not thus reason with yourself, but with all your heart turn to the Lord and ask of Him without doubting, and you will know the multitude of His tender mercies; that He will never leave you, but fulfil the request of your soul. . . . Cleanse, therefore, your heart from all the vanities of this world, and from the words already mentioned, and ask of the Lord and you will receive all, and in none of your requests will you be denied which you make to the Lord without doubting. But if you doubt in your heart, you will receive none of your requests. For those who doubt regarding God are double-souled, and obtain not one of their requests. But those who are perfect in faith ask everything, trusting in the Lord; and they obtain, because they ask nothing doubting. . . . Cleanse your heart, therefore, from all doubt, and put on faith, because it is strong, and trust God that you will obtain from Him all that you ask.[1]

This early Christian text contains a whole list of conditions under which the prayer of a Christian would be heard: the Christian should ask without doubt, cleanse his heart from worldly vanity, and fulfill the commandments of God. However, the author of the book continues, even in that case, one's requests may remain unfulfilled. If God does not fulfill them immediately, he may fulfill them later on:

> And if at any time, after you have asked of the Lord, you are slower in obtaining your request [than you expected], do not doubt because you have not soon obtained the request of your soul; for invariably it is on

---

[1]Shepherd of Hermas, *Mandates* 9 (ANF 2:26). The Shepherd of Hermas is a second-century composition that was placed together with the Gospels and other books of the New Testament in some manuscripts.

account of some temptation or some sin of which you are ignorant that you are slower in obtaining your request. Wherefore do not cease to make the request of your soul, and you will obtain it. But if you grow weary and waver in your request, blame yourself, and not Him who does not give to you.[2]

Thus, both here and in the abovementioned passages from the Gospels of Matthew and Luke, there is a call to persistent prayer. But not one of Jesus' sayings in the Gospels says that a Christian's prayer can remain unfulfilled. In the Sermon on the Mount the promise is phrased with the utmost simplicity: "Ask, and it shall be given you; seek, and ye shall find; knock, and it shall be opened unto you." This is the universal principle that should be unfailingly in effect if a person makes the entire Sermon on the Mount his or her rule of life. If, on the other hand, one exempts oneself from certain parts of Jesus' moral teaching, then his promises also cease to be effective to their full extent.

Subsequent generations of Christians continued to seek to clarify the conditions under which one's prayer would be heard. We find a detailed interpretation of the words of the Sermon on the Mount in the writings of John Chrysostom:

> However, not simply to ask did He command us, but with much assiduity and earnestness. For this is the meaning of "seek". . . . By "seeking," then, He declared this; by "knocking," that we approach with earnestness and a glowing mind. . . . And if thou dost not receive straightway, do not even thus despair. For to this end He said, "knock," to signify that even if He should not straightway open the door, we are to continue there. . . . And if thou continue asking, though thou receive not at once, thou surely wilt receive. For to this end was the door shut, that He may induce thee to knock: to this end He doth not straightway assent, that thou mayest ask. Continue then to do these things, and thou wilt surely receive. . . . Do thou also therefore ask nothing worldly, but all things spiritual, and thou wilt surely receive. . . . Two things now, you

---

[2]Shepherd of Hermas, *Mandates* 9 (ANF 2:26).

see, should be in him that prays, asking earnestly, and asking what he ought.... As it is, surely our asking is a mockery, and the act of drunken rather than of sober men. "What then," saith one, "if I ask even spiritual things, and do not receive?" Thou didst not surely knock with earnestness; or thou madest thyself unworthy to receive; or didst quickly leave off. ... Say not then, "I drew nigh, and did not receive." For in no case is it owing to God that we receive not, God who loves us so much as to surpass even fathers, to surpass them as far as goodness doth this evil nature.[3]

In the seventh century Isaac the Syrian discussed why prayer sometimes remains unheard. The first reason, in his view, lies in the providence of God, according to which he gives to each person according to that person's measure and ability to receive:

> If you should beseech God for a thing and He forbears to hearken to you speedily, do not grieve, for you are not wiser than God. This happens to you either because you are not worthy to obtain your request, or because the pathways of your heart do not accord with your petitions (but rather the contrary), or because you have not reached the measure wherein you could receive the gift you ask for.[4]

Another reason that God does not hear prayer consists in the sins that separate a person from God:

> But since we say that God is plenteous in mercy, why is it that when amidst temptations we unceasingly knock and pray, we are not heard and He disregards our prayer? This we are clearly taught by the Prophet when he says, "The Lord's hand is not little, that it cannot save; nor is He heavy of hearing, that He cannot hear: but our sins have separated us from Him, and our iniquities have turned His face away, that He doth not hearken." Remember God at all times, and He will remember you whenever you fall into evils.[5]

---

[3]John Chrysostom, *Homilies on Matthew* 23.4–5 (NPNF[1] 10:160–161).
[4]Isaac the Syrian, *Ascetical Homilies* 3 (trans. Holy Transfiguration Monastery, 136).
[5]Isaac the Syrian, *Ascetical Homilies* 5 (trans. Holy Transfiguration Monastery, 161).

An exposition of the patristic teaching on prayer is not our present task. However, it seemed important to us to give some examples of how Jesus' commandment to pray fervently was interpreted in the Christian tradition, from apostolic times to the church fathers of the fourth through seventh centuries. These interpretations provide the key to understanding the significance of Jesus' commandment for people today.

Isaac the Syrian, miniature, 15th century

Anyone who has experience in prayer knows that God sometimes responds to a request very quickly, but sometimes "bears long" with his answer, and sometimes leaves the request unfulfilled altogether. On the one hand, we have Jesus' completely clear and unconditional promise: "Ask, and it shall be given you." On the other hand, we have a whole series of qualifications that go back to the first generation of his disciples. These qualifications and clarifications help us to understand why prayer is not always heard.

Prayer is a creative process, the result of which is not always predictable. Jesus did not set himself the task of systematically laying the foundations for a doctrine of prayer. He addressed the topic of prayer often, but even all of his sayings on this topic taken together do not give a complete system according to which one can structure one's prayer life and communication with God.

In the Sermon on the Mount Jesus begins with the examples of the Pharisees and the heathen to show how one should *not* pray (Mt 6.5–8). Then he gives the disciples a model for prayer (Mt 6.9–13). Finally, he speaks of how one *should* pray, emphasizing the importance of persistence and perseverance (Mt 7.7–11). He leaves everything else to the creative discretion of the person praying, who must learn from experience how God responds to prayer and what effect prayer has on his or her life.

Chapter 12

THE "GOLDEN RULE"

In the Sermon on the Mount the instruction to pray with perseverance is followed by the so-called "Golden Rule,"[1] which contains the fundamental principle according to which interpersonal relationships should be built:

> Therefore all things whatsoever ye would that men should do to you, do ye even so to them: for this is the law and the prophets. (Mt 7.12)

The word "therefore" (*oun*) must indicate a connection between this saying and what precedes it. However, we do not observe a direct connection, since the preceding topic was prayer. It is more likely that this word indicates a connection between the "Golden Rule" and the words "Judge not, that ye be not judged," which is a specific application of the rule, or a connection with the general context of the Sermon on the Mount speaking of relations between people, or with Jesus' moral teaching as a whole.

We find an analogous saying in the Gospel of Luke (Lk 6.31), but there it is placed between the exhortations to love one's enemies, to turn the other cheek, and to give to everyone who asks, which precede the saying, and the law of retaliation, which follows it. The overall context of Jesus' speech in Luke is love for one's enemies. The "Golden Rule" appears exactly in the middle of this speech and is naturally woven into its context.

At first glance, this saying contrasts sharply with the radical exhortations to love your enemies, to bless those who curse you, to do good to those who hate you, and to pray for those who offend you: while those exhortations develop the idea of doing good without being reciprocated

[1] The expression "Golden Rule" was first used by the English philosopher Charles Gibbon in the beginning of the seventeenth century.

for it, the saying that we are discussing is based precisely on the principle of reciprocity. Certain scholars think that the "historical Jesus" could not have pronounced such a saying, which embodies the "princely principle of pragmatism." According to them, "it is more likely a prime example of a popular maxim of Greco-Roman ethics, already assimilated into Judaism, that was secondarily placed on the lips of Jesus by Christian Jews who revered him, among other things, as their ethical master."[2]

Meanwhile, in fact, the contradiction turns out to be imaginary. The reciprocity in this rule is not *reactive*, as it is when a person does good in response to good. It is really about taking a *proactive* stance in life, which presupposes that a person would desire for others that which he desires for himself. The "Golden Rule" perfectly fulfills the commandment to love one's enemies and in no way negates or cancels it.

Moreover, this rule derives directly from the commandment that Jesus put in second place after the commandment to love God: "Thou shalt love thy neighbor as thyself" (Lev 19.18). "On these two commandments," in Jesus' words, "hang all the law and the prophets" (Mt 22.38–40). The mention of "the law and the prophets" connects the second commandment with the "Golden Rule," of which it is also said, "for this is the law and the prophets." Jesus is emphasizing, so to speak, that the rule of reciprocity has its roots in the morality of the Old Testament. In this case he is not reforming the Old Testament law: he is merely summarizing it, reducing it to a certain fundamental principle.

The call to love one's neighbor as oneself is recorded in multiple places in the New Testament (Mt 19.19; 22.39; Mk 12.31, 33; Lk 10.27; Rom 13.9).[3] In the Epistle of James it is called the "royal law" (Jas 2.8), while the apostle Paul says of it, "For all the law is fulfilled in one word, even in this: thou shalt love thy neighbor as thyself" (Gal 5.14). The multiple references to this

---

[2]Meier, *Marginal Jew*, 4:557.

[3]In the Western text-type manuscripts of the New Testament, the book of Acts preserves a negative form of the Golden Rule in a speech of the apostle James, delivered to the apostolic council in Jerusalem, positing that gentile Christians should abstain from idolatry, sexual immorality, and eating blood, and "that they should not do to others what they would not wish to be done to themselves," which was accepted by the council, and repeated in the letter they send out to the churches (Acts 15.20, 29). English Bibles do not include this textual variant.

"law" on the pages of the New Testament writings compel us to consider it one of the most important aspects of Christian ethics. But to love one's neighbors as oneself also means to treat them as one would like others to treat oneself.

Researchers have noted more than once that the "Golden Rule" is a universal moral principle reflected in some form or other in the major religious and philosophical systems of the ancient world, including ancient Greek philosophy, Judaism, Christianity, Islam, Confucianism, and Buddhism. It is also reflected in modern philosophy, particularly in Kant's "categorical imperative."[4] We will not

Immanuel Kant, Johann Gottlieb Becker, 1775

cite here all the well-known parallels, since they are quite numerous. But we must note that, with the exception of ancient Greek philosophy and Hinduism, with which Jesus could hardly have been in contact, all these parallels belong to the era that followed the emergence of Christianity.

As for the Old Testament (and it was precisely the Old Testament, as we have seen, that was the foundation on which Jesus built the Sermon on the Mount), we do not find a direct parallel to the "Golden Rule" in it. Among the 613 commandments of the law of Moses, there is neither the "Golden Rule" nor anything close to it.[5] The closest indirect parallel is found in these words from the book of Tobit: "Do that to no man which thou hatest" (Tob 4.15). We may also recall the following advice from the book of the Wisdom of Sirach: "Mind thy neighbor's things by thyself" (Sir 31.15). However, in the first case we have the "Golden Rule" only in the negative form, while in the second the principle is formulated so generally that it is impossible to speak of a direct connection between it and Jesus' saying in the Sermon on the Mount. Thus, it is obvious that when

[4]Immanuel Kant, *Grounding for the Metaphysics of Morals: With, On a Supposed Right to Lie because of Philanthropic Concerns*, trans. James W. Ellington, 3rd ed. (Indianapolis, IN: Hackett, 1993), 30.

[5]R. G. Apresyan, "Talion i zolotoe pravilo (Kriticheskiy analiz sopryazhennykh kontekstov)" [Talion and the Golden Rule (a critical analysis of interconnected contexts)], *Voprosy filosofii* [Questions of philosophy] 3 (2001): 82.

he formulated such an important ethical principle, Jesus did not have any literary primary source in mind.

In the Babylonian Talmud, which was compiled between the third and fourth centuries after Christ, but which reflects the disputes between the followers of Shammai and Hillel that took place in the time of Jesus, there is the story of how one gentile went to Shammai and asked him to retell the entire Torah while standing on one leg. Shammai chased him away with a stick. Then the gentile went to Hillel with the same request, and received the following reply: "What is hateful to you, do not do to your neighbor; that is the whole Torah, while the rest is commentary; go and learn it" (b. Shabbat 31a).[6]

Even if this story truly took place in the time of Shammai and Hillel and is not a later anecdote, the "Golden Rule" is expressed in it only in the negative form. If, on the other hand, we take into account the period in which the Babylonian Talmud was compiled, we cannot exclude the possibility that Christian ethics had influenced its compilers and editors, even if only indirectly.

The "Golden Rule," in the form in which it is expressed by Jesus in the Sermon on the Mount, continues to serve as one of the fundamental moral reference points in Christian ethics. As the link between the Christian and Old Testament ethical systems, it simultaneously connects Christianity with many other philosophical and religious movements, both earlier and later. If a whole series of commandments in the Sermon on the Mount (including, first of all, the commandment to love one's enemies) defines the unique character of Christian morality as a supernatural moral law, then this particular rule stands firmly within the bounds of natural law.

The concept of "natural law" (Latin *lex naturalis*), or "natural right" (*ius naturale*), has an important meaning in Latin theology. It presupposes the presence in human nature of moral attitudes that are common to all mankind and rooted in the concept of "conscience." We will not enter here into an examination of the theory of natural law itself, since it is interpreted in various ways depending on the context—ancient Greek philosophy, medi-

---

[6]English translation from *The Gospel of Mark*, by John R. Donahue and Daniel J. Harrington, Sacra Pagina Series 2 (Collegeville, MN: Liturgical Press, 2002), 356.

eval Latin thought, or modern philosophy. We will limit ourselves merely to this saying of the apostle Paul, which lies at the basis of the medieval understanding of natural law: "For when the Gentiles, which have not the law, do by nature the things contained in the law, these, having not the law, are a law unto themselves, which show the work of the law written in their hearts, their conscience also bearing witness, and their thoughts the mean while accusing or else excusing one another" (Rom 2.14–15).

The general context of Paul's speech is the relationship between the law of Moses and the spiritual and moral attitudes that existed in the gentile world. As he examines this relationship, Paul comes to a very radical conclusion: while the gentiles do not have an absolute law of divine origin, they nevertheless have a law written on their hearts. This law is the voice of conscience, which allows them to distinguish good from evil.

This idea seemed revolutionary to the first generation of Christians, as did all of Paul's activity in drawing gentiles to the Church and his insistence on abolishing foundational Jewish customs, such as circumcision, for the gentiles. For this reason "no small dissension and disputation" arose between Paul and Barnabas, on the one hand, and "certain men which came down from Judaea," on the other hand, which required the convocation of an extraordinary council of all the apostles (Acts 15.1–6).

However, in this case, the apostle Paul did not say anything essentially new in comparison with what had already been formulated by Jesus as a fundamental universal moral principle. Jesus derived it from the law of Moses, insisting that "this is the law and the prophets." Paul merely went one step further, asserting that fundamental moral principles were not limited to the letter of the law of Moses: God placed moral sense not just in the Jews through the law and the prophets, but also in the gentiles.

The Sermon on the Mount is not a systematic exposition of Christian morality. It does, however, bear a programmatic character. All of its precepts are interdependent. The beginning of the Sermon, in particular the Beatitudes and the six antitheses, is distinguished by its radicalism and novelty: Jesus overturns many postulates of natural human morality. In the concluding part of the Sermon on the Mount, however, he shows that the standards he prescribes do not contradict natural morality, but should be

The Sermon on the Mount, Prince G. G. Gagarin, 19th century

in harmony with the latter, complementing and developing it, bringing it to new and ever greater heights, but not abolishing it completely.

In light of what we have said above, we can return to Jesus' words that "one jot or one tittle shall in no wise pass from the law, till all be fulfilled" (Mt 5.18). In the passage of the Sermon on the Mount where these words are found, the words seem to be discordant with the content of the Sermon: how can one speak of a literal observation of the law when Jesus reinterprets one commandment after another from the law of Moses and introduces his own commandments instead? However, the concluding part of the Sermon on the Mount to some extent balances that which at first glance may have seemed incompatible: the law of Moses, which came from God but was based on natural law, and the new law, which also comes from God but, alongside natural standards, contains supernatural standards as well. While the fulfillment of natural standards does not demand from Christians anything beyond that which is expected of any other person, the supernatural standards require spiritual rebirth and moral labor.

Chapter 13

CONCLUDING
SECTIONS

The Sermon on the Mount concludes with three sections that are thematically, structurally, and terminologically connected with each other: a section on the two ways, a section on false prophets and the Last Judgment, and a section on the house on sand and the house on the rock. Thematically, all three sections are united by the idea of posthumous recompense and the prospect of the Last Judgment. Terminologically, the first and second sections are linked by the verb *eiserchomai* ("enter"), and the second and third are linked by the frequent usage of the verb *poieō* (in the sense of "bring forth," "fulfill," or "do"). All three sections make use of antitheses, which is characteristic also of other parts of the Sermon on the Mount and of Jesus' language and thought in general: the narrow gate is contrasted with the wide one, the narrow way with the broad, the few with the many, the good tree with the corrupt, the good fruit with the evil, the one who does the will of the heavenly Father with the one who says "Lord, Lord," the wise man with the foolish, the house on a rock with the house on the sand. The predominant tone is one of warning.[1]

---

[1] Luz, *Matthew 1–7*, 369.

1. The Two Ways

In the first of the three concluding sections of the Sermon on the Mount, the concept of the two ways, which has Old Testament roots, is developed:

> Enter ye in at the narrow gate. For wide is the gate, and broad is the way, that leadeth to destruction, and many there be who go in through it. Because narrow is the gate, and narrow is the way, which leadeth unto life, and few there be that find it. (Mt 7.13–14)

A condensed version of this saying is found in the Gospel of Luke, which tells of how someone asked Jesus, "Lord, are there few that be saved?" Jesus replied, "Strive to enter in at the narrow gate: for many, I say unto you, will seek to enter in, and shall not be able" (Lk 13.23–24). In both instances, the image of a gate is used, but only in Matthew's version do we read about the two ways, and only in Matthew is the way to life contrasted with the way to destruction.

The teaching about the two ways is contained in the words of God in the law of Moses: "I have set before you life and death, blessing and cursing: therefore choose life" (Deut 30.19). Here the term "way" is not used, but two approaches to life are clearly presented, of which the people of Israel are ordered to choose only one.

The word "way" in the sense of "way of life" is encountered multiple times in the Psalter. Already Psalm 1 speaks of the difference between two ways: "For the Lord knoweth the way of the righteous, and the way of the ungodly shall perish" (Ps 1.6). We find a similar contrast between two ways in Psalm 118: "Remove from me the way of unrighteousness, and with thy law have mercy on me. I have chosen the way of truth, and thy judgments have I not forgotten" (Ps 118.29–30). According to the Psalmist, God shows a person the "ways of life" (Ps 15.11), makes for him a "blameless path" (Ps 17.33), sets a law for those who sin in the way and teaches the meek his ways (Ps 24.8–9), and instructs a person in the way that he shall go (Ps 31.8). In contrast, the wicked person sets out on his way on his own initiative (Ps

35.5). Hatred for the "ways of unrighteousness" (Ps 118.104, 128) proceeds out of love for God's commandments.

How do the metaphors of the way and the gate relate to each other? Does the gate open up access to the way, or, conversely, does the way lead to the gate? Either interpretation is possible, but the second seems preferable. The image of a gate is used in the Bible to indicate not the beginning but the end of a path: as a rule, gates correspond to the idea of entering, not exiting. In this sense we can understand the expression "the gate of heaven" (Gen 28.17): it leads into the courts of the Lord (Ps 99.4) and the righteous enter into it (Ps 117.20). The "gates of death" (Job 38.17; Ps 67.21; 106.18) and the "gates of the grave" (Is 38.10), on the contrary, lead to Sheol, to destruction, to the nether regions. In Jesus' speech the "gates of hell" (Mt 16.18) refer to the entrance into hell, not the exit out of it. In the saying from the Sermon on the Mount that we are discussing, the verb "enter" is used with exactly the same meaning as it has when it is used in other passages in the Gospel of Matthew: to signify entrance into the kingdom of heaven (Mt 5.20; 7.21) or life eternal (Mt 18.8–9; 19.17). The two ways lead to two gates, one of which is the entrance to "life," and the other the entrance to "destruction."

The concept of the two ways became widespread in the early Christian Church. The apostles called the teaching of Jesus the "way of the Lord" (Acts 18.25–26; 19.9, 23). The Epistle to the Hebrews says that Christians have boldness to enter into the sanctuary "by the blood of Jesus, by a new and living way, which he hath consecrated for us, through the veil, that is to say, his flesh" (Heb 10.19–20). The "way of righteousness" (2 Pet 2.21) is contrasted with the way of a sinner (Jas 5.20). This contrast is especially pronounced in the *Didache*, which begins with these words: "There are two ways, the one of life and the one of death; the difference between the ways is great."[2]

In Jesus' speech the word "way" has a multifaceted meaning. At the Last Supper he says to his disciples, "And whither I go ye know, and the way ye know." The words of the Teacher confuse Thomas: "Lord, we know not whither thou goest; and how can we know the way?" To this Jesus replies,

---

[2]*Didache* 1.1 (PPS 41:35).

The Last Supper,
A. A. Ivanov,
1850s

"I am the way, the truth, and the life. No man cometh unto the Father, but by me" (Jn 14.4–6). Of the three terms used in the part of the Sermon on the Mount that we are discussing, two are present here: "way" and "life." The term "truth" is characteristic only of the Gospel of John, where grace and truth, which have come through Jesus Christ, are contrasted with the law, which was given through Moses (Jn 1.17). To the Jews who have believed in him, Jesus says, "If ye continue in my word, then are ye my disciples indeed; and ye shall know the truth, and the truth shall make you free" (Jn 8.31–32).

The words from the Sermon on the Mount about the narrow way that leads to life ought to be interpreted from the starting point of the overall context of Jesus' preaching. "Life" here is understood to mean the kingdom of heaven—the end goal of the journey. However, the kingdom of heaven, as we recall, is connected not just with the idea of posthumous recompense: it is acquired here and now, and it is none other than Jesus himself. To follow the narrow way that leads to life means to be a disciple of Jesus, to fulfill his commandments.

Here it is appropriate to recall the image of the door, which Jesus applies to himself. In his conversation with the Jews, he speaks of the sheepfold that the shepherd enters into through a door: "To him the porter openeth; and the sheep hear his voice; and he calleth his own sheep by name, and leadeth them out. . . . And a stranger will they not follow, but will flee from him; for they know not the voice of strangers." The Jews do not understand the meaning of the parable, so Jesus then explains it: "Verily, verily, I say unto you, I am the door of the sheep. . . . I am the door: by me if any man enter in, he shall be saved, and shall go in and out, and find pasture" (Jn 10.1–9).

The sheepfold symbolizes the Church, the sheep are Jesus' followers, and Jesus himself fulfills two functions in the parable: he is both the Shepherd and the door into the sheepfold. The image of the door is semantically close to the image of the gate that is used in the Sermon on the Mount. The gate to the kingdom of heaven is also Jesus himself: it is only through him and thanks to him that it is possible to enter into this kingdom.

The Good Shepherd, Philippe de Champaigne, 17th century

The way to life, therefore, is the spiritual and moral teaching of Jesus, which is set forth in the Sermon on the Mount in particular. To go by the narrow way means to be poor in spirit, to weep, to be meek, to hunger and thirst after righteousness, to be merciful, to be pure in heart, to be a peacemaker, to be persecuted for righteousness' sake. To go by the narrow way means to endure persecution for Jesus' sake, to be the salt of the earth and the light of the world, to not become angry, to respect marital fidelity, to not return evil for evil, to love one's enemies, to avoid superficial righteousness, to not judge others, to forgive them their debts, to not lay up treasures on earth, to not attempt to serve both God and mammon, to not worry about tomorrow, to seek first the kingdom of God and his righteousness.

In a generalized sense, the way to life is Jesus himself. In order to be his disciple, it is not enough to simply carry out a certain number of moral prescriptions: it is necessary to also be a member of his community—the Church. A disciple of Jesus does not walk the narrow way of fulfilling Jesus' commandments alone: together with him or her walks the entire community of disciples, at the head of which stands Jesus.

It is noteworthy that in Luke's version the words about the narrow way constitute the answer to the question, "Lord, are there few that be saved?" The term "salvation" is absent in the Gospels of Matthew, Mark, and John, but it is encountered multiple times in the corpus of Luke's writings (Lk 1.69, 77; 2.30; 19.9–10; Acts 4.11; 7.25; 13.26; 13.47; 28.28), in the Catholic Epistles (Jas 1.5, 9–10; 1 Pet 2.2; Jude 3), and in the Epistles of the apostle Paul (Rom 1.16; 10.1, 10; 11.11; 13.11, and elsewhere). As for the verbs "save" and "be saved," they are found in the entire corpus of New Testament writings, including in all four Gospels. The idea of salvation, therefore, occupies a central place in the New Testament. It is encountered in Jesus' direct speech as well (Mt 18.11; Mk 3.4; Lk 6.9; 19.10; Jn 12.47).

The synonym for "salvation" is "life" in the sense in which this term is used in the fragment of the Sermon on the Mount that we are discussing; the antonym is "destruction" (*apōleia*). This latter term is encountered in the entire corpus of the Gospels twice: for the first time in the Sermon on the Mount, and for the second time in Jesus' words concerning Judas Iscariot, who is called the "son of perdition [or 'destruction,' *apōleias*]" (Jn 17.12).

The trajectory of Judas' life is a clear example of the broad way that leads to spiritual death. He had the same starting point as the other disciples: he was chosen by Jesus as one of the Twelve, received the same instruction as the other apostles did, and was a witness to the same miracles. However, the choice he made turned out to be different from that of the other disciples. In spite of all their human weaknesses, they remained faithful to the Teacher, but Judas betrayed him for thirty pieces of silver. Though he repented of his deed, he did not ask the Teacher or the other apostles for forgiveness, nor did he return to the community, but he killed himself. He was mercilessly expunged from the memory of the Church, which is testified to by Peter's words: "For he was numbered with us, and had obtained part of this ministry. Now this man purchased a field with the reward of iniquity, and falling headlong, he burst asunder in the midst, and all his bowels gushed out. And it was known unto all the dwellers at Jerusalem" (Acts 1.17–19).

Judas' Kiss, Cimabue, late 13th century

A person makes his or her own choice between the way to life and the way to destruction. The way to destruction is, in the narrow sense, the orientation toward the values that Jesus subverts in the Sermon on the Mount and in his other teachings. Their collective name is mammon, and a clear example of following the way of destruction is found in the Pharisees with their hypocrisy and false righteousness. The way to destruction is a life choice made contrary to Jesus and his community. Of this choice Jesus would say to his disciples in his last instruction, "Go ye into all the world, and preach the gospel to every creature. He that believeth and is baptized shall be saved; but he that believeth not shall be damned" (Mk 16.15–16).

We should also pay attention to the antithesis of "many" and "few" in the passage from the Sermon on the Mount. Jesus often uses similar antitheses in other instances as well; for example: "Many be called, but few chosen" (Mt 20.16; 22.14; Lk 14.24); "The harvest truly is plenteous, but the laborers are few" (Mt 9.37; Lk 10.2). It seems that the criterion of *quantity* was never fundamental for Jesus. He did not try to make his moral teaching maximally convenient to follow for as many people as possible: if he had had that goal, he would have formulated different commandments that differed less radically from the basic postulates of the "natural law." Rather, it was the other way round: focusing on the *quality* of his community, Jesus emphasized that following his way would be the lot of a few chosen ones.

Can a community conceived as the "salt of the earth" and the "light of the world" (Mt 5.13, 17) be large in number, or is it doomed to forever remain a "little flock" (Lk 12.32)? Can the narrow way that Jesus commands us to walk become attractive for many, or will it remain the domain of a select few? The history of the Church gives an answer to this. In Jesus' time the community of his disciples was truly a "little flock." Over the course

The Holy Hierarch John Chrysostom, miniature, 13th century

of the next three centuries, this community grew steadily but continued to remain a minority that was surrounded by a pagan majority. The situation changed in the fourth century when, thanks to the Edict of Milan issued by the emperor Constantine, Christianity was legalized in the Roman Empire, and millions of people surged into the Church. It might appear that the narrow way suddenly became broad, and that the Church was able to adapt Jesus' essentially exclusive teachings to the new reality.

An attempt was indeed made to open up the text of the Gospels anew, to interpret it for a new generation of Christians, who lived no longer under persecution but in relative prosperity. The church fathers of this period, such as John Chrysostom, turned to the text of the Gospels with the goal of making it accessible under these new conditions. However, the moral radicalism of Jesus' preaching did not go away, and Chrysostom's commentaries on the Gospels were in no way received by his contemporaries as being intended to soften Jesus' teachings or to make them more palatable to the masses.

Like many preachers of his time, Chrysostom was dealing with a large audience. But it was precisely in this period that the question of the *quality* of the Christian community, first posed by Jesus himself, was particularly acute. Was it sufficient for salvation to simply be a member of the Church? Was it possible to be a member of the Church and at the same time not follow, or only partially follow, the way that Jesus commanded his followers to walk in everyday life? It turned out that this was possible. The Constantinian and post-Constantinian eras revealed the internal dichotomy between the majority and the minority that permeates all of Jesus' preaching. The majority readily adopted the external forms of piety that were offered by the Church, but only a minority turned out to be capable of fully meeting the moral demands that Jesus placed on the members of his community. This is why John Chrysostom, when he was applying the text of the Gospels to the situation in which his listeners found themselves, was so often compelled to

admonish them for deviating from the narrow way
that Jesus commanded his followers to walk.

It is never possible to precisely determine the
ratio of nominal to real Christians: we have no rel-
evant statistics from the fourth century or any other
period in the life of the Church. In this respect the
twenty-first century is no exception. The narrow way
continues to be narrow, and those who walk along it
continue to be few, even if many declare themselves
as members of the Church. Identifying themselves
with the Church culturally, some people participate
in its liturgical and sacramental life, but few are ready
to apply the evangelical moral ideal to their everyday
lives. The number of divorces and abortions among
Christians is only one illustration of how very many of those who associate
themselves with the Church refuse to follow what the Church teaches.

*The Holy Hierarch John
Chrysostom, mosaic,
9th century*

In the fourth century the refusal of the majority to follow the narrow
way that Jesus commanded led to the appearance within the Church of a
community of people who resolved to put into practice the ideal outlined
by Jesus as literally as possible. The monastics of this period applied the
phrase "the narrow way" to their way of life.[3] For them, to follow the narrow way meant to imitate Jesus, rejecting many good things that were
accessible to regular people, including material wealth and marriage.

In this same period the idea began to take shape that saints are a special
class of persons within the Church, who had turned out to be capable of
putting the evangelical ideal into practice in all its fullness. In the first generation of Christians the term "saints" was applied to all members of the
Christian community (Acts 9.41; 26.10; Rom 16.15; 1 Cor 6.1–2; 14.33; 16.1;
2 Cor 9.1, 12; 13.12; Eph 3.8; Phil 4.22). In the post-Constantinian period,
however, this term took on a meaning that persists to this day: Christians began to call "saints" those who distinguished themselves from other

---

[3]See *The Sayings of the Desert Fathers*, Ammonas 11 (*Give Me a Word: The Alphabetical
Sayings of the Desert Fathers*, tr. John Wortley, Popular Patristics Series 52 [Yonkers, NY: St
Vladimir's Seminary Press, 2014], 63); Poemen 111 (PPS 52:246).

Christians by the level of the spiritual perfection they had achieved. At the same time, the term "saints" was not reserved exclusively for monks: non-monastic bishops could be considered saints, as could married priests and laypeople, including those kings and princes who were distinguished by especial piety.

The concept of the "narrow way" does not just apply to monks or saints. It continues to retain its significance for the entire community of Christians, just as the Sermon on the Mount and Jesus' other instructions retain their significance for the entire Church and not just for some part of it. Like road signs, these instructions serve as reference points for every Christian. However, not all follow these reference points and get onto the narrow way; and of those who have resolved to go along the narrow way, not all reach the goal—the gate that opens into the kingdom of heaven. Whether a person gets onto the narrow way depends on the choice he or she makes. How much of the way he or she goes and how far away the goal is depends not only on that person's efforts, but also on God's assistance and the help of other members of the community.

2. False Prophets

The next part of the Sermon on the Mount is connected to the previous part by the theme of the broad way that leads to destruction. While Jesus is the teacher on the narrow way, the broad way has its own teachers, against whom Jesus warns his disciples:

> Beware of false prophets, which come to you in sheep's clothing, but inwardly they are ravening wolves. Ye shall know them by their fruits. Do men gather grapes from thorns, or figs from thistles? Even so every good tree bringeth forth good fruit; but a corrupt tree bringeth forth evil fruit. A good tree cannot bring forth evil fruit, neither can a corrupt tree bring forth good fruit. Every tree that bringeth not forth good fruit is hewn down, and cast into the fire. Wherefore by their fruits ye shall know them.

Not every one that saith unto me, "Lord, Lord," shall enter into the kingdom of heaven, but he that doeth the will of my Father which is in heaven. Many will say to me in that day, "Lord, Lord, have we not prophesied in thy name? And in thy name have cast out devils? And in thy name done many wonderful works?" And then will I profess unto them, "I never knew you. Depart from me, ye that work iniquity." (Mt 7.15–23)

The expression "wolf in sheep's clothing" has become an idiom. The word "wolf" is used in the Old Testament with the epithet "ravenous" (Gen 49.27): the wolf is a symbol of cruelty and lack of restraint (Hab 1.6–8), it attacks people (Jer 5.6), devours its prey (Ezek 22.27), and does not leave a single bone by the morning (Zeph 3.3). Sheep, on the contrary, are a symbol of meekness (Is 53.7). According to the prophet Isaiah, the coming of the Messiah would result in the reconciliation of the irreconcilable: "The wolf also shall dwell with the lamb" (Is 11.6); "The wolf and the lamb shall feed together" (Is 65.25). In the Sermon on the Mount the images of the wolf and the sheep are also used as contrasting images, but here it is not the sheep and the wolf themselves that are being contrasted with each other, but the sheep's appearance with the wolf's essence. In this respect the false prophets are like the Pharisees, of whom Jesus says that they "make clean the outside of the cup and of the platter, but within they are full of extortion and excess" (Mt 23.25).

The image of the tree that is hewn down and cast into the fire is adopted word for word from the preaching of John the Baptist, who said to those who came to him: "And now also the axe is laid unto the root of the trees. Therefore every tree which bringeth not forth good fruit is hewn down, and cast into the fire" (Mt 3.10; Lk 3.9). Jesus began his preaching with the verbatim repetition of the words that were the leitmotif of the Forerunner's preaching: "Repent ye, for the kingdom of heaven is at hand" (Mt 3.2; 4.17). The Sermon on the Mount, in the form in which it is recorded in Matthew, is Jesus' first public address. Notwithstanding its complete originality as a whole, in its concluding section we again hear the voice of the Forerunner. It is true that the Forerunner's words about the trees that are hewn

John the Baptist, icon
(detail), 15th century

down and cast into the fire had a different subtext: they referred to the people who did not bring forth fruits of repentance. Jesus, on the other hand, uses a similar image to refer to false prophets.

We find a parallel to this text in the Gospel of Luke, where it appears in a more concise and generalized form:

> For a good tree bringeth not forth corrupt fruit; neither doth a corrupt tree bring forth good fruit. For every tree is known by his own fruit. For men do not gather figs from thorns, nor do they gather grapes from a bramble bush. . . .

And why call ye me, "Lord, Lord," and do not the things which I say? (Lk 6.43–44, 46)

Here there is no reference at all to false prophets or to the Last Judgment. On the basis of this, supporters of the hypothesis that Matthew and Luke worked with a single common original source (the Q hypothesis) assert that Luke's text, being shorter, is the more authentic one, while Matthew has added to and expanded this text for the benefit of his own community.[4] As in other instances, we do not see any basis for such a treatment of the work of Matthew, and believe that Jesus could easily have said similar things—sometimes longer, sometimes shorter, and with different emphases—to different audiences.

The image of the good tree and the corrupt tree is encountered twice in the Gospel of Matthew in Jesus' speech. Responding to the Jews' accusation that he had cast out demons "by Beelzebub the prince of the demons," Jesus says, "Either make the tree good, and his fruit good, or else make the tree corrupt, and his fruit corrupt. For the tree is known by his fruit. O generation of vipers, how can ye, being evil, speak good things? For out of

---

[4]For example, Rudolf Schnackenburg, *The Gospel of Matthew*, trans. Robert R. Barr (Grand Rapids, MI: Eerdmans, 2002), 78: "Matthew has revised the 'Lord, Lord' logion (Luke 6:46) to suit himself (Matt. 7:21). . . . Obviously he is expanding its scope to include partisans of the false prophets or other persons in the community."

the abundance of the heart the mouth speaketh" (Mt 12.24, 33–34). Here the image of the tree is used in a completely different context than in the Sermon on the Mount: the good tree that bears good fruit is understood here to refer to Jesus' activity, which is contrasted with the evil fruit of the activity of the Pharisees. Recall that the expression "generation of vipers" was first used in relation to the Pharisees by John the Forerunner: again we see how firmly his phraseology has entered Jesus' speech.

The repetition of the formula "by their fruits ye shall know them" is meant to emphasize that it is precisely the fruit, that is, the results of the activity of a false prophet, that should be the main sign by which he can be distinguished from a true prophet (the verb *epignōsesthe*, translated as "ye shall know," can also be translated as "ye shall discern").

Note that in Matthew, in contrast with Luke, different terms are used to designate the "corrupt" tree and its fruit: *sapros* ("rotten," "spoiled," "unsuitable") is used for the tree, and *ponēros* ("evil," "wicked") is used for the fruit. The first term is used to describe objects and produce, while the second is used to describe people. In both instances in Luke we find the term *sapros*. To designate the "good" tree and its fruit, Matthew also uses two different terms: *kalos* ("winsomely good") and *agathos* ("intrinsically good") respectively. Luke uses the term *kalos* in both instances. Thus in Luke the good tree does not produce corrupt fruit, and the corrupt tree does not produce good fruit. In Matthew the (intrinsically) good tree produces (winsomely) good fruit, while the corrupt tree produces evil fruit. By using Greek terms of a clearly expressed ethical nature to translate Jesus' words, Matthew emphasizes the conventionality of the comparison. At the same time, by doing so, he strengthens the contrast between the images: recall that the term "good" (*agathos*) in Jesus' speech is applied to God (Mt 19.17: "There is none good [*agathos*] but one, that is, God"), while the term "evil" is applied to the devil (we have already seen how "evil" in Mt 13.19 is identical to "Satan" in Mk 4.15 and "the devil" in Lk 8.12).

We do not find any Old Testament parallels to the segment of the Sermon on the Mount that we are discussing. However, certain images could have been inspired by the Old Testament, such as the comparison of the

The Last Judgment,
K. V. Lebedev, Church
Archaeology Department
of the Moscow Theological
Academy

righteous person to a tree that bears fruit in Psalm 1, where this comparison abuts the theme of the two ways:

> Blessed is the man that hath not walked in the counsel of the ungodly, nor stood in the way of sinners, nor sat in the seat of the pestilent. But his will is rather in the law of the Lord, and in his law will he meditate day and night. And he shall be like the tree which is planted by the streams of the waters, which shall bring forth its fruit in its season; and its leaf shall not fall, and all things whatsoever he may do shall prosper. Not so are the ungodly, not so; but rather they are like the chaff which the wind doth hurl away from the face of the earth. For this reason shall the ungodly not stand up in judgment, nor sinners in the council of the righteous. For the Lord knoweth the way of the righteous, and the way of the ungodly shall perish. (Ps 1.1–6)

While searching for possible sources for the concluding sections of the Sermon on the Mount, we came upon the following passage from the book of the prophet Jeremiah:

> Stand in the gate of the LORD's house, and proclaim there this word, and say, "Hear the word of the LORD, all ye of Judah, that enter in at these gates to worship the LORD." Thus saith the LORD of hosts, the God of Israel, "Amend your ways and your doings, and I will cause you to dwell in this place. Trust ye not in lying words, saying, 'The temple of the LORD, the temple of the LORD, the temple of the LORD, are these.' For if ye throughly amend your ways and your doings; if ye throughly execute judgment between a man and his neighbor; if ye oppress not the stranger, the fatherless, and the widow, and shed not innocent blood in this place, neither walk after other gods to your hurt,

then will I cause you to dwell in this place, in the land that I gave to your fathers, forever and ever." (Jer 7.2–7)

What this passage and the concluding sections of the Sermon on the Mount have in common is, first of all, the image of the gate and the image of the ways. Second, the prophet speaks of false hope expressed through the thrice-repeated words "The temple of the Lord," which reminds us of the twofold "Lord, Lord," which expresses the idea of false hope for salvation in the Sermon on the Mount. Third, the thrust of the prophet's speech resonates with the overall tone of the Sermon on the Mount, which is likewise a call to correction and repentance, and which also contains specific instructions on how this correction should be expressed.

Who are the false prophets of whom Jesus speaks? The supporters of the hypothesis that the evangelist known as Matthew, who worked at the end of the first century or even at the beginning of the second century, edited Jesus' speech and adapted it to the needs of his own community, propose a wide range of options—from Jews who had infiltrated the Christian community from the outside to Gnostic heretics. However, in our analysis, we proceed from the assumption that the evangelist has given us Jesus' words in the form in which they were uttered. Under this approach, the term "false prophets" has a generalized meaning: it refers to all who distort the teachings of Jesus. The activity of these false prophets is characterized by their prophesying, driving out demons, and doing miracles in the name of Jesus. However, Jesus categorically dissociates himself from them as from those who "work inquity."

Jesus' words about those who "work iniquity," who drive out demons and do miracles in his name, at first glance contradict what we read in the following episode from the Gospel of Mark. In this episode John, the son of Zebedee, says to Jesus, "Master, we saw one casting out devils in thy name, and he followeth not us: and we forbade him, because he followeth not us." Jesus replies, "Forbid him not, for there is no man which shall do a miracle in my name, that can lightly speak evil of me. For he that is not against us is on our side" (Mk 9.38–40). How can we reconcile these two seemingly mutually exclusive statements?

The Last
Judgment,
V. M. Vasnetsov,
1904

It seems to us that the key to this puzzle lies in the meaning of the terms "false prophets" and "many" as they are used in the Sermon on the Mount and also in the overall context of both statements. In the account from the Gospel of Mark, what is being described is a single incident, from which a general conclusion is made: a certain person is not a member of the community of Jesus' disciples and nevertheless works miracles in his name. In the Sermon on the Mount Jesus speaks of "many" who "in that day," that is, at the Last Judgment, would refer to miracles done in his name. We do not know anything about the posthumous fate of the miracle worker from the Gospel of Mark. Jesus merely says to his disciples not to forbid him, but the final result of this miracle worker's activity is unknown to us—whether he would join the community of Jesus' disciples or remain outside it; whether Jesus would recognize him as his disciple at the Last Judgment or reject him as a false prophet.

It is only in the eschatological long term, at the Last Judgment, that the final division between the sheep and the goats will take place (Mt 25.32–33),

and the identity of the true prophets and false prophets will be revealed.
Jesus touches on this more than once in his teachings. Luke cites Jesus'
conversation with the Jews in the synagogue. The text of the conversation
is quite close to the excerpt from the Sermon on the Mount that we are
discussing, but the emphases are placed differently:

> When once the master of the house is risen up, and hath shut the door,
> and ye begin to stand outside, and to knock at the door, saying, "Lord,
> Lord, open unto us"; and he shall answer and say unto you, "I know
> you not whence ye are." Then shall ye begin to say, "We have eaten and
> drunk in thy presence, and thou hast taught in our streets." But he shall
> say, "I tell you, I know you not whence ye are; depart from me, all ye
> workers of unrighteousness." (Lk 13.25–27)

Here the workers of unrighteousness do not appeal to prophecy, or
to the driving out of demons, or to the "wonderful works" that they have
done. They merely say that they had been contemporaries of Jesus and
heard his word. He will reject them at the Last Judgment because they were
not doers of the word but hearers only (Jas 1.22). The doors of the kingdom
of God are shut to "evil workers" (Phil 3.2).

Who are the ones who "work iniquity" in Matthew, or the "workers of
unrighteousness" in Luke? The term "unrighteousness" (*adikia*) is close in
meaning to the term "iniquity" (or "lawlessness"—*anomia*), which comes
from the word for "law" (*nomos*) and which refers foremost to the non-
observance of the law of Moses. In the Psalms the transgressors (those who
do not observe the law) are contrasted with the righteous: the former will be
"utterly destroyed," while the latter will be saved (Ps 36.37–39). In the Sermon
on the Mount, the term "iniquity" refers to the conscious departure from
the law of God as it is presented in Jesus' preaching. It is possible to trace
the semantic link between this term and Jesus' words about how he has "not
come to destroy, but to fulfill" the law of Moses. At the same time, the entire
Old Testament law, according to Jesus, is contained in the commandment to
love God and one's neighbor (Mt 22.37–40). Speaking of the last days, Jesus
connects the multiplication of iniquity with the cooling of love (Mt 24.12).[5]

[5]Luz, *Matthew 1–7*, 380.

We see that while the beginning of the Sermon on the Mount was dedicated to the interpretation of various aspects of the law and the presentation of the new law by which Jesus' disciples should live, in the concluding part of the Sermon, he speaks of what awaits those who do not want to follow his teaching.

The words "depart from me, ye that work iniquity" is a quote from the Psalter (Ps 6.9: "Depart from me, all ye that work vanity"). The expression "ye that work iniquity" is not completely synonymous with the term "false prophets," although it is also used in the Sermon on the Mount with reference to the latter. Those who work iniquity are all who draw near to God with their lips and honor him with their tongues, but whose hearts are far from him (Mt 15.8; Is 29.13). They say to Jesus, "Lord, Lord," but do not fulfill the will of his Father. The warnings from the concluding sections of the Sermon on the Mount apply to all such people.

As for the term "false prophets," on Jesus' lips and in the usage of the early Church, it has a very specific meaning. In the Gospels this term is encountered four times in total, three times in Matthew. In Jesus' discourse about the last days, which precedes the passion narrative in Matthew, he speaks of "many false prophets" who would impersonate him:

> Take heed that no man deceive you. For *many* shall come in my name, saying, "I am Christ"; and shall deceive *many*. . . . And *many false prophets* shall rise, and shall deceive *many*. . . . Then if any man shall say unto you, "Lo, here is Christ," or "there"; believe it not. For there shall arise false Christs, and false prophets, and shall shew great signs and wonders; insomuch that, if it were possible, they shall deceive the very elect. (Mt 24.4–5, 11, 23–24; emphasis added)

In this discourse Jesus is speaking about the time when he would no longer be on earth. The persistent repetition of the word "many" cannot but remind us of the broad way by which many would walk, and of other instances where this term refers to those who would be outside the kingdom of heaven. It is clear that in the Sermon on the Mount the lesson about the "many" who worked miracles in Jesus' name, but who would be rejected at the Last Judgment, applies through all time up until his second coming. The term "false prophets" here is found alongside the term "false Christs," which is used in this discourse (Mt 24.24; Mk 13.22) and not encountered anywhere else on the pages of the New Testament. However, in the Epistles of John we encounter multiple uses of the term "antichrist," which is similar in meaning, in the plural as well as in the singular:

> Little children, it is the last time. And as ye have heard that antichrist shall come, even now are there many antichrists, by which we know that it is the last time. They went out from us, but they were not of us; for if they had been of us, they would no doubt have continued with us; but they went out, that they might be made manifest that they were not all of us. . . . Who is a liar but he that denieth that Jesus is the Christ? He is antichrist, that denieth the Father and the Son. (1 Jn 2.18–19, 22)

The apostle insists on the necessity of "testing the spirits," warning against false prophets as Jesus did:

> Beloved, believe not every spirit, but test the spirits whether they are of God, because many false prophets are gone out into the world. Hereby know ye the Spirit of God: every spirit that confesseth that Jesus Christ is come in the flesh is of God, and every spirit that confesseth not that Jesus Christ is come in the flesh is not of God. And this is that spirit of antichrist, whereof ye have heard that it should come, and even now already is it in the world. (1 Jn 4.1–3)

The main criterion by which a genuine prophet can be distinguished from a false prophet is, according to John, the confession or non-confession of Jesus Christ who has come in the flesh. This agrees with what John, the son of Zebedee, heard from Jesus in reply to his question about the person who was doing miracles in Jesus' name but not walking together with his disciples: "There is no man which shall do a miracle in my name, that can lightly speak evil of me." However, in the Sermon on the Mount, Jesus says that merely confessing his lordship would not be sufficient for salvation: it is necessary to put his teachings into practice and fulfill the will of his Father. It turns out that it is possible to confess Jesus as Lord and even do miracles, but at the same time go against the will of God and,

The Last
Judgment,
mosaic in the
Baptistery of
St John,
Florence, Italy,
1300

as a result, end up at the Last Judgment not on the right hand, but on the left hand of the Judge.

The problem of false prophets was very significant for the early Church.[6] All of early Christian literature is filled with warnings against false prophets and false miracles. The apostle Paul speaks of the "iniquity" that would come in the last days:

> For the mystery of iniquity doth already work: only he who now restraineth will restrain it, until he be taken out of the way. And then shall that wicked one be revealed, whom the Lord shall consume with the spirit of his mouth, and shall destroy with the brightness of his coming, even him, whose coming is after the working of Satan with all power and signs and lying wonders. (2 Thess 2.7–9)

Therefore, there are not only genuine miracles and signs, but false ones also. In and of itself, a person's ability to do great miracles does not make him an heir of the kingdom of heaven, as Isaac the Syrian emphasizes:

[6]Eduard Schweizer, "Matthew's Church," in *The Interpretation of Matthew*, ed. Graham Stanton, Issues in Religion and Theology 3 (Philadelphia, PA: Fortress; London: SPCK, 1983), 130.

Many have accomplished mighty acts, raised the dead, toiled for the conversion of the erring, and have wrought great wonders; and by their hands they have led many to the knowledge of God. Yet after these things, these same men who quickened others, fell into vile and abominable passions and slew themselves, becoming a stumbling-block for many. . . . For they were still sickly in soul, but instead of caring for their souls' health, they committed themselves to the sea of this world in order to heal the souls of others, being yet in ill health; and, in the manner I have stated, they lost their souls and fell away from their hope in God.[7]

Here, as in the Sermon on the Mount, the emphasis is on a person's inner self-perfection. The external effects, including miracles and signs, cannot take the place of the inner work that Jesus requires of a person. It is this work that constitutes the essence of the Christian life; it is this work that is the "narrow path" that is capable of leading a person to the goal—the kingdom of heaven.

Jesus' warning against false prophets has retained its relevance in all times. Even in our age of rationalism and nihilism, people have not only not lost the ability to believe in miracles—on the contrary, this ability has only become more acute in comparison with ancient times. In the modern world unbelief coexists with all possible kinds of superstitions. A significant niche in mass media is occupied by advertisements for various kinds of healers, sorcerers, and psychics who promise to heal diseases, remove "jinxes" or the "evil eye," and solve family problems (for example, return a wayward husband to his wife). Some of these healers really possess various paranormal abilities and work "false wonders and signs." Moreover, they often use religious symbols: icons, candles, and spells that mention the name of God.

The Church, which possesses the ability to "test the spirits," has always warned about the danger of these practices, recalling that sometimes "Satan himself is transformed into an angel of light. Therefore it is no great thing if his ministers also be transformed as the ministers of

---

[7]Isaac the Syrian, *Ascetical Homilies* 4 (trans. Holy Transfiguration Monastery, 145).

righteousness" (2 Cor 11.14–15). The New Testament paints a picture of the struggle between good and evil, between God and the devil. At the same time, on the pages of the New Testament, we encounter many warnings against false prophets and other wolves in sheep's clothing—people who do evil under the guise of good and work miracles in the name of God while being servants of Satan. The battle between good and evil will end with the victory of good when the devil is "cast into the lake of fire and brimstone, where the beast and the false prophet are, and shall be tormented day and night forever and ever" (Rev 20.10).

3. The House on the Rock and the House on the Sand

The Sermon on the Mount concludes with a brief parable, the content of which stems from the preceding exhortations about the necessity of not only confessing Jesus as Lord in words, but also fulfilling his commands in deed. At the same time, this parable summarizes the entire Sermon on the Mount:

> Therefore whosoever heareth these sayings of mine, and doeth them, I will liken him unto a wise man, which built his house upon a rock, and the rain descended, and the floods came, and the winds blew, and beat upon that house; and it fell not: for it was founded upon a rock. And every one that heareth these sayings of mine, and doeth them not, shall be likened unto a foolish man, which built his house upon the sand, and the rain descended, and the floods came, and the winds blew, and beat upon that house; and it fell, and great was the fall of it. (Mt 7.24–27)

Parable was one of the main literary genres that Jesus used to elucidate various aspects of his teachings. Every parable is built on the principle of comparison or likening: a particular reality is described with the help of imagery taken from another sphere, which helps listeners better understand what their teacher is saying to them. Parables make use of memorable images that are taken, as a rule, from the surrounding reality.[8]

In this case the image used is that of a house, which plays an important role in the Old Testament. In biblical usage a house is not simply a commonplace structure made of stone or wood: a house always belongs to a specific person and is the dwelling of this person and his family. Often the term "household" (Hebrew *bayit*) is used broadly to mean a family (Gen 45.11) or a kingdom (2 Sam 7.6). The expressions "the house of Israel" (Ex 16.31) and "the house of Judah" (2 Sam 2.7) are applied to the entire people of Israel or to all the inhabitants of Judah respectively. The posterity of a particular person was also called his "house" (for example, the twelve houses, or tribes, of Israel). Joseph, the husband of Mary, the mother of Jesus, was "of the house of David" (Lk 1.27).

A similar parable concludes the Sermon on the Plain in the Gospel of Luke (Lk 6.47–49). Here the image is more detailed: one builder digs and goes deep and lays a foundation (*themelion*) on the rock, while the other builds on the earth without a foundation.[9] Matthew gives a more general image: he says nothing about a foundation, and the difference between the two builders consists not so much in the use of different construction techniques as in the choice of construction site—one builds on solid ground, while the other builds on unstable ground. Nevertheless, this does not change the meaning of the parable. At the same time, the parallelism that is expressed in the repetition of everything that pertains to the positive character in reference to the negative character, but reversed, is preserved in Luke's version as well. Such parallelism is characteristic of Semitic speech.

---

[8]More details on the peculiarities of the parable genre will be given in the fourth volume of the series *Jesus Christ: His Life and Teaching*.

[9]See Arland J. Hultgren, *The Parables of Jesus: A Commentary*, The Bible in Its World (Grand Rapids, MI: Eerdmans, 2000), 135–136. For a comparison between the two versions of the parable, see Klyne Snodgrass, *Stories with Intent: A Comprehensive Guide to the Parables of Jesus* (Grand Rapids, MI: Eerdmans, 2008), 330–331; Ivor H. Jones, *The Matthean Parables: A Literary and Historical Commentary*, Supplements to Novum Testamentum 80 (New York, NY: Brill, 1995), 173–189.

It is no coincidence that the parable of the house on the rock and the house on the sand stands at the very end of the Sermon on the Mount: "key aspects of the Sermon on the Mount find in it a point of convergence."[10] A number of Old Testament texts of a programmatic nature conclude with placing two alternatives before the listener: to obey the admonitions contained in these texts and thereby receive a blessing, or to not obey them and thereby receive a curse. The presentation of God's commandments in the book of Leviticus concludes with these words:

> If ye walk in my statutes, and keep my commandments, and do them; then I will give you rain in due season, and the land shall yield her increase, and the trees of the field shall yield their fruit.... And I will set my tabernacle among you, and my soul shall not abhor you. And I will walk among you, and will be your God, and ye shall be my people. ... But if ye will not hearken unto me, and will not do all these commandments, and if ye shall despise my statutes, or if your soul abhor my judgments, so that ye will not do all my commandments, but that ye break my covenant, I also will do this unto you: I will even appoint over you terror, consumption, and the burning fever, that shall consume the eyes, and cause sorrow of heart; and ye shall sow your seed in vain, for your enemies shall eat it. (Lev 26.3–4, 11–12, 14–16)

The exposition of God's commandments in the book of Deuteronomy concludes in a similar way: here a series of blessings for obeying God and fulfilling his commandments precedes a series of curses for disobeying him and failing to observe his commandments (Deut 28.1–68).

In the two concluding sections of the Sermon on the Mount, the verb *poieō* in the sense of "produce" (good fruit) or "carry out" (the will of the heavenly Father, Jesus' words) is used nine times. The literal meaning of this verb is "do," "create." The first book of the Bible begins with this verb: "In the beginning God *created* the heaven and the earth" (Gen 1.1). With this same verb Jesus defines his mission on earth: "For I came down from heaven, not to *do* mine own will, but the will of him that sent me" (Jn 6.38). The verb *ergazomai* ("do," "create," "work") is close to it in meaning. Jesus

---

[10]Jones, *Matthean Parables*, 185.

uses it here: "My Father worketh until now, and I work" (Jn 5.17). Both verbs are used in the question posed to Jesus: "What shall we do, that we might work the works of God?" The words of the Teacher are the answer: "This is the work of God, that ye believe on him whom he hath sent" (Jn 6.28–29).

The creative process of God, which began with the creation of the world, has not ceased on earth, and the earthly ministry of the Son of God is its direct continuation. The Son of God came in order to carry out the will of the Father—to complete the work that the Father had entrusted to him (Jn 17.4). But the disciples of Jesus have their own work as well: their work is to believe in Jesus. Belief in him involves not only the conviction that Jesus is the Christ, the Son of God, but also putting into action that which he taught his followers. To carry out Jesus' words means to carry out the will of God the Father. The one who not only hears but also does is like the man who built his house on a solid foundation.

This foundation, this rock which "the builders rejected" but "is become the head of the corner" (Mt 21.42; Mk 12.10; Lk 20.17; Ps 117.22), is Jesus himself. And the house, according to the interpretation of Christian writers, is the Church that he founded. The First Epistle of Peter speaks of this: "To whom coming, as unto a living stone, rejected indeed of men, but chosen by God, and precious, ye also, as living stones, are built up a spiritual house, a holy priesthood" (1 Pet 2.4–5). In the words of Origen, the wise man who built his house on the rock is understood to be "the Lord himself, who built the Church on the rock, that is, on his firmness and strength. . . . All the persecutions were directed at that house and achieved nothing, for it was built on the rock."[11]

The persecutions of the first centuries of the Christian era were a test of endurance for the Church and its members. The Church itself as a "spiritual house," as the "Body of Christ," as the totality of all believers in their union with God, endured these tribulations, and the gates of hell did not prevail against it (Mt 16.18). However, there were individual members of the Church who did not withstand the persecutions. Hearing Jesus' words but not doing them, calling themselves Christians but not living in a Christian

---

[11]Origen, *Fragments on Matthew* 153 (GCS 41/1:76). Translation by present translator.

manner, these people built their houses on sand. Before the rain came and the wind blew and the river flooded, their houses appeared to stand quite fast. But when persecutions began, only those who had built their houses on the firm foundation of fulfilling Jesus' commandments endured. While in times of prosperity both nominal and genuine Christians coexist in the Church, in times of persecution the space for nominal Christians becomes extremely narrow, and many of them fall away from the Church.

History repeats itself, and at each new stage of its development the Church realizes yet again the relevance of Jesus' warnings. When persecutions descended upon the Church in Russia after the Bolsheviks came to power in 1917, very many nominal Christians left the Church, and some of those who had earlier called themselves members of the Church embarked on the path of militant atheism. These persecutions were the day of reckoning that separated the sheep from the goats—the genuine Christians, who were ready to die for their faith, from those who did not wish to walk the narrow way fraught with sufferings and the confession of faith, but went instead by the broad way that leads to perdition. As for those who walked the narrow way to the end, their martyrdom was the gate that opened to them the entrance into the kingdom of heaven.

The image of the house built on the rock is fully applicable to the work that Jesus Christ undertook on earth. Here he built his house—the Church, which is able to accommodate all his followers. He built it on the firm foundation of the Old Testament, including the law of Moses and the testimony of the prophets. The Sermon on the Mount was one of the stages of this creative process, which would continue in Jesus' subsequent ministry, in his death and resurrection, and then in the ministry of the apostles as well.

4. "He Taught Them as One Having Authority"

The audience's reaction to the Sermon on the Mount is described in Matthew in a single sentence:

> And it came to pass, when Jesus had ended these sayings, the people were astonished at his doctrine: for he taught them as one having authority, and not as the scribes. (Mt 7.28–29)

Mark described the audience's reaction to Jesus' preaching in the synagogue in Capernaum in a similar way: "And they were astonished at his doctrine: for he taught them as one that had authority, and not as the scribes" (Mk 1.22). In the parallel passage in Luke we read: "And they were astonished at his doctrine: for his word was with authority" (Lk 4.32). In all three instances, the word "authority" (Greek *exousia*), is used: with this word the evangelists emphasize the difference between Jesus' teaching and the teachings of the scribes.

The latter relied on the authority of the law; they interpreted it and appealed to it, considering themselves "Moses' disciples" (Jn 9.28). Jesus did not appeal to the law or to Moses or to any other authority besides his own, equating it with the authority of God. Therefore, his preaching seemed unprecedented. The servants of the Pharisees and chief priests said of him with amazement, "Never man spake like this man" (Jn 7.46).

The meaning and content of the Sermon on the Mount, as with Jesus' spiritual and moral teaching as a whole, can be understood only under one condition: if his words are received as he himself intended them to be received—as the words of God. Any other reading would reduce his preaching to ordinary moralizing, with which one may agree in some aspects and not in others, which can be criticized, disputed, rejected.

Some humanist writers who do not recognize Jesus as God nevertheless sincerely admire his teaching. Leo Tolstoy, who denied the divinity of Jesus, opposed the Church, and blasphemed the sacraments of the

Church, nevertheless believed that "the words of chapters 5, 6, and 7 of the Gospel of Matthew are so holy, so divine from beginning to end" that nothing could be added to them.[12] After a few unsuccessful attempts at a commentary on the Sermon on the Mount, he limited himself to retelling it, giving this paraphrase the title *The Sermon to the People by our Lord Jesus Christ.*[13] Tolstoy belonged to the number of humanists who did not see in Jesus' teaching anything besides an exposition of a universal human morality. Therefore, he placed Jesus on a par with other teachers of morality such as Buddha, Muhammad, and Socrates.

Yet Jesus himself never placed himself on a par with other teachers. His preaching differed starkly from the exhortations of the Old Testament prophets, including Moses, not only in content but also in tone. While in the books of the prophets we often encounter God speaking directly, the prophet himself always appears as an intermediary: God speaks to people *through* the prophet, *by the lips* of the prophet, but not a single prophet would have ever thought of equating himself with God. Jesus, on the contrary, considered it possible to speak in the capacity of a final, absolute authority for his listeners, which was reflected in these striking expressions: "Ye have heard that it was said . . . but I say unto you. . . ." It was this tone that both astounded and frightened his listeners (the verb *exeplēssonto* can be translated as both "astonished" and "frightened"). They had never encountered anything like this, neither in real life, where they had the opportunity to listen to the teachings of the Pharisees and scribes, nor in the written texts of the Old Testament, which they heard in the synagogues.

In his preaching on the kingdom of heaven, John the Baptist anticipated the preaching of Jesus. But the kingdom of heaven itself began to be revealed to mankind at the moment when the Son of God went out to preach, "opened his mouth," and began to teach. Through the words of the Sermon on the Mount, this enigmatic and mysterious, simultaneously alluring and frightening kingdom began to take on a concrete outline. And

---

[12]Tolstoy, *Polnoe sobranie sochineniy* [Complete works], 85:52. Translation by present translator.

[13]Tolstoy, *Polnoe sobranie sochineniy* [Complete works], 25:530–531.

it turned out that the kingdom of heaven was not some faraway, other-worldly, or eschatological reality. Like sunlight penetrating thick clouds, it penetrates the earthly existence of a person, manifesting itself in the events of everyday life. And it manifests itself first and foremost in how a person conducts himself in relation to God and his neighbor.

Herein lies the entire difference between the law of Moses and the preaching of Jesus, between the books of the prophets and the words of Jesus captured in the Gospels, between the Old and New Testaments. The Old Testament was also a revelation of God, but the messengers of this revelation were ordinary people, and the revelation itself was adjusted for the needs and realities of a specific people at a specific stage of their histori-cal existence. The words of Jesus Christ, which have come down to us in the Gospels, were the direct speech of God—transmitted not through an ordinary person, but through the Son of God; addressed not to one nation, but to all people; retaining its relevance not for some specific period of time only, but for all time.

Moreover, it is in the Church that these words can be realized to their full extent. When he delivered the Sermon on the Mount, Jesus was addressing his disciples first of all, but all the people were able to hear him (Mt 5.1; 7.28). This serves to emphasize, so to speak, the fact that Jesus' commandments are of a universal nature; however, it is precisely the community of his disciples and followers that is the direct addressee of his preaching. It is this community that must become the arena for the testing of human potentialities, since some of Jesus' commandments, particularly the commandment to love one's enemies, stand at the limits of these potentialities. The fulfillment of Jesus' commandments demands effort, sacrifice, and self-denial beyond the strength of an ordinary person: they are impossible to fulfill without the help of God's grace and without the assistance of the church community.

Jesus was the first to fulfill his own commandments, leaving his own person as an example for imitation for all time. But he did not limit him-self to this. He founded the Church and, as "the head of the body, the Church" (Col 1.18), remained in it as a guarantee of the practicability of his commandments. Through the experience of communing with him, which is possible only in the Church, including through participation in the sacraments, a person receives supernatural spiritual strength, which is necessary for putting into action that which Jesus commanded. And it is only within the church experience, in which human activity is linked with God's activity in an indissoluble and incomprehensible manner, that a person is able not only to realize fully the meaning of the Sermon on the Mount, but also to put it into practice.

In the Epistle to the Hebrews a parallel is drawn between Jesus and Moses. Recalling the circumstances in which the law was given from Sinai, the author of the Epistle contrasts Moses with Jesus as the founder of the Church and the mediator of the new covenant:

> For ye are not come unto the mount that might be touched, and that burned with fire, nor unto blackness, and darkness, and tempest, and the sound of a trumpet, and the voice of words, which voice they that heard entreated that the word should not be spoken to them any more[14] (for they could not endure that which was commanded, "And if so much as a beast touch the mountain, it shall be stoned, or thrust through with a spear";[15] and so terrible was the sight, that Moses said, "I exceedingly fear and quake");[16] but ye are come unto mount Sion, and unto the city of the living God, the heavenly Jerusalem, and to an innumerable company of angels, to the general assembly and Church of the firstborn, which are written in heaven, and to God the Judge of all, and to the spirits of just men made perfect, and to Jesus the mediator of the new covenant. (Heb 12.18–24)

Throughout the entire corpus of the New Testament—from the Sermon on the Mount to the Epistle to the Hebrews—one idea can be traced: the new Moses is Jesus, who came to renew the covenant established by God with the people of Israel. He is the one of whom God spoke to Moses, whom the prophets foretold, to whom John the Baptist referred. On him are focused all the expectations and hopes permeating all of Old

[14]Ex 20.18–19.
[15]Ex 19.13.
[16]Ps 54.6.

Testament history; in him is realized the purpose and meaning of all this history that was worked by the hands of God and man. His second coming is the conclusion of the earthly history of all mankind and the beginning of "a new heaven and a new earth" (Rev 21.1)

* * *

With this chapter we have concluded our examination of the Sermon on the Mount. But all the same the following questions remain: is the ethics presented in it an ideal or a standard? What can explain the uncompromising nature of the gospel? Can the ethics of the Sermon on the Mount be built into the law and become a guide for action?

The Russian philosopher Nicolas Berdyaev gives his own version of an answer to these questions in the book *The Destiny of Man*. One chapter of this book is dedicated to the ethics of the Gospel. In the words of the philosopher, "The Gospel makes a complete change in our moral valuations. ... The morality of the Kingdom of God proves to be unlike the morality of the fallen world. ... The ethics of redemption is in every way opposed to the ideas of this world." Berdyaev believes the gospel to be "absolute and uncompromising, but there is nothing harsh about it. Uncompromising moralism is false because it is uncompromising towards other people and insists on their carrying out the law. It is pitiless and condemns everyone." The gracious absolutism of the gospel, on the contrary, "merely reveals to us the Kingdom of God and opens the way to it, but it gives no rules and norms. One must be uncompromising with oneself and not with others. To be strict to oneself and kind to others—this is the truly Christian attitude."[17]

He further asserts that Christianity is opposed to a legalistic division of people into good and evil:

"He maketh his sun to rise on the evil and on the good, and sendeth rain on the just and on the unjust." Until those words were spoken the ethics of law, which knows not grace or redemption, assumed that the sun rises over the just only and the rain falls on them alone. But the

[17]Berdyaev, *Destiny of Man*, 109–111.

Nicolas Berdyaev,
photograph

Gospel equalizes in the sight of God the righteous and the unrighteous, the good and the evil. The good and the righteous can no longer pride themselves on their goodness and righteousness. The old legalistic valuations of good and evil apply no more. "The publicans and the harlots go into the Kingdom of God before you." They go before the Pharisees, before those who consider themselves good and righteous. No system of ethics had ever sided with harlots and publicans, with the sinful and unrighteous.... "He that is without sin among you let him first cast a stone at her." But the moralists of this world, the champions of the pharisaic ethics of law, regard it their duty to throw a stone at the sinner. ... It is perfectly obvious that true Christianity does not allow of dividing mankind into two camps—"the good" and "the wicked", "the righteous" and "the sinners." The wicked and sinful may become good and righteous.[18]

The chief argument against the gospel, continues Berdyaev, is "that it is impracticable and opposed to the very laws of life." The key to understanding the "absolute, transcendental and uncompromising character of the truth proclaimed in the Gospel" is the teaching about the kingdom of God, which is "the essence both of the Gospel and of Christianity as a whole." It is in the kingdom of God that "everything in it proves to be unlike the relative life of the world. The Gospel morality is not a norm or a law because it is the morality of paradise and is beyond our good and evil, beyond our legalistic distinctions between good and evil."[19]

The Christian call to perfection as an inner work, which is not directly connected with specific external prescriptions, is revealed in the context of the teaching concerning the kingdom of God:

Christ came to bring down fire on earth, and everything that men regard as valuable, all the kingdoms built up by them, are consumed in

[18]Berdyaev, *Destiny of Man*, 112.
[19]Berdyaev, *Destiny of Man*, 123.

that fire. Be perfect as your Father in heaven is perfect. Is that a norm and a rule of life? Of course not. The perfection of the Heavenly Father cannot be the norm for a sinful world; it is absolute, while a law or rule is always relative to sin. It is a revelation of an absolute, divine life, different from the sinful life of the world. Thou shalt do no murder, thou shalt not steal, thou shalt not commit adultery—all this can be a norm or a rule for the sinful life of the world and is relative to it. But the perfection of the Heavenly Father and the Kingdom of God are not relative to anything and cannot be made into a rule. The gospel appeals to the inner, spiritual man and not to the outer man, a member of society. It calls not for external works in the social world but for the awakening and regeneration of the spiritual life, for a new birth that is to bring us into the Kingdom of God.[20]

The ethics of the gospel is deeply Christocentric, and it is in Christ and through Christ that it becomes possible to fulfill:

Everything in the Gospel is connected with the person of Christ and is incomprehensible apart from that connection. The injunctions of the Gospel are utterly unrealizable and impossible as rules of action. But what is impossible for man, is possible for God. Only in and through Christ is the perfection similar to the perfection of the Heavenly Father realized, and the Kingdom of God actually comes. The Gospel is based not upon law, even if it be a new law, but upon Christ Himself, upon His personality. Such is the new ethics of grace and redemption.[21]

Berdyaev sharply refutes the distorted understanding of the Christian worldview that was expressed by the German philosopher Friedrich Nietzsche. Nietzsche saw Christianity foremost as a religion of slaves who had decided to normalize their humiliated state and find a justification for their downtrodden position:

There is *master-morality* and *slave-morality*. ... Supposing that the abused, the oppressed, the suffering, the unemancipated, the weary,

[20]Berdyaev, *Destiny of Man*, 123–124.
[21]Berdyaev, *Destiny of Man*, 124.

and those uncertain of themselves, should moralise, what will be the
common element in their moral estimates? Probably a pessimistic
suspicion with regard to the entire situation of man will find expression, perhaps a condemnation of man, together with his situation. The
slave has an unfavourable eye for the virtues of the powerful. . . . On
the other hand, *those* qualities which serve to alleviate the existence
of sufferers are brought into prominence and flooded with light; it is
here that sympathy, the kind, helping hand, the warm heart, patience,
diligence, humility, and friendliness attain to honour.[22]

The idea of Christianity as a religion of slaves was not solely an inven-
tion of Nietzsche. This idea arose in the depths of German materialism and
was firmly established in atheist philosophy and the history of philosophy
of the nineteenth century. For example, the well-known Marxist theoreti-
cian Karl Kautsky saw the sources of Christian ethics in the struggle of the
proletariat against slaveholders. According to him, the Christian community "originally embraced proletarian elements almost exclusively, and was
a proletarian organization." It is this that supposedly explains the attacks on
the rich that are scattered across the entire corpus of the New Testament.
"Few are the occasions on which the class hatred of the modern proletariat
has assumed such fanatical forms as that of the Christian proletariat."[23]

Berdyaev opposed this view with all the force of his polemical genius:

> Christian morality is aristocratic in the spiritual sense and not slavish,
> it is the morality of the strong in spirit and not of the weak. Christian-
> ity calls us to follow the line of the greatest resistance to the world and
> demands heroic efforts. Christianity rose against the slavish sense of
> injury. . . . Christianity wants to eradicate resentment from the human
> soul and heal man from envy and wounded self-love. Christianity alone
> knows the remedy against it. Nietzsche's idea of strength and weakness
> was much too superficial. . . . Christian morality, interpreted not legal-

---

[22]Friedrich Nietzsche, *Beyond Good and Evil: Prelude to a Philosophy of the Future*, trans.
Helen Zimmern (New York, NY: Macmillan, 1907), 227–230.

[23]Karl Kautsky, *Foundations of Christianity: A Study of Christian Origins* (London: George
Allen & Unwin, 1925), 323, 329.

istically but in the inner, spiritual sense, means acquisition of spiritual power in all things. Christian virtue is not compliance to norm and duty but strength and power. . . . Normative idealism is impotent; it does not know whence to draw the power for realizing the good law. The law and the norm are powerless because they are without grace. But Christianity traces back all good to the source of power, that is, to God. Sinful man is powerless without Christ, but he is strong in Christ, for Christ has overcome the world.[24]

Christianity is by no means a religion of slavery. To imagine Christianity to be a religion of any particular class or category of people, including slaves, is to slander Christianity. Freedom is the most important category in Christian morality. To the Jews who believed in him, Jesus said, "If ye continue in my word, then are ye my disciples indeed; and ye shall know the truth, and the truth shall make you free." The audience did not understand his words: "We are Abraham's seed, and were never in bondage to any man. How sayest thou, 'Ye shall be made free'?" But Jesus answered them, "Verily, verily, I say unto you, whosoever committeth sin is the servant of sin. And the servant abideth not in the house forever. But the Son abideth ever. If the Son therefore shall make you free, ye shall be free indeed" (Jn 8.31–36).

Christianity is a religion of freedom. It frees a person from a pharisaical understanding of morality as the sum of laws and regulations whose scrupulous fulfillment leads a person to God. It frees a person from any form of dependence, including dependence on sin. It teaches that freedom is not defined by one's origin or social position.

For the Christian, freedom is an internal, not external, category. Berdyaev speaks of this in another of his seminal works, *The Philosophy of Freedom*:

Freedom in the Christian religion is not a formal principle, as it is in political liberalism; it is not an indifferent, vacuous freedom. . . . For Christianity, the content of religious conscience cannot be indifferent,

---

[24]Berdyaev, *Destiny of Man*, 115–116.

and what Christianity values is not an empty form of freedom that can be filled with any content at all. . . . Freedom is immeasurably dear to the Christian, because freedom is the spirit of his faith, because Christ is freedom. . . . The way of truth is the way of freedom in Christ, for the Son sets free. In the religion of Christ, freedom is limited only by love; Christianity is a religion of free love and a religion of loving freedom. The New Testament is a covenant of love and freedom. Love and freedom is the entire content of the New Testament faith, which overcomes Old Testament legalism and pagan naturalism.[25]

In the very first generation of Christians, the exhortation of the apostle Paul was heard: "For, brethren, ye have been called unto liberty." This exhortation was addressed to different categories of persons—free and slave, Jew and gentile, rich and poor. But Paul then immediately specified what he meant by freedom: "only use not liberty for an occasion to the flesh, but by love serve one another." And he repeated the words that were uttered by Jesus: "For all the law is fulfilled in one word, even in this: 'Thou shalt love thy neighbor as thyself.'" Then he added, "But if ye bite and devour one another, take heed that ye be not consumed one by one another" (Gal 5.13–15).

The capacity that people have for a happy life does not depend on external conditions but on whether they are able to learn to love each other. Christianity is a religion of love, and it is on the idea of love that all of Christian morality is built. Christianity makes human beings creators of their own happiness, teaching them love, including love for their enemies, and thereby protects them from self-destruction. But happiness, like freedom, is understood in Christianity not as an external category: one's happiness depends on one's inner world, on how one builds one's relationships with other people and with God. And it turns out that happiness (or "blessedness," if we use the language of the Sermon on the Mount) is accessible to any person—free or slave, rich or poor, sick or healthy. It is not tied at all to a person's social position or to the conditions of his or her earthly existence.

[25]Nicolas Berdyaev, *Filosofiya svobody* [The philosophy of freedom] (Moscow, 1911), 214–215. Translated by present translator.

Herein lies the deepest chasm between Christian morality and morality that is based on a materialistic worldview, whether in its Marxist or Nietzschean incarnation. Against the universalism of Christianity, materialistic philosophy has set particularism, creating utopian theories about how one group of people can become happy at the cost of the destruction of other people. Marxism promised to make the proletariat happy at the cost of the destruction of class differences. Nietzscheanism lay at the basis of the idea of the superiority of one race over other races that could be sacrificed for the superior race's

The Savior of the World,
El Greco, circa 1600

happiness and welfare. Both projects—the Marxist and the Nietzschean—were tested in practice and resulted in millions of innocent victims.

Christianity survived both these projects. Under the conditions of the totalitarian regimes of the twentieth century, it was able to find its own mode of existence, as it had done from its very inception, when all the punitive power of the Roman Empire was directed at its destruction. Over the course of two thousand years, Christianity proved its resilience and hardiness as it endured under very different regimes.

The strength of Christianity consists in the fact that it gives people spiritual and moral reference points that are not tied to a specific era or tailored for a certain class of people. Christian morality has a universal and timeless nature. There is no doubt that it is an uncompromising morality. But it is not utopian, unlike many theories that were supposed to make humanity happy but which resulted in great tragedies. Christian morality is realistic, and this has been demonstrated by the life and labors of many people, beginning with Christ himself and the early Christian martyrs—and all the way to the saints of our time.

CONCLUSION

Our time poses a question with special keenness: what price must Christians pay for their faith?

It seemed to many in the nineteenth century that the era of persecutions against the Church had faded into the past for good. The term "persecution" itself, like the term "martyrdom," was applied primarily to the era of the ancient Church and was used mainly in scholarly works dedicated to early Christianity.

Theologians of a liberal orientation, who developed New Testament scholarship in comfortable offices in German universities, formulated an entire system of ideas that completely distanced historical Christianity from the "historical Jesus." They dismembered the Gospel text into a multitude of fragments, each of which they ascribed to real or imagined authors who lived at the end of the first or beginning of the second century and wrote for a specific Christian congregation. In this picture a place was found for the sayings that were ascribed to the "historical Jesus," but the degree of their authenticity remained a subject of debate in scholarly circles. The opinion that the real voice of the real historical Jesus had been forever lost to mankind became all but universally accepted in the liberal scholarship of the West: in the Gospels we allegedly have only some echoes of this voice, which had been subjected to significant editorial reworking.

In this context even the absolute value of what Jesus said and taught was called into question. How can we be sure that he spoke exactly thus and not in a different way? How can we be sure that what the evangelists have reported to us are his words and not their own speculations and inventions? Having cast doubt on the authenticity of the testimony of the Gospels regarding the historical Jesus, researchers then dismantled all of his moral teaching, declaring some parts of it inauthentic and other parts impracticable.

The achievements of nineteenth-century liberal scholarship fully con-
formed to the general direction of the philosophical and political thinking
of that era, which was becoming increasingly anti-church and anti-Christian. From the rejection of the presence of God in human history to the
complete rejection of his very existence—such was the spectrum of philosophical views that formed the background against which New Testament
scholarship of the time developed. Deist philosophers removed God from
the world that he created and took as axiomatic his non-interference in
the affairs of the world and, consequently, the right of a person to arrange
his life in his own way. Scholars who worked in the field of New Testament
research removed the historical Jesus from the Church that he founded,
opposing its teaching to that which, in their opinion, Jesus in fact said or
could have said.

In particular, many principles of the Sermon on the Mount were subjected to critical analysis in light of the growing influence of secular ideology. They began to be viewed as an unattainable ideal at best, and, at worst,
as obviously unrealistic standards that were beyond human capabilities.
People began to speak of Jesus as a preacher of moral radicalism and rigor-
ism, and they tried to find an explanation for his approach in the culture of
his time, in the eschatological character of his preaching, in the peculiarities of the life of the Church at the beginning of the first century, and in
other secondary factors of a similar sort.

It was precisely in the nineteenth century that the model of "Christianity
lite" was created, which involved only a selective acceptance of the moral
truths contained in the Sermon on the Mount and in Jesus' other teachings. Christianity without effort, without ascesis, without labor, began to
actively develop in various Protestant communities. The entire spiritual
and moral code of Christianity was subjected to complete review. In the
conditions of prosperity and comfort in which a significant part of Western society lived, the idea of Christianity as a narrow path, of the Christian
community as a persecuted minority, was forgotten for a long time.

The twentieth century introduced serious correctives to the idea that
the history of persecutions could not repeat itself. A series of revolutions

shook many states in Europe, Asia, and Latin America, provoking a mighty wave of violence against Christians.

In Turkey the beginning of the twentieth century was marked by the extermination of Armenians, Assyrians, and members of other Christian peoples. The government of the Young Turks, which had come to power, unleashed genocide on the Christian populations of the Ottoman Empire, and this continued after the fall of the empire. Violent executions, massacres, and mass deportations affected more than a million people.

In Russia the October Revolution of 1917 sparked the mass repression of the clergy, monks, and laypeople. In 1918 the Soviet authorities published the "Decree on the Freedom of Conscience, and on Clerical and Religious Societies," which asserted the principle of the separation of the Church from the state and schools. Religious organizations were deprived of their status as legal entities and did not have the right to possess property or collect donations. The first Soviet Constitution of 1917 defined the clergy and monastics as non-working elements that had no right to vote. The children of priests were not allowed to enroll in institutions of higher learning. The authorities, in the persons of Lenin and Stalin, initiated purges of their own people on an unprecedented scale, the victims of which numbered in the tens of millions. The Church was subjected to almost total ruin: bishops and priests were shot without trial or investigation, churches were blown up, and monasteries and religious schools were closed down.

The "Decree on the Separation of the Church from the State and the School from the Church" and the "Law on Religious Associations" of 1929 made the Russian Orthodox Church effectively illegal. Persecutions against the clergy and believers would wane at times and then break out with renewed vigor, in the periods both before and after the Second World War. In the number of martyrs who suffered for the faith, the Russian Church surpassed by many times the host of Christian martyrs who suffered in the first centuries of the persecutions under the pagan Roman Empire.

In the twentieth century the new martyrs and confessors of the Russian Church were put to death not for some particular qualities or actions or for certain acts or misdemeanors or crimes: they were deliberately and systematically destroyed solely because they believed in Jesus Christ as

The demolition
of the Cathedral
of Christ
the Savior
(Moscow), 1931

God and Savior. Christian churches were blown up for no other reason than that they were Christian, and icons were burned on bonfires because they depicted the likenesses of Christ and the Christian saints.

In Hitler's Germany and the Spanish Republic of the 1930s, Christians of different confessions were subjected to varying degrees of persecution. The persecution of the Catholic Church in Mexico in the 1920s was cruel and bloody: if it had not been for Graham Greene's novel *The Power and the Glory*, few would have known of it. In the middle of the twentieth century, the Cultural Revolution in China resulted in the mass repression of Christian clergy. The list could go on and on.

The persecuted Christians discovered again for themselves the power and relevance of the words that Jesus addressed to his disciples, and through them to all generations of his followers in all times: that they would be persecuted, hunted, killed, and tortured for his name's sake. The fate of millions of Christians in the twentieth century was a repetition of the situation in which the Christian community found itself in the first three centuries of its existence, up to the Edict of Milan in 313 (and beyond the borders of the Roman Empire, for a much longer time). Again every Christian faced the choice between being faithful to Christ or renouncing the faith, compromising one's conscience to serve mammon.

In the era of persecutions there were mass renunciations of the faith. But the feat of martyrdom was also undertaken on an unprecedented scale. In the Russian Church alone more than 1,500 new martyrs and confessors are commemorated by name—these are the ones whose martyrdom was learned of through archival work. The total number of martyrs and confessors of the twentieth century who are counted among the number of the saints, known and unknown by name, is estimated as likely in the hundreds of thousands. As they died in suffering and obscurity, they were comforted by the words of Jesus in the Sermon on the Mount: "Rejoice, and be exceeding glad: for great is your reward in heaven" (Mt 5.12).

At the beginning of the twenty-first century, we have become witnesses of a new wave of persecutions and harassment against Christians in countries of the Middle East and Africa. Again the blood of martyrs is being poured out, again Christian churches are being burned, again hundreds of thousands of people are being compelled to abandon their native land, where their forebears had lived for many centuries. Terrible scenes of mass executions are uploaded onto the Internet by terrorists who take cover under the name of Allah and have as their goal the complete annihilation of Christianity in the Middle East and, in the long term, the whole world, as well as the creation of a worldwide "Islamic Caliphate," in which there would be no place at all for Christ and the Church, just as no place for them remains in the territories that these people have occupied.

Under these circumstances, what Jesus said concerning the persecution of his followers acquires a new keenness and relevance. For a countless multitude of Christians in Iraq, Sudan, Libya, Egypt, Syria, Nigeria, Afghanistan, Pakistan, Algeria, and a number of other countries, the choice between confessing Christ and rejecting him is a choice between life and death. Many have preferred death to renouncing the faith and have been added to the global list of Christian martyrs known to God alone, which at the present time includes millions of names of people of various nationalities who have lived in various eras.

Christianity is subject to persecution of a different kind in countries that until recently were a part of so-called "Christian civilization." In Western Europe, North America, Australia, and some other regions of the

world, militant secularism, which actively opposes itself to any manifestation of religion, gathers more and more strength.

Secularism is the worldview that is the basis for modern secular—that
is to say, nonreligious—society. Secularism is not against religion as such: it
is against the Church having an influence on societal processes and inter-
acting with the worlds of politics, art, science, and culture. The endeavor to
displace religion from the public sphere, to assign it a place on the outskirts
of human everyday life, to reduce it exclusively to the realm of the private
life of separate individuals—that is the program striven for by representatives of the modern secular worldview, who would like religion to be
separated not only from the state but from society also.

This program has dealt especially severe blows to Christianity. A pur-
poseful, well thought-out policy for weakening Christian churches and
dismantling the Christian value system is being conducted in the countries
of Western Europe, in North America, in Australia, and in some countries
of Eastern Europe and Latin America. This program is based on certain
principles perceived as axioms and imposed on the populace through mass
media, legislation, and the educational system: (1) religion is a strictly private affair, and religion must not have any external expression in the public
sphere; a person's actions in everyday life and conduct in society must not
be religiously motivated; (2) an absolute system of values does not exist; all
value systems are relative; each person is free to choose his or her values;
the only restriction on the freedom of a person is the freedom of another
person; (3) the notion of sin is outdated; there is nothing that is sinful in
itself, with the exception of criminally punishable offenses; (4) Christian
churches must review their moral teaching to agree with modern standards, otherwise they will fall behind the times and go out of fashion.

Christian communities react in different ways to this ideology. The
Orthodox Church and a significant portion of the Catholic Church continue to adhere to traditional Christian morality, not fearing being subjected
to massive criticism from liberal society. A certain portion of Protestant
and Anglican communities also take the traditional positions on moral
questions. However, a different, fairly significant portion of Protestant and
Anglican communities in the North and West have embarked on the path

of revising moral teachings with the goal of bringing them closer to the prevailing liberal trends. In these communities, a whole theology has been created for the justification of actions that are sinful and immoral from the point of view of traditional Christian morality.

Today it is all the more difficult to speak of "Christianity" as a unified system of spiritual and moral values accepted by all Christians across the globe. Today it is more appropriate to speak of "Christianities"—of different versions of Christianity exhibited by different communities.

It is possible, very conditionally, to divide all existing versions of Christianity into two large groups: traditional and liberal. The chasm that exists today does not so much divide Orthodox and Catholics, or Catholics and Protestants, as much as "traditionalists" and "liberals." Some Christian leaders say that marriage between a man and a woman is no longer the only way to create a Christian family, that other models exist, and that the Church must become "inclusive" enough to recognize alternative standards of behavior and officially bless them. Others suggest that human life is no longer an absolute value, that it can be cut off in its mother's womb, or that a person can leave this life of his or her own will, and that Christian "traditionalists" must revise their views in order to keep in step with the times.

Some Protestant communities have already revised them. They have come to stand on the same level as the modern secular world, but they have lost the evangelical foundation on which the life of the Christian churches has been built for centuries.

Christianity does not impose itself on anyone, just as Jesus did not impose his teaching on anyone. But not a single church community has the right to lower the high standard that Jesus set in the Sermon on the Mount, in his parables, and in his discourses on moral topics. One can interpret Jesus' teaching and search for ways to apply it in modern life, but church communities do not have the right to reinterpret it so as to reverse the meaning of what Jesus said, otherwise they cease to be the "salt of the earth" and the "light of the world." The task of a church community is to be the guardian and interpreter of Jesus' teaching, to be the space in which it is brought to life.

To be a Christian means to follow Jesus' teaching everywhere and always, whether in one's personal spiritual practice, in one's social or professional activities, or in one's family life. To be a Christian means to be searching always and everywhere for the higher dimension that is opened up by Jesus, by his person and by his preaching. To be a Christian means "to rise from being of this world to being other than the world" at Jesus' command.[1]

Rejection of being of this world presupposes a readiness to swim against the current. This always requires spiritual valor, and in a situation of direct persecution, it requires martyrdom. Jesus was the first to walk the way along which he leads his followers. And he has not shown them any other way.

[1]Albert Schweitzer, *Out of My Life and Thought: An Autobiography*, trans. Antje Bultmann Lemke, 60th Anniversary ed. (Baltimore, MD: The Johns Hopkins University Press, 2009), 58.

ABBREVIATIONS

ANF   The Ante-Nicene Fathers. Edited by Alexander Roberts and
        James Donaldson. Buffalo, 1885–1887. 10 vols. Repr., Peabody,
        MA: Hendrickson, 1994.

CCSL   Corpus Christianorum: Series Latina. Turnhout: Brepols,
        1953–

CSCO   Corpus Scriptorum Christianorum Orientalium. Edited by Jean
        Baptiste Chabot et al. Paris, 1903–

CSEL   Corpus Scriptorum Ecclesiasticorum Latinorum. Vienna,
        1866–2012; Berlin: de Gruyter, 2012–

GCS   Die griechischen christlichen Schriftsteller der ersten [drei] Jah-
        rhunderte. Leipzig; Berlin. 1897–

NPNF[1] The Nicene and Post-Nicene Fathers, Series 1. Edited by Philip
        Schaff. New York, 1886–1889. 14 vols. Repr., Peabody, MA: Hen-
        drickson, 1994.

NPNF[2] The Nicene and Post-Nicene Fathers, Series 2. Edited by Philip
        Schaff and Henry Wace. New York, 1890. 14 vols. Repr., Peabody,
        MA: Hendrickson, 1994.

PG   Patrologia Graeca. Edited by J.-P. Migne. 162 vols. Paris,
        1857–1886.

PL   Patrologia Latina. Edited by J.-P. Migne. 217 vols. Paris,
        1844–1864.

PPS   Popular Patristics Series. Crestwood, NY [Yonkers, NY]: St
        Vladimir's Seminary Press, 1996–

SC   Sources chrétiennes. Paris: Les Éditions du Cerf. 1942–

TUGAL   Texte und Untersuchungen zur Geschichte der altchristlichen
        Literatur.

BIBLIOGRAPHY[1]

1. The Old and New Testaments

Biblia Hebraica Stuttgartensia. 4th ed. Karl Elliger and Wilhelm Rudolph, eds.
Stuttgart: Deutsche Bibelgesellschaft, 1990.

The Holy Bible: King James Version. Standard text ed. Cambridge: Cambridge University Press, 1995.

Novum Testamentum Graece. 28th rev. ed. Eberhard Nestle, Erwin Nestle, and
Kurt Aland, eds. Stuttgart: Württembergische Bibelanstalt, 1963.

Septuaginta: id est, Vetus Testamentum graece iuxta LXX interpretes. Editio
minor. Rahlfs, Alfred, ed. Stuttgart: Deutsche Bibelgesellschaft, 1979.

*Synopsis Quattor Evangeliorum: Locis parallelis evangeliorum apocryphorum et
partum adhibitis.* 13th rev. ed. Kurt Aland, ed. Stuttgart: Deutsche Bibelgesellschaft, 1988.

2. Works of the Fathers and Teachers of the Church[2]

Ambrose of Milan. *Exposition of the Christian Faith.* PL 16:527–698.

Athanasius the Great. *Fragments on Matthew.* PG 27:1364–1389.

Augustine of Hippo. *The City of God.* PL 41:13–801.

_____. *The Gift of Perseverance.* PL 45:993–1054.

_____. *Harmony of the Gospels.* PL 34:1041–1230.

_____. *On Rebuke and Grace.* PL 44:915–946.

_____. *On the Visitation of the Sick.* PL 40:1147–1158.

_____. *Our Lord's Sermon on the Mount.* PL 34:1229–1308.

[1]This bibliography includes only published works that have been cited in this volume.

[2]The titles of these works have been given in English, with an indication of the sources in the Greek, Latin, or other original language, where available. The bibliography entries for specific English *translations* of these works that have been quoted in the present volume are found in Section 2b of this bibliography, except where the translation is from the NPNF or ANF series.—Trans.

_____. *The Predestination of the Saints*. PL 44:959–992.

Barnabas. SC 172.

Basil the Great. *Homily against Anger*. PG 31:353–372.

_____. *Homily Explaining That God Is Not the Cause of Evil*. PG 31:329–354.

_____. *Shorter Responses*. PG 31:1051–1306.

Clement of Alexandria. *Stromata*. In *Clemens Alexandrinus*, edited by Otto Stählin and Ludwig Frühtel, 4th ed., Bde. 2–3. GCS 15, 17. Leipzig: Hinrichs, 1985.

_____. *The Instructor*. PG 8:560A.

_____. *Who Is the Rich Man That Shall Be Saved?* PG 9:603–652.

Clement of Rome. *First Epistle to the Corinthians*. In *Patres Apostolici*, edited by Franz Xavier Funk, 2nd ed., vol. 1, 98–183. Tübingen: Laupp, 1901.

_____. *Second Epistle to the Corinthians*. In *Patres Apostolici*, edited by Franz Xavier Funk, 2nd ed., vol. 1, 184–210. Tübingen: Laupp, 1901.

Cyprian of Carthage. *Treatise on the Lord's Prayer*. In *Opera omnia*, by Cyprian of Carthage, edited by W. Hartel, CSEL 3/1, 187–205. Vienna, 1868.

Cyril of Alexandria. *Fragments on Matthew*. Matthäus-Kommentare aus der griechischen Kirche, edited by Joseph Reuss. TUGAL 61:153–269. Berlin: Akademie-Verlag, 1957.

Cyril of Jerusalem. *Mystagogical Catecheses*. PG 33:1065–1131.

Didache. SC 248.

Dorotheos of Gaza. *Discourses*. SC 92.

Ephrem the Syrian. *Commentary on the Diatessaron*. In *Commentaire de l'Évangile concordant texte syriaque (Manuscrit Chester Beatty 709)*, by Ephrem the Syrian, edited and translated by Louis Leloir, Chester Beatty Monographs 8. Dublin: Hodges Figgis, 1963.

Epistle to Diognetus. SC 33.

Gregory of Nazianzus. *Epistles*. PG 37:21–388.

_____. *Oration 2: Apology on the Priesthood*. PG 35:500–518.

_____. *Oration 4: First Invective against Julian*. PG 35:531–663.

_____. *Oration 27: Against the Eunomians; First Theological Oration*. PG 36:11–26.

_____. *Poems on Scripture 25 [On Anger]*. PG 37:813–851.

Gregory of Nyssa. *The Beatitudes*. PG 44:1193–1302.

_____. *The Life of Moses*. PG 44:297–430.

_____. *The Lord's Prayer*. PG 44:1119–1194.

_____. *On Perfection.* PG 46:252–285.

Hilary of Poitiers. *Commentary on Matthew.* PL 9:917–1078.

Hippolytus of Rome. *On the Apostolic Tradition.* SC 11.

Ignatius of Antioch. *Epistle to the Ephesians.* SC 10:66–93.

_____. *Epistle to Polycarp.* SC 10:170–181.

_____. *Epistle to the Romans.* SC 10:124–139.

Irenaeus of Lyons. *Against Heresies.* SC 100; 152–153; 263–264; 293–294; 210–211.

_____. *Epistle to Victor, Bishop of Rome.* Cited by Eusebius in *Ecclesiastical History* 5.24.12 (NPNF² 1:243).

Isaac the Syrian. *Ascetical Homilies.* In *De perfectione religiosa*, by Isaac of Nineveh [Isaac the Syrian], edited by Paul Bedjan. Paris: Harrossowitz, 1909.

_____. *Chapters on Knowledge* (unpublished). Selected chapters translated into Russian in *O bozhestvennykh taynakh i o dukhovnoy zhizni: Novootkrytye teksty* [On the divine mysteries and spiritual life: newly discovered texts], by Isaac the Syrian, translated by Metropolitan Hilarion (Alfeyev), 75–85. St Petersburg, 2003.

_____. *The Second Part.* In *"The Second Part": Chapters IV–XLI*, by Isaac of Nineveh [Isaac the Syrian], edited and translated by Sebastian Brock. 2 vols. CSCO 554–555. Louvain: Peeters, 1995.

Isidore of Pelusium. *Letters.* PG 78:177–1646.

Jerome. *Commentary on Ezekiel.* PL 25:15–490.

John Chrysostom. *Commentary on the Psalms.* PG 55:35–498.

_____. *Homilies on 1 Corinthians.* PG 61:11–382.

_____. *Homilies on John.* PG 59.

_____. *Homilies on Matthew.* PG 57–58.

_____. *Homilies on Repentance.* PG 49:277–350.

_____. *Homilies on Romans.* PG 60:391–682.

_____. *On the Priesthood.* PG 48:623–692.

John Climacus. *The Ladder of Divine Ascent.* PG 88:631–1164.

Justin Martyr. *First Apology.* PG 6:327–440.

Macarius of Egypt. *On the Freedom of the Mind.* PG 34:935–968.

_____. *Homilies* [Collection 1]. In *Makarios/Symeon: Reden und Briefe; Die Sammlung I des Vaticanus Graecus 694 B.*, edited by Heinz Berthold, 2 vols. Berlin: Akademie-Verlag, 1973.

_____. *Spiritual Homilies* [Collection 2]. In *Die 50 geistlichen Homilien des Makarios*, by Pseudo-Macarius, edited by Hermann Dörries, Erich Klostermann, and Matthias Kroeger, Patristische Texte und Studien 4. Berlin: De Gruyter, 1964.

Maximus the Confessor. *Disputation with Pyrrhus*. PG 91:287–354.

Origen. *Against Celsus*. SC 132; 136; 147; 150.

_____. *Commentary on the Psalms*. In *Analecta sacra spicilegio solesmensi parata*, ed. Jean Baptiste Pitra, 8 vols., 2:444–483, 3:1–236, 242–245, 248–364. Venice: 1876–1891.[3]

_____. *Fragments on Matthew*. In *Origenes Werke*, vol. 12, by Origen, edited by E. Klostermann and E. Benz, GCS 41/1, 13–235. Leipzig: Teuber, 1941.

_____. *Homilies on Luke*. PG 13:1801–1902.

_____. *Homilies on the Song of Songs*. In *Origenes Werke*, vol. 8, by Origen, edited by W. A. Baehrens, GCS 33, 26–60. Leipzig: Teubner, 1925.

_____. *On First Principles*. PG 11:115–414.

_____. *Prayer*. PG 11:415–562.

Philaret of Moscow. "Slovo v nedelyu 19 po Pyatidesyatnitse" [Homily on the 19th Sunday after Pentecost]. In *Slova i rechi* [Homilies and speeches], vol. 1, 285–289. Moscow, 1873.

Polycarp of Smyrna. *Epistle to the Philippians*. SC 10:202–222.

Pseudo-Chrysostom. *Commentary on Matthew*. PG 56:611–946.

Sayings of the Desert Fathers. PG 65:71–442.

Shepherd of Hermas. In *Patres Apostolici*, edited by Franz Xavier Funk, 2nd ed., vol. 1, 414–639. Tübingen: Laupp, 1901.

Symeon the New Theologian. *Catechetical Discourses*. SC 96; 104; 113.

_____. *Ethical Discourses*. SC 122; 129.

Tertullian. *Against Marcion*. CCSL 1:441–726.

_____. *Apology*. CCSL 1:85–171.

_____. *On Exhortation to Chastity*. CCSL 2:1015–1035.

_____. *On Idolatry*. CCSL 2:1101–1124.

_____. *On Prayer*. CCSL 1:255–274.

_____. *To Scapula*. CCSL 2:1127–1132.

Theodore the Studite. *Great Catechesis*. In *Patris nostri Theodori Studitae parvae et magnae catecheseos sermones*, by Theodore the Studite, edited by Josephus Cozza-Luzi, T. 9, pt. 1–2 of *Nova patrum bibliotheca*. Rome, 1888.

_____

[3]The composition belongs to Evagrius Ponticus; see *Clavis Patrum Graecorum* 2455.

_____. *Iambs*. In *Theodoros Studites: Jamben auf verschiedene Gegenstände*. By Theodore the Studite. Edited by Paul Speck. Supplementa Byzantina 1. Berlin: de Gruyter, 1968.

Theophilus of Antioch. *To Autolycus*. PG 6:1023–1168.

2b. English Translations of Works of the Fathers and Teachers of the Church

Basil the Great. *The Asketikon of St Basil the Great*. Translated by Anna M. Silvas. Oxford Early Christian Studies. Oxford: Oxford University Press, 2005.

_____. *On the Human Condition*. Translated by Nonna Verna Harrison. Popular Patristics Series 30. Crestwood, NY: St Vladimir's Seminary Press, 2005.

_____. *The Rule of St. Basil in Latin and English: A Revised Critical Edition*. Translated by Anna M. Silvas. Collegeville, MN: Liturgical Press, 2013.

Cyril of Jerusalem. *Lectures on the Christian Sacraments: Greek Original and English Translation*. Translated by Maxwell E. Johnson. Popular Patristics Series 57. Yonkers, NY: St Vladimir's Seminary Press, 2017.

Dorotheos of Gaza. *Discourses and Sayings*. Translated by Eric P. Wheeler. Cistercian Studies Series 33. Kalamazoo, MI: Cistercian Publications, 1977.

Give Me a Word: The Alphabetical Sayings of the Desert Fathers. Translated by John Wortley. Popular Patristics Series 52. Yonkers, NY: St Vladimir's Seminary Press, 2014.

Gregory of Nazianzus. *Poems on Scripture*. Translated by Brian Dunkle. Popular Patristics Series 46. Yonkers, NY: St Vladimir's Seminary Press, 2012.

Gregory of Nyssa. *Ascetical Works*. Translated by Virginia Woods Callahan. Fathers of the Church 58. Washington, DC: Catholic University of America Press, 1967.

_____. *St Gregory of Nyssa: Catechetical Discourse*. Translated by Ignatius Green. Popular Patristics Series 60. Yonkers, NY: St Vladimir's Seminary Press, 2019.

_____. *The Life of Moses*. Translated by Abraham J. Malherbe and Everett Ferguson. Classics of Western Spirituality. New York, NY: Paulist Press, 1978.

_____. *The Lord's Prayer; The Beatitudes*. Translated by Hilda C. Graef. Ancient Christian Writers 18. Mahwah, NJ: Paulist Press, 1954.

Hilary of Poitiers. *Commentary on Matthew*. Translated by D. H. Williams. Fathers of the Church 125. Washington, DC: Catholic University of America Press, 2012.

Hippolytus of Rome. *On the Apostolic Tradition*. 2nd ed. Translated by Alistair Stewart. Popular Patristics Series 54. Yonkers, NY: St Vladimir's Seminary Press, 2015.

Ignatius of Antioch: The Letters. Translated by Alistair Stewart. Popular Patristics Series 49. Yonkers, NY: St Vladimir's Seminary Press, 2013.

Incomplete Commentary on Matthew (Opus imperfectum). Vol. 1. Translated by James A. Kellerman. Edited by Thomas C. Oden. Ancient Christian Texts. Downers Grove, IL: InterVarsity, 2010.

Isaac the Syrian. *The Ascetical Homilies of Saint Isaac the Syrian*. Translated by Holy Transfiguration Monastery. Rev. 2nd ed. Boston, MA: Holy Transfiguration Monastery, 2011.

Isaac of Nineveh (Isaac the Syrian). *"The Second Part": Chapters IV–XLI*. Translated by Sebastian Brock. CSCO 555, Scriptores syri 225. Louvain: Peeters, 1995.

John Chrysostom. *On Repentance and Almsgiving*. Translated by Gus George Christo. Fathers of the Church 96. Washington, DC: Catholic University of America Press, 1998.

———. *Six Books on the Priesthood*. Translated by Graham Neville. Popular Patristics Series 1. Crestwood, NY: St Vladimir's Seminary Press, 1977.

John Climacus. *The Ladder of Divine Ascent*. Translated by Holy Transfiguration Monastery. Revised ed. Boston, MA: Holy Transfiguration Monastery, 2001.

Julian the Emperor, Containing Gregory Nazianzen's Two Invectives and Libanius' Monody, with Julian's Extant Theosophical Works. Translated by C. W. King. London: George Bell and Sons, 1888.

Maximus the Confessor. *The Disputation with Pyrrhus of our Father among the Saints Maximus the Confessor*. Translated by Joseph P. Farrell. South Canaan, PA: St. Tikhon's Seminary Press, 1990.

On the Two Ways: Life or Death, Light or Darkness: Foundational Texts in the Tradition. Translated by Alistair Stewart. Popular Patristics Series 41. Yonkers, NY: St Vladimir's Seminary Press, 2011.

Origen. *An Exhortation to Martyrdom, Prayer and Selected Works*. Translated by Rowan A. Greer. Classics of Western Spirituality. Mahwah, NJ: Paulist Press, 1979.

———. *Homilies on Luke; Fragments on Luke*. Translated by Joseph T. Lienhard. Fathers of the Church 94. Washington, DC: Catholic University of America Press, 1996.

———. *On First Principles*. Translated by G. W. Butterworth. Edited by Tania M. Geist. Notre Dame, IN: Ave Maria Press, 2013.

———. *The Song of Songs: Commentary and Homilies*. Translated by R. P. Lawson. Ancient Christian Writers 26. Westminster, MD: Newman Press, 1957.

Pseudo-Macarius. *The Fifty Spiritual Homilies and the Great Letter*. Translated by George A. Maloney. Classics of Western Spirituality. New York, NY: Paulist Press, 1992.

Saint Ephrem's Commentary on Tatian's Diatessaron: An English Translation of Chester Beatty *Syriac MS 709 with Introduction and Notes*. Translated by Carmel McCarthy. Journal of Semitic Studies Supplement 2. Oxford: Oxford University Press, 1993.

Symeon the New Theologian. *The Discourses*. Translated by C. J. deCatanzaro. Classics of Western Spirituality. Mahwah, NJ: Paulist Press, 1980.

———. *On the Mystical Life: The Ethical Discourses*. Vol. 1, *The Church and the Last Things*, translated by Alexander Golitzin. Popular Patristics Series 14. Crestwood, NY: St. Vladimir's Seminary Press, 1995.

———. *On the Mystical Life: The Ethical Discourses*. Vol. 2, *On Virtue and Christian Life*, translated by Alexander Golitzin. Popular Patristics Series 15. Crestwood, NY: St. Vladimir's Seminary Press, 1996.

Tertullian, Cyprian & Origen: On the Lord's Prayer. Translated by Alistair Stewart-Sykes. Popular Patristics Series 29. Crestwood, NY: St Vladimir's Seminary Press, 2004.

3. Other Sources

Calvin, John. *Institutes of the Christian Religion*. Vol. 2, translated by Ford Lewis Battles and edited by John T. McNeill. The Westminster Press, 1960. Reissued, Louisville, KY: Westminster John Knox, 2006.

Josephus, Flavius. *The Antiquities of the Jews*. Translated by William Whiston. In *The Works of Flavius Josephus*. Auburn and Buffalo, NY: John E. Beardsley, 1895.

_____. *The Wars of the Jews*. Translated by William Whiston. In *The Works of Flavius Josephus*. Auburn and Buffalo, NY: John E. Beardsley, 1895.

Kant, Immanuel. *Grounding for the Metaphysics of Morals: With, On a Supposed Right to Lie because of Philanthropic Concerns*. Translated by James W. Ellington. 3rd ed. Indianapolis, IN: Hackett, 1993.

Kantor, Marvin, and Richard S. White, trans. *The Vita of Constantine and the Vita of Methodius*. Michigan Slavic Materials 13. Ann Arbor, MI: Dept. of Slavic Languages and Literature, University of Michigan, 1976.

Luther, Martin. *Commentary on the Sermon on the Mount*. Translated by Charles A. Hay. Philadelphia, PA: Lutheran Publication Society, 1892.

_____. *On the Bondage of the Will*. In *Luther and Erasmus: Free Will and Salvation*, edited and translated by E. Gordon Rupp, A. N. Marlow, Philip S. Watson, and B. Drewery, 101–334. The Library of Christian Classics. The Westminster Press, 1969. Reissued, Louisville, KY: Westminster Fort Knox Press, 2006.

The Mishnah. Edited and translated by Herbert Danby. Oxford: Oxford University Press, 1933.

Moscow Patriarchate. *The Basis of the Social Concept of the Russian Orthodox Church* Vol. 5. The document was presented at the Bishops' Council, Moscow, August 13–16, 2000; online version at https://mospat.ru/en/documents/social-concepts/viii/.

Philo of Alexandria. *Apology for the Jews*. In *The Works of Philo: Complete and Unabridged*, by Philo of Alexandria, translated by C. D. Yonge, updated ed., 742–746. Peabody, MA: Hendrickson, 1993.

Puech, Émile, ed. *Qumrân Grotte 4.XVIII: Textes Hébreux (4Q521–4Q528, 4Q576–4Q579)*. Discoveries in the Judaean Desert 25. Oxford: Clarendon Press, 1998.

Simonetti, Manlio, ed. *Matthew 1–13*. Ancient Christian Commentary on Scripture New Testament 1a. Downers Grove, IL: InterVarsity, 2001.

Socrates Scholasticus. *Ecclesiastical History*. NPNF[2] 2:1–178.

Thomas Aquinas. *Summa Theologiae*. In *Opera Omnia*, by Thomas Aquinas, vols. 4–12. Rome, 1888–1906.

Tolstoy, Leo. *The Four Gospels Harmonized and Translated*. Vol. 2. Croydon: The Brotherhood Pub. Co., 1896.

_____. *Polnoe sobranie sochineniy* [Complete works]. 90 vols. Moscow: Gos. izd-vo khudozh. lit-ry, 1928–1958.

4. Cited Literature

Albright, W. F., and C. S. Mann, ed. and trans. *Matthew: Introduction, Translation, and Notes by W. F. Albright and C. S. Mann*. Anchor Yale Bible 26. New Haven, CT: Yale University Press, 2011. First published 1971 by Doubleday (Garden City, NY).

Allison, Dale C., Jr. *The Sermon on the Mount: Inspiring the Moral Imagination*. Companions to the New Testament. New York, NY: Crossroad, 1999.

Apresyan, R. G. "Talion i zolotoe pravilo (Kriticheskiy analiz sopryazhennykh kontekstov)" [Talion and the Golden Rule (a critical analysis of interconnected contexts)]. *Voprosy filosofii* [Questions of philosophy] 3 (2001): 72–84.

Barackman, Floyd H. *Practical Christian Theology: Examining the Great Doctrines of the Faith*. 3rd ed. Grand Rapids, MI: Kregel, 1998.

Barth, Karl. *Church Doctrine*. Vol. 4, *The Doctrine of Reconciliation*, pt. 3.2, translated by G. W. Bromiley and edited by T. F. Torrance. New York, NY: T&T Clark International, 2004.

Barton, Stephen C. *Discipleship and Family Ties in Mark and Matthew*. Society for New Testament Studies Monograph Series 80. Cambridge: Cambridge University Press, 1994.

Beare, Francis Wright. *The Gospel according to Matthew: A Commentary*. Oxford: Blackwell, 1981.

Berdyaev, Nicolas. *The Destiny of Man*. Translated by Natalie Duddington. London: G. Bles, The Centenary Press, 1937.

_____. *Filosofiya svobody* [The philosophy of freedom]. Moscow, 1911.

_____. "The Kingdom of God and the Kingdom of Caesar." Translated by Stephen Janos. Berdyaev Online Bibliotek Library. 2001. http://www.berdyaev.com/berdiaev/berd_lib/1925_303.html.

_____. *O naznachenii cheloveka: Opyt paradoksal'noy etiki*. Paris: Sovremennye zapisi, 1931.

_____. "Tsarstvo Bozhie i tsarstvo kesarya" [The kingdom of God and the kingdom of Caesar]. In *Izbrannye filosofskie sochineniya 1920-x gg.* [Selected philosophical works of the 1920s], 13–48. Moscow: DirectMEDIA, 2015.

Betz, Hans Dieter. *Essays on the Sermon on the Mount.* Translated by L. L. Welborn. Philadelphia, PA: Fortress, 1985.

Black, Matthew. *An Aramaic Approach to the Gospels and Acts.* 2nd ed. Oxford: Clarendon Press, 1954.

Bock, Darrell L. *Jesus according to Scripture: Restoring the Portrait from the Gospels.* Grand Rapids, MI: Baker Academic, 2002.

Bockmuehl, Markus. *Seeing the Word: Refocusing New Testament Study.* Grand Rapids, MI: Baker Academic, 2006.

Bonhoeffer, Dietrich. *Discipleship.* Translated by Barbara Green and Reinhard Krauss. Minneapolis, MN: Fortress Press, 2015.

Bornkamm, Günther. *Jesus of Nazareth.* Translated by Irene McLuskey, Fraser McLuskey, and James M. Robinson. New York, NY: Harper & Row, 1960.

Bornkamm, Günther, Gerhard Barth, and Heinz Joachim Held. *Tradition and Interpretation in Matthew.* Translated by Percy Scott. The New Testament Library. Philadelphia, PA: Westminster, 1963.

Brake, Donald L., and Todd Bolen. *Jesus, a Visual History: The Dramatic Story of the Messiah in the Holy Land.* Grand Rapids, MI: Zondervan, 2014.

Bray, Gerald. *Yours is the Kingdom: A Systematic Theology of the Lord's Prayer.* Notthingham, England: Inter-Varsity Press, 2007.

Brooke, George J. *The Dead Sea Scrolls and the New Testament.* Minneapolis, MN: Fortress, 2005.

Bultmann, Rudolf. *The History of the Synoptic Tradition.* Translated by John Marsh. Oxford: Blackwell, 1963.

_____. *Theology of the New Testament.* Translated by Kendrick Grobel. 2 vols. Waco, TX: Baylor University Press, 2007.

Carlston, Charles E., and Craig A. Evans. *From Synagogue to Ecclesia: Matthew's Community at the Crossroads.* Wissenschaftliche Untersuchungen zum Neuen Testament 334. Tübingen: Mohr Siebeck, 2014.

Childs, Brevard S. *Biblical Theology of the Old and New Testaments: Theological Reflection on the Christian Bible.* Minneapolis, MN: Fortress, 1993.

Clark-Soles, Jaime. *Death and the Afterlife in the New Testament.* New York, NY: T&T Clark, 2006.

Clines, David J. A., ed. *The Dictionary of Classical Hebrew.* 9 vols. Sheffield: Sheffield Academic, 1993–2016.

Cohen, David. *Law, Sexuality, and Society: The Enforcement of Morals in Classical Athens.* Cambridge: Cambridge University Press, 1991.

Cook, Edward M. *Dictionary of Qumran Aramaic.* Winona Lake, IN: Eisenbrauns, 2015.

Crossan, John Dominic. *The Greatest Prayer: Rediscovering the Revolutionary Message of the Lord's Prayer.* New York, NY: HarperOne, 2010.

Cullmann, Oscar. *Christ and Time: The Primitive Christian Conception of Time and History.* Translated by Floyd V. Filson. Revised ed. London: SCM Press, 1962.

Dalman, Gustaf. *Die Worte Jesu.* 2nd ed. Bd. 1, *Einleitung und wichtige Begriffe.* Leipzig: J. C. Hinrichs, 1930.

Davies, W. D., and Dale C. Allison. *A Critical and Exegetical Commentary on the Gospel according to Saint Matthew.* 3 vols. Edinburgh: T&T Clark, 1988–1997.

Davies, W. D. *The Setting of the Sermon on the Mount.* Cambridge: Cambridge University Press, 1964.

Davis, James F. *Lex Talionis in Early Judaism and the Exhortation of Jesus in Matthew 5.38–42.* Journal for the Study of the New Testament, Supplement Series 281. New York, NY: T&T Clark International, 2005.

Deines, Roland. "Not the Law but the Messiah: Law and Righteousness in the Gospel of Matthew—An Ongoing Debate." In *Built upon the Rock: Studies in the Gospel of Matthew,* edited by Daniel M. Gurtner and John Nolland, 53–84. Grand Rapids, MI: Eerdmans, 2008.

Deutsch, Celia. *Hidden Wisdom and the Easy Yoke: Wisdom, Torah and Discipleship in Matthew 11.25–30.* Journal for the Study of the New Testament Supplement Series 18. Sheffield: JSOT Press, 1987.

Di Luccio, Pino. *The Quelle and the Targums: Righteousness in the Sermon on the Mount/Plain.* Analecta Biblica 175. Rome: Pontificio Istituto Biblico, 2009.

Dibelius, Martin. "Die Bergpredigt." In *Botschaft und Geschichte,* Bd. 1, 79–174. Tübingen: Mohr, 1953.

Dodd, C. H. "The Primitive Catechism and the Sayings of Jesus." In *New Testament Essays: Studies in Memory of Thomas Walter Manson, 1893–1958,* edited by A. J. B. Higgins, 106–118. Manchester: Manchester University Press, 1959.

Donahue, John R., and Daniel J. Harrington. *The Gospel of Mark*. Sacra Pagina Series 2. Collegeville, MN: Liturgical Press, 2002.

Dunn, James D. G. *A New Perspective on Jesus: What the Quest for the Historical Jesus Missed*. Grand Rapids, MI: Baker Academic, 2005.

Dupont, Jacques. *Les Béatitudes*. New ed. Vol. 1, *Le problème littéraire: les deux versions du Sermon sur la montagne et des Béatitudes*. Bruges: Abbaye de Saint-André, 1958.

Ehrman, Bart D. *Misquoting Jesus: The Story behind Who Changed the Bible and Why*. New York, NY: HarperCollins, 2005.

Elchaninov, Alexander. *Zapisi* [Notes]. Moscow, 1992.

Evans, Craig A. *Matthew*. New Cambridge Bible Commentary. Cambridge: Cambridge University Press, 2012.

Fedotov, G. P., ed. *A Treasury of Russian Spirituality*. New York, NY: Sheed & Ward, 1948.

Fiebig, Paul. *Das Vaterunser: Ursprung, Sinn und Bedeutung des christlichen Hauptgebetes*. Gütersloh: C. Bertelsmann, 1927.

Fitzmyer, Joseph A. *The Dead Sea Scrolls and Christian Origins*. Studies in the Dead Sea Scrolls and Related Literature. Grand Rapids, MI: Eerdmans, 2000.

――――. *The Gospel according to Luke: Introduction, Translation and Notes*. Vol. 2, *Luke X–XXIV*, Anchor Bible 28A. Garden City, NY: Doubleday, 1985.

France, R. T. *The Gospel of Matthew*. The New International Commentary on the New Testament. Grand Rapids, MI: Eerdmans, 2007.

Gardner, Richard B. *Matthew*. Believers Church Bible Commentary. Scottsdale, PA: Herald, 1991.

Gerhardsson, Birger. "The Matthean Version of the Lord's Prayer (Matt 6:9b–13): Some Observations." In *The New Testament Age: Essays in Honor of Bo Reicke*, edited by William C. Weinrich, vol. 1, 207–220. Macon, GA: Mercer University Press, 1984.

Goldsmith, Martin. *Matthew and Mission: The Gospel through Jewish Eyes*. Carlisle, UK: Paternoster, 2001.

Goulder, M. D. "The Composition of the Lord's Prayer." *Journal of Theological Studies* 14 (1963): 32–45.

Grassi, Joseph A. *Informing the Future: Social Justice in the New Testament*. New York, NY: Paulist Press, 2003.

Green, Joel B., Scot McKnight, and I. Howard Marshall, eds. *Dictionary of Jesus and the Gospels: A Compendium of Contemporary Biblical Scholarship.* Downers Grove, IL: InterVarsity, 1992.

Guelich, Robert A. *The Sermon on the Mount: A Foundation for Understanding.* Waco, TX: Word Books, 1982.

Gundry, Robert H. *Matthew: A Commentary on His Literary and Theological Art.* Grand Rapids, MI: Eerdmans, 1982.

Hannan, Margaret Ann. *The Nature and Demands of the Sovereign Rule of God in the Gospel of Matthew.* Library of New Testament Studies 308. New York, NY: T&T Clark, 2006.

Hauerwas, Stanley. *Matthew.* Brazos Theological Commentary on the Bible. Grand Rapids, MI: Brazos, 2006.

Hays, Richard B. *The Moral Vision of the New Testament: Community, Cross, New Creation; A Contemporary Introduction to New Testament Ethics.* San Francisco, CA: HarperSanFrancisco, 1996.

Hengel, Martin. *The Four Gospels and the One Gospel of Jesus Christ: An Investigation of the Collection and Origin of the Canonical Gospels.* 1st North American ed. Harrisburg, PA: Trinity Press International, 2000.

Hilarion (Alfeyev), [Metropolitan]. *Dukhovnyy mir prepodobnogo Isaaka Sirina* [The spiritual world of St Isaac the Syrian]. 6th ed. Moscow: Veche, 2013.

_____. *Jesus Christ: His Life and Teaching.* Vol. 1, *The Beginning of the Gospel,* translated by Christopher Hill and Brenda Seah Mikitish. Yonkers, NY: St Vladimir's Seminary Press, 2018.

_____. *St Symeon the New Theologian and Orthodox tradition.* Oxford: Oxford University Press, 2000.

_____. *Orthodox Christianity,* volume 2: *Doctrine and Teaching of the Orthodox Church.* Yonkers, NY: St Vladimir's Seminary Press, 2012.

_____. *Orthodox Christianity,* volume 4: *The Worship and Liturgical Life of the Orthodox Church.* Yonkers, NY: St Vladimir's Seminary Press, 2012.

Hill, David, ed. *The Gospel of Matthew.* New Century Bible. London: Oliphants, 1972.

Holmås, Geir Otto. *Prayer and Vindication in Luke-Acts: The Theme of Prayer within the Context of the Legitimating and Edifying Objective of the Lukan Narrative.* Library of New Testament Studies 433. New York, NY: T&T Clark, 2011.

Honeyman, A. M. "The Etymology of Mammon." *Archivum linguisticum* 4 (1952): 60–65.

Horsley, Richard A. *Jesus and the Spiral of Violence: Popular Jewish Resistance in Roman Palestine.* San Francisco, CA: Harper & Row, 1987.

Hultgren, Arland J. *The Parables of Jesus: A Commentary.* The Bible in Its World. Grand Rapids, MI: Eerdmans, 2000.

Jeremias, Joachim. *Abba: Studien zur neutestamentlichen Theologie und Zeitgeschichte.* Göttingen: Vandenhoeck & Ruprecht, 1966.

_____. *Jerusalem in the Time of Jesus: An Investigation into Economic and Social Conditions during the New Testament Period.* Translated by F. H. Cave and C. H. Cave. Philadelphia, PA: Fortress, 1969.

_____. *Jesus and the Message of the New Testament.* Edited by K. C. Hanson. Fortress Classics in Biblical Studies. Minneapolis, MN: Fortress, 2002.

_____. *The Sermon on the Mount.* Translated by Norman Perrin. London: Athlone Press, 1961.

Jones, Ivor H. *The Matthean Parables: A Literary and Historical Commentary.* Supplements to Novum Testamentum 80. New York, NY: Brill, 1995.

Käsemann, Ernst. *New Testament Questions of Today.* Translated by W. J. Montague. Philadelphia, PA: Fortress, 1969.

Kautsky, Karl. *Foundations of Christianity: A Study of Christian Origins.* London: George Allen & Unwin, 1925.

Keener, Craig S. *The Gospel of Matthew: A Socio-Rhetorical Commentary.* Grand Rapids, MI: Eerdmans, 2009.

Kierkegaard, Søren. *The Lily of the Field and the Bird of the Air.* Translated by Bruce H. Kirmmse. Princeton, NJ: Princeton University Press, 2016.

Kingsbury, Jack Dean. *Matthew: Structure, Christology, Kingdom.* Philadelphia, PA: Fortress, 1975.

Kissinger, Warren S. *The Sermon on the Mount: A History of Interpretation and Bibliography.* ATLA Bibliography Series 3. Metuchen, NJ: Scarecrow, 1975.

Kister, Menahem. "Words and Formulae in the Gospels in the Light of Hebrew and Aramaic Sources," In *The Sermon on the Mount and Its Jewish Setting,* ed. Hans-Jürgen Becker and Serge Ruzer, Cahiers de la Revue biblique 60, 117–147. Paris: Gabalda, 2005.

Koehler, Ludwig, and Walter Baumgartner. *Hebräisches und aramäisches Lexikon zum Alten Testament.* 3rd ed. Edited by Walter Baumgartner and Johann Jakob Stamm. 5 Lfg. and 1 Supplementband. Leiden: Brill, 1967–1996.

Köstenberger, Andreas J., L. Scott Kellum, and Charles L. Quarles. *The Cradle, the Cross, and the Crown: An Introduction to the New Testament.* Nashville, TN: B&H Academic, 2009.

Kümmel, Werner Georg. *Theology of the New Testament according to Its Major Witnesses: Jesus—Paul—John.* Translated by John E. Steely. Nashville, TN: Abingdon, 1973.

Ladd, George Eldon. *A Theology of the New Testament.* Revised ed. Edited by Donald A. Hagner. Grand Rapids, MI: Eerdmans, 1993.

Latham, James E. *The Religious Symbolism of Salt.* Théologie Historique 64. Paris: Éditions Beauchesne, 1982.

Lee, Dorothy A. *Transfiguration.* New Century Theology. New York, NY: Continuum, 2004.

Lloyd-Jones, D. Martyn. *Studies in the Sermon on the Mount.* 2nd ed. Grand Rapids, MI: Eerdmans, 1976.

Luz, Ulrich. *Matthew 1–7: A Commentary.* Translated by James E. Crouch. Edited by Helmut Koester. Hermeneia. Minneapolis, MN: Fortress, 2007.

_____. *The Theology of the Gospel of Matthew.* Translated by J. Bradford Robinson. New Testament Theology. Cambridge: Cambridge University Press, 1995.

Maier, Gerhard. *Der Brief des Jakobus* (Wuppertal: Brockhaus, 2004).

Manns, F., and E. Alliata, eds. *Early Christianity in Context: Monuments and Documents.* Collectio Maior 38. Jerusalem: Franciscan Printing Press, 1993.

Manson, T. W. *The Sayings of Jesus: As Recorded in the Gospels according to St. Matthew and St. Luke; Arranged with Introduction and Commentary.* London: SCM, 1949.

Massey, Isabel Ann. *Interpreting the Sermon on the Mount in the Light of Jewish Tradition as Evidenced in the Palestinian Targums of the Pentateuch: Selected Themes.* Studies in the Bible and Early Christianity 25. Lewiston, NY: E. Mellen, 1991.

McNamara, Martin. "Some Targum Themes." In *Justification and Variegated Nomism,* edited by D. A. Carson, Peter T. O'Brien, and Mark A. Seifrid, vol. 1, *The Complexities of Second Temple Judaism,* 303–356. Grand Rapids, MI: Baker Academic, 2001.

Meier, John P. *A Marginal Jew: Rethinking the Historical Jesus.* 5 vols. Anchor Bible Reference Library (vols. 1–3) and Yale Anchor Bible Reference Library (vols.

4–5). New York, NY: Doubleday, 1991–2001 (vols. 1–3) and New Haven, CT: Yale University Press, 2009–2016 (vols. 4–5).

_____. *Law and History in Matthew's Gospel: A Redactional Study of Mt. 5:17–48.* Analecta Biblica 71. Rome: Biblical Institute Press, 1976.

_____. *Matthew.* New Testament Message. Collegeville, MN: Liturgical Press, 1990.

_____. *The Vision of Matthew: Christ, Church, and Morality in the First Gospel.* Crossroad, 1991. Reprint, Eugene, OR: Wipf & Stock, 2004.

Metzler, Norman. "The Lord's Prayer: Second Thoughts on the First Petition." In *Authenticating the Words of Jesus*, edited by Bruce Chilton and Craig A. Evans, 187–202. Boston, MA: Brill, 2002.

Moloney, Francis J. *"A Hard Saying": The Gospel and Culture.* Collegeville, MN: Liturgical Press, 2001.

Montefiore, C. G. *The Synoptic Gospels.* 2 vols. London: Macmillan, 1909.

Morris, Leon. *The Gospel According to Matthew.* The Pillar New Testament Commentary. Grand Rapids, MI: Eerdmans, 1992.

Muretov, M. D. *Evangelie po Matfeyu* [The Gospel of Matthew]. In *Izbrannye trudy* [Selected works], 193–279. Moscow: Izd. Svyato-Vladimirskogo Bratstva, 2002.

Neumann, Frederick. *The New Heart: An Introduction to the Sermon on the Mount.* Princeton, NJ: Princeton University Press, 1991.

Neusner, Jacob, Bruce D. Chilton, and Baruch A. Levine. *Torah Revealed, Torah Fulfilled: Scriptural Laws in Formative Judaism and Earliest Christianity.* New York, NY: T&T Clark, 2008.

Newman, Barclay M. and Philip C. Stine. *A Handbook on the Gospel of Matthew.* UBS Helps for Translators. New York, NY: United Bible Societies, 1992.

Neyrey, Jerome H. *Honor and Shame in the Gospel of Matthew.* Louisville, KY: Westminster John Knox, 1998.

Nietzsche, Friedrich W. *The Antichrist.* Translated by H. L. Mencken. New York, NY: Alfred A. Knopf, 1920.

_____. *Beyond Good and Evil: Prelude to a Philosophy of the Future.* Translated by Helen Zimmern. New York, NY: Macmillan, 1907.

Nolland, John. *The Gospel of Matthew: A Commentary on the Greek Text.* New International Greek Testament Commentary. Grand Rapids, MI: Eerdmans, 2005.

Oakman, Douglas E. "The Lord's Prayer in Social Perspective." In *Authenticating the Words of Jesus*, edited by Bruce Chilton and Craig A. Evans, 137–186. Boston, MA: Brill, 2002.

Pennington, Jonathan T. *Heaven and Earth in the Gospel of Matthew*. Supplements to Novum Testamentum 126. Leiden: Brill, 2007. Reprint, Grand Rapids, MI: Baker Academic, 2009.

_____. *Reading the Gospels Wisely: A Narrative and Theological Introduction*. Grand Rapids, MI: Baker Academic, 2012.

Perrin, Norman. *Jesus and the Language of the Kingdom: Symbol and Metaphor in New Testament Interpretation*. London: SCM, 1976.

Reisinger, Ernest C. *The Law and the Gospel*. Phillipsburg, NJ: Presbyterian & Reformed Pub. Co., 1997.

Renan, Ernest. *The Life of Christ*. Translated by Charles Edwin Wilbour. New York, NY: Carleton, 1864.

Reumann, John. *Jesus in the Church's Gospels: Modern Scholarship and the Earliest Sources*. Philadelphia, PA: Fortress, 1968.

Ridderbos, Herman N. *Matthew*. Translated by Ray Togtman. Bible Student's Commentary. Grand Rapids, MI: Zondervan, 1987.

Robinson, James M., Paul Hoffmann, and John S. Kloppenborg, eds. *The Critical Edition of Q: Synopsis Including the Gospels of Matthew and Luke, Mark and Thomas with English, German, and French Translations of Q and Thomas*. Hermeneia. Minneapolis, MN: Fortress, 2000.

Roh, Taeseong. *Die familia dei in den synoptischen Evangelien: eine redaktions- und sozialgeschichtliche Untersuchung zu einem urchristlichen Bildfeld*. Novum testamentum et orbis antiquus 37. Fribourg: Universitätsverlag; Göttingen: Vandenhoeck & Ruprecht, 2001.

Rowe, Robert D. *God's Kingdom and God's Son: The Background in Mark's Christology from Concepts of Kingship in the Psalms*. Arbeiten zur Geschichte des antiken Judentums und des Urchristentums 50. Leiden: Brill, 2002.

Sanders, E. P. *Jesus and Judaism*. Philadelphia, PA: Fortress, 1985.

Sawicki, Marianne. *Crossing Galilee: Architectures of Contact in the Occupied Land of Jesus*. Harrisburg, PA: Trinity Press International, 2000.

Schnackenburg, Rudolf. *The Gospel of Matthew*. Translated by Robert R. Barr. Grand Rapids, MI: Eerdmans, 2002.

Schnelle, Udo. *Theology of the New Testament*. Translated by M. Eugene Boring. Grand Rapids, MI: Baker Academic, 2009.

Schrage, Wolfgang. *The Ethics of the New Testament*. Translated by David E. Green. Philadelphia, PA: Fortress, 1988.

Schubert, Kurt. "The Sermon on the Mount and the Qumran Texts." In *The Scrolls and the New Testament*, edited by K. Stendahl, 118–28. New York, NY: Harper & Brothers, 1957.

Schweitzer, Albert. *Out of My Life and Thought: An Autobiography*. Translated by Antje Bultmann Lemke. 60th Anniversary ed. Baltimore, MD: The Johns Hopkins University Press, 2009.

Schweizer, Eduard. *The Good News according to Matthew*. Translated by David E. Green. Atlanta, GA: John Knox, 1975.

———. "Matthew's Church." In *The Interpretation of Matthew*, edited by Graham Stanton. Issues in Religion and Theology 3:129–155. Philadelphia, PA: Fortress; London: SPCK, 1983.

Seifrid, Mark A. "Righteousness Language in the Hebrew Scriptures and Early Judaism." In *Justification and Variegated Nomism*, ed. D. A. Carson, Peter T. O'Brien, and Mark A. Seifrid, vol. 1, *The Complexities of Second Temple Judaism*, 415–442. Grand Rapids, MI: Baker Academic, 2001.

Senior, Donald. *Matthew*. Abingdon New Testament Commentaries. Nashville, TN: Abingdon, 1998.

Shillington, V. George. *The New Testament in Context: A Literary and Theological Textbook*. New York, NY: T&T Clark, 2008.

Sigal, Phillip. *The Halakhah of Jesus of Nazareth according to the Gospel of Matthew*. Studies in Biblical Literature 18. Atlanta, GA: Society of Biblical Literature, 2007.

Snodgrass, Klyne. *Stories with Intent: A Comprehensive Guide to the Parables of Jesus*. Grand Rapids, MI: Eerdmans, 2008.

Sophrony (Sakharov), [Archimandrite]. *Saint Silouan the Athonite*. trans. Rosemary Edmonds. Crestwood, NY: St Vladimir's Seminary Press, 1999.

Spencer, F. Scott. *What Did Jesus Do?: Gospel Profiles of Jesus' Personal Conduct*. Harrisburg, PA: Trinity Press International, 2003.

Stanton, Graham N. *A Gospel for a New People: Studies in Matthew*. Edinburgh: T&T Clark, 1992.

———. "Matthew's Sermon on the Mount." In *Tradition and Interpretation in the New Testament: Essays in Honor of E. Earle Ellis for His 60th Birthday*, edited by Gerald F. Hawthorne and Otto Betz, 181–192. Grand Rapids, MI: Eerdmans, 1987.

Stein, Robert H. *Jesus the Messiah: A Survey of the Life of Christ.* Downers Grove, IL: InterVarsity, 1996.

Stevenson, Kenneth W. *The Lord's Prayer: A Text in Tradition.* Minneapolis, MN: Fortress, 2004.

Stock, Augustine. *The Method and Message of Matthew.* Collegeville, MN: Liturgical Press, 1994.

Storkey, Alan. *Jesus and Politics: Confronting the Powers.* Grand Rapids, MI: Baker Academic, 2005.

Strecker, Georg. *The Sermon on the Mount: An Exegetical Commentary.* Translated by O. C. Dean Jr. Edinburgh: T&T Clark, 1988.

Subramanian, J. Samuel. "The Lord's Prayer in the Gospel of Matthew." In *Resourcing New Testament Studies: Literary, Historical, and Theological Essays in Honor of David L. Dungan,* edited by Allan J. McNicol, David B. Peabody, and J. Samuel Subramanian, 107–122. New York, NY: T&T Clark International, 2009.

Swartley, Willard M. *Covenant of Peace: The Missing Piece in New Testament Theology and Ethics.* Studies in Peace and Scripture 9. Grand Rapids, MI: Eerdmans, 2006.

Taft, Robert F. *A History of the Liturgy of St. John Chrysostom.* Vol. 5, *The Precommunion Rites.* Orientalia Christiana Analecta 261. Rome: Pontificio Istituto Orientale, 2000.

Talbert, Charles H. *Matthew.* Paideia. Grand Rapids, MI: Baker Academic, 2010.

———. *Reading the Sermon on the Mount: Character Formation and Decision Making in Matthew 5–7.* Grand Rapids, MI: Baker Academic, 2006.

Tomson, Peter J. *"If This Be from Heaven . . .": Jesus and the New Testament Authors in Their Relationship to Judaism.* Biblical Seminar 76. Sheffield: Sheffield Academic Press, 2001.

Turner, David L. *Matthew.* Baker Exegetical Commentary on the New Testament. Grand Rapids, MI: Baker Academic, 2008.

van Banning, Joop, ed. *Opus imperfectum in Matthaeum.* CCSL 87b. Turnhout: Brepols, 1988.

———. "Il Padre Nostro nell'*Opus Imperfectum in Matthaeum.*" *Gregorianum* 71, no. 2 (1990): 293–313.

Vermes, Geza. *The Complete Dead Sea Scrolls in English.* Revised ed. New York, NY: Penguin, 2011.

Viviano, Benedict T. *Matthew and His World: The Gospel of the Open Jewish Christians; Studies in Biblical Theology*. Novum Testamentum et orbis antiquus 61. Fribourg: Academic Press; Göttingen: Vandenhoeck & Ruprecht, 2007.

Wierzbicka, Anna. *What Did Jesus Mean?: Explaining the Sermon on the Mount and the Parables in Simple and Universal Human Concepts*. Oxford: Oxford University Press, 2001.

Windisch, Hans. *The Meaning of the Sermon on the Mount*. Translated by S. MacLean Gilmour. Philadelphia, PA: Westminster, 1951.

Wright, Christopher J. H. *Old Testament Ethics for the People of God*. Downers Grove, IL: IVP Academic, 2004

Yancey, Philip. *The Jesus I Never Knew*. Grand Rapids, MI: Zondervan, 1995.

Yoder, John H. *He Came Preaching Peace*. Scottdale, PA: Herald, 1985.